# Women and Power in American History:
## A Reader
## Vol. II from 1870

### Edited by
### Kathryn Kish Sklar
### and
### Thomas Dublin

Prentice Hall, Upper Saddle River, New Jersey 07458

**Library of Congress Cataloging-in-Publication Data**

Women and power in American history : a reader/ edited by Kathryn
  Kish Sklar and Thomas Dublin.
      p.  cm.
    Includes bibliographical references and index.
    ISBN 0-13-962218-7 (v. 1). — ISBN 0-13-962234-9 (v. 2)
      1. Women—United States—History.  2. Women—United States—Social
  conditions.  I. Sklar, Kathryn Kish.  II. Dublin, Thomas.
  HQ1410.W643  1991
  305.4'0973—dc20                                                                90-7941
                                                                                      CIP

*To our students—past, present, and future*

Editorial production supervision and
  interior design: Tally Morgan, WordCrafters
Cover design: Lundgren Graphics, Ltd.
Manufacturing buyers: Debbie Kesar/Mary Ann Gloriande

Printed in the United States of America
10   9   8

ISBN 0-13-962234-9

PRENTICE-HALL INTERNATIONAL (UK) LIMITED, *LONDON*
PRENTICE-HALL OF AUSTRALIA PTY. LIMITED, *SYDNEY*
PRENTICE-HALL CANADA INC., *TORONTO*
PRENTICE-HALL HISPANOAMERICANA, S.A., *MEXICO*
PRENTICE-HALL OF INDIA PRIVATE LIMITED, *NEW DELHI*
PRENTICE-HALL OF JAPAN, INC., *TOKYO*
PEARSON EDUCATION ASIA PTE. LTD., *SINGAPORE*
EDITORA PRENTICE-HALL DO BRASIL, LTDA., *RIO DE JANEIRO*

# Contents

# Preface

These volumes demonstrate the phenomenal growth of the field of U.S. women's history during the past twenty years. Kathryn Kish Sklar began teaching American women's history at the University of Michigan in 1971, Thomas Dublin at Wellesley College in 1975. Since then the field has blossomed into one of the most vital areas of historical study in the late twentieth century. With the founding of the International Federation for Research in Women's History in 1987, its impact has become evident on a global scale. The introduction of women's experience has irrevocably changed the discipline of history, in the United States and throughout the world.

This transformation occurred as the result of collective action taken in classrooms, at conferences, and in professional organizations. These volumes build on a legacy of struggle to achieve a more complete and democratic representation of human experience. Within that struggle two groups have been particularly meaningful to us, and we wish to thank them here. First and foremost, our own students, at the undergraduate and graduate levels, have provided a constituency for women's history. Their insistent demand for answers to questions about the history of women gave this new scholarship a reason for being. Their questions sprang from the stuff of life itself in the late twentieth century—participation in social movements in the 1960s and 70s, the transformation in women's labor force participation in the 1970s and 80s, and new forms of family and social relationships.

Second, our colleagues in women's history have steadily supported our efforts to bring new research findings in women's history into the classroom. Beginning in 1977, the UCLA Workshop on the Teaching of Women's History provided a splendid forum for the discussion of problems and strategies in the teaching of U.S. women's history. Drawing on scholarly talent in the far West and Southwest, from Washington to Texas, this dedicated group of college teachers shaped our approach to classroom teaching. Our debt to them is very great. Later at the graduate level, the 1988 NEH-Wingspread Conference on Graduate Training in U.S. Women's History helped us synthesize the needs of graduate and undergraduate teaching. These resources have been sustained by the Berkshire Conference in Women's History, which at triennial national conferences since 1973 has nurtured the development of women's history.

This all goes to show that historians of women have benefitted from the same processes that have shaped the lives of average American women. Like them, historians of women have responded to the circumstances of their lives and times. Like them, historians of women have expressed their commitment to social goals. Like them, historians of women have responded to new opportunities to assert their interests. Since 1970 changes in the historical discipline have brought historians of women into close conjunction with the lives of average women. These volumes reflect and celebrate that conjunction.

Binghamton, New York

# Contributors

Suzanne M. Bianchi is a demographer at the Center for Demographic Studies at the U.S. Bureau of the Census and is co-author of *American Women in Transition*.

Ruth Bordin is an independent scholar in Ann Arbor, Michigan. Her most recent book is *Frances Willard: A Biography*.

Elizabeth Clark-Lewis is Professor of History at Northern Virginia Community College. She is the producer of a documentary video, "Freedom Bags," which explores the migration of African-American women from the rural south in the period 1900–1930.

Laurie Coyle is an independent film-maker living in San Francisco. She recently completed "Fenix Rising," a documentary film on Mexico's first nuclear accident.

Sara Evans is Professor of History at the University of Minnesota. She recently completed *Born for Liberty: A History of Women in America* and *Wage Justice: Comparable Worth and the Paradox of Technocratic Reform*.

Dana Frank is Assistant Professor of History at the University of Missouri-St. Louis. She is completing a study entitled *Labor and the Politics of Consumption: Seattle, Washington, 1919–1929*.

Estelle Freedman is Professor of History at Stanford University. She recently co-authored *Intimate Matters: A History of Sexuality in America*.

Linda Gordon is Florence Kelley Professor of History at the University of Wisconsin-Madison. She is the author of *Heroes of Their Own Lives: The Politics and History of Family Violence*.

Gail Hershatter teaches History at Williams College. She is author of *The Workers of Tianjin, 1900–1949* and coeditor of *Personal Voices: Chinese Women in the 1980's*.

Emily Honig is Assistant Professor of History at Yale University. She is author of *Sister and Strangers: Women in the Shanghai Cotton Mills, 1919–1949* and coeditor of *Personal Voices: Chinese Women in the 1980's*.

Julie Roy Jeffrey is Elizabeth Todd Professor and chair of the History Department at Goucher College. She is author of *Frontier Women: The Trans-Mississippi West, 1840–1880* and has just completed a forthcoming biography of the missionary Narcissa Whitman.

Christine A. Littleton is Professor of Law at the University of California, Los Angeles. She is the author of "Reconstructing Sexual Equality, *California Law Review*, vol. 1975 (1987), pp. 1279–1337.

Ruth Milkman is Professor of Sociology at the University of California,

Los Angeles. She is author of *Gender at Work: The Dynamics of Job Segregation by Sex During World War II.*

Mary J. Oates is Professor of Economics at Regis College. She is editor of *Higher Education for Catholic Women: An Historical Anthology.*

Kathy Peiss is Associate Professor of History at University of Massachusetts. She is author of *Cheap Amusements: Working Women and Leisure in Turn-of-the-Century New York* and coeditor of *Passion and Power: Sexuality in History.*

Jessie M. Rodrique is a doctoral student at the University of Massachusetts at Amherst and assistant editor of the Margaret Sanger Papers Project at Smith College.

Mary Logan Rothschild teaches History at Arizona State University and is author of *A Case of Black and White: Northern Volunteers and the Southern Freedom Summers, 1964–1965.*

Christina Simmons teaches History at the University of Windsor. She is coeditor of *Passion and Power: Sexuality in History.*

Daphne Spain teaches Sociology and Environmental Planning at the University of Virginia. She is co-author of *American Women in Transition.*

Rosalyn Terborg-Penn is Professor of History at the Morgan State University. She is founder of the Association of Black Women Historians and the author and editor of numerous works on Black women's history, including the anthology *Women in Africa and the African Diaspora.*

Carole Turbin is an Associate Professor at Empire State College of the State University of New York. She is author of a forthcoming book on gender, family, and labor activism among the collar workers of Troy, New York.

# Introduction: Power as a Theme in Women's History

One of the biggest challenges facing historians of American women is the task of identifying the causes and consequences of long-term changes in women's lives. That task looms large not only because it is central to the historian's chief calling—analyzing change over time—but also because the turning points of historical change for women differ from those that have mattered most to men. When history is history seen from the perspective of women's experience, then new categories of analysis are clearly needed, since wars and other political events that have marked the standard historical divisions have usually been less important in the lives of average women than changes in family values, social movements, or the organization of the paid labor force. Thus during the first twenty years of its existence as an academic discipline, the field of U.S. women's history has focused more attention on women's family lives, their working lives, and their community activism than on the larger themes of power that pervade male-centered treatments of American history.

Yet the need to analyze change over time in U.S. women's history has grown more urgent as the field itself has grown. Its abundant diversity, embracing women of all classes, ethnicities, races, religions, and regions, poses serious challenges as to how this diversity can be meaningfully synthesized into a coherent whole. In their search for unifying themes, historians of American women have found new uses for the most fundamental category of analysis known in the discipline of history—the study of social power, its components, causes, and consequences.

Power is a very useful means of depicting change in women's lives over time. First, it is a theme capable of linking changes in the three fundamental dimensions of women's lives—family, work, and community experiences. We know that changes in these three arenas of women's experience overlap and influence one another, but to understand that process we need tools of analysis that cut across all three. Themes relating to power do that effectively since they embrace personal relations of the sort found in family life as well as collective identities located in community activities and the workplace.

Second, power is a valuable theme for connecting women's history with other dimensions of American history. The field's effectiveness as an illuminator of all American history hinges on its use of a Promethean new category of historical analysis—gender as a principle of social organization.

Since women can never be studied totally in isolation from men, gender relations are central to women's history, bringing with them the experience of men and their relations with women. In this context, power is a key category of analysis because it illuminates the relationships between men and women.

Thirdly, power is a helpful vehicle for understanding relations among women of different social standing. Most differences among women are socially constructed. Differences of class, race, ethnicity, religion, or region are generated by social structures. Much as they may appear to be natural, they are created by social values and social institutions that reinforce social hierarchies and distribute power unevenly. Women's history needs to take account of differences among women and the way social disparities translate into differences of power.

For these and other reasons historians of women are increasingly using power as a leading category of analysis. This collection of writings in American women's history is the first to focus centrally on themes of power in women's lives. It seeks to convey the diverse perspectives from which this theme can fruitfully be viewed, as well as the wide variety of female experiences the theme can integrate.

What do historians of women mean by "power?" The newness of the term's application to women can be seen in historians' tendency to leave it undefined. Many dictionaries define power as the "possession of control, authority, or influence over others."* Yet an important aspect of women's power has been expressed in their ability to exercise control over their own bodies, to limit men's access to their sexuality and to control their own reproductive lives. From the perspective of women's history, then, a more suitable definition of power is the ability to control the distribution of social resources. Women's power has often rested in their ability to control the distribution of things or services rather than persons. Put another way, the essence of women's power has historically rested in their control of goods or services through which they frequently, albeit indirectly, have controlled persons. Women's power has often been expressed through a withdrawal of their services. For example, the meat boycott led by Jewish housewives in 1917, described in this volume's article by Dana Frank, expressed women's power as consumers and demonstrated their ability to control the distribution of their grocery money. At another level of power, women reformers affected the access of women workers to trade union organizing and the eight-hour day.

Short introductions to each article in this collection provide a guide to how each historian analyzes themes of power. Less evident are the ways that women's power changed over time. It is useful to identify four principles of change that shape the period between 1869 and 1990—that is, between the emergence of the woman suffrage movement and the present.

---

*Webster's Ninth New Collegiate Dictionary* (Springfield, Mass.: Merriam-Webster, 1989).

The first principle concerns the interconnectedness of the major arenas of women's activities—family, work, and community life. Changes in one of these dimensions have invariably been linked to changes in the others. Thus, for example, changes in women's family status, as reflected in higher divorce rates after 1960, were closely related to the sharp increase in women's labor force participation rates, which gave many women an increased sense of their own worth and to an unprecedented degree made it possible for them to assume financial responsibility for their children. Both of these changes, in turn, were reflected in the reemergence of feminism in the 1960s. How the causal arrows point within the triad of family, work, and community life depends upon the circumstances at any given moment, but those connections have been central to women's experience of change over time.

Another important principle is that change in female experience is often excruciatingly slow. Perhaps because gender constitutes the most fundamental form of social organization—the one upon which all others are built—changes in gender relations involve a multitude of other categories of change, and these, in turn, require their own sets of causes, many of which are long in the making. For example, the dramatic decline in birthrates experienced by American women between 1800 and 1940, which reduced the average number of children born to women of all races, classes, and regions, was caused by factors so pervasive that they continue to elude historical analysis today. Historians used to attribute the long-term decline to industrialization and urbanization. But recent research has shown that rural Americans accounted for most of that decline in its most intensive decade—the 1850s. Recently, historians have turned to even larger and more elusive causes, such as the growth of the market economy and its mirror image, the decline of subsistence agriculture. The new valuation placed on each individual child was also important, historians now believe, along with religious beliefs that made human agency the cause of salvation. Since each of these and other causal components of fertility decline had its own chain of causes, fertility decline rested upon a pyramid of other historical changes. Taken together, they constituted an almost total transformation in American life—a transformation that took more than one hundred years to achieve.

Other less complex changes in women's lives also need to be measured by decades rather than years. For example, the women's rights movement, born in Seneca Falls, New York, in 1848, took more than seventy years to achieve its goal of woman suffrage in 1920, making it the longest-lived continuous social movement in U.S. history. Similarly, changes in women's labor force participation, surely the single most important transformation in women's lives in the twentieth century, occurred in a series of stages between 1880 and 1980.

This does not mean that women's history lacks turning points or that it forms one long progression of achievement. Rather, it shows us that when turning points do occur, they usually involve a multitude of causes that have deep social roots and extend across more than one generation.

Another key principle of change over time in women's history involves differences among women. The social construction of dissimilarities among women may change to reflect changing social, economic, or political structures. For example, the passage of the Woman Suffrage Amendment in 1920 nominally extended voting rights to all women citizens, but actually created new differences between white and African-American women in regions where all blacks were excluded from voting. Conversely, changing social, political, or economic realities have also eroded differences among women. For example, the massive entrance of married white women into the paid labor force between 1950 and 1980 has made their life-cycle working patterns more similar to those historically experienced by black women. Thus differences and similarities among women are constantly changing, reflecting, and influencing changes in the larger society, polity, and economy.

Finally, and perhaps most importantly, women's agency—that is, their ability to influence changes in their lives and in their society—commands our attention as a crucial principle in the interpretation of change over time in women's history. No one proposition is more widely held in the field of women's history than the view that women have not been merely passive victims, but have played a part in shaping their historical destiny. No women were totally lacking in agency; even poor immigrant women made choices that enhanced their ability to control their life circumstances.

The extent to which women have been able to shape the circumstances of their lives has itself changed over time, offering us one of the most fruitful avenues of historical inquiry. For example, the ability of women to control their reproductive lives increased significantly after the 1973 U.S. Supreme Court decision in *Roe v. Wade* ruled unconstitutional all state laws prohibiting abortion.

By viewing women's agency over time we gain a clearer understanding of the other principles of change evident in examining women's history: the interrelationships among family, work, and community life; the tendency for changes in women's lives to reflect long-term, deeply rooted alterations; and the shifting relationships between different groups of women. For example, the empowerment of women's political culture through the Woman's Christian Temperance Union between 1874 and 1900 buttressed a steady expansion of women's agency in family and community life. The American Birth Control League, seeking greater agency for women in their ability to control their reproductive lives, both reflected and reinforced the long-term decline in fertility in the United States since 1800. Finally, woman's agency was highly visible in the civil rights movement of the 1960s, which did much to erode racial differences between women.

The history of American women is a history of struggle. We can understand that struggle better by viewing the changing dimensions of power in women's lives.

\* \* \*

These essays reveal dramatic changes in all areas of women's lives during the past one hundred years. Women's working lives, their family experiences, their expression of sexuality, and their political culture underwent profound transformation in the decades between 1870 and 1990. Affecting different groups of women in different ways, these changes dramatically altered women's experience in the twentieth century, their ability to control their life circumstances, and their access to social resources.

Growing labor force participation has served as the most important engine of change bringing new forms of power into women's lives. Before 1900 the vast majority of women wage earners were young and unmarried. This meant that they faced enormous difficulties in engaging in collective action to improve their working conditions. Historians, such as Carole Turbin, have recently shed new light on the experience of women workers by investigating occasions when women succeeded in organizing unions. These successful occasions highlight the factors that helped women prevail over the demographic facts of their youth and their temporary status in the waged labor force. Nevertheless, in the early twentieth century most working women remained unorganized; in 1920 one out of every five working men was a trade union member, but only one out of fifteen women. That difference reflected occupational distinctions in which women were excluded from the vast majority of jobs open to men—especially high-paying skilled jobs—and were crowded into few, relatively unskilled occupations.

Crowding is a key concept that historians and sociologists have used to describe women's waged work and the powerlessness that has persistently accompanied it. Despite many significant changes in women's labor force participation between 1870 and 1990, the crowding of women workers into relatively few sex-segregated occupations remains constant. Crowding has meant that women strenuously competed against one another for the few jobs available to them. It has rendered their skills less meaningful and has kept their wages low.

A good example of the effects of crowding can be found among Catholic sisters in Massachusetts in the early twentieth century, as described by Mary Oates. Their increased crowding into school teaching was accompanied by a loss of their religious community's control over the terms of their labor and a reduction in their income.

For many African-American women, sex-segregated work has also been race segregated. For example, although the proportion of women who worked as household servants declined dramatically between 1900 and 1940, the proportion of wage-earning black women who worked as servants actually increased because their exclusion from manufacturing jobs crowded them into domestic service. Nevertheless, as Elizabeth Clark-Lewis's article shows, these women found ways to enhance their ability to control their life circumstances and increase their contribution to community organizations.

Ethnic segregation has been another feature of the female labor force, as demonstrated by the Mexican and Mexican-American women garment workers employed by the Farah Manufacturing Company in the 1970s. While their ethnic identity aided in the workers' solidarity during their strike, and their consciousness of their power was enhanced by collective action, these workers are examples of the continuing exploitation of minority women in the labor force. The growing Latina population in the United States in the 1990s means that this problem too will grow.

While many problems related to women's exploitation in the paid labor force remain, there is no doubt about the single most visible change in women's labor force participation in the twentieth century—the considerable increase in the proportion of women who work for wages. World War II is often taken for a turning point in the history of women's waged labor, but as Ruth Milkman's essay argues, women's work experience remained sex-segregated even under those unusual conditions. As Suzanne Bianchi and Daphne Spain's article demonstrates, the most important change in women's labor force participation in the twentieth century are visible in the numbers of women working for wages rather than in changes in the occupations in which they have worked.

Have these increases in women's wage-earning activities significantly enhanced women's ability to control their life circumstances? For many women the answer to this question is no; wage-earning work has merely absorbed them into the same unrewarding routine that men have long known, the chief difference being that they now do two jobs—one at the workplace, one at home. Nonetheless, women's increased earnings have laid the foundation for new sorts of power in their lives, flowing from their dramatically greater ability to contribute to their own and their family's support.

Important changes in women's family and sexual experience preceded this rapid rise in their labor force participation. While the 1970s witnessed transforming changes in the proportion of women who worked outside the home, the 1920s introduced thoroughgoing and enduring changes into women's family and sexual lives. The first and most obvious of these might be called "the revival of heterosexuality." Victorian sexual values were strongly shaped by the long-term decline in fertility called the "demographic transition." Beginning in 1800 and continuing until 1940, this decline had an even more profound effect on women's lives than their movement into the paid labor force after 1950, since it reduced from seven to two the average number of children born to women who survived to the age of fifty. Two-thirds of this decline occurred before 1880 without the use of artificial contraceptive techniques. Relying on sexual abstinence to lengthen the intervals between births, couples were aided by Victorian sexual values, which discouraged the expression of sexual desire and granted women unprecedented control over their own bodies. These values also exaggerated the differences between the sexes and treated women as morally superior to men. In this context the proportion of women who never married rose to an all-time high between 1870 and 1910 (much greater than today), and many women—married and unmarried—formed what historians have come to call "homosocial" relationships with other women.

Toward the end of the demographic transition, around 1920, these Victorian values gave way to the new sexual values described by Christina Simmons: companionship between men and women—before and after marriage—and an intolerance for close relations between women. As Kathy Peiss's essay indicates, the heterosexual leisure culture of turn-of-the-century working-class women suggests that they were in the vanguard of changing sexual mores. All that remained to make this change complete was the access to birth control techniques described in articles by Linda Gordon and Jessie Rodrique. Gordon analyzes the strong support Margaret Sanger drew from middle-class women, who by the 1920s relied on artificial birth control techniques to limit their fertility. Rodrique shows that African-American women, though not as active in the American Birth Control League as white women, controlled their fertility in ways that reflected post-1920 assumptions about separating sexuality from reproduction. These four articles demonstrate the importance of women's actions in defining their own reproductive lives. They also illustrate some of the forces opposed to these actions. Ultimately they show that this "personal" issue is also political.

Margaret Sanger was one of a multitude of women reformers who exemplified the power of women's political culture that arose from women's separate institutions between 1870 and 1930. Launched in the antebellum era, women's political culture was energized through women's service in the Civil War. Many new institutions—the women's club movement, the Woman's Christian Temperance Union, and the social settlement movement to name only a few—emerged in the decades after 1870 to create the social space within which women attempted to bridge racial, class, and regional differences; train women leaders; and articulate women's issues. Forces promoting the extension of women's political culture extended into rural as well as urban areas. Nevertheless, the success of women's separate institutions can only partly be explained by women's triumphant mobilization in these decades. Equally important were the opportunities open to women in the U.S. political domain. Many of these opportunities were created by traditions of limited government that empowered the voluntary sector in which women played so important a part. For example, the U.S. Sanitary Commission during and after the Civil War empowered women in positions that in Europe were occupied by male bureaucrats. Under the Sanitary Commission women held important positions in the administration of hospital care and the awarding of widows' and other forms of war pensions.

Other gaps engendered by traditions of limited government became more apparent as American society underwent rapid industrialization and urbanization after 1880. In addition to its work for prohibition the Woman's Christian Temperance Union offered shelter, food, and medical care to needy women, men, and children. Women on state charity boards urged more attention to the problems of the poor, and the social settlement movement found new ways to advocate the redistribution of social resources to meet the needs of working class people. Not surprisingly in this context, the woman suffrage movement justified its goals in social justice terms—women voters would end political corruption, reorient public policy, and eliminate social injustice.

While women's political culture depended upon coalition building, women's assumptions about gender-based solidarity were often disappointed by the persistence of class, ethnic, and racial distinctions within their political cultures. Viewed positively, these distinctions were an inherent feature of women's collective action because they expressed an essential aspect of women's lives. Thus the raucous consumer boycotts through which Jewish immigrant women expressed their own view of social justice built on ethnic as well as gender identities. Likewise, the political culture of African-American women was rooted in their distinctive experience of the social construction of race in the United States. Yet, as Rosalyn Terborg-Penn's essay shows, white women's political culture often buttressed social distinctions that discriminated against black women. The Nineteenth Amendment did not bring suffrage to black women as readily as it did to white—especially in regions where black men did not vote. By accepting that outcome, the white-dominated suffrage movement reinforced the barriers between itself and black women's political culture. In the Civil Rights Movement of the 1960s, however, those barriers were significantly eroded.

Just as a multitude of causes led to the empowerment of women's political culture in the early nineteenth century, a confluence of many causes eroded its power in the 1920s. The dispute over whether to pursue strategies for women's advancement based on women's difference from men or on their similarities to men, accentuated by the Equal Rights Amendment (ERA) proposed in 1922, debilitated the women's movement during the interwar years.

The reemergence of feminism in the 1960s built on four decades of growing equality between the sexes as illustrated by women's labor force participation rates, their place in family life, and their sexual identity. As a result, the new feminists championed equality rather than difference as the mode by which they advanced women's interests. A telling landmark in this shift was the endorsement of the ERA by women members of the United Automobile Workers and by the U.S. Women's Bureau in 1972.

Nevertheless, in the late 1980s the need for some recognition of gender differences reemerged in legal causes fostering the advancement of women's interests in the paid labor force. As Christian Littleton argues in her article on feminist legal theory, notions of gender equality often measure women by male norms. A better basis for public policy decisions, she argues, are notions that accept difference as part of equality. Thereby women do not have to become like men in order to be treated equally with men. Thus American feminists in the 1990s face the important challenge of merging the best attributes of nineteenth- and twentieth-century feminism— of devising methods that permit them to acknowledge the valuable aspects of female experience while aspiring to transcend the limitations traditionally associated with female experience.

# 1

## Separatism as Strategy: Female Institution Building and American Feminism, 1870–1930

### Estelle Freedman

*For a variety of reasons, partly because of their exclusion from male organizations and partly because of cultural beliefs that emphasized differences between women and men, women's political culture flourished in separate institutions. Estelle Freedman analyzes some of the causes and effects of that separation. Accounting for much of the power of women's political culture before 1920, women's institutions declined thereafter, leading to an overall decline in women's social and cultural power. Not until women's institutions were again reconstructed on the new material basis of women's greatly expanded labor force participation in the 1960s, 1970s, and 1980s did women regain the political power they collectively wielded before 1920.*

### SCHOLARSHIP AND STRATEGIES

The feminist scholarship of the past decade has often been concerned, either explicitly or implicitly, with two central political questions: the search for the origins of women's oppression and the formulation of effective strategies for combating patriarchy. Analysis of the former question helps us to answer the latter; or as anthropologist Gayle Rubin has wryly explained:

> If innate male aggression and dominance are at the root of female oppression, then the feminist program would logically require either the extermination of the offending sex, or else a eugenics project to modify its character. If sexism is a by-product of capitalism's relentless appetite for profit, then sexism would wither away in the advent of a successful socialist revolution. If the world historical defeat of women occurred at the hands of an armed patriarchal revolt, then it is time for Amazon guerrillas to start training in the Adirondacks.[1]

Another anthropologist, Michelle Zimbalist Rosaldo, provided an influential exploration of the origins-strategy questions in her 1974 theoretical overview of women's status.[2] Rosaldo argued that "universal sexual asymmetry" (the lower value placed on women's tasks and roles in all

This article is reprinted from *FEMINIST STUDIES*, Volume 5, Number 3 (Fall 1979): 512–29, by permission of the publisher FEMINIST STUDIES, Inc., c/o Women's Studies Program, University of Maryland, College Park, MD 20742.

*Woman suffrage demonstration. Library of Congress.*

cultures) has been determined largely by the sexually defined split between domestic and public spheres. To oversimplify her thesis: the greater the so-cial distance between women in the home and men in the public sphere, the greater the devaluation of women. The implications for feminist strat-egy become clear at the end of Rosaldo's essay in which she says that greater overlap between domestic and public spheres means higher status for women. Thus to achieve an egalitarian future, with less separation of female and male, we should strive not only for the entrance of women into the male-dominated public sphere, but also for men's entry into the female-dominated domestic world.

Rosaldo also discusses an alternative strategy for overcoming sexual asymmetry, namely, the creation of a separate women's public sphere; but she dismisses this model in favor of integrating domestic and public spheres. Nonetheless, the alternative strategy of "women's societies and Af-rican queens" deserves further attention.[3] Where female political leaders have power over their own jurisdiction (women), they also gain leverage in tribal policy. Such a separate sexual political hierarchy would presumably offer women more status and power than the extreme male-public/female-domestic split, but it would not require the entrance of each sex into the sphere dominated by the other sex. At certain historical periods, the cre-ation of a public female sphere might be the only viable political strategy for women.

I would like to argue through historical analysis for the alternative strategy of creating a strong, public female sphere. A number of feminist historians have recently explored the value of the separate, though not necessarily public, female sphere for enriching women's historical experience. Carroll Smith-Rosenberg's research[4] has shown how close personal relationships enhanced the private lives of women in the nineteenth century. At the same time, private "sisterhoods," Nancy Cott has suggested, may have been a precondition for the emergence of feminist consciousness.[5] In the late nineteenth and early twentieth centuries, intimate friendships provided support systems for politically active women, as demonstrated by the work of both Blanche Cook and Nancy Sahli.[6] However, the women's culture of the past—personal networks, rituals, and relationships—did not automatically constitute a political strategy. As loving and supportive as women's networks may have been, they could keep women content with a status which was inferior to that of men.

I do not accept the argument that female networks and feminist politics were incompatible. Rather, in the following synthesis of recent scholarship in American women's history, I want to show how the women's movement in the late nineteenth and early twentieth centuries provides an example of the "women's societies and African queens" strategy that Rosaldo mentioned. The creation of a separate, public female sphere helped mobilize women and gained political leverage in the larger society. A separatist political strategy, which I refer to as "female institution building," emerged from the middle-class women's culture of the nineteenth century. Its history suggests that in our own time, as well, women's culture can be integral to feminist politics.[7]

## WHAT HAPPENED TO FEMINISM?

My desire to restore historical consciousness about female separatism has both a personal and an intellectual motivation. As a feminist working within male-dominated academic institutions, I have realized that I could not survive without access to the feminist culture and politics that flourish outside of mixed institutions. How, I have wondered, could women in the past work for change within a men's world without having this alternative culture? This thought led me to the more academic questions. Perhaps they could not survive when those supports were not available; and perhaps this insight can help explain one of the most intriguing questions in American women's history: What happened to feminism after the suffrage victory in 1920?

Most explanations of the decline of women's political strength focus on either inherent weaknesses in suffragist ideology or on external pressures from a pervasively sexist society.[8] But when I survey the women's movement before suffrage passed, I am struck by the hypothesis that a major strength of American feminism prior to 1920 was the separate female community that helped sustain women's participation in both social reform and political activism. Although the women's movement of the late nineteenth century contributed to the transformation of women's social roles, it did not reject a separate, unique female identity. Most feminists did not adopt the radical demands for equal status with men that originated at the Seneca Falls Convention of 1848. Rather, they preferred to retain membership in a separate female sphere, one which they did not believe to be inferior to men's sphere and one in which women could be free to create their own forms of personal, social, and political relationships. The achievements of feminism at the turn of the century came less through gaining access to the male domains of politics and the professions than in the tangible form of building separate female institutions.

The self-consciously female community began to disintegrate in the 1920s just as "new women" were attempting to assimilate into male-dominated institutions. At work, in social life, and in politics, I will argue, middle-class women hoped to become equals by adopting men's values and integrating into their institutions. A younger generation of women learned to smoke, drink, and value heterosexual relationships over female friendships in their personal lives. At the same time, women's political activity epitomized the process of rejecting women's culture in favor of men's promises of equality. The gradual decline of female separatism in social and political life precluded the emergence of a strong women's political bloc which might have protected and expanded the gains made by the earlier women's movement. Thus the erosion of women's culture may help account for the decline of public feminism in the decades after 1920. Without a constituency a movement cannot survive. The old feminist leaders lost their following when a new generation opted for assimilation in the naive hope of becoming men's equals overnight.

To explore this hypothesis, I shall illustrate episodes of cultural and political separatism within American feminism in three periods: its historical roots prior to 1870; the institution building of the late nineteenth century; and the aftermath of suffrage in the 1920s.


## HISTORICAL ROOTS OF SEPARATISM

In nineteenth-century America, commercial and industrial growth intensified the sexual division of labor, encouraging the separation of men's and women's spheres. While white males entered the public world of wage labor, business, the professions and politics, most white middle-class women remained at home where they provided the domestic, maternal, and spiritual care for their families and the nation. These women underwent inten-

sive socialization into their roles as "true women." Combined with the restrictions on women which denied them access to the public sphere, this
training gave American women an identity quite separate from men's.
Women shared unique life experiences as daughters, wives, childbearers,
childrearers, and moral guardians. They passed on their values and traditions to their female kin. They created what Smith-Rosenberg has called
"The Female World of Love and Ritual," a world of homosocial networks
that helped these women transcend the alienation of domestic life.[9]

The ideology of "true womanhood" was so deeply ingrained and so
useful for preserving social stability in a time of flux that those few women
who explicitly rejected its inequalities could find little support for their
views. The feminists of the early women's rights movement were certainly
justified in their grievances and demands for equal opportunity with men.
The Seneca Falls Declaration of Sentiments of 1848, which called for access
to education, property ownership, and political rights, has inspired many
feminists since then, while the ridicule and denial of these demands have
inspired our rage. But the equal rights arguments of the 1850s were apparently too radical for their own times.[10] Men would not accept women's entry
into the public sphere, but more importantly, most women were not interested in rejecting their deeply rooted female identities. Both men and
women feared the demise of the female sphere and the valuable functions
it performed. The feminists, however, still hoped to reduce the limitations
on women within their own sphere, as well as to gain the right of choice—
of autonomy—for those women who opted for public rather than private
roles.

Radical feminists such as Elizabeth Cady Stanton and Susan B. Anthony recognized the importance of maintaining the virtues of the female
world while eliminating discrimination against women in public. As their
political analysis developed at mid-century, they drew upon the concepts of
female moral superiority and sisterhood, and they affirmed the separate
nature of woman. At the same time, their disillusionment with even the
more enlightened men of the times reinforced the belief that women had
to create their own movement to achieve independence. The bitterness that
resulted when most male abolitionists refused to support women's rights in
the 1860s, and when they failed to include Woman Suffrage in the Fifteenth
Amendment (as well as the inclusion of the term "male citizen" in the Four-
teenth Amendment) alienated many women reformers. When Frederick
Douglass proclaimed in defense that "This is the Negro's Hour," the more
radical women's rights advocates followed Stanton and Anthony in with-
drawing from the reform coalition and creating a separatist organization.
Their National Woman Suffrage Association had women members and officers; supported a broad range of reforms, including changes in marriage
and divorce laws; and published the short-lived journal, *The Revolution*. The
radical path proved difficult, however, and the National Woman Suffrage

Association merged in 1890 with the more moderate American Woman Suffrage Association.

### FEMALE INSTITUTION BUILDING

The "transition period" that Stanton and Anthony invoked lasted from the 1870s to the 1920s. It was an era of separate female organization and institution building, the result on the one hand, of the negative push of discrimination in the public, male sphere, and on the other hand, of the positive attraction of the female world of close, personal relationships and domestic institutional structures. These dual origins characterized, for instance, one of the largest manifestations of "social feminism" in the late nineteenth century—the women's club movement.

The club movement illustrated the politicization of women's institutions as well as the limitations of their politics. The exclusion of women reporters from the New York Press Club in 1868 inspired the founding of the first women's club, Sorosis. The movement then blossomed in dozens and later hundreds of localities, until a General Federation of Women's Clubs formed in 1890. By 1910, it claimed over one million members. Although club social and literacy activities at first appealed to traditional women who simply wanted to gather with friends and neighbors, by the turn of the century women's clubs had launched civic reform programs. Their activities served to politicize traditional women by forcing them to define themselves as citizens, not simply as wives and mothers. The clubs reflected the societal racism of the time, however, and the black women who founded the National Association of Colored Women in 1896 turned their attention to the social and legal problems that confronted both black women and men.[11]

The Women's Christian Temperance Union had roots in the social feminist tradition of separate institution building. As Ellen DuBois has argued, the WCTU appealed to late nineteenth-century women because it was grounded in the private sphere—the home—and attempted to correct the private abuses against women, namely, intemperance and the sexual double standard.[12] Significantly, though, the WCTU, under Frances Willard's leadership, became a strong prosuffrage organization, committed to righting all wrongs against women, through any means, including the vote.

The women's colleges that opened in these same decades further attest to the importance of separate female institutions during this "transition period." Originally conceived as training grounds of piety, purity, and domesticity, the antebellum women's seminaries, such as Mary Lyon's Mt. Holyoke and Emma Willard's Troy Female Academy, laid the groundwork for the new collegiate institutions of the postwar era. When elite male institutions refused to educate women, the sister colleges of the East, like their counterparts elsewhere, took on the task themselves. . . . At the same time, liberal arts and science training provided tools for women's further development, and by their examples, female teachers inspired students to use their skills creatively. As Barbara Welter noted when she first described the "Cult of True Womanhood,"[13] submissiveness was always its weakest link. Like other women's institutions, the colleges could help subvert that element of the Cult by encouraging independence in their students.

The most famous example of the impact of women's colleges may be Jane Addams's description of her experience at Rockford Seminary where she and other students were imbued with the mission of bringing their female values to bear on the entire society. While Addams later questioned the usefulness of her intellectual training in meeting the challenges of the real world, other women did build upon academic foundations when increasingly, as reformers, teachers, doctors, social workers, and in other capacities they left the home to enter public or quasi-public work. Between 1890 and 1920, the number of professional degrees granted to women increased 226 percent, at three times the rate of increase for men. Some of these professionals had attended separate female institutions such as the women's medical colleges in Philadelphia, New York, and Boston. The new female professionals often served women and children clients, in part because of the discrimination against their encroachment on men's domains, but also because they sincerely wanted to work with the traditional objects of their concern. As their skills and roles expanded, these women would demand the right to choose for themselves where and with whom they could work. This first generation of educated professional women became supporters of the suffrage movement in the early twentieth century, calling for full citizenship for women.

The process of redefining womanhood by the extension, rather than by the rejection, of the female sphere may be best illustrated by the settlement house movement. Although both men and women resided in and supported these quasi-public institutions, the high proportion of female participants and leaders (approximately three-fifths of the total), as well as the domestic structure and emphasis on service to women and children, qualify the settlements as female institutions. . . . Thus did Jane Addams learn the techniques of the political world through her efforts to keep the neighborhood clean. So too did Florence Kelley of Hull House welcome appointment as chief factory inspector of Illinois, to protect women and children workers; and Julia Lathrop, another Hull House resident, entered the public sphere as director of the United States Children's Bureau; while onetime settlement resident Katherine Bement Davis moved from the superintendency of the Bedford Hills reformatory for women to become in 1914 the first female commissioner of corrections in New York City. Each of these women, and other settlement workers who moved on to professional and public office, eventually joined and often led branches of the National American Woman Suffrage Association.[14] They drew upon the networks of personal friends and professional allies that grew within separate female institutions when they waged their campaigns for social reform and for suffrage.

Separate female organizations were not limited to middle-class women. Recent histories have shown that groups hoping to bridge class lines between women existed within working-class or radical movements. In both the Women's Trade Union League and the National Consumers League, middle-class reformers strived for cooperation, rather than condescension, in their relationships with working women. Although in neither organization were they entirely successful, the Women's Trade Union League did provide valuable services in organizing women workers, many of whom were significant in its leadership. The efforts of the Consumers League, led by Florence Kelley, to improve working conditions through the use of middle-class women's buying power was probably less effective, but efforts to enact protective legislation for women workers did succeed. Members of both organizations turned to suffrage as one solution to the problems workers faced. Meanwhile, both in leftist organizations and in unions, women formed separate female organizations. Feminists within the Socialist Party met in women's groups in the early twentieth century, while within the clothing trades, women workers formed separate local unions which survived until the mid-1920s.[15]

As a final example of female institution building, I want to compare two actual buildings—the Woman's Pavillion at the 1876 Centennial Exposition in Philadelphia, analyzed recently by Judith Paine, and the Woman's Building at the 1893 World Columbian Exposition in Chicago. I think that the origins and functions of each illustrate some of the changes that occurred in the women's movement in the time interval between those two celebrations.

Originally, the managers of the 1876 Centennial had promised "a sphere for woman's action and space for her work" within the main display areas. In return women raised over $100,000 for the fair, at which point the management informed the Women's Centennial Executive Committee that there would not be any space for them in the main building. The women's response surprised the men: they raised money for a separate building, and although they hoped to find a woman architect to design it, there was no such professional at the time. From May through October, 1876, the Woman's Pavillion displayed achievements in journalism, medicine, science, art, literature, invention, teaching, business, and social work. It included a library of books by women; an office that published a newspaper for women; and an innovative kindergarten annex, the first such day school in the country. Some radical feminists, however, boycotted the building. Eliza-

beth Cady Stanton claimed that the pavillion "was no true exhibit of woman's art" because it did not represent the product of industrial labor or
protest the inequalities of "political slavery."[16]

By 1893, there was less hesitation about the need for a woman's building and somewhat less conflict about its functions. Congress authorized the
creation of a Board of Lady Managers for the Columbian Commission, and
the women quickly decided on a separate Woman's Building, to be designed
by a woman architect chosen by nationwide competition. Contests were also
held to locate the best women sculptors, painters, and other artists to complete the designs of the building. The Lady Managers also planned and
provided a Children's Building that offered nursery care for over ten thousand young visitors to the fair. At this exposition, not only were women's
artistic and professional achievements heralded, but industrial organizations were "especially invited to make themselves known," and women's
industrial work, as well as the conditions and wages for which they worked,
were displayed. Feminists found this exhibit more agreeable; Antoinette
Brown Blackwell, Julia Ward Howe, and Susan B. Anthony all attended,
and Anthony read a paper written by Elizabeth Cady Stanton at one of the
women's symposia. The Board of Lady Managers fought long and hard to
combine their separate enterprise with participation in the rest of the fair.
They demanded equal representation of women judges for the exhibitions
and equal consideration of women's enterprises in all contests.[17] While they
had to compromise on some goals, their efforts are noteworthy as an indication of a dual commitment to separate female institutions, but only if they
had equal status within the society at large.

## THE POLITICAL LEGACY

The separate institution building of the late nineteenth century rested
on a belief in women's unique identity which had roots in the private female
sphere of the early nineteenth century. Increasingly, however, as its participants entered a public female world, they adopted the more radical stance
of feminists such as Stanton and Anthony who had long called for an end
to political discrimination against women.

The generation that achieved suffrage, then, stood on the border of
two worlds, each of which contributed to its ideology and politics. Suffragists argued that women needed the vote to perform their traditional
tasks—to protect themselves as mothers and to exert their moral force on
society. Yet they also argued for full citizenship and waged a successful, female-
controlled political campaign to achieve it.

The suffrage movement succeeded by appealing to a broad constituency—mothers, workers, professions, reformers—with the vision of the
common concerns of womanhood. The movement failed, however, by not

extending fully the political strengths of woman bonding. For one thing, the leadership allowed some members to exploit popular racist and nativist sentiments in their prosuffrage arguments, thus excluding most black and immigrant women from a potential feminist coalition. They also failed to recognize that the bonds that held the constituency together were not "natural," but social and political. The belief that women would automatically use the vote to the advantage of their sex overlooked both the class and racial lines that separated women. It underestimated the need for continued political organization so that their interests might be united and realized.

Unfortunately, the rhetoric of equality that became popular among men and women (with the exception of the National Woman's Party) just after the passage of the Suffrage Amendment in 1920 subverted the women's movement by denying the need for continued feminist organization. Of course, external factors significantly affected the movement's future, including the new Freudian views of women; the growth of a consumer economy that increasingly exploited women's sexuality; and the repression of radicalism and reform in general after World War I.[18] But at the same time, many women, seemingly oblivious that these pressures necessitated further separate organizing, insisted on striving for integration into a male world— sexually, professionally, and politically.

Examples of this integrationist approach can be found in the universities, the workplace, and politics. In contrast to an earlier generation, the women who participated in the New York World's Fair of 1937 had no separate building. Woman, the Fair Bulletin explained, "will not sit upon a pedestal, not be segregated, isolated; she will fit into the life of the Exposition as she does into life itself—never apart, always a part." The part in this World's Fair, however, consisted primarily of fashion, food, and vanity fair.[19] In the universities, the success of the first generation of female academics did not survive past the 1920s, not only because of men's resistance, but, as Rosalind Rosenberg has explained, "Success isolated women from their culture of origin and placed them in an alien and often hostile community." Many academics who cut off their ties to other women "lost their old feminine supports but had no other supports to replace them."[20]

The lessons of women's politics in the 1920s are illustrated by the life of one woman, Emily Newell Blair, who learned first hand the pitfalls of rejecting a separatist basis for feminism.[21] Blair's life exemplified the transformation of women's roles at the turn of the century. Educated at a woman's college, Goucher, this Missouri-born, middle-class woman returned to her hometown to help support her family until she married and created her own home. Between 1900 and 1910 she bore two children, supported her husband's career, and joined in local women's club activities. In her spare time, Blair began writing short stories for ladies' magazines. Because she found the work, and particularly the income, satisfying, she became a free-lance writer. At this point, the suffrage movement revived in Missouri, and Blair took over state publicity, editing the magazine *Missouri Woman* and doing public relations. Then, in World War I, she expanded her professional activities further by serving on the Women's Council of the U.S. Council of National Defense. These years of training in writing, feminist organizing, and public speaking served Blair well when suffrage passed and she entered politics.

In 1920, women faced three major political choices: they could become a separate feminist political force through the National Woman's Party, which few did; they could follow the moderates of the NAWSA into the newly formed, nonpartisan League of Women Voters, concentrating on citizen education and good government; or they could join the mainstream political parties. Emily Newell Blair chose the last, and rose through the Democratic Party organization to become national vice-chairman of the party in the 1920s.

Blair built her political life and her following on the belief that the vote had made women the political equals of men. Thus, the surest path to furthering women's goals was through participation in the party structure. Having helped to found the League of Women Voters, Blair then rejected nonpartisanship, while she urged women not to vote as women but as citizens. In a 1922 lecture on "What Women May Do with the Ballot," Blair argued that "reactions to political issues are not decided by sex but by intellect and emotion. . . ." Although she believed that lack of political experience and social training made women differ from men temporarily, she expected those differences to be eliminated after a few years of political activity. To hasten women's integration into the mainstream of party politics, Blair set up thirty "schools of democracy" to train the new voters during the early twenties, as well as over one thousand women's clubs. Her philosophy, she claimed, was one of "Boring from Within." Blair rejected the "sex conscious feminists" of the Woman's Party and those who wanted "woman cohesiveness." Although she favored the election of women, she wanted them to be chosen not as women but as politicians. "Give women time," she often repeated, and they would become the equals of men in politics.

By the late 1920s, however, women had not gained acceptance as men's political equals, and Blair's views changed significantly. Once she had claimed that the parties did not discriminate against women, as shown by her own powerful position. After she retired from party office in 1928, however, Blair acknowledged that the treatment of women by the parties had deteriorated since the years immediately after suffrage passed. As soon as male politicians realized that there was no strong female voting bloc or political organization, they refused to appoint or elect powerful women, and a "strong masculine prejudice against women in politics" surfaced.

Now they chose women for party office who seemed easiest to manage or who were the wives of male officeholders.

By 1931, Blair's former optimism had turned to disillusionment. She felt herself "ineffective in politics as a feminist," a term that she began to use positively. Blair realized that women could not command political power and the respect of their male colleagues unless, like the suffrage leaders, they had a visible, vocal following. "Unfortunately for feminism," she confessed, "it was agreed to drop the sex line in politics. And it was dropped by the women." In the pages of the *Woman's Journal,* Blair called for a revival of feminism in the form of a new politics that would seek to put more women into office. Reversing her former stance, she claimed that *women* voters should back *women* candidates, and use a *women's* organization to do so. They could remain in the parties, but should form "a new organization of feminists devoted to the task of getting women into politics."

The development of Emily Newell Blair's feminist consciousness may have been unique for her time, but it is a familiar process among educated and professional women today. Having gained access to formerly male institutions, but still committed to furthering women's struggles, today's "new women" are faced with political choices not dissimilar to the generation that achieved suffrage. The bitterness of Stanton and Anthony in their advice to the younger generation in 1881, and the strategy that Emily Newell Blair presented in 1931, may serve as lessons for the present.

## THE LESSONS OF SEPARATISM

The strength of female institutions in the late nineteenth century and the weaknesses of women's politics after the passage of the Suffrage Amendment suggest to me that the decline of feminism in the 1920s can be attributed in part to the devaluation of women's culture in general and of separate female institutions in particular. When women tried to assimilate into male-dominated institutions, without securing feminist social, economic, or political bases, they lost the momentum and the networks which had made the suffrage movement possible. Women gave up many of the strengths of the female sphere without gaining equally from the man's world they entered.

This historical record has important implications for the women's movement today. It becomes clearer, I think, why the separate, small women's group, organized either for consciousness raising or political study and action, has been effective in building a grass-roots movement over the past ten years. The groups helped to reestablish common bonds long veiled by the retreat from women's institutions into privatized families or sexually integrated, but male-dominated, institutions. The groups encouraged the reemergence of female networks and a new women's culture which in turn have given rise to female institution building. . . .

The history of separatism also helps explain why the politics of lesbian feminism have been so important in the revival of the women's movement. Lesbian feminism, by affirming the primacy of women's relationships with each other and by providing an alternative feminist culture, forced many nonlesbians to reevaluate their relationships with men, male institutions, and male values. In the process, feminists have put to rest the myth of female dependence on men and rediscovered the significance of woman bonding. . . . [22]

I find two kinds of political lessons in the history of the separatist trend. In the past, one of the limitations of separate female institutions was that they were often the only places for women to pursue professional or political activities, while men's institutions retained the power over most of the society. Today it is crucial to press for feminist presence both outside and within the bastions of male dominance, such as politics, the universities, the professions, the unions. But it is equally important for the women within mixed institutions to create female interest groups and support systems. Otherwise, token women may be coopted into either traditionally deferential roles, or they will assimilate through identification with the powers that be. In the process, these women will lose touch with their feminist values and constituencies, as well as suffer the personal costs of tokenism. . . .

I argue for a continuation of separatism not because the values, culture, and politics of the two sexes are biologically, irreversibly distinct, but rather because the historical and contemporary experiences that have created a unique female culture remain both salient for and compatible with the goal of sexual equality. Our common identities and heritage as women can provide enormous personal and political strength as long as we claim the power to define what women can be and what female institutions can achieve. I argue for renewed female institution building at this point in the contemporary women's movement because I fear that many feminists— faced with the isolation of personal success or dismayed by political backlash—may turn away from the separate women's politics that have achieved most of our gains in the past decade. And I argue as well for both greater respect for women's culture among political feminists and greater political engagement on the part of cultural feminists because we now face both external resistance and internal contradictions that threaten to divide our movement.

## NOTES

1. Gayle Rubin, "The Traffic in Women: Notes on the 'Political Economy' of Sex," in *Toward an Anthropology of Women,* ed. Rayna R. Reiter (New York and London: Monthly Review Press, 1975), pp. 157–58.

2. Michelle Zimbalist Rosaldo, "Woman, Culture, and Society: A Theoretical Overview," in *Woman, Culture and Society,* eds. Michelle Zimbalist Rosaldo and Louise Lamphere (Stanford, Calif.: Stanford University Press, 1974), pp. 17–42.

3. Ibid., pp. 37–38. Rosaldo lists women's trading societies, church clubs, "or even political organizations" and cites both the Iroquois and West African societies in which "women have created fully articulated social hierarchies of their own."

4. Carroll Smith-Rosenberg, "The Female World of Love and Ritual: Relationships between Women in Nineteenth-Century America," *Signs* 1, no. 1 (Autumn 1975): 1–29.

5. Nancy F. Cott, *The Bonds of Womanhood: "Women's Sphere" in New England, 1780–1835* (New Haven: Yale University Press, 1977).

6. Blanche Wiesen Cook, "Female Support Networks and Political Activism: Lillian Wald, Crystal Eastman, Emma Goldman," *Chrysalis,* no. 3 (1977): 43–61; and Nancy Sahli, "Smashing: Women's Relationships Before the Fall," *Chrysalis,* no. 8 (Summer 1979): 17–27.

7. Feminist historians need clear definitions of women's culture and women's politics to avoid such divisions between the personal and political. Women's culture can exist at both private and public levels. Women's politics, too, can be personal (intrafamilial, through friendship and love, for example) as well as public (the traditional definition of politics). The question of when women's culture and politics are *feminist* has yet to be fully explored. At this time, I would suggest that any female-dominated activity that places a positive value on women's social contributions, provides personal support, and is not controlled by antifeminist leadership has feminist political potential.

8. These theories are surveyed in Estelle B. Freedman, "The New Woman: Changing Views of Women in the 1920s," *Journal of American History* 61 (September 1974): 372–93.

9. Smith-Rosenberg, "The Female World of Love and Ritual."

10. See Ellen DuBois, "The Radicalism of the Woman Suffrage Movement: Notes Toward the Reconstruction of Nineteenth-Century Feminism," *Feminist Studies* 3 (Fall 1975): 63–71. On opposition to women's rights from a "traditional" woman, see Kathryn Kish Sklar, *Catharine Beecher: A Study in American Domesticity* (New Haven: Yale University Press), pp. 266–67.

11. William O'Neill, ed., *The Woman Movement: Feminism in the United States and England* (Chicago: Quadrangle Books, 1969), pp. 47–54; and Gerda Lerner, ed., *Black Women in White America* (New York: Vintage, 1972), chap. 8.

12. DuBois, "Radicalism," p. 69.

13. Barbara Welter, "The Cult of True Womanhood, 1820–1860," *American Quarterly* 18 (Summer 1966): 150–74.

14. For biographical data on these and other reformers, see the entries in *Notable American Women, 1607–1950,* eds. Edward T. James, Janet Wilson James, and Paul S. Boyer (Cambridge, Mass.: Harvard University Press, 1971).

15. On women in labor and radical movements, see: Nancy Schrom Dye, "Feminism or Unionism? The New York Women's Trade Union League and the Labor Movement," and Robin Miller Jacoby, "The Women's Trade Union League and American Feminism," in *Feminist Studies* 3, no. 1–2 (Fall 1975): 111–40; Allis Rosenberg Wolfe, "Women, Consumerism, and the National Consumers League in the Progressive Era, 1900–1923," *Labor History* 16 (Summer 1975), 378–92; Mary Jo Buhle, "Women and the Socialist Party, 1901–1914," *Radical America* 4, no. 2 (February 1970): 36–55. . . .

16. Judith Paine, "The Women's Pavillion of 1876," *Feminist Art Journal* 4, no. 4 (Winter 1975–76): 5–12; and *The Woman's Building, Chicago, 1893/The Woman's Building, Los Angeles, 1973* (Los Angeles, 1975).

17. Bertha Honoré Palmer, "The Growth of the Woman's Building," in *Art and Handicraft in the Woman's Building of the World's Columbian Exposition,* ed. Maud Howe Elliott (New York, 1893), pp. 11–12.

18. See Ryan, *Womanhood in America,* for an exploration of these trends.

19. The New York World's Fair Bulletin 1, no. 8 (December 1937): 20–21; the *New York City World's Fair Information Manual,* 1939, index. Amy Swerdlow kindly shared these references and quotations about the 1937 fair from her own research on women in the World's Fairs.

20. Rosalind Rosenberg, "The Academic Prism: The New View of American Women," in *Women of America: A History,* eds. Carol Ruth Berkin and Mary Beth Norton (Boston: Houghton Mifflin, 1979), pp. 318–38.

21. The following account of Blair is drawn from research for a biographical essay that appeared in *The Dictionary of American Biography,* suppl., vol. 5 (New York: Charles Scribner, 1977), pp. 61–63. For examples of her writings see "What Women May Do with the Ballot" (Philadelphia, 1922); "Boring from Within," *Woman Citizen* 12 (July 1927): 49–50; "Why I am Discouraged About Women in Politics," *Woman's Journal* 6 (January 1931): 20–22.

22. Radicalesbians, "The Woman-Identified Woman," *Notes from the Third Year: Women's Liberation* (reprinted in *Radical Feminism,* ed. Anne Koedt, Ellen Levine and Anita Rapone [New York: Quadrangle, 1973] pp. 240–45); Lucia Valeska, "The Future of Female Separatism," *Quest* 2, no. 2 (Fall 1975) 2–16; Charlotte Bunch, "Learning from Lesbian Separatism," in *Lavender Culture,* eds. Karla Jay and Allen Young (New York: Jove Books, 1978), pp. 433–44.

# 2

# And We Are Nothing but Women: Irish Working Women in Troy

## Carole Turbin

*Most accounts of working women stress the subordination of women within a family wage economy and the failure of women to organize to improve their wages and working conditions. Carole Turbin, in her study of collar laundry workers in Troy, New York, offers a contrasting view. She finds that working women were successful at organizing an effective trade union and in mobilizing labor in Troy in support of their efforts. She offers a thoughtful explanation for the power exercised by these women workers in the post–Civil War years.*

> You know what a union is . . . you know full well the value of cooperation; we have been out of money six weeks and but two of our number have given in. I fancy but there are few men's organizations that can show such a record, and we are nothing but women.
>
> > Esther Keegan, Vice President of the Collar Laundry Union of Troy, New York, to the Workingmen's Union of New York City, July 2, 1869. (New York *World,* July 3, 1869).

It has often been observed that women's labor activity in the United States in the mid-nineteenth century was sporadic, short-lived, and unsuccessful. As dependents whose proper sphere was fireside and nursery, working women's role in the labor force was incompatible with the conditions necessary for permanent trade union organization. Women did not devote time and money to union activity because they did not regard themselves as permanent members of the work force. Moreover, they were occupied with household duties after their hours of wage labor and were too shy and retiring to participate in organizations that required speaking in public and assuming leadership. Also, since women were the most unskilled, low-paid workers of the day, they lacked the leverage to bargain with employers and the resources to weather hard times and strikes. Finally, some women workers faced hostility from working men because men believed that women competed for their jobs and reduced their wages to the low level of women's earnings. As helpless, degraded workers on the lowest levels of the working class, most women wage earners did not engage in labor activity to protect their interests as workers.[1]

Woman Ironing *(1882). Edgar Degas; National Gallery of Art, Washington; Collection of Mr. and Mrs. Paul Mellon.*

The Collar Laundry Union of Troy, New York, does not fit this characterization. Other working women periodically went on strike and some organized small unions that lasted as long as a year. But the laundresses' union was larger and more permanent than many men's locals during these decades. This women's union consisted of at least 400 members at its peak and existed for almost 6 years (from February 1864 to September 1869). Other women workers improved wages and working conditions from time to time. But the laundresses raised their wages to a level almost equal to the average earnings of working men. Also, they accumulated a fund large enough to provide security during strikes, illness, or death in the family. Further, the laundresses did not face hostility from male workers, but formed a close alliance with the male-led labor movement. Male unionists considered the Collar Laundry Union the only "'bona fide' female union in the country."[2] In light of the obstacles to labor organization that women faced, why was the Collar Laundry Union so successful?

The women who organized the Collar Laundry Union were not transient workers who had little reason to attempt to improve their condition as workers. Like other working women in the nation, the Troy laundresses as a group were permanent members of the industrial work force. Although individual women may not have remained in the labor force all their working days, women were essential to industrial production, and by the mid-nineteenth century they were a substantial percentage of the industrial labor force. Labor historian David Montgomery points out that by 1870 one-quarter of the wage earners in nonagricultural occupations were female. Of these, 70 percent were domestic servants. But of the remaining 30 percent, most were industrial workers. Over four-fifths of women industrial workers were employed in some branch of apparel making, including hoopskirt making and parasol and umbrella sewing. The remaining one-fifth were schoolteachers, clerks in stores, or worked in numerous other industrial occupations employing women, such as paper box making, cigar making, and printing.[3]

Troy's laundresses were an important part of that city's permanent industrial work force. They were not domestic servants or washerwomen who did personal laundry, as the term laundress suggests, but industrial workers who ironed newly manufactured detachable collars in commercial laundries. Employing about 600 women, Troy's approximately 14 laundries performed one step in the production of detachable collars for the city's prosperous shirt, collar, and cuff industry. In keeping with the increasing division of labor of the day, the laundering process was divided into separate steps—washing, starching, and ironing—and individual workers specialized in only one operation. And in keeping with craft unionism, each group of workers formed separate organizations, although sometimes they engaged in labor activity together. Also in keeping with craft unionism, the women who formed the union were the most skilled workers in the shops—the ironers. In Troy the union was often referred to as the Collar Ironers' Union.

Troy's shirt, collar, and cuff industry was not a minor local industry in a backwater town. Troy was an important industrial center with two major industries—shirt, collar, and cuff manufacturing and the iron industry. These industries' products, as well as textiles and other goods produced in surrounding Albany and Cohoes, were shipped all over the United States via the Hudson River and the Erie Canal, which connected the East to the Midwest through the Great Lakes. The relatively small-scale collar laundries were interdependent with Troy's shirt, collar, and cuff factories, which produced most of the detachable collars and cuffs sold in the nation. The 15 factories employed a total of 3,128 women. Although it was a local industry, it was seventh in capital investment of all the 23 apparel industries in the state, including New York City's already vast clothing industry. Today Troy is still nicknamed "Collar City."[4]

Many members of the Collar Laundry Union were not permanent workers. Working men and women agreed with other Americans that ideally women should remain at home in their proper sphere and husbands should earn enough to support their families. Thus, in Troy as in other communities, less than 1 percent of the women in the labor force were wives living with their husbands.[5] Another much larger group (about 17 percent of the Troy laundresses in 1865) were widows with small children. But by far the largest group of working women in the nation were young single women who lived with their families. Some of these women may not have been willing to devote time and money to trade union activity because they did not regard themselves as permanent workers. Young single women who anticipated marrying and raising children probably regarded their employment as temporary. Even widows dependent entirely on their own earnings probably hoped to remarry and leave the work force. Yet the collar laundresses did seek to improve their condition through trade union activity. To understand this, we must look more closely at the significance of women's temporary role in the work force.

The fact that Troy's laundresses worked only temporarily did not mean that their occupation was a fleeting moment in their lives, not worth improving through trade unionism. These working women were not laboring to buy themselves luxuries; many were the sole supporter of their family. Augusta Lewis, President of the Women's Typographical Union No. 1 of New York City, observed that many of the laundresses "had aged parents, younger brothers and sisters, and some had their own children besides themselves depending on their wages." In 1865 Kate Mullaney, the laundresses' president, was supporting herself as well as her mother, Bridget, age 55, and two younger sisters.[6] Many others had to work even when the male head of household was employed. . . . Clearly, working-class women's proper role included the role of provider.

For women like Troy's laundresses, some form of employment was a familiar experience in every stage of life. In many working-class families, daughters joined the work force as soon as they reached a suitable age, often entering the same occupation as their older sisters or other female relatives.

Those who married in their early twenties probably did not work for more than five to seven years. But women who did not marry remained in the work force much longer. Because most working-class women were employed at one time or another, and because at any given time some female family members were working for wages, working-class women were constantly reminded of the necessity of earning a decent living. Although they may not have been permanent workers as individuals, they had good reason to protect their rights as workers.

The collar laundresses' position in the work force and the community was worth defending. Like many industrial workers during this period, the collar laundry women were largely of Irish background. In fact, over three-quarters of the laundresses were of Irish descent. In contrast, only one-half of other female industrial workers, and about 30 percent of sewing women were Irish-born or the children of Irish immigrants. Only domestic servants were more overwhelmingly of Irish background than collar laundresses.

Mid-nineteenth-century immigration patterns in the United States partially explain the overwhelming proportion of Irish women employed in the laundries. Many Irish immigrants found their way to Troy because the Hudson River provided convenient transportation from New York City, and Troy's industries promised employment. By 1865 Irish immigrants constituted almost one-quarter of Troy's population; the American-born children of these residents made the proportion even higher. Since most of these people were working class, probably more than one-half of Troy's working class was of Irish decent.[7]

This is not to say that Troy's laundresses came from the city's poorest families. Irish workers did labor in the most menial occupations, such as day labor and domestic service, but many Irish families achieved a much higher status through employment in Troy's iron industry. This industry included several large iron and steel works and many smaller foundries that produced stoves, ranges, bells, wheels, and other iron products. Some skilled occupations, like pattern-makers in the foundries and nailers and spikers in Burden's nail factory, employed largely workers of American background. But men of Irish descent constituted the largest number of workers in each of the three largest skilled branches of the iron foundries— molders, puddlers, and heaters and rollers. Since most of these men arrived in America with few industrial skills, they experienced considerable upward mobility through the iron industry.[8]

Troy's laundresses were part of a well-organized labor movement led by these highly skilled, largely Irish iron molders. In the 1860s and 1870s the most well-organized workers were highly skilled, well-paid men of American background. But in Troy the most well-organized workers were skilled iron workers, chiefly stove and range molders. From about 1860 to the 1880s the Troy Iron Molders' Union No. 2 was one of the most influential locals in the International Iron Molders' Union, and this national union was in turn one of the three or four most powerful national trade unions. In Troy the molders helped organize strikes, meetings, and trade union picnics that contributed to other workers' labor activity or celebrated working-class solidarity.[9] The Troy *Press* viewed one picnic as a symbol of this unity: "Capital, with her high head, proud mein and plethoric purse, is at Saratoga or Newport. Labor, with her brawny arms, independent spirit and moderate share of greenbacks is at Winnie's Grove. Hurrah for Winnie's!"

What was the collar laundresses' status in this working-class community? Although many laundresses came from the families of unskilled workers, an even larger group came from families on the highest levels of the working class. For example, in 1865 about 30 percent of the laundresses' male relatives were unskilled workers like laborers or porters, but only about 11 percent of sewing women's male relatives were unskilled. Also, about half (52 percent) of laundresses' male relatives were skilled workers like carpenters, blacksmiths, or molders. This figure is about the same for other Troy working women—for example, 59 percent for sewing women's male relatives. The laundresses' status was consistent with both the low status of Irish workers in general and the relatively high status of many Irish families in Troy.

The characteristics of the laundresses' occupation itself fit in with their mixed status in Troy's working class. In general, work in commercial laundries carried less status than other industrial occupations like needlework. Although laundering was probably not any more fatiguing and health-impairing than sewing and factory work, working conditions involved strenuous physical labor. Esther Keegan reported that laundresses stood on their feet almost all of their 11 to 14 hours of labor in shops as small as 16 feet square. Temperatures reached the "nineties" in the winter, and in the summer it was so hot that laundresses often had to "forgo their work for two or three weeks at a time from sheer inability to perform it." Ironers were required to continually lift hot heavy irons, and starchers' fingers became sore from constant immersion in starchy water. Keegan asserted that because of these conditions, laundresses frequently contracted consumption: "None but the strongest could stand it."

Laundering was also less ladylike than other women's occupations. While women from prosperous families may have done their own fine needlework, they rarely did their own laundry. People invariably compared laundry work to taking in washing, which was one of the most menial, poorly paid women's occupations. Thus, although laundry work was an industrial occupation, it was less genteel and respectable than dress-making, millinery, or even routine hand-stitching. Women of American background who had more options for employment probably preferred the more ladylike occupations of sewing or light industrial work.

Collar laundering was, however, more prestigious than domestic service. Working-class women considered the work of cooks, chambermaids, and housekeepers degrading because it involved serving or cleaning up after others and did not provide the independence of a wage. Women who needed servants bemoaned the fact that most Americans "would rather want bread than *serve* to gain it."[10] Therefore, while laundry work was not a prestigious occupation for women of American background who could get other work, it was a good occupation for Irish women who wished to rise above employment in service occupations.

Unlike taking in washing and domestic service, laundering offered the independence of a wage and regular employment. Also, thanks to the union, laundresses' earnings were comparatively high. In 1872 the average earnings of working women amounted to $299.00 per year, or $1.16 per day, $6.96 per week, a figure close to the average earnings of working men ($13.44 per week). Collar laundering combined the disadvantages of unlady-like labor with the advantages of industrial work. It attracted women from lower levels of the working class who were able to get better employment than domestic service, and those from higher levels who were willing to endure hard physical labor for high wages.

Of the several laundering steps, collar ironing was the most presti-gious. It was not a skilled trade, since it involved a task familiar to many women and did not require knowledge of many complicated processes. Nevertheless, handling the heavy hot irons required physical strength, en-durance, and a skill that could only be acquired through two to four weeks of intensive training. According to employers, good ironers were not easy to come by, and the ironing skill was worth more than that of starchers and washers. In the small world of commercial laundries, ironers were the aristocracy of labor.[11]

The collar laundresses' organizational structure and level of skill helped them to defend their right to earn a living in the occupation in which they were trained. The ironers organized by the work they did in their shop as well as by sex. This organizational structure was typical of craft unionism; workers who did different kinds of labor in one industry almost always organized separately. But it was also useful for women to organize separately because women who organized into men's locals were at a disad-vantage. They faced male workers' antagonisms more directly and were more reluctant to speak up at meetings and take leadership roles. The few women who did belong to men's locals, like women cigar makers, were less effective unionists because their interests were submerged and isolated.[12] Working women like the laundresses who formed separate organizations could develop their own leaders and adopt strategies and tactics tailored to their particular work situation.

Kate Mullaney was aware that it was important for working women to organize independently from men. A reporter who interviewed Mullaney in September 1868 argued that the organization of New York City's working women lagged because women were not confident of their own abilities to be "presidents and secretaries" of trade unions. In defense of her sisters, Mullaney responded that "there are numbers of ladies connected with the laundry union who were just as competent as any gentlemen." Probably because she realized that some women were at first reluctant to speak up at meetings or take leadership roles, she offered to send laundry union members to New York City to help women organize. If "ladies from New York" were not "competent," she would "send some from Troy and pay their expenses until such time as they were able to educate some of their own." According to Mullaney, New York's working women could overcome these difficulties with the help of other women workers rather than male trade unionists. Clearly, the laundresses' strategies were shaped partly by their status as women.

The ironers also used their position as semiskilled workers in strategies that contributed to their union's success. In this period, skilled workers were the most well organized partly because their skill was a valuable commodity that they could withhold from employers.[13] An incident that occurred early in September 1868 indicates that employers could not maintain a profitable level of production with inexperienced hands. Having given in to wage increases since 1864, the laundry proprietors tried to undermine the union by persuading nonunion ironers in the city's largest laundry to train new hands to replace workers in union shops. It would not have been necessary for the owners to use this tactic to weaken the union if they could have simply fired the union ironers and replaced them with new hands. Mullaney reported that the employers' tactics failed because the nonunion ironers, "seeing what the result would finally be, for their own protection, joined the union in a body." The owners' need for experienced labor enabled the ironers to strengthen their union even further. The laundry proprietors could not maintain full production levels during a strike even while scab workers were being trained. As employers themselves admitted, it took "some time to teach the newcomers the business." Even with a few weeks of training, the inexperienced workers' skill was not equal to the dexterity and speed of the striking ironers.

This tactic of withholding labor was successful partly because laundry proprietors were relatively vulnerable to employees' concerted action. As operators of a small-scale service industry, the laundry owners had fewer resources than the collar manufacturers with which to weather reduced production during strikes. Even more important, the laundry owners' position in the business community enabled them to pass on any increased labor costs to the collar manufacturers. The manufacturers had to absorb these costs. Despite the manufacturers' extensive resources and markets, they were dependent on the laundries' services to prepare their products for sale. The ironers' three-month strike in 1869 demonstrates the importance of these factors in the union's success. In previous strikes the laundresses had conflicted only with the laundry proprietors, but in 1869 they faced a more formidable foe. That year the laundry proprietors combined with the much more powerful collar manufacturers. More than any other factor, the manufacturers' resources and strategies determined the strike's outcome— the demise of the Collar Laundry Union.

The strike officially began on May 29, and on June 1 the manufac- turers met publicly to plan their resistance. Their strategies were carried out on two fronts. They pressured the proprietors into holding out indefi- nitely by refusing to send new collars and cuffs to any laundry employing union ironers, and they helped the laundry owners obtain a new work force by helping them recruit and train new hands. Also, the manufacturers at- tempted to undermine directly the union's efforts to weather the strike. They tried to create a negative image of the union through the local press, which they virtually controlled. They prevented the few collar manufac- turers in other cities from patronizing the union's cooperative laundry even though it claimed it could provide the same services for 25 percent less. Under these circumstances, the collar ironers' tactics were much less useful.

The collar manufacturers and laundry owners combined to prevent future wage increases. They aimed to do this not simply by opposing the present increase, but by finally eliminating the union. One indication that this was their motivation is the substantial evidence that the conflict was actually initiated by the laundry owners.[14] The ironers had demanded and received a wage increase in July 1868, and the starchers received an increase in March 1869. The third conflict began when the laundry owners de- manded that the ironers equalize wages paid for work on different-size col- lars within each shop. When the ironers complied by decreasing rates for some work and increasing rates for other work, there was a general increase of about $1\frac{1}{2}$ cents per dozen collars. Although the proprietors had de- manded the equalization, they refused to pay the increase.

The manufacturers claimed through the local press that this increase was the issue of the strike. They maintained that the ironers already re- ceived extraordinarily high wages for only ten hours of light labor per day, and that women foolish enough to be influenced by "outside busybodies" deserved to lose their jobs. Troy's collar factories, they argued, were already being undersold by the few collar manufacturers in other cities. If the iron- ers continued their unreasonable demands, Troy's collar industry would be destroyed and thousands of residents would suffer. The Troy *Daily Whig* asked, will "this new collar-a" prevail?

Although Troy's press was not as biased as the strikers claimed, it did suppress an essential fact that was revealed in New York City's newspapers: Once the ironers went on strike for the increase, some employers offered to rehire them at slightly higher wages on the condition that they give up their union. Kate Mullaney told the Workingmen's Union of New York City on July 2, 1869, that the laundry union's employers "do not care for the money." They were willing to pay the increased wages, but insisted that the ironers "must give up" their union. Esther Keegan maintained that the iron-ers would make "every concession," but "it would never do to give up" their union. "We are determined not to yield." From a trade unionist's point of view, the strike was a lockout in which employers would not rehire union members unless they gave up their union. Like the iron molders' Great Lockout of 1866, the issue of the ironers' strike was "union or no union."

Partly because the combination of employers was so formidable, the ironers also chose another strategy for obtaining their rights: They formed a producers' cooperative, essentially a joint stock company financed through selling shares. In the late 1860s many prominent trade unionists believed that strikes could eliminate only the worst effects of wage slavery. They ar-gued that producers' cooperatives enabled workers to escape wage slavery permanently by transforming themselves into small businessmen.[15] Iron molders were among the most enthusiastic advocates of cooperation, and their iron foundries in Troy were among the most successful cooperative enterprises in the nation. Following the example of molders and others, the collar ironers laid plans for a cooperative laundry in early June. In July, when it was apparent that local manufacturers prevented out-of-town manu-facturers from supplying the cooperative with newly made collars, the union expanded the project to include a cooperative collar-and-cuff manu-factory. As Mullaney wrote in a letter to Susan B. Anthony which appeared in *The Revolution* in April 1870, the "girls" hoped "to proceed on a purely business basis, by doing the work . . . themselves." They hoped eventually to "buy up all the stock and hold it for their own benefit." If the project had succeeded, the laundresses would have transformed themselves into small businesswomen who were not dependent on wages for survival.

Despite the ironers' determination and the trade union movement's generous support, the union was dissolved in early September 1869, and the cooperative was disbanded in 1870. The cooperative was doomed largely because of problems inherent in this form of producers' coopera-tive, and partly because it could not compete with Troy's powerful collar manufacturers. But the project's failure was probably also due to the fact that the ironers were women. No matter how efficient the ironers' enter-prise was, and no matter how much expertise and financial aid male trade unionists contributed, prospective buyers were not likely to take women seriously as manufacturers.

The demise of the union and the cooperative does not mean that the laundresses were helpless women or degraded workers who had no bargain-ing power. They successfully resisted employers' appropriation of an unfair share of the profits their labor produced for a much longer period than most male workers did in these decades. They could do this for the same reasons that working men were able to improve wages and working condi-tions—by making the most of their employers' need for trained labor, and by taking advantage of the owners' vulnerability and their position in the

business community. The ironers lost this leverage only when the proprietors increased their strength by combining with the manufacturers. The
ironers' leverage was decreased even further a few years later when collar
manufacturers found a more effective way to avoid absorbing laundry owners' increased labor costs: By the late 1870s the manufacturers incorporated
the laundries into the collar manufactories. The collar ironers were "nothing but women" who faced more disadvantages than male workers. But like
other relatively successful women and men unionists, they faced their employers primarily as workers.

The laundresses withstood employers' efforts to break their union for
several months because their alliance with other workers—male trade
unionists—made their strategies and tactics more effective. Male unionists
cooperated with the ironers despite the fact that the antagonisms between
men and women workers were as deep as other hostilities dividing American wage earners. Just as working men were threatened by unskilled "green
hands," especially if they were black or Chinese, they were also threatened
by women workers. Working men not only believed that women took men's
jobs and reduced their earnings, but they also thought that women wage
earners were out of their natural sphere.[16] Because of these beliefs, sometimes male workers were not willing to provide women wage earners with
the aid that unskilled or semiskilled workers urgently needed to organize
effectively. Yet they did aid the laundresses.

How firm was this alliance between collar laundresses and male trade
unionists? The ironers' relationship with the male-led trade union movement began with their friendship with Troy's iron molders. This relationship in turn began with the laundresses' first efforts to organize, lasted until
at least 1870, and continued into the 1880s, if not longer. Esther Keegan
reported that the molders' union introduced the laundresses to the principles of trade unionism in February 1864. During the period of economic
difficulties just after the beginning of the Civil War, their "weeks' wages
could only buy a pair of shoes." They "asked higher wages," but "were not
listened to." But when they organized into a union on the advice of the
molders, they "got the advance they asked for." By 1869 almost all shops
were organized and the union included about 430 members.

In the ensuing years the laundresses showed their appreciation and
the molders reciprocated. At the first molders' picnic on July 18, 1864,
about 4,000 people watched the presentation of a blue silk banner to Henry
Rockefeller, the Troy molders' president. The banner pictured on one side
a furnace in full blast with men "pouring off" the molten metal and on the
other side a figure of justice below an eagle. Ribbons on one side of the
banner bore the inscription: "Presented by the Collar Laundry Union of
Troy to the Iron Molders' Association." Two years later, in April 1866, the
laundresses donated the enormous sum of 1,000 dollars to the molders during their Great Lockout. In return, in September 1868, William Sylvis, Presi-

dent of the National Labor Union and the IMIU, appointed Kate Mullaney Assistant Secretary of the NLU. Remembering the laundresses' loyalty, the molders were the ironers' staunchest supporters during their 1869 strike.

Trade unionists in New York City and elsewhere also stood by the iron- ers in 1869. In early July Kate Mullaney and Esther Keegan visited New York City in order to solicit contributions for their cooperative and strike fund from the city's prosperous unions. Almost every union in the city responded with generous amounts of cash. By September, contributions totaled 4,510 dollars.

The state's trade unions generously aided the ironers in part because the strike was one of the few that was officially endorsed by the New York State Workingmen's Assembly. Trade unionists resented "begging expedi- tions" that visited New York, because contributing to strikes depleted their treasuries and weakened their ability to resist their own employers. In re- sponse to this problem William Jessup, President of the New York State Workingmen's Assembly, instituted a policy of investigating conflicts when strikers requested aid in order to determine whether they were worthy of contributions. If he deemed them worthy, Jessup issued an official circular explaining the strike's cause. The ironers' 1869 strike was one of only two conflicts that year endorsed in this manner. Significantly, the other worthy strike was the New York City Bricklayers' strike for the eight-hour day. Troy's iron molders, Troy's labor movement, and New York State's trade unions were the ironers' loyal allies.

Since most working men were threatened by women workers, why did male unionists rally behind the laundresses' union? A New York State Bu- reau of Labor Statistics Report of 1886 suggests that the iron molders and laundresses were allied because the laundry women were an important source of income for molders' families. The census manuscript adds some support to this argument. While 14 percent of the laundresses' male rela- tives were molders in 1865, molders constituted only 8 percent of collar sewers' male relatives, and 5 percent of sewing women's male relatives. Al- though 14 percent does not represent very many individuals, slightly more laundry women than other working women were related to molders. These family ties may have reduced antagonisms between male and female work- ers in collar laundries and iron foundries. Shared ethnic identity may have augmented these ties. Living in the same neighborhoods and participating in Irish political and nationalist organizations, Troy's Irish working-class community was particularly close-knit.[17] Troy's laundresses and molders probably had more ethnic and family ties than other female and male workers.

But family ties and shared ethnic identity cannot provide a full expla- nation for this alliance. If the alliance was based entirely on these ties, then the ironers' union would have to be viewed as an isolated example that depended on the external aid of relatives or membership in an ethnic community. The union's strength, commitment to trade unionism, and firm alliance with male trade unionists could not have been based on external aid alone, but must have also depended on the ironers' own efforts as wage earners. Also, family ties and ethnic identity cannot explain why workers organize, because these ties do not necessarily lead to a commitment to trade unionism. In order to organize successfully the laundresses also had to develop a commitment to trade unionism through their own experiences in bargaining with employers. In order to form firm alliances with other workers the laundresses had to have common interests as wage earners who were attempting to counter the power of capital. These common interests also explain the laundresses' alliance with the national trade union movement.

It was possible for some male workers to ally with women on the basis of shared interests as wage earners and for others to be hostile to working women because working men's situation as men and as trade unionists was inconsistent. As American workers, male unionists were threatened by women working for wages. However, working men also recognized that women worked because they had to, that women workers had a right to protect themselves from employers, and that working women, like men, could obtain this protection only through trade unionism.

But working men's fear of women's competition was so strong that working men could cooperate with women wage earners only under circumstances that mitigated this threat to their livelihood. Three kinds of circumstances seemed necessary for this cooperation: With few exceptions, male and female wage earners cooperated only when male workers believed that women were not directly competing with men; this kind of cooperation occurred when working women were not helpless but proved the unionists' adage that "those who would be free must themselves strike the first blow"; most important, working men cooperated with women workers when they derived some direct benefit from working women's labor activity.

Most male-female cooperation in the 1860s and 1870s occurred between men and women who labored in different branches of the same industry. For example, members of the Daughters of St. Crispin stitched shoes in the same shops as male Crispins. In these situations male and female wage earners were not competitors, because they did work strictly reserved for either sex. Their cooperation strengthened the bargaining position of both sexes, since their efforts were aimed at the same employers.

In Troy and other communities cooperation also occurred between women and men who were employed in entirely different industries with different employers. In this case, women's unions were beneficial to men in another equally important way: They made substantial contributions to the solidarity of the working-class community. Troy's trade union movement was a major center of labor activity partly because iron molders and other skilled workers not only protected their own interests, but also helped draw other less-skilled workers into the local trade union movement. The molders helped establish Troy's Trades' Assembly in 1864 and organized huge picnics and demonstrations that mobilized thousands of workers in Troy and neighboring communities. Not only did they help the collar ironers organize, but they also aided others who were less likely to organize on their own, such as day laborers, tailoresses, and dressmakers. Unlike needlewomen in other communities, these Troy sewing women were continuously organized for at least a year.[18] Workers of different backgrounds, levels of skill, and stages of organization could depend on each other for support. . . .

The ironers and other female trade unionists in Troy not only received aid but also made their own contributions to the unity of labor against capital. The dressmakers' and milliners' unions contributed to the bookkeepers' strike for a wage increase in 1864. The ironers not only supported the molders in 1866, but donated the large sum of 500 dollars to the New York City Bricklayers' strike in 1868. As a Troy molder put it, "The ironers . . . have always been noted for their liberality in assisting other trade unions on strike."

The laundresses also contributed to the solidarity of the national trade union movement. Their contribution to the molders' lockout was a donation not to a local conflict, but to Sylvis's strategy to counter a national association of manufacturers formed to weaken the IMIU. Similarly, the bricklayers' strike was part of the strategy of the state's eight-hour movement to enforce an eight-hour law recently passed by the state legislature. Like their allies, the laundresses protected not only themselves and their neighbors, but also the working-class movement as a whole.

The ironers' 1869 strike and their cooperative were major contributions to this movement. . . . Despite the fact that the strike failed and the cooperative foundered, the ironers' leaders continued to be committed to trade unionism, and male trade unionists continued to stand by them. As valuable members of the trade union movement, the ironers continued to be deserving of support. Sharing the interests of wage earners who sought to protect themselves through trade unionism, the collar ironers were "bona fide" trade unionists.

The women who formed the Collar Laundry Union overcame formidable obstacles to trade union organization. Women who overcame these barriers must have been forceful individuals who developed the abilities to articulate clearly their conclusions and to plan strategies and tactics to achieve their goals. But the laundresses' success was not due to the fact that some were exceptional individuals. They were successful because they shared more characteristics that enabled workers in general to form permanent unions than did other female industrial workers. The laundresses were successful for the same reasons that male trade unionists were.

The factors contributing to the laundresses' success reveal that they organized primarily as workers rather than women. Coming from the same

level of the working class as many male unionists, their organization reflected the characteristics of their occupation and their employers, divisions
between workers based on level of skill, nationality, religion, and sex, and
characteristics of the labor movement in their community. They came to
the same conclusions about the relationship between labor and capital,
adopted the same strategies and tactics, and formed the same alliances as
male unionists.

An important conclusion about women trade unionists' consciousness
of themselves as workers and as women emerges from this examination of
male and female trade unions. Esther Keegan's address to the Workingmen's Union indicates that Keegan, like other women unionists, viewed herself primarily as a wage earner who was also a working-class woman—that is,
Keegan recognized that the laundresses were "nothing but women" whose
dependent status shaped their ability to organize as successfully as men. But
this status was in turn fundamentally shaped by the disadvantages they
shared with working-class men who were also dependent on wages for their
livelihood. Thus, to the extent that women trade unionists organized as
women, they identified with other working-class women, not with women
of other social classes. Conscious of their identity as wage earners, they did
not identify with women's rights advocates who would probably never have
to work for wages. Women trade unionists like Troy's laundresses organized
as women within their own social class.

This conclusion is not meant to argue that working women in the mid-
nineteenth century did not identify with issues relevant to women of all
levels of society. Women unionists did not agree with suffragists that "the
ballot, in the World of work is [woman's] only shield and protection." But
they did firmly believe that in principle women should have the ballot. Further, this conclusion is not meant to argue that all working women in all
times and places will always identify primarily with working-class men
rather than with women of other social groups.[19] These conclusions indicate
that for these women at this time and place, class interests were more important than interests shared with women of other social groups.

## NOTES

1. John B. Andrews and W. P. D. Bliss, *History of Women in Trade Unions,* Arno Press, New
York, 1974 (reprint of 1911 edition), pp. 17–18, 45–49, 140–145; Theresa Wolfson, *The Woman
Worker and the Trade Unions,* International Publishers, New York, 1926, pp. 90–97, 157–158;
Eleanor Flexner, *Century of Struggle,* Atheneum, New York, 1970, Chap. 9, especially p. 137.

2. For basic facts about these unions, see: Flexner, *Century of Struggle,* pp. 131–141; and
Andrews and Bliss, *Women in Trade Unions,* pp. 105–110. The following essay is based primarily
on fuller information found in newspapers published in Troy and New York City, the labor
press, Susan B. Anthony's *The Revolution* (New York, 1868–1872), and proceedings of meetings
of the National Labor Union and the New York State Workingmen's Assembly. This quote is
from the *Workingman's Advocate,* June 26, 1869.

3. David Montgomery, *Beyond Equality: Labor and the Radical Republicans, 1862–1872,* Vintage Books, New York, 1967, p. 33.

4. Daniel Walkowitz, "Statistics and the Writing of Working Class Culture: A Statistical Portrait of the Iron Workers in Troy, New York, 1860–1880," *Labor History*, 15 (Summer 1974), 416–460; *New York State Census*, 1865, p. 478.

5. All percentages for age, birthplace, occupation of male relatives, and marital status are based on the manuscript censuses for Troy in 1865 and 1870.

6. The description of Mullaney and her family and the following discussion of work patterns are drawn from the manuscript census for Troy in 1865 and 1870.

7. Montgomery, *Beyond Equality*, pp. 35–40; Walkowitz, "Statistics," p. 422; *New York State Census*, pp. 11–12, 151–152.

8. Walkowitz, "Statistics," pp. 435–444.

9. Walkowitz, "Statistics," pp. 426–428.

10. Oscar Handlin, *Boston's Immigrants, 1790–1880,* Atheneum, New York, 1972, p. 61.

11. Norman Ware, *The Industrial Worker, 1840–1860,* Quadrangle Books, Chicago, 1964, pp. xviii–xxi; Montgomery, *Beyond Equality*, pp. 140–148.

12. Flexner, *Century of Struggle*, p. 137.

13. Montgomery, *Beyond Equality*, pp. 140–148.

14. There is some evidence that the collar manufacturers were behind the initiation of the strike, but there is not enough data to confirm the role they played at this stage.

15. Montgomery, *Beyond Equality*, pp. 154–155, 227–229.

16. Montgomery, *Beyond Equality*, p. 147.

17. Walkowitz, "Statistics," pp. 433–435.

18. Walkowitz, "Statistics," pp. 426–428.

19. *The Revolution,* January 15, 1868 (quote); New York *World,* September 18, 1868.

# 3
# Woman's Mighty Realm of Philanthropy
## Ruth Bordin

*The expansion of women's political culture after the Civil War laid the foundation for the greatest political mobilization of women in American history—the Woman's Christian Temperance Union (WCTU). Between the time of its founding in 1874 and the height of its influence twenty years later, the WCTU became an umbrella organization for a multitude of social undertakings, including woman suffrage, which it endorsed as early as 1880. The WCTU's history lends support to Estelle Freedman's argument in "Separatism as Strategy" stressing the importance of separate female institutions to women's political culture before 1920. In this reading, Ruth Bordin tells how WCTU members responded to their society's need for new social welfare institutions capable of meeting the twin challenges of rapid industrialization and urbanization.*

No problem was too complicated, no solution too innovative to find a hearing in [the councils of the Woman's Christian Temperance Union (WCTU)] of the late nineteenth century. Again, as with home protection, Frances Willard provided the pithy slogan—Do Everything—which aptly described the breathtaking sweep of the Union's concerns, but the membership matched her in range of interest. The WCTU of the 1870s had concerned itself primarily with temperance and temperance-related causes. The WCTU of the 1880s and 1890s added most of the social problems of the day to the list of issues it embraced. Willard articulated this change of emphasis in her address to the national convention in 1891, proclaiming, "Woman's mighty realm of philanthropy encroaches each day upon the empire of sin, disease and misery that has so long existed, we thought it must endure forever."[1] That "realm of philanthropy" had indeed begun to encroach upon most of the nation's sins. Social action had replaced prayer as woman's answer to distress. Although the argument can be made that social action to the WCTU often meant charity—as in Willard's "philanthropy"—and the Union's missions and lodging houses for the indigent or its work with young boys plying street trades can certainly be seen in this light, Do Everything also moved the WCTU into legislative halls where it lobbied for institutional change, and in this sense Do Everything was a program of social reform.

... The Union's attention to improving the police force, the prison,

The chapter title is from Frances Willard's 1891 presidential address, transcribed in the *Minutes* of the convention, 93.

Excerpted from "Woman's Mighty Realm of Philanthropy," Chapter 6 of *Woman and Temperance: The Quest for Power and Liberty, 1873–1900* by Ruth Bordin. Copyright © 1981 by Temple University Press. Reprinted by permission.

and the reformatory; its work with and for indigent children; its concern for the working woman; its attention to problems of public health (of which it properly saw alcohol abuse as one), were all designed to find solutions to problems created by burgeoning cities and a rapidly changing economy. The Union literally tried to take on most of society's problems.

The openness of the WCTU contrasted with the line taken by militant suffragists during the same period. Susan B. Anthony was convinced she must stick to a single issue to be effective. Before the Civil War she had advocated a number of causes simultaneously, but she believed she had learned an important lesson when she adopted the short-skirted bloomer costume for a brief period in the 1850s: people looked at her clothes rather than listened to her words. "If I wished my hearers to consider the suffrage question I must not present the temperance, the religious, the dress or any other besides, but must confine myself to suffrage."[2] While Elizabeth Cady Stanton never approved of reducing the woman suffrage movement to a single goal, the broad perspective of the earlier period was abandoned in the last quarter of the nineteenth century. During its first years, from 1868 to 1871, the National Woman Suffrage Association, the militant wing led by Anthony and Stanton, had addressed itself to broad social and economic questions, but it gave up public expression on these issues by 1871 because of the opposition it inspired among women, an opposition that it believed would jeopardize the suffrage goal.[3]

Although neither prohibition nor the vote for women was achieved until these campaigns became single-issue movements, the nineteenth-century WCTU did not conceive the temperance issue narrowly. Instead it approached temperance as part of a complex of related issues that should be dealt with simultaneously. Part of the Union's appeal in the closing decades of the nineteenth century was its eclecticism. The WCTU offered some way for almost every woman to relate to the movement, from encouraging young children to sign the time-honored pledge of abstinence to advocating a new socialist society. The Union's eclecticism may have hurt its usefulness to the temperance cause (prohibition efforts lost ground during the 1890s), but it helped make possible the WCTU's impressive numerical growth and thereby its importance as a vehicle for the woman's movement. Do Everything made the Union strong and gave it depth. It attracted women who pioneered in the professions and business; it provided a channel through which women who were deeply concerned with social problems could find a constituency and a forum. When it reverted to a single-minded temperance stance in the twentieth century, the Union lost many of these women.

Do Everything was operationally possible because of the large measure of organizational local autonomy that the constitution of the WCTU provided from the beginning. Aside from a commitment to teetotaling temperance and a willingness to pay nominal national dues, each local, county, or state union had no nationally authorized duties and could decide for itself what aspects of the program it wished to pursue. A national program was adopted by majority vote of delegates to national conventions, but any union or union member could choose not to implement any part of that program or even deny it tacit support. The reluctant South need not advocate the vote for women. No member was compelled to cease wearing feathered hats or discard her corset-stays to conform to dress reform standards. No local union was forced to emulate Frances Willard's growing ecumenical outreach to the Catholic community. There was a large measure of grass-roots support for most of the national program, but support of its more radical aspects was always thin, especially when a new program task was first adopted. At the same time there was room for militant and radical women to work effectively within the organizational framework. Devotion to the temperance cause was the cement that held the conglomerate together.

In 1882, of the twenty departments (each headed by a superintendent) into which the work of the national union was then organized, only three— the franchise, prisons and jails, and juvenile affairs—were not solely concerned with promoting the temperance cause.[4] The next year the number had risen to nine out of thirty-one, and by 1896 twenty-five departments out of a total of thirty-nine were dealing wholly or in major part with nontemperance issues.[5] In 1889 the WCTU in a single city, Chicago, was sponsoring two day nurseries, two Sunday schools, an industrial school, a mission that sheltered four thousand homeless or destitute women in a twelve-month period, a free medical dispensary that treated over sixteen hundred patients a year, a lodging house for men that had to date provided temporary housing for over fifty thousand men, and a low-cost restaurant.[6] The national convention that same year passed an antivivisection resolution, petitioned Congress to prohibit the manufacture of cigarettes, petitioned the Czar for more humane treatment of Siberian exiles, petitioned state legislatures for free public kindergartens, and agreed to continue work for reformatories for women and the employment of police matrons and women administrators for women's correctional institutions.[7] Small local unions were also engaged in social action projects. For example, the little Harriman, Tennessee, local in 1891 was working to secure athletic facilities for young men and a Saturday half-holiday in factories.[8] The WCTU of Hampden, Massachusetts, established in 1890 a residential vocational school for inebriate and "fallen" women at South Hadley in the pleasant twelve-room house of a union member.[9]

Generally speaking, however, it would seem that state and local unions paid less attention than the national organization to broad social issues. In September and October 1893, at the depth of the financial panic, when the *Union Signal* was devoted much editorial space to economic and social problems, the reports it published from state unions described primarily temperance activities. Five states reported only temperance activity, although one of these reports was from the Illinois Union, where Chicago alone had several nontemperance projects running. A few state unions reported a variety of other projects ranging from home placement of orphaned children to cooperation with the Knights of Labor.[10]

... The Chicago Union sponsored a lodging house for transient women that provided a clean bed in a dormitory and a nightdress for ten cents, and a light breakfast at low rates.[11] Coffee tanks were placed in factories that employed women, in order to discourage the use of gin and beer, the only liquids previously available.[12] Shelters for homeless men and cheap coffeehouses and restaurants that served a well-balanced meal were aimed at helping the drinker resist the temptation of the saloon's free lunch.

Most importantly, by the 1890s the WCTU leadership had moved close to seeing alcoholism as disease rather than sin.[13] In 1891 Willard unexpectedly devoted a large proportion of her annual address to the question of whether drunkenness was a disease or a moral aberration. She argued that it was both: the drunkard was sick and should be treated with all the remedies science could devise, but "the flask in his pocket should also be replaced with a Bible."[14] ... The WCTU slowly replaced gospel temperance with the recognition that alcoholism was a serious public health problem. Eventually it was also to see poverty as a cause rather than result of drink.

Prison reform was the first nontemperance issue to attract widespread attention from the WCTU. That attention was originally triggered by the gospel temperance meetings in jails, but in a very few years a department for prison, jail and almshouse work was petitioning for rehabilitative reformatories and police matrons, establishing halfway houses for released women prisoners, and demanding women be appointed to state boards of charities and corrections. A strong element of social feminism had crept into the work. As early as 1882 the national Superintendent of Prison and Police Work commented, "It is a standing rebuke to our civilization that women are arrested and given into the hands of men to be searched and cared for, tried by men, sentenced by men, committed to ... institutions where only men have access to them."[15] Pressure from the WCTU put four police matrons in Philadelphia station houses by 1885, and increased the number employed by Chicago from ten in 1885 to twenty-one in 1890. By that year, largely through Union efforts, matrons were employed in thirty-six United States cities, the larger cities employing several.[16] Willingness to participate in the work of this WCTU department was almost universal; there were active departments in forty-five states and territories as early as 1889.[17] In most cases pressure was put on state and local governments to improve and reform services, but several unions supported halfway houses themselves. The Arkansas Union paid the salary of a police matron, and almost everywhere unions demanded and stocked prison libraries, which had been almost nonexistent before.[18] Some efforts were frivolous, if touching. The Arkansas Union entertained at a strawberry festival at the state prison in June, complete with buttonhole bouquets and an organ recital.[19]

Prison work was slowest to move beyond the gospel temperance syndrome in the South. The Louisiana Union found it difficult to find recruits for prison work because all the women who became superintendents soon found that their husbands disapproved of their visiting prisons.[20] Nonetheless two Union women, Rebecca Felton of Georgia and Julia Tutweiler of Alabama, led the fight against the convict lease system in the South in the 1880s.[21] The *Union Signal* carried full accounts of the sessions of the National Prison Association and the National Conference of Charities and Corrections, and by 1894 Willard strongly recommended support for policewomen—not matrons but women on the beat.[22] Because of pressure from the Woman's Alliance and the WCTU, the Chicago city council as early as 1889 authorized the commissioner of health to appoint five women to the sanitary police force that inspected tenements and factories.[23] A WCTU member actually served as police chief of El Cajon in San Diego County at the turn of the century.[24]

Another area into which the WCTU moved early was work with children. Again the Union began with temperance-oriented activity, the organization of juvenile unions whose young members signed the pledge and assisted the temperance cause. The juvenile temperance movement had begun in Great Britain in 1830. It was formally organized in 1847 as the Bands of Hope and was open to children under sixteen. Children's temperance clubs were popular because little formal entertainment was available for youngsters, and the excursions, lantern slide shows, and other club-sponsored outings filled this lack. There is no evidence of organized work with children in the United States before the Civil War. The WCTU began juvenile work in the mid-1870s, and the department formed for the purpose reported to the national convention for the first time in 1878. Membership of children's groups varied and was erratically reported since it had no representation in national conventions, but in 1880 Massachusetts reported twenty-six juvenile unions, with over 15,000 members; New York, fifty-nine, with over 7,000 members; and Michigan, sixty-one, with 10,000 members.[25] Many juvenile unions, some later called Loyal Temperance Legions rather than Bands of Hope, were affiliated with Sunday schools, and their exhibitions of marching and song were always favorite entertainments at WCTU conventions. The members of Bands of Hope and Loyal Temperance Legions were not always the sons and daughters of temperance women; the San Diego WCTU organized a Band of Hope in 1889 among derelict children on the waterfront.[26] The Loyal Temperance Legion was strongest in the 1880s. It met strong competition in the 1890s from the United Boys' Brigade, a quasi-militaristic, uniformed marching and drilling organization frequently sponsored by churches, which lured the young away from the gentler temperance cause.[27]

From organizing Sunday-school children the WCTU moved on to work with bootblacks, telegraph messengers, newsboys, and street urchins.

Street trades were normally plied in the late nineteenth century by children, an impoverished, abused, scruffy lot, who—with little else to comfort them—were frequently habitual users of alcohol and tobacco. Reading rooms and coffeehouses were provided by the WCTU for their use as well as that of their elders, and food and entertainments were arranged at intervals. For example, the New Orleans WCTU gave a holiday "Robin Dinner" for four hundred news, telegraph and messenger boys, including "about forty young tramps." They fed them on donated ham, turkey, tongue, and chicken and lobster salads, cake, fruit, and coffee. Of course, they invited them to attend their Sunday gospel temperance meetings and sign the pledge. Some forty obliged.[28]

A corollary of work with street boys was the "kitchen garden" program for girls. Beginning in 1882, training schools in the domestic arts, nutrition, food preparation, and simple sewing were initiated in poor neighborhoods, almshouses, and orphanages. Usually this program was the responsibility of the Young Woman's Christian Temperance Unions, known as Y's. By 1883 schools had been started in eight cities. Yonkers had one class for black children. Occasionally the kitchen garden program was designed for middle-class children, as in Louisville, and tuition charged, the proceeds being used to support the work among the poor.[29] The program was discontinued in 1887, but the convention expressed the hope that Y's would continue the work.[30] (The settlement-house movement soon initiated similar training programs.) In the mid-1880s the WCTU began to emphasize industrial training schools for girls rather than weekly classes in the domestic arts. The curriculum was broader, including printing, drawing, telegraphy, typewriting, and stenography, as well as housekeeping skills. Frequently these schools were residential institutions in rural settings, designed to remove the young from urban temptations. They were usually privately supported but occasionally recieved public funds. The *Union Signal* published frequent items in 1888 on the new industrial schools.[31]

In 1891 the national Union created a department for work with homeless children, which promoted finding foster and permanent homes for orphans and dependent children rather than institutionalizing them. Where possible the department cooperated with state agencies and private institutions. By 1894 the unions of twenty-one states were engaged in the program, and states not participating were those where the need was already being filled by active Children's Aid Societies or Societies for the Prevention of Cruelty to Children.[32] Child abuse was always a concern of temperance women and was seen as proper cause for terminating parental rights. Incidents of child abuse were regularly reported in the *Union Signal* and almost invariably blamed on drunkenness.

One of the WCTU's major social contributions in the 1880s was its enthusiastic promotion of the kindergarten movement. Willard found this cause especially rewarding. She called it the "greatest theme, next to salvation by faith, that can engage a woman's heart and brain."[33] San Francisco's Golden Gate Kindergarten Association founded the first free WCTU kindergarten in 1880, and by 1890 that center alone had over fifteen hundred children enrolled.[34] The Baltimore Union sponsored a free kindergarten, manned by volunteers and a paid teacher and assistant, that clothed and fed fifty children "from homes of wretched poverty," where four-year-olds "who used tobacco" were cleaned up and cured of their bad habits. Twelve additional children, too young for kindergarten, were cared for in a day nursery.[35] The sponsorship of kindergartens was largely an urban movement and was specifically designed for the children of working mothers who would otherwise be forced to leave their children alone in locked rooms. Usually children were served three meals a day and spent twelve hours, from 7:00 A.M. to 7:00 P.M., at the "creche." Ten cents a day was charged mothers who could afford to pay. The San Diego Union, only three years old at the time, established a day nursery for the children of working mothers in 1887, which they expanded by 1890 to a day-care and residential facility for orphans. The older children attended public school and the younger ones a kindergarten class on the premises. Parents who were able paid a nominal fee, the state paid the cost for its wards, and the city supervisors paid for those placed by the city. Part of the time women without resources were accepted with their children. The institution lasted well into the twentieth century and is an example of a WCTU social welfare project on the local level that was both meaningful and permanent.[36] Frequently, training programs for teachers were attached to WCTU kindergartens.[37]

Although some WCTU locals lobbied for public kindergartens as early as the mid-1880s, the national WCTU began to promote kindergartens as part of the public school system in the 1890s.[38] It is incorrect or at most partially right to attribute Willard's support of the kindergarten movement to its usefulness as an appeal through children to solicit women for the temperance cause.[39] The WCTU supported kindergartens as a necessary service for working-class mothers and children. Temperance recruitment was a small part of the motivation.

The WCTU first addressed itself to equal rights for women, as it did everything else, from the vantage point of temperance. The need to reform or restrain the drunken husband who abused or abandoned his legally helpless wife and children was the redundant chorus of its publications, public meetings, and prayers in its early years. But as Frances Willard summarized the Union's changed attitudes,

> The Crusaders wrought only for their tempted husbands and fathers, brothers and sons; but behold seventeen years later all this work has tended more toward the liberation of women than it has toward the extinction of the saloon.[40]

Change occurred first in the WCTU's attitude toward women's place within the family. Not only was the wife entitled to a sober husband, but she was entitled to a share of the income of any husband, however exemplary. In "A Word to Husbands" in 1886 the *Union Signal* exhorted,

> Your wife is entitled to a share of your income. It is her income as well as yours. . . . To dole out money grudgingly to your wife is more than ungenerous, it is unjust. The treasury is a common treasury. You and she are, commercially speaking, partners. She has a right to a reasonable portion of your income; to have it regularly; and to have it without hesitation . . . and not to be called on to account for each dollar.[41]

Willard called for putting "a money value" on homemaking chores and for giving this money directly to the wife, to be "hers out of the common income and collectible by law."[42] This campaign continued into the 1890s. The *Signal* also agitated for educating boys in "husbanding" as well as the professions and world of work.[43]

Willard believed women had a right to refuse sex in marriage, that enforced motherhood was a crime, and that there should be no accidental children or forced pregnancies.[44] This was more than tacit acceptance of the fact that women, as the nineteenth century progressed, exercised more control over their own bodies within the marriage relationship. It had within it a strong plea for equal rights, perhaps even unilateral rights for women that superseded those of men.[45] A woman's legal right to her children was an issue that the WCTU continually championed. The Minnesota WCTU fought hard against a statute passed by the legislature in 1889 that made the father sole guardian of his minor children and permitted him "to will away his children" even before they were born.[46] Willard distressingly pointed out that in thirty-six states in 1890, the married mother was not the legal "owner" of her child.[47] These concerns naturally reinforced the Union's equal-rights position. . . .

The WCTU's first approach to the problems of labor offered a simple solution: drunkenness breeds poverty; eliminate drunkenness and the economic problems of the working class will disappear. As late as 1886 Willard stated that the central question of labor reform was not "how to get higher wages," but "how to turn present wages to better account." She believed the labor movement must learn that lesson and that only the WCTU could teach it.[48] The Union's reports and publications emphasized the large average per capita expenditure on drink by the working man.[49] The Union began its practical efforts to aid the working man by asking the new industrial giants to require total abstinence from their employees.[50] Efforts were spotty and confined largely to public transportation companies at first, where a sound case could be made for stringent rules on the basis of safety. But the WCTU also attempted to reach the working man directly. The gospel temperance approach was tried among lumbermen and miners as well as railroad workers in the mid-1880s with at best indifferent success. Lumbermen were most responsive to these missionary efforts, because they provided some small respite from the lonely boredom of the pineries in winter.

The severe depression of the mid-1880s and the attendant economic distress and labor unrest slowly convinced the WCTU that it needed to take a second look at the causes of poverty. In the same presidential address in 1886 that voiced her belief that abstention from liquor could solve the laborer's money problems, Willard endorsed the eight-hour day as a way to reduce unemployment and made her first overtures toward organized labor, expressing sympathy with its methods when it used arbitration, cooperation, and the ballot box. Terence Powderly and the Knights of Labor had won her admiration with their equal rights stance, a membership ban on liquor dealers, and advocacy of temperance.[51] . . . Clearly the Union's design was no longer simply to convert, or coerce through management, but to explore the possibility of a working alliance between the WCTU and organized labor.

The first approach by the WCTU to organized labor had been made in June 1886, when the general officers sent a delegation at Willard's behest to bring greetings to the Knights of Labor convention in Cleveland; Mary Woodbridge carried the message. The Knights were surprised at this overture but received Woodbridge kindly with frequent applause, and Powderly later wrote that it was the first time a representative of another organization had been admitted to their conventions.[52] The 1886 convention endorsed and continued this overture, and Willard composed a letter addressed to the Knights of Labor, trades unions, and other labor organizations, that expressed sympathy with the labor movement, saluted it as an ally, and especially commended its stand on women: equal pay for equal work, admitting women to membership, and support of woman suffrage. . . . Powderly responded positively, saying he had read her address with pleasure and would publish it in the Knights' official organ.[53]

Thus began an informal alliance that was to persist for several years. In February 1887 Powderly agreed to distribute through his locals 95,000 petitions for the protection of women. Later that month the Knights cooperated with the WCTU in its lobbying effort on behalf of Senator Henry Blair's bill for federal aid to public elementary schools.[54] Meanwhile Willard was conferring with the leadership of the Knights and addressing labor meetings. In many ways this was a strange partnership, and one that surely would not have existed without Willard's initiative. Most of the rank and file of the WCTU were not radical, and organized labor was viewed with alarm by even the enlightened middle classes in the 1880s. The prominent feminist Lucy Stone watched Willard's approaches to the Knights of Labor "with fear and trembling"; she saw the Knights as extremely disruptive to business and looked with horror at their strikes.[55] . . .

Willard, who was actually inducted into the Knights in 1887, did not lead the WCTU down the labor union path without opposition. By the end of 1887 considerable protest against Willard's romance with the Knights of Labor was developing in the columns of the *Union Signal.* Some questioned fraternal ties with a secret society, others feared the alienation of conservative friends of the WCTU.[56] Willard felt compelled to answer her opponents in her presidential address in the fall of that year, and she mentions her labor union ties briefly in *Glimpses,* where she also provides a transcript of her 1886 open letter to the Knights and other labor organizations. Although there must have been many WCTU members who found organized labor a strange bedfellow, Willard calmed the Union's misgivings by emphasizing the Knights' commitment to temperance and woman suffrage. Religious groups were aghast at the affiliation.... Nonetheless Anna Sneed Cairns, superintendant of the Department of the Relation of Temperance to Labor, reported the unions of eighteen states were engaged in some variety of cooperative effort with either labor unions or militant farmers' groups, and Cairns herself urged the rank and file to join the Farmers' Alliance or the Knights of Labor.[57] Strikes and violence posed a stumbling block; even Willard found it difficult to condone the Homestead rioters, and the *Union Signal* hedged, avoiding outright support of the strike but condemning the use of Pinkerton men and troops.[58] Officially the WCTU, like the Knights for that matter, was committed to arbitration and conciliation rather than the strike as the way to settle labor disputes.

During the years when it began to establish its tentative alliance with the labor movement, the WCTU also moved toward a radically changed position on poverty and economic distress. Its old assumption that temperance would cure poverty was sharply challenged during the depression winter of 1885. A *Union Signal* editorial described homeless men walking back and forth in railroad tunnels trying to keep warm. Thousands were unemployed in Chicago alone, and thousands of children lived "in homes bare of food and fire." ... In 1889 Willard publicly reversed her stance and attributed intemperance to bad working conditions and long hours, stating that overwork drove men to drink and that poor working conditions sent the factory girl to the saloon at night.[59] The *Union Signal* had paved the way the previous winter by running a long series of articles on the evils of child labor that showed how the use of stimulants flowed naturally from wretchedness and deprivation, and by pursuing an editorial policy that called for the "study of poverty as a cause of intemperance."[60] By the 1890s the vocal elements within the Union were practically unanimous in accepting the view that poverty breeds intemperance. Annie Jackson wrote in the *Union Signal,* "Men and women, overworked, with a state of low vitality and innumerable difficulties to meet, naturally turn toward anything that will afford temporary relief.... In the midst of misery, drinking is almost inevitable." ...

Meanwhile Frances Willard believed she had found the real solution to poverty. In 1889 she stated in her annual address that "the land and all resources of the earth [must] be held and controlled in some way by the community as a whole."[61] Willard had been converted to Christian socialism. The instrument of her conversion had been Edward Bellamy's *Looking Backward*, which had had a profound effect on several among the WCTU leadership. . . . Willard advocated that fundamental reform of the economic system begin with relief for the unemployed, the five-and-a-half-day week, free technical education, free school lunches, and gradual nationalization or municipal ownership of the railroads, the telegraph, public utilities, and factories.[62] She adopted these views long before her association with the English Fabians, who simply reinforced positions she already held. The economic dislocations that followed the panic of 1893 brought others within the WCTU to espouse her position. The *Union Signal* deplored the concentration of economic power in the hands of a few capitalists and advocated "a change of ownership. [The general benefit of mankind] cannot be expected as long as these great wealth producing interests are in the hands of individuals or private corporations. The only other ownership is, of course, the national government."[63] . . .

Willard's Do Everything policy, "that woman's mighty realm of philanthropy," began with a strong emphasis on temperance and temperance-related causes and ended with the Union leadership's commitment to revolutionary changes in the structure and organization of the economic system, a commitment less widely shared by the membership. Nonetheless, Do Everything embodied strong feminist goals that found general acceptance at all levels. Do Everything may have begun in some measure as domestic feminism. Its rhetoric was aimed at establishing woman's position in the home, but Do Everything from the beginning emphasized pragmatic or social feminism. It aimed at solving specific societal problems. Certainly the Union ended the century with a large proportion of its membership committed to militant feminism, equal rights, and full participation in the political process. In this sense the Union was the cutting edge of the feminist cause in the nineteenth century. Broad social reform was equated with feminism more strongly and clearly in the Union than anywhere else. . . . Of all major women's organizations, the nineteenth-century WCTU came closest to advocating sweeping societal reform. But for a variety of reasons, despite its limited goals, the suffrage movement rather than the Union was to lead women to nominal political power and the vote.

NOTES

1. *Minutes, 1891 Convention*, 93.
2. Ida Husted Harper, *The Life and Work of Susan B. Anthony* (Indianapolis: Bobbs-Merrill, 1899), v. 1, 117.
3. See Ellen DuBois, "The Radicalism of the Woman Suffrage Movement, Stanton-Anthony Wing, 1867–1875," in Zillah R. Eisenstein, *Capitalist Patriarchy and the Case for Socialist Feminism* (New York: Monthly Review Press, 1979), 138–50; Barbara Harris, *Beyond Her Sphere:*

*Women and the Professions in American History* (Westport, Conn.: Greenwood Press, 1978), 86, 129; and Lois Banner, *Elizabeth Cady Stanton: A Radical for Woman's Rights* (Boston: Little, Brown, 1980), 103, 116–17.

4. *Minutes, 1882 Convention,* i–lxvi.

5. *Minutes, 1883 Convention,* 5–7; *Minutes, 1896 Convention,* 1–8, 169–408.

6. *Union Signal,* April 3, 1890, 3.

7. *Minutes, 1890 Convention,* 55–60.

8. *Union Signal,* June 11, 1891, 5.

9. *Union Signal,* July 24, 1890, 9.

10. *Union Signal,* September 14, 23, 28, October 3, 1893.

11. *Union Signal,* March 10, 1887, 3.

12. *Minutes, 1883 Convention,* xi–-xiv.

13. In contrasting the nineteenth- and twentieth-century attitudes toward alcohol, Gusfield asserts that in the nineteenth century "the drunkard was neither sick or foolish, he was sinful" (*Symbolic Crusade, 30*). This is only partly true even earlier in the century. The WCTU emphasized alcohol as an unhealthful, destructive poison from the beginning, and Benjamin Rush much earlier had viewed alcohol abuse as simply a health problem.

14. *Minutes, 1891 Convention,* 145.

15. *Minutes, 1882 Convention,* xiii.

16. *Union Signal,* December 2, 1886, 5; *Minutes, 1885 Convention,* iv; *Minutes, 1890 Convention,* 332.

17. *Minutes, 1889 Convention,* xxxiii–xl.

18. *Minutes, 1890 Convention,* 286–88.

19. *Union Signal,* July 9, 1885, 11.

20. *Union Signal,* January 20, 1887, 10.

21. Anne Firor Scott, *The Southern Lady: From Pedestal to Politics, 1830–1930* (Chicago: University of Chicago Press, 1970), 148.

22. *Minutes, 1894 Convention,* 171.

23. *Union Signal,* August 1, 1889, 1.

24. Miriam E. Rains, scrapbook, 1898–1942, San Diego Historical Society Library, Serra Museum, Presidio Park, San Diego.

25. *Minutes, 1880 Convention,* 136–37.

26. *San Diego Union,* June 17, 1890, 8.

27. Clipping, *Cleveland Leader,* November 22, 1894, scrapbook 70, p. 7, WCTU Series, reel 42.

28. *Union Signal,* January 25, 1883, 10.

29. *Minutes, 1883 Convention,* xxiii–xxvi.

30. *Minutes, 1887 Convention,* 12.

31. Frances Willard wrote her presidential address at one of the more successful of the schools in 1888. Its superintendent was the former WCTU state president of North Carolina (*Union Signal,* August 2, 1888, 9).

32. *Minutes, 1894 Convention,* 263–71.

33. *Union Signal,* March 27, 1890, 8.

34. *Union Signal,* March 20, 1890, 8. By 1895 over 18,000 children had been served.

35. *Union Signal,* April 30, 1885, 9.

36. See Jan Lundie, "To Provide a Home" (an unpublished paper) and clipping file on San Diego Children's Home, both in San Diego Historical Society Library, Serra Museum, Presidio Park, San Diego.

37. *Union Signal,* March 4, 1886, 12; *Minutes, 1885 Convention,* xxx–xxxvi.

38. See Superintendent Emma Wheeler's report, *Minutes, 1890 Convention,* 354–57.

39. See Mary Earhart, *Frances Willard: From Prayers to Politics* (Chicago: University of Chicago Press, 1944), 188, for an example of this misconception.

40. President's address, *Minutes, 1891 Convention,* 87.

41. *Union Signal,* March 18, 1886, 15.

42. President's address, *Minutes, 1886 Convention,* 78.

43. *Union Signal,* January 8, 1891, 7.

44. *Minutes, 1889 Convention,* 123.

45. See Daniel Scott Smith, "Family Limitation, Sexual Control and Domestic Feminism in Victorian America," in Mary Hartman and Lois Banner, eds., *Clio's Consciousness Raised: New*

*Perspectives on the History of Women* (New York: Harper Torchbooks, 1974), 119–36. Smith sees the steady drop in the birthrate in the nineteenth century as stemming from what he calls "domestic feminism," women's increasing insistence on control of their own bodies through family limitation, frequency of sex, or coitus interruptus. He argues that women moved from concern with their status in the marriage relationship to causes outside the home. See also Linda Gordon, *Woman's Body, Woman's Right: A Social History of Birth Control in America* (New York: Penguin, 1977). Gordon attributes the decline at least in part to early contraceptive devices.

46. *Union Signal,* July 3, 1890, 1. By "will" the *Union Signal* meant that a father could provide whatever guardian he chose in the case of his death, even if the mother was living and competent.

47. President's address as reproduced in *Union Signal,* November 27, 1890, 7. "Owner" is an awkward word, but it was the word used in connection with parental rights at the time.

48. *Minutes, 1886 Convention,* 85.

49. The WCTU put this at $70 per capita in 1886 (*Minutes, 1886 Convention,* ciii). Jon M. Kingsdale, "The 'Poor Man's Club': Social Functions of the Urban Working Class Saloon," *American Quarterly* 25 (October 1973): 482, disputes this assumption. He estimates that liquor consumption never accounted for more than 5 percent of the working man's annual budget and that it generally contributed little to working-class poverty. Other historians of temperance, among them Norman Clark, do not necessarily agree; but it should be remembered that distilled spirits were cheap in the nineteenth century.

50. The Committee on Inducing Corporations to Require Total Abstinence reported for the first time in 1881 (*Minutes, 1881 Convention,* cxxii–xxiii). Resolutions had been passed in 1880 appealing to railroad and steamship companies to require employee abstinence as a safety measure (*Minutes, 1880 Convention,* 65–66).

51. *Minutes, 1886 Convention,* 86–87.

52. *Union Signal,* June 3, 1886, 20; Terence V. Powderly, *Thirty Years of Labor, 1859–1889* (Columbus: Excelsior Publication House, 1890), 601.

53. Powderly to Willard, December 12, 1886, WCTU Series, reel 14. A copy of Willard's letter, distributed as a printed document, is found in scrapbook 12, pp. 478–80, WCTU Series, reel 31, and in Frances Willard, *Glimpses of Fifty Years: An Autobiography of An American Woman* (published by Woman's Temperance Publishing Association, 1889; reprinted New York: Source Book Press, 1970), 363.

54. *Union Signal,* February 3, 1887, 1; February 10, 8.

55. Stone to Willard, March 28, 1887, as quoted in Earhart, *Willard,* 246.

56. See especially *Union Signal,* December 22, 1887, 5.

57. *Minutes, 1890 National Convention,* 368–73.

58. *Union Signal,* July 14, 1892, 1; August 4, 9.

59. President's address, *Minutes, 1889 Convention,* 114.

60. *Union Signal,* December 1888–February 1889; April 4, 1889, 7.

61. President's address, *Minutes, 1889 Convention,* 116.

62. President's address, *Minutes, 1889 National Convention,* 117.

63. *Union Signal,* February 23, 1893, 8.

# 4

## Hull House in the 1890s:
## A Community of Women Reformers

### Kathryn Kish Sklar

*In the movement for woman suffrage and in myriad reform movements at the turn of the twenti-eth century, women reformers exercised a degree of political power previously (some might add, subsequently) unknown in American society. Foremost among these women reformers was a generation of women active in the social settlement movement. Hull House, founded by Jane Addams in Chicago in 1889, was the leading institution in that movement. Through a case study of women reformers at Hull House, Kathryn Kish Sklar offers a window into the experi-ences that motivated and empowered this remarkable generation of reformers. She shows how our understanding of their substantial exercise of power within the broader social, economic, and political life of the nation can be illuminated through an appreciation of the community they constructed among themselves.*

What were the sources of women's political power in the United States in the decades before they could vote? How did women use the political power they were able to muster? This essay attempts to answer these ques-tions by examining one of the most politically effective groups of women reformers in U.S. history—those who assembled in Chicago in the early 1890s at Hull House, one of the nation's first social settlements, founded in 1889 by Jane Addams and Ellen Gates Starr. Within that group, this study focuses on the reformer Florence Kelley (1859–1932). Kelley joined Hull House in 1891 and remained until 1899, when she moved to Lillian Wald's Henry Street Settlement on the Lower East Side of New York, where she lived for the next twenty-seven years. According to Felix Frankfurter, Kelley "had probably the largest single share in shaping the social history of the United States during the first thirty years of this century," for she played "a powerful if not decisive role in securing legislation for the removal of the most glaring abuses of our hectic industrialization following the Civil War."[1] It was in the 1890s that Kelley and her colleagues at Hull House developed the patterns of living and thinking that guided them throughout their lives of reform, leaving an indelible imprint on U.S. politics.[2] This essay attempts to determine the extent to which their political power and activities flowed from their collective life as coresidents and friends and the degree to which this power was attributable to their close affiliation with male reformers and male institutions.

Excerpted from "Hull House in the 1890s: A Community of Women Reformers," in *SIGNS* 10 (1985): 658–77. By permission of the University of Chicago Press.

*Jane Addams, c. 1890. Sophia Smith Collection, Smith College.*

The effects of both factors can be seen in one of the first political campaigns conducted by Hull House residents—the 1893 passage and the subsequent enforcement of pathbreaking antisweatshop legislation mandating an eight-hour day for women and children employed in Illinois manufacturing. This important episode reveals a great deal about the sources of this group's political power, including their own collective initiative, the support of other women's groups, and the support of men and men's groups. Finally, it shows how women reformers and gender-specific issues they championed helped advance class-specific issues during a time of fundamental social, economic, and political transition.

One of the most important questions asked by historians of American women today is, To what degree has women's social power been based on separate female institutions, culture, and consciousness, and to what degree has it grown out of their access to male spheres of influence, such as higher education, labor organization, and politics?[3] This essay advances the commonsense notion that women's social power in the late nineteenth century depended on both sources of support. Women's institutions allowed them to enter realms of reality dominated by men, where, for better or for worse, they competed with men for control over the distribution of social resources. Thus although their own communities were essential to their social strength, women were able to realize the full potential of their collective power only by reaching outside those boundaries.

* * *

The community of women at Hull House made it possible for Florence Kelley to step from the apprenticeship to the journeyman stage in her reform career. A study of the 1893 antisweatshop campaign shows that the community provided four fundamental sources of support for her growth as a reformer. First, it supplied an emotional and economic substitute for traditional family life, linking her with other talented women of her own class and educational and political background and thereby greatly increasing her political and social power. Second, the community at Hull House provided Kelley with effective ties to other women's organizations. Third, it enabled cooperation with men reformers and their organizations, allowing her to draw on their support without submitting to their control. Finally, it provided a creative setting for her to pursue and develop a reform strategy she had already initiated in New York—the advancement of the rights and interests of working people in general by strengthening the rights and interests of working women and children.

As a community of women, Hull House provided its members with a lifelong substitute for family life. In that sense it resembled a religious order, supplying women with a radical degree of independence from the claims of family life and inviting them to commit their energies elsewhere. When she first crossed the snowy threshold of Hull House "sometime between Christmas and New Year's," 1891, Florence Kelley Wischnewetzky was fleeing from her husband and seeking refuge for herself and her three children, ages six, five, and four. "We were welcomed as though we had been invited," she wrote thirty-five years later in her memoirs.[4] The way in which

Kelley's family dilemma was solved reveals a great deal about the sources of support for the political activity of women reformers in the progressive era: help came first and foremost from women's institutions but also from the recruited support of powerful men reformers. Jane Addams supplied Kelley with room, board, and employment and soon after she arrived introduced her to Henry Demarest Lloyd, a leading critic of American labor policies who lived with his wife Jessie and their young children in nearby Winnetka. The Lloyds readily agreed to add Kelley's children to their large nursery, an arrangement that began a lifelong relationship between the two families.[5] A sign of the extent to which responsibility for Kelley's children was later assumed by members of the Hull House community, even after her departure, was the fact that Jane Addams's closest personal friend, Mary Rozet Smith, regularly and quietly helped Kelley pay for their school and college tuition.[6]

A bit stunned by her good fortune, the young mother wrote her own mother a summary of her circumstances a few weeks after reaching Hull House: "We are all well, and the chicks are happy. I have fifty dollars a month and my board and shall have more soon as I can collect my wits enough to write. I have charge of the Bureau of Labor of Hull House here and am working in the lines which I have always loved. I do not know what more to tell you except this, that in the few weeks of my stay here I have won for the children and myself many and dear friends whose generous hospitality astonishes me."[7] This combination of loving friendship and economic support served as a substitute for the family life from which she had just departed. "It is understood that I am to resume the maiden name," she continued to her mother, "and that the children are to have it." It did not take Kelley long to decide to join this supportive community of women. As she wrote Friedrich Engels in April 1892, "I have cast in my lot with Misses Addams and Starr for as long as they will have me."[8] To her mother she emphasized the personal gains Hull House brought her, writing, "I am better off than I have been since I landed in New York since I am now responsible *myself* for what I do." Gained at great personal cost, Kelley's independence was her most basic measure of well-being. Somewhat paradoxically, perhaps, her autonomy was the product of her affiliation with a community.

One significant feature of Hull House life was the respect that residents expressed for one another's autonomy. Although each had a "room of her own," in Kelley's case this room was sometimes shared with other residents, and the collective space was far more important than their small private chambers.[9] Nevertheless, this intimate proximity was accompanied by a strong expression of personal individuation, reflected in the formality of address used at Hull House. By the world at large Kelley was called Mrs. Kelley, but to her close colleagues she was "Sister Kelley," or "Dearest F. K.," never Florence. Miss Addams and Miss Lathrop were never called Jane or Julia, even by their close friends, although Kelley occasionally took the liberty of calling Addams "gentle Jane." It was not that Hull House was bleak and business-like, as one resident once described male settlements in New York, but rather that the colleagues recognized and appreciated one another's individuality. These were superb conditions for social innovation since the residents could draw on mutual support at the same time that they were encouraged to pursue their own distinct goals.

This respect for individuality did not prevent early Hull House residents from expressing their love for one another. Kelley's letters to Jane Addams often began "Beloved Lady," and she frequently addressed Mary Rozet Smith as "Dearly Beloved," referring perhaps to Smith's special status in Addams's life. Kelley's regard for Addams and Addams's for her were revealed in their correspondence after Kelley left in 1899. Addams wrote her, "I have had blows before in connection with Hull House but nothing like this"; and Mary Rozet Smith added, "I have had many pangs for the dear presiding lady." Later that year Addams wrote, "Hull House sometimes seems a howling wilderness without you." Kelley seems to have found the separation difficult since she protested when her name was removed from the list of residents in the *Hull House Bulletin.* Addams replied, "You overestimate the importance of the humble Bulletin," but she promised to restore Kelley's name, explaining that it was only removed to "stop people asking for her." Fourteen years later in 1913 Addams wrote "Sister Kelley," "It is curious that I have never gotten used to you being away from [Hull House], even after all these years!"[10]

One source of the basic trust established among the three major reformers at Hull House in the 1890s—Jane Addams, Julia Lathrop, and Florence Kelley—was similarity of family background. Not only were they all of the upper middle class, but their fathers were politically active men who helped Abraham Lincoln found and develop the Republican Party in the 1860s. John Addams served eight terms as a state senator in Illinois, William Lathrop served in Congress as well as in the Illinois legislature, and William Kelley served fifteen consecutive terms in Congress. All were vigorous abolitionists, and all encouraged their daughters' interests in public affairs. As Judge Alexander Bruce remarked at the joint memorial services held for Julia Lathrop and Florence Kelley after their deaths in 1932, "Both of them had the inspiration of great and cultured mothers and both had great souled fathers who, to use the beautiful language of Jane Addams in speaking of her own lineage, 'Wrapped their little daughters in the large men's doublets, careless did they fit or no.'"[11]

These three remarkable women were participating in a political tradition that their fathers had helped create. While they were growing up in the 1860s and 1870s, they gained awareness through their fathers' experience of the mainstream of American political processes, thereby learning a great deal about its currents—particularly that its power could be harnessed to fulfill the purposes of well-organized interest groups.

Although Hull House residents have generally been interpreted as reformers with a religious motivation, it now seems clear that they were more strongly motivated by political goals. In that regard they resembled a large proportion of other women social settlement leaders, including those associated with Hull House after 1900, such as Grace and Edith Abbot, whose father was Nebraska's first lieutenant governor, or Sophonisba Breckinridge, daughter of a Kentucky congressman.[12] Women leaders in the social settlement movement seem to have differed in this respect from their male counterparts, who were seeking alternatives to more orthodox religious, rather than political, careers. In, but not of, the Social Gospel movement, the women at Hull House were a political boat on a religious stream, advancing political solutions to social problems that were fundamentally ethical or moral, such as the right of workers to a fair return for their labor or the right of children to schooling.

Another source of the immediate solidarity among Addams, Lathrop, and Kelley was their shared experience of higher education. Among the first generation of American college women, they graduated from Rockford College, Vassar College, and Cornell University, respectively, in the early 1880s and then spent the rest of the decade searching for work and for a social identity commensurate with their talents. Addams tried medical school; Lathrop worked in her father's law office; Kelley, after being denied admission to graduate study at the University of Pennsylvania, studied law and government at the University of Zurich, where she received a much more radical education than she would have had she remained in Philadelphia. In the late 1880s and early 1890s, the social settlement movement was the right movement at the right time for this first generation of college-educated women, who were able to gain only limited entry to the male-dominated professions of law, politics, or academics.[13]

While talented college women of religious backgrounds and inclinations were energetically recruited into the missionary empires of American churches, those seeking secular outlets for their talents chose a path that could be as daunting as that of a missionary outpost. Except for the field of medicine, where women's institutions served the needs of women physicians and students, talented women were blocked from entering legal, political, and academic professions by male-dominated institutions and networks. In the 1890s the social settlement movement supplied a perfect structure for women seeking secular means of influencing society because it collectivized their talents, it placed and protected them among the working-class immigrants whose lives demanded amelioration, and it provided them with access to the male political arena while preserving their independence from male-dominated institutions.

Since Hull House drew on local sources of funding, often family funds supplied by wealthy women,[14] Jane Addams found it possible to finance the settlement's activities without the assistance or control of established religious or educational institutions. In 1895 she wrote that Hull House was modeled after Toynbee Hall in London, where "a group of University men . . . reside in the poorer quarter of London for the sake of influencing the people there toward better local government and wider social and intellectual life." Substituting "college-trained women" for "University men," Hull House also placed a greater emphasis on economic factors. As Addams continued, "The original residents came to Hull House with a conviction that social intercourse could best express the growing sense of the economic unity of society." She also emphasized their political autonomy, writing that the first residents "wished the social spirit to be the undercurrent of the life of Hull-House, whatever direction the stream might take."[15] Under Kelley's influence in 1892, the social spirit at Hull House turned decisively toward social reform, bringing the community's formidable energy and talents to bear on a historic campaign on behalf of labor legislation for women and children.[16]

Meredith Tax's *Rising of the Women* contains the most complete account of this campaign, which culminated in the passage of landmark state legislation in 1893. There Tax justly reproves Jane Addams for assigning Hull House more than its share of the credit for the campaign. The settlement did play a critical leadership role in this venture, but it was never alone. Indeed it was part of a complex network of women's associations in Chicago in the 1890s.[17] About thirty women's organizations combined forces and entered into local politics in 1888 through the Illinois Women's Alliance, organized that year by Elizabeth Morgan and other members of the Ladies Federal Union no. 2073 in response to a crusading woman journalist's stories in the *Chicago Times* about "City Slave Girls" in the garment industry.[18] The alliance's political goals were clearly stated in their constitution: "The objects of the Alliance are to agitate for the enforcement of all existing laws and ordinances that have been enacted for the protection of women and children—as the factory ordinances and the compulsory education law. To secure the enactment of such laws as shall be found necessary. To investigate all business establishments and factories where women and children are employed and public institutions where women and children are maintained. To procure the appointment of women, as inspectors and as members of boards of education, and to serve on boards of management of public institutions."[19] Adopting the motto "Justice to Children, Loyalty to Women," the alliance acted as a vanguard for the entrance of women's interests into municipal and state politics, focusing chiefly on the passage and enforcement of compulsory education laws. One of its main accomplishments was the agreement of the city council in 1889 "to appoint five lady inspectors" to enforce city health codes.[20]

The diversity of politically active women's associations in Chicago in the late 1880s was reflected in a list of organizations associated with the alliance.[21] Eight bore names indicating a religious or ethical affiliation, such as the Woodlawn branch of the Woman's Christian Temperance Union and the Ladies Union of the Ethical Society. Five were affiliated with working women or were trade unions, such as the Working Women's Protective Association, the Ladies Federal Union no. 2703, and (the only predominantly male organization on the list) the Chicago Trades and Labor Assembly. Another five had an intellectual or cultural focus, such as the Hopkins Metaphysical Association or the Vincent Chatauqua Association. Three were women's professional groups, including the Women's Press Association and the Women's Homeopathic Medical Society. Another three were female auxiliaries of male social organizations, such as the Lady Washington Masonic Chapter and the Ladies of the Grand Army of the Republic. Two were suffrage associations, including the Cook County Suffrage Association; another two were clubs interested in general economic reform, the Single Tax Club and the Land Labor Club no. 1; and one was educational, the Drexel Kindergarten Association.

Florence Kelley's 1892 entrance into this lively political scene was eased by her previous knowledge of and appreciation for the work of the alliance. Soon after its founding she had written the leaders a letter that was quoted extensively in a newspaper account of an alliance meeting, declaring, "The child labor question can be solved by legislation, backed by solid organization, and by women cooperating with the labor organizations, which have done all that has thus far been done for the protection of working children."[22] In Chicago Kelley was perceived as a friend of the alliance because in 1889 and 1890 she had helped organize the New York Working Women's Society's campaign "to add women as officials in the office for factory inspection." According to Kelley, the Society, "a small group of women from both the wealthy and influential class and the working class, . . . circulated petitions, composed resolutions, and was supported finally in the years 1889 and 1890 in bringing their proposal concerning the naming of women to factory inspectorships to the legislature, philanthropic groups and unions."[23] As a result in 1890 the New York legislature passed laws creating eight new positions for women as state factory inspectors. This was quite an innovation since no woman factory inspector had yet been appointed in Great Britian or Germany, where factory inspection began, and the only four previously appointed in the United States had been named within the last two years in Pennsylvania.[24] Writing in 1897 about this event, Kelley emphasized the political autonomy of the New York Working Women's Society: "Their proposal to add women as officials in the office for factory inspection was made for humanitarian reasons; in no way did it belong to the goals of the general workers' movement, although it found support among the unions."[25] Thus when Kelley arrived at Hull House, she had already been affiliated with women's associations that were independent of trade unions even though cooperating with them.

For Kelley on that chilly December morning the question was not whether she would pursue a career in social reform but how, not whether she would champion what she saw as the rights and interests of working women and children but how she would do that. The question of means was critical in 1891 since her husband was unable to establish a stable medical practice, even though she had spent the small legacy inherited on her father's death the year before on new equipment for his practice. Indeed so acute were Kelley's financial worries that, when she decided to flee with her children to Chicago, she borrowed train fare from an English governess, Mary Forster, whom she had probably befriended at a neighborhood park.[26] Chicago was a natural choice for Kelley since Illinois divorce laws were more equitable, and within its large population of reform-minded and politically active women she doubtlessly hoped to find employment that would allow her to support herself and her children. Although the historical record is incomplete, it seems likely that she headed first to a different community of women—that at the national headquarters of the Woman's Christian Temperance Union (WCTU).[27] She had been well paid for articles written for their national newspaper, the *Union Signal*—the largest women's newspaper in the world, with a circulation in 1890 of almost 100,000—and the WCTU was at the height of its institutional development in Chicago at that time, sponsoring "two day nurseries, two Sunday schools, an industrial school, a mission that sheltered four thousand homeless or destitute women in a twelve-month period, a free medical dispensary that treated over sixteen hundred patients a year, a lodging house for men that had . . . provided temporary housing for over fifty thousand men, and a low-cost restaurant."[28] Just after Kelley arrived, the WCTU opened its Women's Temple, a twelve-story office building and hotel. Very likely it was someone there who told Kelley about Hull House.

The close relationship between Hull House and other groups of women in Chicago was exemplified in Kelley's interaction with the Chicago Women's Club. The minutes of the club's first meeting after Kelley's arrival in Chicago show that on January 25, 1892, she spoke under the sponsorship of Jane Addams on the sweating system and urged that a committee be created on the problem.[29] Although a Reform Department was not created until 1894, minutes of March 23, 1892, show that the club's Home Department "decided upon cooperating with Mrs. Kelly [sic] of Hull House in establishing a Bureau of Women's Labor." Thus the club took over part of the funding and the responsibility for the counseling service Kelley had been providing at Hull House since February. (Initially Kelley's salary for this service was funded by the settlement, possibly with emergency monies given by Mary Rozet Smith.) In this way middle- and upper-middle-class clubwomen were drawn into the settlement's activities. In 1893 Jane Addams successfully solicited the support of wealthy clubwomen to lobby for the antisweatshop legislation: "We insisted that well-known Chicago women should accompany this first little group of Settlement folk who with trade-unionists moved upon the state capitol in behalf of factory legislation." Addams also described the lobbying Hull House residents conducted with other voluntary associations: "Before the passage of the law could be secured, it was necessary to appeal to all elements of the community, and a little group of us addressed the open meetings of trades-unions and of benefit societies, church organizations, and social clubs literally every evening for three months."[30] Thus Hull House was part of a larger social universe of voluntary organizations, and one important feature of its political effectiveness was its ability to gain the support of middle-class and working-class women.

In 1893 the cross-class coalition of the Illinois Women's Alliance began to dissolve under the pressure of the economic depression of that year, and in 1894 its leaders disbanded the group. Hull House reformers inherited the fruits of the alliance's five years of agitation, and they continued its example of combining working-class and middle-class forces. In 1891 Mary Kenney, a self-supporting typesetter who later became the first woman organizer to be employed by the American Federation of Labor, established the Jane Club adjacent to the settlement, a cooperative boardinghouse for young working women. In the early 1890s Kenney was a key figure in the settlement's efforts to promote union organizing among working women, especially bookbinders.[31] Thus the combination of middle-class and working-class women at Hull House in 1892–93 was an elite version of the type of cross-class association represented by the Illinois Women's Alliance of the late 1880s—elite because it was smaller and because its middle-class members had greater social resources, familiarity with American political processes, and exposure to higher than average levels of education, while its working-class members (Mary Kenney and Alzina Stevens) were members of occupational and organizational elites.[32]

By collectivizing talents and energies, this community made possible the exercise of greater and more effective political power by its members. A comparison of Florence Kelley's antisweatshop legislation, submitted to the Illinois investigate committee in February 1893, with that presented by Elizabeth Morgan dramatically illustrates this political advantage. The obvious differences in approach indicate that the chief energy for campaigning on behalf of working women and children had passed from working-class to middle-class social reformers.[33] Both legislative drafts prohibited work in tenement dwellings. Morgan's prohibiting all manufacturing, Kelley's all garment making. Both prohibited the labor of children under fourteen and regulated the labor of children aged fourteen to sixteen. Kelley's went beyond Morgan's in two essential respects, however. Hers mandated an eight-hour day for women in manufacturing, and it provided for enforcement by calling for a state factory inspector with a staff of twelve, five whom were to be women. The reasons for Kelley's greater success as an innovator are far from clear, but one important advantage in addition to her greater education and familiarity with the American political system was the larger community on which she could rely for the law's passage and enforcement.

Although Elizabeth Morgan could draw on her experience as her husband's assistant in his work as an attorney and on the support of women unionists, both resources were problematic. Thomas Morgan was erratic and self-centered, and Elizabeth Morgan's relationship with organized women workers was marred by sectarian disputes originating within the male power structure of the Chicago Trades and Labor Assembly. For example, in January 1892, when she accused members of the Shirtwaist Union of being controlled by her husband's opposition within the assembly, "a half dozen women surrounded [her] seat in the meeting and demanded an explanation. She refused to give any and notice was served that charges would be preferred against her at the next meeting of the Ladies' Federation of Labor."[34] Perhaps Morgan's inability to count on a supportive community explains her failure to provide for adequate enforcement and to include measures for workers over the age of sixteen in her legislative draft. Compared to Kelley's, Morgan's bill was politically impotent. It could not enforce what it endorsed, and it did not affect adults.

Kelley's draft was passed by the Illinois legislature in June 1893, providing for a new office of enforcement and for an eight-hour day for women workers of all ages. After Henry Demarest Lloyd declined an invitation to serve as the state's first factory inspector, reform governor John Peter Altgeld followed Lloyd's recommendations and appointed Kelley. Thus eighteen months after her arrival in Chicago, she found herself in charge of a dedicated and well-paid staff of twelve mandated to see that prohibitions against tenement workshops and child labor were observed and to enforce a pathbreaking article restricting the working hours of women and children.

Hull House provided Kelley and other women reformers with a social vehicle for independent political action and a means of bypassing the control of male associations and institutions, such as labor unions and political parties; at the same time they had a strong institutional framework in which they could meet with other reformers, both men and women. The drafting of the antisweatshop legislation revealed how this process worked. In his autobiography, Abraham Bisno, pioneer organizer in the garment industry in Chicago and New York, described how he became a regular participant in public discussions of contemporary social issues at Hull House. He joined "a group ... composed of Henry D. Lloyd, a prominent physician named Bayard Holmes, Florence Kelley, and Ellen G. [Starr] to engage in a campaign for legislation to abolish sweatshops, and to have a law passed prohibiting the employment of women more than eight hours a day."[35] Answering a question about the author of the bill he endorsed at the 1893 hearings, Bisno said, "Mrs. Florence Kelly [sic] wrote that up with the advice of myself, Henry Lloyd, and a number of prominent attorneys in Chicago."[36] Thus as the chief author of the legislation, Florence Kelley drew on the expertise of Bisno, one of the most dedicated and talented union organizers; of Lloyd, one of the most able elite reformers in the United States; and, surely among the "prominent attorneys," of Clarence Darrow, one of the country's most able reform lawyers. It is difficult to imagine this cooperative effort between Bisno, Kelley, and Lloyd without the existence of the larger Hull House group of which they were a part. Their effective collaboration exemplified the process by which members of this remarkable community of women reformers moved into the vanguard of contemporary reform activity, for they did so in alliance with other groups and individuals.

What part did the Hull House community, essential to the drafting and passage of the act, have in the statute's enforcement? Who benefited and who lost from the law's enforcement? Answers to these questions help us view the community more completely in the context of its time.

During the four years that Kelley served as chief factory inspector of Illinois, her office and Hull House were institutionally so close as to be almost undistinguishable. Kelley rented rooms for her office across the street from the settlement, with which she and her three most able deputies were closely affiliated. Alzina Stevens moved into Hull House soon after Altgeld appointed her as Kelley's chief assistant. Mary Kenney lived at the Jane Club, and Abraham Bisno was a familiar figure at Hull House evening gatherings. Jane Addams described the protection that the settlement gave to the first factory inspection office in Illinois, the only such office headed by a woman in her lifetime: "The inception of the law had already become associated with Hull House, and when its ministration was also centered there, we inevitably received all the odium which these first efforts entailed. . . . Both Mrs. Kelley and her assistant, Mrs. Stevens, lived at Hull-House; . . . and one of the most vigorous deputies was the President of the Jane Club. In addition, one of the early men residents, since dean of a state law school, acted as prosecutor in the cases brought against the violators of the law."[37] Thus the law's enforcement was just as collective an undertaking as was its drafting and passage. Florence Kelley and Alzina Stevens were usually the first customers at the Hull House Coffee Shop, arriving at 7:30 for a breakfast conference to plan their strategy for the day ahead. Doubtlessly these discussions continued at the end of the day in the settlement's dining hall.

One important aspect of the collective strength of Kelley's staff was the socialist beliefs shared by its most dedicated members. As Kelley wrote to Engels in November 1893, "I find my work as inspector most interesting; and as Governor Altgeld places no restrictions whatever upon our freedom of speech, and the English etiquette of silence while in the civil service is unknown here, we are not hampered by our position and three of my deputies and my assistant are outspoken Socialists and active in agitation."[38] In his autobiography Bisno described the "fanatical" commitment that he, Florence Kelley, and most of the "radical group" brought to their work as factory inspectors. For him it was the perfect job since his salary allowed him for the first time to support his wife and children and his work involved direct action against unfair competition within his trade. "In those years labor legislation was looked on as a joke; few took it seriously," he later wrote. "Inspectors normally . . . were appointed from the viewpoint of political interest. . . . There were very few, almost no, court cases heard of, and it was left to our department to set the example of rigid enforcement of labor laws."[39] Although they were replaced with "political interests" after the election of 1896, this group of inspectors shows what could be accomplished by the enactment of reform legislation and its vigorous enforcement. They demonstrated that women could use the power of the state to achieve social and economic goals.

What conclusions can be drawn about the Hull House community from this review of their activities on behalf of antisweatshop legislation? First, and foremost, it attests to the capacity of women to sustain their own institutions. Second, it shows that this community's internal dynamics promoted a creative mixture of mutual support and individual expression. Third, these talented women reformers used their institution as a means of allying with male reformers and entering the mainstream of the American political process. In the tradition of earlier women's associations in the United States, they focused on the concerns of women and children, but these concerns were never divorced from those of men and of the society as a whole. Under the leadership of Florence Kelley, they pursued gender-specific reforms that served class-specific goals.

In many respects the Hull House community serves as a paradigm for women's participation in Progressive reform. Strengthened by the support of women's separate institutions, women reformers were able to develop their capacity for political leadership free from many if not all of the constraints that otherwise might have been imposed on their power by the male-dominated parties or groups with which they cooperated. Building on one of the strengths of the nineteenth-century notion of "women's sphere"—its social activism on behalf of the rights and interests of women and children—they represented those rights and interests innovatively and effectively. Ultimately, however, their power encountered limits imposed by the male-dominated political system, limits created more in response to their class-specific than to their gender-specific reform efforts.

## NOTES

1. Quoted in the foreword, Josephine Goldmark, *Impatient Crusader* (Urbana: University of Illinois Press, 1953), p. 5.
2. The best brief source on Jane Addams is Anne Firor Scott's entry in Edward James, Janet Wilson James, and Paul Boyer, eds., *Notable American Women, 1607–1950*, 3 vols. (Cambridge, Mass.: Harvard University Press, 1971), 1:16–22. For biographical information about

Florence Kelley, see Louise C. Wade's entry in ibid., 2:316–19; Goldmark; and Dorothy Rose Blumberg, *Florence Kelley: The Making of a Social Pioneer* (New York: Augustus M. Kelley, 1966).

3. See esp. Estelle Freedman, "Separatism as Strategy: Female Institution Building and American Feminism, 1870–1930," *Feminist Studies* 5, no. 3 (Fall 1979): 512–29; and Rosalind Rosenberg, "Defining Our Terms: Separate Spheres" (paper presented at the Organization of American Historians, Los Angeles, April 1984).

4. Florence Kelley, "I Go to Work," *Survey* 58, no. 5 (June 1, 1927): 271–77, esp. 271.

5. Nicholas Kelley, "Early Days at Hull House," *Social Service Review* 28, no. 4 (December 1954): 424–29.

6. Mary Rozet Smith sent money to Kelley on many occasions. See Mary Rozet Smith to Florence Kelley, October 6, 1899, Jane Addams Papers, University of Illinois at Chicago; Florence Kelley to Dearly Beloved [Mary Rozet Smith], February 4, 1899, Swarthmore College Peace Collection, Jane Addams Papers; Mary Rozet Smith to Florence Kelley, July 12, 1900, Addams Collection, University of Illinois at Chicago.

7. Florence Kelley to Caroline Kelley, Hull House, February 24, 1892, Nicholas Kelley Papers, New York Public Library (hereafter cited as NK Papers).

8. Florence Kelley to Friedrich Engels, Hull House, December 29, 1887, Archiv, Institute of Marxism-Leninism, Moscow, fund I, schedule 5. I am grateful to Dorothy Rose Blumberg for the use of her microfilm copy of these letters, some of which have been printed in her "'Dear Mr. Engels': Unpublished Letters, 1884–1894, of Florence Kelley (-Wischnewetsky) to Friedrich Engels," *Labor History* 5, no. 2 (Spring 1964): 103–33. Kelley's correspondence with Engels began in 1884, when she decided to translate his *Condition of the English Working Class in 1844* (New York: J. W. Lovell Co., 1887). Until 1958 hers was the only English translation of this classic work.

9. See Dolores Hayden, *The Grand Domestic Revolution: A History of Feminist Designs for American Homes, Neighborhoods, and Cities* (Cambridge, Mass.: MIT Press, 1981), pp. 162–74.

10. Jane Addams to Florence Kelley, [June 1899], NK Papers; Mary Rozet Smith to Florence Kelley, September 14, 1899, Addams Papers; and Jane Addams to Florence Kelley, November 8, 1899, NK Papers. Also Jane Addams to Florence Kelley, November 22, 1899, NK Papers; and Jane Addams to Florence Kelley, July 5, 1913, Special Collections, Columbia University.

11. See the biographies of Addams, Lathrop, and Kelley in James et al., eds. (n. 2 above); and Rebecca Sherrick, "Private Visions, Public Lives: The Hull-House Women in the Progressive Era" (Ph.D. diss., Northwestern University, 1980). Judge Bruce's remarks are in the transcription "Memorial Services for Mrs. Florence Kelley, Miss Julia C. Lathrop, Hull House, Chicago, May 6, 1932," Anita McCormick Blaine Papers, State Historical Society of Wisconsin, Madison (typescript, 1932), pp. 20–21. In this description of her lineage, Addams adapted lines from Elizabeth Browning's *Aurora Leigh*.

12. The political and secular backgrounds of women social settlement leaders can be seen in the biographies of the twenty-six listed as settlement leaders in the classified index of James et al., eds. (n. 2 above), vol. 3. More than a third had fathers who were attorneys or judges or held elected office. Only one was the daughter of a minister—Vida Scudder, whose father died when she was an infant.

13. For the most complete study of the settlements, see Allen F. Davis, *Spearheads for Reform: The Social Settlements and the Progressive Movement, 1890–1914* (New York: Oxford University Press, 1967).

14. Jane Addams, "Hull-House: A Social Settlement," in *Hull House Maps and Papers* (Boston: Thomas Crowell & Co., 1895), pp. 207–30, esp. p. 230.

15. Ibid., pp. vii, 207–8.

16. For Kelley's singular influence on Addams's shift from philanthropist to reformer in 1892, see Allen F. Davis, *American Heroine: The Life and Legend of Jane Addams* (New York: Oxford University Press, 1973), p. 77.

17. Meredith Tax, *The Rising of the Women: Feminist Solidarity and Class Conflict, 1880–1917* (New York: Monthly Review Press, 1979), pp. 23–89, 302, n. 40. The number and variety of women's organizations in Chicago in the 1890s can be seen in the multitude whose remaining records are listed in Andrea Hinding, Ames Sheldon Bower, and Clark A. Chambers, eds., *Women's History Sources: A Guide to Archives and Manuscript Collections in the United States,* vol. 1, *Collections* (New York: R. R. Bowker Co., 1979), pp. 228–57.

18. See Ralph Scharnau, "Elizabeth Morgan, Crusader for Labor Reform," *Labor History* 14, no. 3 (Summer 1973): 340–51.

19. Newspaper clipping, [November] 1888, Thomas J. Morgan Papers, University of Illinois at Urbana-Champaign, box 4, vol. 2.

20. Alliance motto in the *Chicago Daily Interocean* (November 2, 1889), Morgan Papers; women inspectors are mentioned in the *Chicago Tribune* (July 26, 1889).

21. The list is reprinted in Tax, p. 301.

22. Newspaper clipping, November 1888, Morgan Papers, box 4, vol. 2.

23. Florence Kelley, "Die Weibliche Fabrikinspektion in den Vereinigten Staaten," in *Archiv für soziale Gesetzgebung und Statistik,* ed. H. Braun (Tübingen: Edgar Jaffe, 1897), 11:128–42, 130, translated by J. Donovan Penrose as "Women as Inspectors of Factories in the United States" (typescript).

24. Ibid.

25. Ibid.

26. Florence Kelley to Caroline Kelley, February 24, 1892, NK Papers.

27. In "Early Days at Hull House" (n. 5 above), Nicholas Kelley wrote that his mother "became a resident at Hull House almost at once after we came to Chicago" (p. 427).

28. Ruth Bordin, *Woman and Temperance: The Quest for Power and Liberty, 1873–1900* (Philadelphia: Temple University Press, 1981), pp. 90, 98, 142.

29. Minutes of board meeting, March 23, 1892, Chicago Women's Club Papers, Chicago Historical Society. See also Henriette Greenbaum Frank and Amalie Hofer Jerome, comps., *Annuals of the Chicago Women's Club for the First Forty Years of Its Organization, 1876–1916* (Chicago: Chicago Women's Club, 1916), p. 120. Kelley defined "sweating" as "the farming out by competing manufacturers to competing contractors the material for garments, which, in turn, is distributed among competing men and women to be made up. The middle-man, or contractor, is the sweater (though he also may be himself subjected to pressure from above), and his employees are the sweated or oppressed" ("Sweating System in Chicago," *Seventh Biennial Report of the Bureau of Labor Statistics of Illinois, 1892* [Springfield, Ill.: State Printer, 1893]).

30. Jane Addams, *Twenty Years at Hull-House* (New York: Macmillan Publishing Co., 1912), pp. 202, 201.

31. See Eleanor Flexner and Janet Wilson James's entry for Mary Kenney O'Sullivan in James et al., eds. (n. 2 above), 2:655–56.

32. A typesetter and leading labor organizer, Alzina Parsons Stevens became Kelley's chief deputy in 1893, moving into Hull House that year. See Allen F. Davis's entry for Stevens in James et al., eds. (n. 2 above), 3:368–69.

33. Testimony of Florence Kelley and Elizabeth Morgan, *Report and Findings of the Joint Committee to Investigate the "Sweat Shop" System, together with a Transcript of the Testimony Taken by the Committee* (Springfield, Ill.: State Printer, 1893), pp. 144–50, 135–40, respectively.

34. Newspaper clipping, Morgan Papers, box 4, vol. 6.

35. Abraham Bisno, *Abraham Bisno, Union Pioneer: An Autobiographical Account of Bisno's Early Life and the Beginnings of Unionism in the Women's Garment Industry* (Madison: University of Wisconsin Press, 1967), pp. 202–3.

36. *Report and Findings ...* , p. 239.

37. Addams, *Twenty Years at Hull-House,* p. 207.

38. Florence Kelley to Friedrich Engels, November 21, 1893, Archiv, Institute of Marxism-Leninism.

39. Bisno, pp. 148–49.

# 5

## Women in the Southern Farmers' Alliance: A Reconsideration of the Role and Status of Women in the Late Nineteenth-Century South

### Julie Roy Jeffrey

*In 1880 three-fourths of the American people lived in settlements of less than 2,500 inhabitants. Julie Roy Jeffrey examines the political culture of some of these rural women. Her findings overturn our notions of southern women as passive and subservient. As was true in so many other examples of women's political activism, women in the Southern Farmers' Alliance responded eagerly to the opportunity to participate more fully in their community's political life, but also thereby encountered new limits of their involvement. In this respect Alliance women constitute a case study of the way in which women's political culture changes over time.*

In the spring of 1891, Mrs. Brown, secretary of the Menola Sub-Alliance in North Carolina, welcomed an audience of delegates to the quarterly meeting of the Hertford County Farmers' Alliance. After introductory remarks to both the women and men in the audience, Brown addressed her female listeners directly.

> Words would fail me to express to you, my Alliance sisters, my appreciation of woman's opportunity of being co-workers with the brethren in the movement which is stirring this great nation. Oh, what womanly women we ought to be, for we find on every hand, fields of usefulness opening befor us. Our brothers . . . are giving us grand opportunities to show them, as Frances E. Willard says, that "Drudgery, fashion and gossip are no longer the bounds of woman's Sphere."

So enthusiastically was Brown's speech received, that the County Alliance unanimously requested its publication in the official paper of the Farmers' Alliance, the *Progressive Farmer*.[1] In a similar fashion, the Failing Creek Alliance asked the *Progressive Farmer* later that year to reprint a speech Katie Moore had delivered to them. Moore had also spoken before an audience of women and men, and she too had had some special words for the women.

Excerpted from FEMINIST STUDIES, Volume 3, number 1/2 (Fall 1975): 72–91, by permission of the publisher, FEMINIST STUDIES, Inc., c/o Women's Studies Program, University of Maryland, College Park, MD 20742.

*Southern Farm women attend rally of the Southern Tenant Farmers' Union, 1937, continuing traditions dating back to the Southern Farmers Alliance in the early 1890s. Louise Boyle Collection.*

"Tis not enough that we should be what our mothers were," she told them. "We should be more, since our advantages are superior. . . . This is the only order that allows us equal privileges to the men; we certainly should appreciate the privilege and prove to the world that we are worthy to be considered on an equal footing with them."[2]

That the two audiences had approved of these speeches to the point of urging their wider circulation was not surprising. For the slogan of the Southern Farmers' Alliance itself was, "Equal rights to all, special privileges to none." As one Alliance publication explained, "The Alliance has come to redeem women from her enslaved condition, and place her in her proper sphere. She is admitted into the organization as the equal of her brother . . . the prejudice against woman's progress is being removed."[3]

Such statements about the condition of Alliance women were important, for they came from an organization which had millions of members and which was a significant force on the regional and national level in the

1880s and 1890s. In part, the Alliance was a rural protest against the inferior social, economic, and political position its members felt farmers occupied in the emerging urban-industrial society. But, like civil service reformers and other protest groups in the Gilded Age, the Farmers' Alliance argued that the finely balanced two-party system responded only to the demands of special interest groups and political machines rather than to the needs of the people. Alliance members first tried to change this situation by pressing at the state level for control of monopolies and other unfriendly interests and for favorable legislation. Better public schools for rural children, state agricultural colleges, colleges for women, laws controlling the railroads, better prices for farm products were some of the goals the Alliance sought to enable rural classes to survive within a new world. As this strategy proved frustrating, about half of the Alliance membership moved into the Populist party which ran its first presidential candidate in 1892. Although the Populist party ultimately failed, it offered the most serious challenge to the two-party system in the late nineteenth century and contributed to the reshaping of the American political system.[4]

These exhortations and demands emphasizing female equality and opportunity were important, then, because the Alliance was important, but they have an unfamiliar ring in the context of what has generally been known about sex roles and relationships in the post–Civil War South. The accepted interpretation of late nineteenth-century southern society has argued that the model of the southern lady, submissive and virtuous, "the most fascinating being in creation . . . the delight and charm of every circle she moves in," still marked the parameters of appropriate behavior for middle-class women, though the model had been predictably weakened by the traumatic experience of civil war. As for lower-class women, this interpretation suggests, they were "not much affected by role expectations," although "farmers' wives and daughters and illiterate black women . . . in some inarticulate way doubtless helped to shape [society]" and its standards.[5]

Yet an investigation of the Farmers' Alliance in North Carolina, where the Alliance had great success, indicates this explanation does not hold true for that state. If the North Carolina experience is at all typical of other southern Alliance states, and there is little reason to think it is not, the reality of southern attitudes toward women was more complex than recent analyses have allowed. The Civil War had been the initial catalyst for women entering new areas of activities; after the war, poverty and loss of fathers, brothers, husbands, and other male relatives forced many women to run farms, boarding houses, to become seamstresses, postmistresses, and teachers.[6] As the traditional view of woman's sphere crumbled under the impact of the post-war conditions, at least one alternative to the older view emerged in the South—one exemplified by the case of North Carolina. Responsive to social changes stemming from war and defeat, the Alliance in the 1880s and 1890s urged women to adopt a new self-image, one that included education, economic self-sufficiency, one that made a mockery of all false ideas of gentility. The activities and behavior that the Alliance sanctioned were not only considered appropriate for middle-class women but for women on all social levels.[7] Although evidence on the social class composition of the Alliance is limited, recent work suggests that approximately 55 percent of the North Carolina membership owned their land, about 31 percent were tenants, and 14 percent rural professionals. Since many wives and daughters joined the Alliance, it seems reasonable to assume that female membership, like male membership, crossed class lines.[8] Certainly, the new female role was applicable to all of them. Finally, although it was not actually created by Alliance women, the new cultural model was consciously elaborated by some of them, thus offering one way of understanding how middle-class farming women, later deemed "inarticulate" because they left so few written records, perceived and shaped their social role.

Furthermore, a case study of the North Carolina Farmers' Alliance shows that the Alliance also offered numerous rural women the rare privilege of discussing important economic and political issues with men and of functioning as their organizational equals. Few southern institutions offered women similar opportunities. The political party barred them altogether. The Methodist and Baptist churches, which with the Presbyterian claimed a majority of church members, still supported the traditional view that women ought to remain at home although they had allowed women a new area of activity in establishing female missionary societies. This expansion of their sphere was considered to be "no compromise . . . [to] female modesty and refinement," although, in reality, women could and did acquire political experience and skills in them.[9] After 1883, North Carolina women also gained valuable organizational knowledge through their involvement in the Woman's Christian Temperance Union. But the W.C.T.U., the church missionary societies and women's clubs of the 1880s were all-female organizations and thus did not offer women the chance to establish a pragmatic working relationship with men as the Alliance would do.[10]

One other rural organization in the South, the Grange, which reached its height of popularity in North Carolina between 1873 and 1875, admitted both sexes before the Alliance did so. Unlike the Alliance, however, the Grange made clear distinctions between most of the offices and ranks women and men could hold. Nevertheless, the Grange clearly provided women with some practical organizational experience with men and, presumably, offered some kind of rough equality. Still, partly because of its Northern origins, the impact of the Grange was limited in the South. In North Carolina, the Grange's total membership never surpassed the 15,000 mark, and by the 1880s, numbers had dwindled.[11] Moreover, since the Grange was primarily an educational body, it failed to provide the same kind of experience for southern women as the Alliance would in the 1880s and 1890s. Ostensibly apolitical, the Alliance was actually devoted to a discussion of the "science of economical government" and was deeply involved in political questions.[12] Within the North Carolina Alliance, the spheres of women and men drew closer as both sexes voted, held office, and discussed together the stirring issues of the day as they had rarely done before.

Within the framework of the Alliance, then, southern women had the opportunity to discuss pressing economic, political, and social questions, to try out ways of behaving in mixed groups and to gain confidence in newly acquired skills. One might expect that a group of women, and perhaps men, eventually emerge whose Alliance experiences would lead them ultimately to demand or sympathize with the greater expansion of woman's role that the organization officially supported. Yet this never happened. At the same time that the Alliance offered new roles and organizational possibilities for women, the meaning of equality for women was constricted by the organization's major goal of reviving southern agriculture. Political rights within the Alliance were not seen as the first step toward political rights outside of the Alliance. The career of the North Carolina Alliance and its inclusion of women in its membership thus offers another kind of study of the slow progress of the women's rights movement in North Carolina and perhaps gives additional clues for its uncertain course in the South as a whole.

The evidence for this study comes from many sources. Most useful is the State Alliance paper, the *Progressive Farmer*,[13] whose policy it was to publish the views of the Alliance membership. Few of these rural correspondents provided the leading articles for the paper, but rather they contributed letters to the correspondence page. Since these long forgotten farm women and men left virtually no other personal records, their letters, some literary, most artless, provide a crucial insight into the grassroots level of the Alliance and an important view of their responses to the opportunities the Alliance held out to them.

Initial interest in a farmers' organization in North Carolina resulted from the depressed state of southern agriculture in the 1880s. By 1886, Colonel Leonidas Polk, editor of the new agricultural weekly, the *Progressive Farmer,* was vigorously urging the paper's readers to organize local farmers' clubs as the basis for a future statewide organization. From the beginning he visualized at least some women in the clubs, for he advised they could be "elected as honorary members." Yet farmers' clubs were not to have a long life in North Carolina. By May 1887 Alliance organizers from Texas, where the agricultural order had originated, had begun to establish local Alliances in North Carolina, while a Carolinian, J. B. Barry, also began recruiting. Polk, aware of the growth potential of the Alliance, joined one of Barry's Alliances in July 1887, and was soon meeting with Texas Alliance leaders to discuss a merger between the Alliance and his farmers' clubs. After the merger was made the North Carolina Alliance grew by leaps and bounds. In the summer of 1888 the membership stood at 42,000. By 1891 the Alliance claimed 100,000 members in over 2,000 local chapters.[14]

Requirements for membership in the Alliance, formalized in the state constitution adopted in October 1887, were far more positive to female members than Polk's farmers' clubs had been. Membership was open to rural white women and men over sixteen years of age who had a "good moral character," believed in "the existence of a Supreme Being," and showed "industrious habits." While men were to pay fifty cents as an initiation fee in addition to quarterly dues of twenty-five cents, women had no required fee or dues, no doubt a recognition of their marginal economic status and their desirability as members.[15]. . .

Alliance leaders did not leave the issue of female participation in the organization to chance but stressed it forcefully. Harry Tracy, a National Lecturer of the order, urged *"the ladies to come out and hear him,"* and warned Alliance members: "The ladies eligible must join the order before we can succeed." Despite emphatic support from the top, however, letters from local Alliances to the *Progressive Farmer,* now the official organ of the North Carolina Alliance, indicate some male resistance to the idea of female members. As the Secretary of the Davidson College Alliance explained: "I think that the ladies are best suited to home affairs." Verbal opposition to female members led one woman to comment, "They don't want us to join, and think it no place for us." Other, more subtle techniques of discouraging female membership seem to have existed. Holding meetings in places where women would be uncomfortable or feel out of place kept the number of female members down. As the correspondent from Lenoir Alliance noted, his Alliance had fifty men and one woman because meetings were held in the court house. As one frequent contributor to the *Progressive Farmer* who favored female members pointed out: "Each Sub-Alliance needs a hall. . . . We cannot urge the ladies to attend until we can seat them comfortably."[16]

Numerous questions addressed to Polk, now secretary of the state Alliance as well as editor of the *Progressive Farmer,* indicated that even if not opposed to female membership, men were often hesitant and confused about the membership of women. A variety of questions focused on what women were eligible for membership and, if elected, what their rights should be. Were women, in fact, to have the same "rights and privileges of the male members"?[17] Over and over again Polk replied that women were to have equal rights and privileges; they were to vote on new members, participate in all Alliance business and to know "all the secret words and signs" of the order.[18]

If some men were unenthusiastic about female members, so too were some of the women. As one Allianceman explained: "Our female friends seem to repose great confidence in our ability to conduct the affairs of the Alliance without their direct union and assistance. Indeed, our wives, mothers and sisters have as much as they can do to attend their own business." Other letters from men more enthusiastic about female members agreed that women refused to join because they were "too modest, or think it out of their line."[19] The traditional view of woman's sphere, then, constituted a barrier to active female participation in the Alliance, and it was one which female members consciously tried to undermine. When Alliancewomen wrote to the *Progressive Farmer* they frequently urged the other women to overcome feelings of timidity. "Dear Sisters, go to work; don't stay home and die, then say I have something else to do; that will never do," wrote Addie Pigford. "Sisters, what are you doing?" asked Mrs. Carver. "There is work for us to do, and we shall not be found wanting. We can help in many ways, and we must do it."[20]

Opposition and hesitation on the subject of female members obviously existed as the reports of local and county Alliances and male and female correspondents to the *Progressive Farmer* show. But evidence suggests that the message that women were to be encouraged as vigorous participants of the Alliance eventually came through clearly to most local groups. By 1889, for example, the State Line Alliance reported it was planning to discuss the desirability of female members. Rather ruefully, the writer commented: "That indicates *how far we are behind,* but we do not intend to remain there."[21] Questions about membership requirements and privileges, membership breakdowns sent into the *Progressive Farmer,* and local minute books, indicate that women were presenting themselves for membership. Not only did the wives and daughters of male members join but so too did unattached women. As the Alliance grew so did the number of women in the organization. In some cases, women comprised one-third to one-half of local groups.[22] "We can work just as well as the brethren," pointed out one Alliance woman. "If we want to derive good from the Alliance, we must work in love and harmony with our fellow-man."[23]

As thousands of women responded to the Alliance's invitation to join "the great army of reform," there were hints that women felt increasingly at ease in their new organizational role. Although it is difficult to recover the perceptions of these rural women, their letters to the *Progressive Farmer* from 1887 through 1891 can serve as an imperfect measure for their thoughts and feelings about their participation in the Alliance.[24]

One of the most striking aspects of the women's correspondence is the initial hesitation about writing to a newspaper at all. Only one woman communicated to the editor in 1887. Gradually, however, women began to send letters, many of them conscious of departing from past patterns of behavior. "Being a farmer's wife, I am not in the habit of writing for the public prints," wrote the first female correspondent of 1888, a certain Mrs. Hogan who was concerned about stray dogs. Replied the second, "Mr. Editor:—I have never written anything for the public to read, but I feel just now, after reading Mrs. Hogan's trouble . . . that I want to tell her I truly sympathize with her."[25] Other correspondents in 1888 and 1889 often began their letters with the polite request for a "small space" for a few words from a farm woman or with the phrase, "I am but a female." "I suppose your many subscribers will not expect much from a female correspondent," wrote one corresponding secretary, "and if so, they will not be disappointed when they read this article, but if I can be of any service to the Alliance by putting in my little mite, I am willing to do what I can."[26] By 1890 such protestations and expressions of humility had disappeared. A series of letters from Evangeline Usher exemplifies the growing confidence on the part of women that their letters and reports on Alliance activities were appropriate and acceptable. In an early letter, Usher urged other women to write to the paper, with the typical hope that Polk would "give us a little space somewhere." Describing herself as fearful that her letter would go into the wastebasket, she further explained that her feelings of delicacy would prevent her from contributing her Alliance's news regularly. "I already imagine I see Brother 'R' smiling ludicrously at the idea." Within a few months, however, Usher wrote again, confessing "a kind of literary pride in seeing my name in print." By 1889, she could begin her letter, "I feel like I must intrude again, and as I am quite independent of all disfavor, I do not care whether you like the intrusion or not."[27] Though Usher was unusually outspoken, her growing boldness correlates with the straightforward and secure tone women gradually adopted in writing to the paper and suggests their greater feelings of confidence within the organization.

Local reports, letters, and records also give information on another crucial consideration concerning women's involvement in the Alliance. If women only sat on the back benches during Alliance meetings, listening silently while men discussed the great economic and political issues of the day, their membership would have been insignificant. If, on the other hand, women actually helped to run the organization and helped contribute to its success, even if they were not equal in every respect to men, then the Alliance was an important departure from the typical southern organization.

Although there is no indication that women were ever elected to the office of president of local Alliances, they were occasionally, at least, voted into important positions. The Jamestown Alliance Minute Book, for example, records that a year after the subject of female members was first discussed, a woman was elected as assistant secretary; she declined, but two months later was elected as treasurer.[28] Other women held the office of secretary, with the responsibility not only for making "a fair record of all things necessary to be written," but also for "receiving all moneys due" and for communicating with Secretary Polk.[29] Still others became lecturers or assistant lecturers, both crucial positions since they were to give addresses, lead discussions, and furnish "the material of thought for the future consideration of the members."[30] Women as well as men read papers "on subjects of importance for the benefit of the order." In one Alliance, records show that women conducted the business on an Alliance meeting day.[31] At the county level where meetings were held quarterly, women were included in the membership count on which representation was based, were delegates, and at least one was elected vice-president. Others gave key addresses to large audiences.[32] Women could also be found at the annual meetings of the state Alliance. As the *Progressive Farmer* warmly replied to two women who had written to ask if they could go to the meeting, "You are not only *allowed,* but you will be most cordially welcomed to a seat."[33] Though such evidence is fragmentary, it does imply that many women took an active part in running Alliance affairs.

Women participated in the Alliance in a variety of other areas too. Several letters to the *Progressive Farmer* noted that women subscribed to the State Business Agency Fund, an important Alliance effort aimed at eliminating middlemen in purchasing fertilizers, groceries, and agricultural goods. Alliance leaders urged local groups to donate at least fifty cents a member to the fund. A few reports show women carrying their financial share. Women also sent in news to the paper, wrote articles, and worked to increase the subscription list, a job which Polk and other leaders saw as vital to Alliance success since they argued that earlier efforts to arouse farmers had foundered on ignorance and lack of proper information.[34]

If not all women were active members of the Alliance, enough were to be reported and praised in the *Progressive Farmer.* Clearly, many women welcomed the chance to work in the organization. Moreover, as their letters indicate, they shared men's interest in the compelling subjects of the day: agricultural cooperation, the role of combines and trusts in creating the farming crisis, the need to diversify southern agriculture, all standard themes for discussion and instruction in Alliance meetings and reading material.[35] But as much as women were involved with such topics, as much as they enjoyed the social conviviality of the Alliance, many must have agreed with the woman who reminded her Alliance, "This is the only order that allows us equal privileges to the man; we certainly should appreciate the privilege."[36]

North Carolina Alliance's support of "equal rights" for women within the organization and of the new role described for them outside it may seem startling, yet it corresponded to the reality of life for southern women in the late 1880s and early 1890s. It would have been surprising if the changes in southern society following the Civil War had failed to result in some ideological reconsideration of women's status. Yet the Alliance's stance was not merely a response to social change in the South. The National Alliance upheld the concept of equal rights. State leaders recognized that the farmer and his wife worked as an agricultural unit. It made sense to involve both in the Alliance for as one farmer pointed out, "We know we can scarcely dispense with the labor of our wives and children on the farm."[37] . . .

The social composition of the leadership suggests another important reason for the Alliance support for women. Although men like Colonel Polk and Sydenham Alexander, president of the state Alliance, had been or were farmers genuinely concerned with agricultural problems, they were also members of the rural upper-class. Polk had had a long career as a planter, army officer, legislator, commissioner of agriculture, and editor. Alexander had headed the state Grange in the 1870s. Other leaders were teachers, doctors, and clergymen.[38] As members of North Carolina's elite, these men partially accepted the traditional view of woman as the beacon of social morality. "If our organization means anything," one prominent supporter of female members wrote, "it means a moral reformation, morality must be our guide. The ladies are and always have been the great moral element in society; therefore *it is impossible to succeed without calling to our aid the greatest moral element in the country.*"[39]

This was how Alliance leaders conceived of the role and importance of women within their organization. But women themselves had their own ideas about their role, as an examination of their letters to the *Progressive Farmer* reveals. The writers stressed their pride in farm life, the need to throw off female passivity, the vital importance of women to the Alliance effort. "While it has been remarked that women are necessary evil," wrote Fannie Pentecost, "let us by our untiring energy, and zeal show them that it is a mistake. . . . We should devise plans and means by which we can assist those who have to bear the burdens of life." In the Alliance, another woman pointed out, women had the unique opportunity of helping men "in the thickest of the fight" by encouragement, prayers, self-denial, and endurance. Some correspondents clearly saw their role as one of moral support, but others visualized a more active role, using words like helpmate or companion to describe how they saw themselves.[40] One woman shaped the female role curiously: "Let us all put our shoulders to this great wheel, the Alliance. We, as sisters of this Alliance may feel we are silent factors in this work; we know we constantly need something to lean upon. . . . Let us so entwine ourselves around our brothers that *should we be taken away* they will feel they are *tottering.*" Here, encouragement and support had become the vital activity for women. So, too, one woman from Fair Grove commented that women must be "ready to hold the hands of the strong, should they become weak."[41] . . .

. . . Yet, despite these indications that women suspected that they rather than men were possibly the most steadfast and reliable leaders of reform, they were hardly ready to challenge openly the Alliance's basic assumptions because of the positive support the Alliance was already providing for southern women in many areas of life.

. . . A woman's role in the Alliance was understood to parallel the more significant role the Alliance suggested women could enjoy in society at large. The *Progressive Farmer*'s policy of reporting on the achievements of women who were doctors, surgeons, journalists, lawyers, government workers, even pastors, indicated the wide range of possibilities beyond the conventional one of marriage and motherhood.[42] These career options, of course, depended on educating women, a goal that the Alliance and its official newspaper consistently supported as part of the general attempt to improve all educational facilities for "farmers and laborers."[43]. . .

The reason for the Alliance's concern with women's education becomes obvious in the *Progressive Farmer*'s discussions of private girls' schools. Traditionally, these schools had stressed teaching female accomplishments to the would-be southern lady of means. But now the *Progressive Farmer* enthusiastically reported, Salem Female Academy had expanded its offering by establishing a business course featuring music, telegraphy, phonography (shorthand), typing and bookkeeping. Such a course, the *Progressive Farmer* pointed out, was most desirable with its "studies of a practical character, fitting the learners for active avocations when required to depend upon their own efforts in the battle of life." Other schools, the paper urged, ought to follow Salem Academy's example. The fundamental point, the paper emphasized, was that *all* young women of *all* social classes should be prepared for jobs. It was true, of course, that education would help poor girls by enabling them "to make an honest living," but all women ought to learn to be self-sufficient and self-supporting.[44]

Women themselves stressed the importance of economic self-sufficiency. They did not want to "be entirely dependent upon the bounties of others" if they lost their protectors. And, as an additional point in favor of education, one Alliance woman brought up the important question of marriage. Self-sufficiency would allow women to marry because they wanted to, not because they needed financial support. Thus education of a certain kind would help women avoid the "fatal blunder," incompatibility in marriage.[45]

Alliance support for practical education for women was based on a rejection of the concept of gentility which had been such a fundamental component of the idea of the southern lady.[46] The search for a "pale and delicate" complexion, the interest in elaborate clothing and accomplishments were all denounced in the pages of the *Progressive Farmer*. These traditional female concerns were misguided since they undermined the importance of hard work and, thus, the opportunities for female independence. The idea that labor was degrading, the *Progressive Farmer* reminded its readers, was just another unfortunate remnant of slavery, and, in fact, contributed in an important way to poverty itself. True Alliance men and women wanted young people "to see that it is no disgrace, but a high honor, to know how to work and to be able to do it." The feminine ideal was the woman who was independent and practical, educated either to support herself or to marry wisely.[47]

Better education for both sexes was an issue with which many Alliance members sympathized, hoping their children's future would be more promising than their own. Yet the Alliance could not concern itself exclusively with the new options for young women who still had their lives ahead of them. With so many adult female members, the Alliance also considered how to reshape life styles for those women who would never leave the farm for school or a job. "Is the life of the Farmer's wife under present systems, calculated to give her virtue and intelligence full play," asked the Southern Alliance paper, the *National Economist.* "Is she not a slave and a drudge in many cases?" The *Progressive Farmer* gave the answer: there were "thousands and tens of thousands" of farmers' wives "worked to their graves."[48] Improving this dreary situation necessitated a multipronged approach. First, the paper's scientific articles on housekeeping and cooking could show the farm wife how to lighten her work load. Then, too, her husband was to be prodded into helping her out. As one correspondent to the *Progressive Farmer* explained, men needed tough words. "Our Lecturer, in trying to discuss the social feature [of the Alliance], handles husbands quite roughly, but it is received in the proper spirit. If country life is ever made more attractive, there must be more congeniality in spirit and aggressiveness between the one that follows the plow handles and the one of all beings earthly that acts as a helpmeet to man." What were "the conveniences for the good and faithful wife?" asked Colonel Polk. How far did she have to walk to the woodpile or the spring? Had the bloom on her cheeks faded prematurely? These were the subjects, he urged, that ought to be discussed in Alliance circles so that "new life, new energy, new action . . . and new views of life and living" might emerge for both sexes.[49]

The Alliance's concern with helping hardworking farmwomen fused with the order's major objective, the overall improvement of agricultural life. To this end, the Alliance sought to discover "a remedy for every evil known to exist and afflict farmers and other producers."[50] The remedy of improved farming methods was especially important as the number of articles in the *Progressive Farmer* attest. The paper argued that the one-crop system was the obvious and basic cause of the state's agricultural depression. Over and over again, the paper and Alliance meetings focused on the need to farm properly and to stay out of debt. Consider the two kinds of farmers, the *Progressive Farmer* urged. One raised cotton on his land, bought milk, bread, hay and fertilizers on credit. The other chose the Alliance route and would prosper. And "his wife, dear devoted woman, instead of wearing out her life in cooking for a lot of negroes to work cotton, has time to look after the adornment and the beautifying of her home, to attend to her milk and butter, eggs, garden, bees, chickens and other poultry, and with all this they have a little time to spare socially with their neighbors and to go to church."[51]

The *Progressive Farmer* might describe the tasks of the wise farmer's wife enthusiastically, but the list of her activities highlights a crucial problem in the Alliance's approach to women. Although the Alliance supported expanding women's rights and privileges, its over-all objective was to put farmers on an economic, social, and political parity with other occupations. To do so, or to try to do so, had definite implications for women's lives and shaped the Alliance's conception of equality. If the home was to be made attractive enough to discourage children from abandoning farm life, if it was to be "a place of rest, of comfort, of social refinement and domestic pleasure," then women would have to make it so.[52] If the farm was to stay out of debt, if the farmer was to remain free of the supply merchant by raising as many of his necessities as he could, his wife must help. Woman's "judgement and skill in management may be essential to the success of her husband," one article reminded Alliance readers. "And this responsibility . . . continues to the close of her life."[53]

The Alliance proposed a position for women that embodied an equality of sorts, the economic equality of a diligent coworker. In its recognition of the importance and difficulty of woman's work, the role model differed from that of the southern lady. Nor did the model merely update the characters of the yeoman farmer's family. The Alliance's concern with diversifying southern agriculture, with eliminating the disastrous dependency on the one-crop system, was not an attempt to recreate the small farm and agricultural myth of an idealized past but to create a new kind of farm and a new cast of characters. Agricultural reform, in fact, was seen as part of a modernizing process, and it was favored not only by the Alliance but also by leaders of the New South movement. Spokesmen for each group agreed that the South had to end its colonial status both through substantial industrial growth and through agricultural diversification.[54]

But what were the implications of such a view for women? "The housewife, who, by her industry, transforms the milk from her dairy into butter . . . is as truly a manufacturer as the most purse-proud mill-owner of Britian," explained the *National Economist.* Labeled manufacturers or helpmates, women were to carry a heavy burden in creating the new order.[55] The truth was that even though the Alliance talked of a variety of opportunities available for women, most women in North Carolina would continue to live on the farm, and Alliance leaders thought this right in terms of the world they wished to create. . . .

Moreover, women needed to be educated so that, in turn, they could teach Alliance children, first at home and then at school. Rural children, many Alliance members were convinced, needed a special kind of education, one that embraced "the moral, physical and industrial, as well as the mental training of our children." By providing such an education, women could offer an "invaluable service." For "this system will strengthen the attachment of these classes [to agricultural life] instead of alienating [them] from it . . . it will better qualify them for success and happiness in life . . . increase the opportunity and inclination to adorn the home and practice the social virtues."[56]

Other pragmatic considerations led to the support of women's education. Education could provide poor girls with the opportunity "to make an honest living." Most, but not all, women would marry. To prepare for the possibility of spinsterhood, every careful mother must see not only that daughters were trained in their domestic and spiritual responsibilities, but would also "have them taught a trade or profession and thus equip them fully to 'face the world' if this need shall come to them."[57]. . .

The part that the Alliance encouraged women to play in southern life was more expansive than the traditional role of the southern lady at the same time that it had definite limitations. Women need no longer cultivate the appearance of genteel passivity; they required education as the preparation for a useful life. But the Alliance defined utility in terms of the organization's over-all objectives, the profitability of agriculture, the prosperity of the state. Thus, it was vital that women learn to be skilled managers or teachers. Whether spinsters or widows, women must never be parasites on their families or on their state. Beneath the rhetoric, the lifestyle the Alliance supported for women was one of constant hard work and low wages, if women were to be paid for their labor at all. These limitations, harsh though they seem, were realistic both in terms of the Alliance's major goals and in terms of available options in the South. As one northern observer testified, "There is yet no rapid development of opportunity for profitable labor for young white women in the South."[58]

There may be yet another reason for the contradictory meaning of equality that the Alliance proposed for women. Despite the support the Alliance gave to an expanded life style for women, Alliance leaders were affected by the circumstances of time, place, and class. Like other well-born Southerners, they had not rejected the traditional view of women as the source of morality and goodness. Because of their moral qualities, women had to participate in the Alliance, but it is doubtful whether North Carolina Alliance leaders would have supported enlarging women's sphere in any way that might threaten their own social or political position.[59]. . .

There are few indications that this strategy was unacceptable to the majority of Alliance women. Most letters from women indicate that the new parameters for female behavior were thankfully welcomed. Only occasionally can one discern an undercurrent of unrest, when women remarked on men's failure to be vigorous Alliance fighters or when they pointed out how much better a place the world would be had women, long ago, taken a more active part in shaping it.[60] Then, too, a few women dared to write on political matters, giving their own opinions and urging men to take notice.[61] At least one woman realized how far she had stepped out of her place. After mocking Alliance men who were "willing to wave Alliance principles and swallow the whole Democratic party," she observed, "I could say a good deal more on this line, but will stop, for fear some fool will ask: 'Are you a woman?'"[62]

The *Progressive Farmer* not surprisingly steered away from the explosive issue of women's participation in politics.[63] In two unusual references to the question of women's political rights, however, it is clear that the issue had come up in local meetings. At one county rally, the lecturer told the women, "He did not invite them to suffrage, though it was gaining rapidly in public favor and if they had the ballot they would drive out the liquor traffic of this country and other evils." In Almance County, the Alliance lecturer warned his female listeners, "Do not spend your time in longing for opportunities that will never come, but be contented in the sphere the Lord hath placed you in. If the Lord had intended you for a preacher or lawyer He would have given you a pair of pantaloons."[64]

But the desire to maintain the *status quo* did not automatically succeed. Though Alliance leaders delineated definite boundaries to the theoretical and actual position women might occupy in the world, the fact that suffrage was mentioned at all may indicate a turbid undercurrent of half conscious challenge to the leadership. The way the two Alliance speakers spoke of the suffrage issue suggests that some Alliance circles had discussed it. A few letters to the *Progressive Farmer* and other fragmentary evidence point to the same conclusion. On a visit to North Carolina in 1893, for example, a Mrs. Virginia Durant who had established a suffrage organization in South Carolina, reported she found "suffrage sentiment" of an unfocused kind in the state. Perhaps she sensed incipient interest among those women exposed to the Alliance.[65]

Yet there is not enough evidence to resolve the issue. If there were some support for the further expansion of women's activities through the Alliance, however, it never had the time to grow strong and vocal. For although the Alliance lingered on into the twentieth century, by the mid-1890s it had ceased to be an institution of importance. The failure of Alliance cooperative economic ventures, continued hard times, and a split within the organization over the support of the Populist party all contributed to a decline in membership. A changing political climate brought new issues, new questions to the fore; many of them would have conservative implications.[66] By the end of the decade, the shape of southern life would be set. After the Populist challenge, franchise for both poor whites and blacks would be limited and the question of political participation closed. Voting was a privilege, not a right. "Equal rights for all, special privileges for none" was a slogan best forgotten.[67]

Though the Alliance did not survive long enough to dislodge the traditional ideas of woman's sphere, its spirited attempt to work out a new place for her both in theory and practice shows greater complexity in late nineteenth-century attitudes and behavior with respect to sex roles than previously recognized, and suggests that there may have been other attempts to create new roles for women in the South. The Alliance alternative, it is true, fell short of offering women equality in all spheres of life. Primary Alliance goals and the nature of the leadership limited the meaning of equal rights for women. Yet to expect the Alliance to propose full equality for women would be to ignore the influence of both time and place and

to expect consistency of thought and action when such consistency rarely
exists.

## NOTES

1. *Progressive Farmer,* June 23, April 21, 1891.
2. *Progressive Farmer,* December 22, 1891.
3. Nelson A. Dunning, ed., *The Farmer's Alliance History and Agricultural Digest* (Washington:
The Alliance Publishing Co., 1891), pp. 309–310. See also *National Economist,* June 6, 1891.
4. For general information on the Alliance see John D. Hicks, *The Populist Revolt: A History
of the Farmers' Alliance and the People's Party* (Minneapolis: University of Minnesota Press, 1931),
pp. 105, 146; Theodore Saloutos, *Farmer Movements in the South: 1865–1933* (Berkeley: University
of California Press, 1960), pp. 85, 123, 282–83; Hugh Talmage Lefler and Albert Ray Newsome,
*The History of A Southern State: North Carolina* (Chapel Hill: University of North Carolina Press,
1963), p. 513; John M. Dobson, *Politics in the Gilded Age: A New Perspective on Reform* (New York:
Praeger, 1972), pp. 172–75, 183–86.
5. Quoted in Anne Firor Scott, *The Southern Lady: From Pedestal to Politics, 1830–1930* (Chicago: University of Chicago Press, 1970), pp. 4–5, x–xi, and Anne Firor Scott, "Women's Perspective on the Patriarchy in the 1850s," *Journal of American History* 61 (June 1974): 54, note 4.
6. Scott, *Southern Lady,* chapters 4 and 5.
7. Robert Carroll McMath, Jr., "The Farmers' Alliance in the South: The Career of an
Agrarian Institution" (Ph.D. dissertation, University of North Carolina at Chapel Hill, 1972),
pp. 88–89; Robert Carroll McMath, Jr., "Agrarian Protest at the Forks of the Creek: Three
Subordinate Farmers' Alliance in North Carolina," *The North Carolina Historical Review* 51 (January 1974): 47; Philip Roy Muller, "New South Populism: North Carolina, 1884–1900," (Ph.D.
dissertation, University of North Carolina at Chapel Hill, 1971), pp. 33–37, 148–54.
8. McMath, "Farmers' Alliance," pp. 88–89.
9. Quoted in Hunter Dickinson Farish, *The Circuit Rider Dismounts: A Social History of Southern Methodism, 1865–1900* (Richmond: Dietz Press, 1938), pp. 327, 325–26; Scott, *Southern Lady,*
pp. 137–41; Anne Firor Scott, "Women, Religion and Social Change in the South, 1830–1930,"
in *Religion and the Solid South,* ed., Samuel S. Hill, Jr. (Nashville: Abingdon Press, 1972), pp. 93–
115; Marjorie Stratford Mendenhall, "Southern Women of a 'Lost Generation,'" *South Atlantic
Quarterly* 33 (October 1937): 339–41; Emory Stevens Bucke, ed., *The History of American Methodism*
(Nashville: Abingdon Press, 1964), vol. 2, pp. 291–92.
10. Daniel J. Whitener, *Prohibition in North Carolina, 1715–1935* (Chapel Hill: University of
North Carolina Press, 1945), pp. 104–105; Scott, *Southern Lady,* pp. 139–52. Men were admitted
as honorary members to the W.C.T.U.
11. Solon Justus Buck, *The Granger Movement: A Study of Agricultural Organization and Its Political, Economic and Social Manifestations: 1870–1880* (Cambridge: Harvard University Press, 1913),
pp. 41–43, 381; Saloutos, *Farmer Movements,* pp. 30–33, 42; Stuart Noblin, *The Grange in North
Carolina 1929–1954: A Story of Agricultural Progress* (Greensboro: The North Carolina State
Grange, 1954), pp. 2, 3.
12. Saloutos, *Farmer Movements,* pp. 32, 42; Roy V. Scott, *The Reluctant Farmer: The Rise of
Agricultural Extension to 1914* (Urbana: University of Illinois Press, 1970), pp. 42–46; *National
Economist,* March 14, 1889, June 7, 1890; *Progressive Farmer,* December 1, 1887, January 28, 1890.
In 1889, the North Carolina State Alliance decided all political demands were to be sent to
local Alliances for their approval. See "Official Circular No. 6," May 27, 1892, John R. Osborne
Papers, Duke University, where Alliance secretaries are ordered to present the State Alliance
resolution in favor of a secret ballot to their Sub-Alliances "for discussion and ratification."
13. Although major Alliance manuscript collections and records were utilized for this
study, the most useful source for it was the official newspaper of the North Carolina Alliance,
the *Progressive Farmer.* Letters and articles for 1886, the year before the Alliance officially
adopted the paper, are also used since they do not differ in content or tone from what was
published later. The *Progressive Farmer* is the best source for this study of Alliance thought and
practice not only because of its central role in disseminating and reflecting Alliance views, but
because local Alliance records are skimpy, leaders were often concerned with the "major"

issues, and few of the women and men left any lasting remains at all aside from their letters to the paper.

14. *Progressive Farmer,* March 31, 1886; McMath, "Farmers' Alliance," pp. 82–83; John D. Hicks, "The Farmer's Alliance in North Carolina," *The North Carolina Historical Review* 2 (April 1925): 169. It is difficult precisely to estimate membership in the Southern Alliance or its North Carolina branch. The organization claimed a total membership of 362,970 in July 1888, just a year after recruiting began. Of these, 42,496 or 12 percent were women. By 1890, the Alliance reported it had 3,000,000 members, a figure that some believe was inflated (Saloutos, *Farmer Movements,* p. 77). In North Carolina, the Farmers' Alliance *Daybook,* North Carolina State Archives, Raleigh, notes that the number of local Alliances had reached 2,000 in February 1890. See also *Minutes* of the Farmers' State Alliance, 1887–1893, August 14, 1888, North Carolina State Archives, Raleigh; McMath, "Farmers' Alliance," p. 139.

15. *Minutes,* Farmers' State Alliance, October 4, 1887, August 16, 1888.

16. *Progressive Farmer,* July 9, 1889, February 25, 1890, June 23, 1891. *The Sub Alliance and What It Can Accomplish: Report of the Program Committee of the North Carolina Farmers State Alliance* (no date, North Carolina State Archives, Raleigh) emphatically makes the point that female membership is a necessity. (See also *Progressive Farmer,* June 11, 1889; July 10, May 22, 1888; July 30, 1889; February 25, 1890; April 8, 1890; June 25, 1889.

17. *Progressive Farmer,* December 18, June 12, December 4, June 12, July 24, 1888, May 14, 1889.

18. Ibid.; also *Progressive Farmer,* March 13, 1888, March 5, 1889.

19. *Progressive Farmer,* May 22, 1888; October 7, 1890. See also July 30, August 6, 1889, September 23, October 7, 1890.

20. *Progressive Farmer,* December 16, March 25, 1890. See also July 24, 1888, June 11, August 6, October 1, 1889; February 11, September 23, 1890; September 22, December 22, 1890; *National Economist,* June 6, 1891. Of course, men were also encouraged to be more vigorous in their support of the Alliance.

21. *Progressive Farmer,* June 11, November 19, 1889.

22. For membership ratios, see the Bethany Alliance Minute Book, John R. Osborne Papers, Duke University, Jamestown Alliance Minute Book, Duke University, and the Mt. Sylvan Alliance Minute Book, North Carolina State Archives, Raleigh. See also the Account Book of Wake City Alliance, Roll Book of L. L. Polk, Sub Alliance No. 2254, Wake County, Polk Papers, in the Southern Historical Collection, University of North Carolina Library, Chapel Hill, and the *Progressive Farmer, passim.* The Wake County Alliance Account Book, which gives membership figures for about 45 local Alliances in that County, indicates that 36 percent of the County's membership in September 1890 were women. A year later this percentage of women had risen to 38 percent.

23. *Progressive Farmer,* February 11, 1890; August 7, May 15, December 11, 1888; August 13, 1889.

24. *Progressive Farmer,* March 10, 1891. There is, of course, the possibility that any woman writing to the newspaper was atypical.

25. *Progressive Farmer,* January 19, 1887; February 16, March 13, 1888.

26. *Progressive Farmer,* April 16, April 30, 1889; October 1, 1889.

27. *Progressive Farmer,* July 24, December 11, 1888; September 23, 1889; see also her letter of March 19, 1889, and February 25, 1890. Interestingly enough, Polk saved a letter from Usher that can be found in his papers. Evangeline Usher to L. L. Polk, December 25, 1889, Polk Papers, in the Southern Historical Collection, University of North Carolina Library, Chapel Hill.

28. Jamestown Alliance Minute Book. She subsequently left this office. "Organizers Report," November 13, 1889, Polk Papers, in the Southern Historical Collection, University of North Carolina Library, Chapel Hill, notes Miss J. M. E. Midget as treasurer. Unfortunately, inadequate records make it impossible to discover how many women held office. There are enough casual references to women in office, however, to suggest that female office holders were not unusual.

29. *National Farmers' Alliance and Industrial Union Ritual* (Washington, D.C.: National Economist Publishing Co., 1891). *Progressive Farmer,* May 28, October 1, 1889; September 23, October 7, 1890.

30. *Ritual; Progressive Farmer,* August 6, September 24, 1889. President Alexander stressed

the crucial importance of the lecturer's position in characterizing it as "more important than any of the others" (*Minutes,* Farmers' State Alliance, August 13, 1889).

31. *Progressive Farmer,* September 11, 1888; March 31, December 22, 1891.

32. *Progressive Farmer,* June 23, 1891; July 17, October 23, 1888; April 21, 1891. There was clearly some confusion about counting women for representation. W. M. Koonts, secretary of the Davidson County Alliance, wrote to the Bethany Alliance secretary, "You are only entitled to delegates for the *male* members clear on the books." But the previous year Polk, in answer to a question on this very point, had announced that both sexes were to be counted (S. M. Koonts, to John R. Osborne, December 27, 1889, John R. Osborne papers, Duke University), *Progressive Farmer,* July 17, 1888.

33. *Progressive Farmer,* July 9, 1889.

34. "Circular No. 3, North Carolina Farmers' Alliance Business Agency Fund," November 22, 1890, Richard Street Papers, North Carolina State Archives, Raleigh; *Progressive Farmer,* August 13, 1889; July 24, 1888, September 8, 1887; S. B. Alexander to L. L. Polk, November 14, 1885, Polk Papers, Southern Historical Collection, University of North Carolina Library, Chapel Hill; *Progressive Farmer,* May 28, October 1, 1889; Circular, "Important to Sub-Alliances: Please Read at Next Meeting," L. Polk Denmark Collection, North Carolina State Archives, Raleigh.

35. Women reported on crop information and expressed interest in a wide variety of subjects. See *Progressive Farmer,* August 14, November 6, 1888; February 26, April 30, July 9, 1889 for examples.

36. *Progressive Farmer,* December 22, 1891.

37. *Progressive Farmer,* September 11, 1888.

38. See Noblin, *Polk, passim;* Noblin, *The Grange,* p. 3; McMath, "Farmers' Alliance," pp. 84–88; Muller, "New South Populism," pp. 33–37, 148–54.

39. *Progressive Farmer,* July 9, 1889; March 31, 1891; June 25, 1889; November 13, 1888. The Pleasant Garden Alliance Minute Book, William D. Hardin Papers, Duke University, shows the importance members attributed to moral and orderly conduct at meetings. *Progressive Farmer,* March 24, 1891.

40. *Progressive Farmer,* June 11, 1889; June 23, 1891; for similar views from other southern women, see *National Economist,* July 12, July 26, 1889; October 25, 1890; July 25, 1891.

41. *Progressive Farmer,* July 24, 1888, my italics; *Progressive Farmer,* June 4, 1889.

42. These items are generally given without any editorial comments, as were the other items of general interest. For examples, see *Progressive Farmer,* May 18, July 21, October 29, November 17, 1886; February 2, May 8, June 12, July 3, November 6, 1888; August 20, 1889.

43. *Progressive Farmer,* November 10, 1887.

44. *Progressive Farmer,* June 19, 1888, June 23, 1887, January 12, 1888; February 19, 1889. The objectives of the Normal and Industrial School for girls were "(1) to give young women such education as shall fit them to teach; (2) to give instruction in drawing, telegraphy, typewriting, stenography, and such other arts as may be suitable to their sex and conducive to their usefulness." (quoted in Lathrop, *Educate a Woman,* p. xii).

45. *Progressive Farmer,* June 25, 1889; December 16, 1890.

46. Scott, *Southern Lady,* pp. 4–8.

47. *Progressive Farmer,* March 10, June 30, 1886; April 21, 1887; February 26, June 11, 1889; July 7, February 10, 1886; February 2, 1887; November 20, 1888; September 4, 1888; March 24, 1886.

48. *National Economist,* May 4, 1889. See also W. Scott Morgan, *History of the Wheel and Alliance and the Impending Revolution* (Fort Scott: J. H. Rice & Sons, 1889), pp. 197–99; *Progressive Farmer,* June 2, 1886; September 4, 1888.

49. *Progressive Farmer,* January 19, 1887; June 30, 1886; June 5, 1888; February 28, 1888; December 8, 1886. For another southern view, see *National Economist,* June 14, 1890.

50. Dunning, *The Farmers' Alliance,* p. 257; Saloutos, *Farmer Movements,* p. 85.

51. *Progressive Farmer,* March 26, 1889.

52. *Progressive Farmer,* March 10, April 21, 1886. See *National Economist,* May 25, 1889, in which one of the Alabama Alliance's goals is to "adorn and beautify our homes, and render farm life more attractive."

53. *Progressive Farmer,* January 19, 1887; June 2, 1886; May 28, 1889; May 5, 1887. See also *The Sub-Alliance and What It Can Accomplish,* p. 6.

54. Richard H. Abbott, "The Agricultural Press Views the Yeoman: 1819–1859," *Agricultural History* 42 (January 1968): 35–48, suggests that historians have overestimated the importance of the myth of the yeoman farmer. See also, Muller, "New South Populism," p. 23; Paul M. Gaston, *The New South Creed: A Study in Southern Mythmaking* (New York: Alfred A. Knopf, 1970), pp. 64–68, 107–108.

55. *National Economist,* April 5, 1889.

56. *Progressive Farmer,* November 10, 1887; *Minutes,* Farmers' State Alliance, August 11, 1892; *Progressive Farmer,* February 19, 1889.

57. *Progressive Farmer,* July 2, and April 21, 1887.

58. Mayo, "Southern Women," p. 170.

59. As Muller, "New South Populism," notes, p. 149, only men qualified as members of the elite.

60. *Progressive Farmer,* September 22, 1891.

61. *Progressive Farmer,* June 3, September 16, December 23, 1890; July 7, December 15, 1891.

62. *Progressive Farmer,* November 4, 1890.

63. For suffrage discussions, see *National Economist,* March 1, July 12, October 18, October 25, 1890; March 5, November 12, December 24, 1892; January 21, February 18, March 11, 1893.

64. *Progressive Farmer,* September 15, 1891; December 3, 1889. There were occasionally other references to suffrage; see January 22, 1889, for example.

65. Quoted in Taylor, "Woman Suffrage," p. 46.

66. Saloutos, *Farmer Movements,* pp. 122–26; McMath, "Agrarian Protest," pp. 56–63.

67. Gerald Henderson Gaither, "Blacks and the Populist Revolt: Ballots and Bigotry in the New South (Ph.D. dissertation, University of Tennessee, 1972), pp. 151, 201–209; Gaston, *The New South,* pp. 38–39; J. Morgan Kousser, "The Shaping of Southern Politics: Suffrage Restriction and the Establishment of the One Party South, 1880–1910," (Ph.D. dissertation, Yale University, 1971), pp. 139–43; Guion Griffis Johnson, "The Ideology of White Supremacy, 1876–1910," in Fletcher Melvin Green, ed., *Essays in Southern History* (Chapel Hill: University of North Carolina Press, 1949), p. 133.

# 6

# "Charity Girls" and City Pleasures: Historical Notes on Working-Class Sexuality, 1880–1920

## Kathy Peiss

*The emergence of heterosocial public culture and a more open sexuality are two of the major features that distinguish modern American culture from its nineteenth-century Victorian predecessor. In her research on the leisure world of working women in New York City, Kathy Peiss has uncovered evidence of the independent development of working-class sexuality. In the commercial dance halls, amusement parks, and movie theaters of turn-of-the-century New York, young, single working women affirmed a new expressive sexuality that disturbed many middle-class observers. In a world that subordinated women at work and within the family, leisure offered young women an unusual degree of power and social freedom. Peiss shows both the possibilities and the limitations of their new leisure world.*

Uncovering the history of working-class sexuality has been a particularly intractable task for recent scholars. Diaries, letters, and memoirs, while a rich source for studies of bourgeois sexuality, offer few glimpses into working-class intimate life. We have had to turn to middle-class commentary and observations of working people, but these accounts often seem hopelessly moralistic and biased. The difficulty with such sources is not simply a question of tone or selectivity, but involves the very categories of analysis they employ. Reformers, social workers, and journalists viewed working-class women's sexuality through middle-class lenses, invoking sexual standards that set "respectability" against "promiscuity." When applied to unmarried women, these categories were constructed foremost around the biological fact of premarital virginity, and secondarily by such cultural indicators as manners, language, dress, and public interaction. Chastity was the measure of young women's respectability, and those who engaged in premarital intercourse, or, more importantly, dressed and acted as though they had, were classed as promiscuous women or prostitutes. Thus labor investigations of the late nineteenth century not only surveyed women's wages and working conditions, but delved into the issue of their sexual virtue, hoping to resolve scientifically the question of working women's respectability.[1]

*A young wage-earner and her gentleman friend meeting during a lunch break. Lewis Hine Collection, United States History, Local History & Genealogy Division, The New York Public Library, Aston, Lenox, and Tilden Foundations.*

Nevertheless, some middle-class observers in city missions and settlements recognized that their standards did not always reflect those of working-class youth. As one University Settlement worker argued, "Many of the liberties which are taken by tenement boys and girls with one another, and which seem quite improper to the 'up-towner,' are, in fact, practically harmless."[2] Working women's public behavior often seemed to fall between the traditional middle-class poles: they were not truly promiscuous in their actions, but neither were they models of decorum. A boarding-house matron, for example, puzzled over the behavior of Mary, a "good girl": "The other night she flirted with a man across the street," she explained. "It is true she dropped him when he offered to take her into a saloon. But she does go to picture shows and dance halls with 'pick up' men and boys."[3] Similarly, a city missionary noted that tenement dwellers followed different rules of etiquette, with the observation: "Young women sometimes allow young men to address them and caress them in a manner which would offend well-bred people, and yet those girls would indignantly resent any liberties which they consider dishonoring."[4] These examples suggest that we must reach beyond the dichotomized analysis of many middle-class observers and draw out the cultural categories created and acted on by work-ing women themselves. How was sexuality "handled" culturally? What man-ners, etiquette, and sexual style met with general approval? What constituted sexual respectability? Does the polarized framework of the mid-dle class reflect the realities of working-class culture?

Embedded within the reports and surveys lie small pieces of informa-tion that illuminate the social and cultural construction of sexuality among a number of working-class women. My discussion focuses on one set of young, white working women in New York City in the years 1880 to 1920. Most of these women were single wage earners who toiled in the city's facto-ries, shops, and department stores, while devoting their evenings to the lively entertainment of the streets, public dance halls, and other popular amusements. Born or educated in the United States, many adopted a cul-tural style meant to distance themselves from their immigrant roots and familial traditions. Such women dressed in the latest finery, negotiated city life with ease, and sought intrigue and adventure with male companions. For this group of working women, sexuality became a central dimension of their emergent culture, a dimension that is revealed in their daily life of work and leisure.[5]

These New York working women frequented amusements in which fa-miliarity and intermingling among strangers, not decorum, defined normal public behavior between the sexes. At movies and cheap theaters, crowds mingled during intermissions, shared picnic lunches, and commented volu-bly on performances. Strangers at Coney Island's amusement parks often involved each other in practical jokes and humorous escapades, while dance halls permitted close interaction between unfamiliar men and women. At one respectable Turnverein ball, for example, a vice investigator described closely the chaotic activity in the barroom between dances:

> Most of the younger couples were hugging and kissing, there was a general mingling of men and women at the different tables, almost everyone seemed to know one another and spoke to each other across the tables and joined couples at different tables, they were all singing and carrying on, they kept running around the room and acted like a mob of lunatics let lo[o]se.[6]

As this observer suggests, an important aspect of social familiarity was the ease of sexual expression in language and behavior. Dances were adver-tised, for example, through the distribution of "pluggers," small printed cards announcing the particulars of the ball, along with snatches of popular songs or verse; the lyrics and pictures, noted one offended reformer, were often "so suggestive that they are absolutely indecent."[7]

The heightened sexual awareness permeating many popular amuse-ments may also be seen in working-class dancing styles. While waltzes and two-steps were common, working women's repertoire included "pivoting" and "tough dances." While pivoting was a wild, spinning dance that pro-moted a charged atmosphere of physical excitement, tough dances ranged from a slow shimmy, or shaking of the hips and shoulders, to boisterous animal imitations. Such tough dances as the grizzly bear, Charlie Chaplin wiggle, and the dip emphasized bodily contact and the suggestion of sexual intercourse. As one dance investigator commented, "What particularly dis-tinguishes this dance is the motion of the pelvic portions of the body."[8] In contrast, middle-class pleasure-goers accepted the animal dances only after the blatant sexuality had been tamed into refined movement. While cabaret owners enforced strict rules to discourage contact between strangers, man-agers of working-class dance halls usually winked at spieling, tough dancing and unrestrained behavior.[9]

Other forms of recreation frequented by working-class youth incorpo-rated a free and easy sexuality into their attractions. Many social clubs and amusement societies permitted flirting, touching, and kissing games at their meetings. One East Side youth reported that "they have kissing all through pleasure time, and use slang language, while in some they don't behave nice between [*sic*] young ladies."[10] Music halls and cheap vaudeville regularly worked sexual themes and suggestive humor into comedy routines and songs. At a Yiddish music hall popular with both men and women, one reformer found that "the songs are suggestive of everything but what is proper, the choruses are full of double meanings, and the jokes have broad and unmistakable hints of things indecent."[11] Similarly, Coney Island's Stee-plechase amusement park, favored by working-class excursionists, carefully marketed sexual titillation and romance in attractions that threw patrons into each other, sent skirts flying, and evoked instant intimacy among strangers.[12]

In attending dance halls, social club entertainments, and amusement resorts, young women took part in a cultural milieu that expressed and affirmed heterosocial interactions. As reformer Belle Israels observed, "No amusement is complete in which 'he' is not a factor."[13] A common custom involved "picking up" unknown men or women in amusement resorts or on the streets, an accepted means of gaining companionship for an evening's entertainment. Indeed, some amusement societies existed for this very pur-pose. One vice investigator, in his search for "loose" women, was advised by a waiter to "go first on a Sunday night to 'Hans'l & Gret'l Amusement Society' at the Lyceum 86th Str & III Ave, there the girls come and men pick them up."[14] The waiter carefully stressed that these were respectable work-ing women, not prostitutes. Nor was the pickup purely a male prerogative. "With the men they 'pick up,'" writer Hutchins Hapgood observed of East Side shop girls, "they will go to the theater, to late suppers, will be as jolly as they like."[15]

The heterosocial orientation of these amusements made popularity a goal to be pursued through dancing ability, willingness to drink, and eye-catching finery. Women who would not drink at balls and social entertainments were often ostracized by men, while cocktails and ingenious mixtures replaced the five-cent beer and helped to make drinking an acceptable female activity. Many women used clothing as a means of drawing attention to themselves, wearing high-heeled shoes, fancy dresses, costume jewelry, elaborate pompadours, and cosmetics. As one working woman sharply explained, "If you want to get any notion took of you, you gotta have some style about you."[16] The clothing that such women wore no longer served as an emblem of respectability. "The way women dress today they all look like prostitutes," reported one rueful waiter to a dance hall investigator, "and the waiter can some times get in bad by going over and trying to put some one next to them, they may be respectable women and would jump on the waiter."[17]

Underlying the relaxed sexual style and heterosocial interaction was the custom of "treating." Men often treated their female companions to drinks and refreshments, theater tickets, and other incidentals. Women might pay a dance hall's entrance fee or carfare out to an amusement park, but they relied on men's treats to see them through the evening's entertainment. Such treats were highly prized by young working women; as Belle Israels remarked, the announcement that "he treated" was "the acme of achievement in retailing experiences with the other sex."[18]

Treating was not a one-way proposition, however, but entailed an exchange relationship. Financially unable to reciprocate in kind, women offered sexual favors of varying degrees, ranging from flirtatious companionship to sexual intercourse, in exchange for men's treats. "Pleasures don't cost girls so much as they do young men," asserted one saleswoman. "If they are agreeable they are invited out a good deal, and they are not allowed to pay anything." Reformer Lillian Betts concurred, observing that the working woman held herself responsible for failing to wangle men's invitations and believed that "it is not only her misfortune, but her fault; she should be more attractive."[19] Gaining men's treats placed a high premium on allure and personality, and sometimes involved aggressive and frank "overtures to men whom they desire to attract," often with implicit sexual proposals. One investigator, commenting on women's dependency on men in their leisure time, aptly observed that "those who are unattractive, and those who have puritanic notions, fare but ill in the matter of enjoyments. On the other hand those who do become popular have to compromise with the best conventional usage."[20]

Many of the sexual patterns acceptable in the world of leisure activity were mirrored in the workplace. Sexual harassment by employers, foremen, and fellow workers was a widespread practice in this period, and its form often paralleled the relationship of treating, particularly in service and sales jobs. Department store managers, for example, advised employees to round out their meager salaries by finding a "gentleman friend" to purchase clothing and pleasures. An angry saleswoman testified, for example, that "one of the employers has told me, on a $6.50 wage, he don't care where I get my clothes from as long as I have them, to be dressed to suit him."[21] Waitresses knew that accepting the advances of male customers often brought good tips, and some used their opportunities to enter an active social life with men. "Most of the girls quite frankly admit making 'dates' with strange men," one investigator found. "These 'dates' are made with no thought on the part of the girl beyond getting the good time which she cannot afford herself."[22]

In factories where men and women worked together, the sexual style that we have seen on the dance floor was often reproduced on the shop floor. Many factories lacked privacy in dressing facilities, and workers tolerated a degree of familiarity and roughhousing between men and women. One cigar maker observed that his workplace socialized the young into sexual behavior unrestrained by parental and community control. Another decried the tendency of young boys "of thirteen or fourteen casing an eye upon a 'mash.'" Even worse, he testified, were the

> many men who are respected—when I say respected and respectable, I mean who walk the streets and are respected as working men, and who would not under any circumstances offer the slightest insult or disrespectful remark or glance to a female in the streets, but who, in the shops, will whoop and give expressions to "cat calls" and a peculiar noise made with their lips, which is supposed to be an endearing salutation.[23]

In sexually segregated workplaces, sexual knowledge was probably transmitted among working women. A YWCA report in 1913 luridly asserted that "no girl is more 'knowing' than the wage-earner, for the 'older hands' initiate her early through the unwholesome story or innuendo."[24] Evidence from factories, department stores, laundries, and restaurants substantiates the sexual consciousness of female workers. Women brought to the workplace tales of their evening adventures and gossip about dates and eligible men, recounting to their co-workers the triumphs of the latest ball or outing. Women's socialization into a new shop might involve a ritualist exchange about "gentlemen friends." In one laundry, for example, an investigator repeatedly heard this conversation:

> "Say, you got as feller?"
> "Sure, Ain't you got one?"
> "Sure."[25]

Through the use of slang and "vulgar" language, heterosexual romance was expressed in a sexually explicit context. Among waitresses, for example, frank discussion of lovers and husbands during breaks was an integral part of the work day. One investigator found that "there was never any open violation of the proprieties but always the suggestive talk and behavior." Laundries, too, witnessed "a great deal of swearing among the women." A 1914 study of department store clerks found a similar style and content in everyday conversation:

> While it is true that the general attitude toward men and sex relations was normal, all the investigators admitted a freedom of speech frequently verging upon the vulgar, but since there was very little evidence of any actual immorality, this can probably be likened to the same spirit which prompts the telling of risqué stories in other circles.[26]

In their workplaces and leisure activities, many working women discovered a milieu that tolerated, and at times encouraged, physical and verbal familiarity between men and women, and stressed the exchange of sexual favors for social and economic advantages. Such women probably received conflicting messages about the virtues of virginity, and necessarily mediated the parental, religious, and educational injunctions concerning chastity, and the "lessons" of urban life and labor. The choice made by some women to engage in a relaxed sexual style needs to be understood in terms of the larger relations of class and gender that structured their sexual culture.

Most single working-class women were wage-earners for a few years before marriage, contributing to the household income or supporting themselves. Sexual segmentation of the labor market placed women in semi-skilled, seasonal employment with high rates of turnover. Few women earned a "living wage," estimated to be $9.00 or $10.00 a week in 1910, and the wage differential between men and women was vast. Those who lived alone in furnished rooms or boarding houses consumed their earnings in rent, meals, and clothing. Many self-supporting women were forced to sacrifice an essential item in their weekly budgets, particularly food, in order to pay for amusements. Under such circumstances, treating became a viable option. "If my boy friend didn't take me out," asked one working woman, "how could I ever go out?"[27] While many women accepted treats from "steadies," others had no qualms about receiving them from acquaintances or men they picked up at amusement places. As one investigator concluded, "The acceptance on the part of the girl of almost any invitation needs little explanation when one realizes that she often goes pleasureless unless she does accept 'free treats.'"[28] Financial resources were little better for the vast majority of women living with families and relatives. Most of them contributed all of their earnings to the family, receiving only small amounts of spending money, usually 25¢ to 50¢ a week, in return. This sum covered the costs of simple entertainments, but could not purchase higher priced amusements.[29]

Moreover, the social and physical space of the tenement home and boarding house contributed to freer social and sexual practices. Working women living alone ran the gauntlet between landladies' suspicious stares and the knowing glances of male boarders. One furnished-room dweller attested to the pressure placed on young, single women: "Time and again when a male lodger meets a girl on the landing, his salutation usually ends with something like this: 'Won't you step into my place and have a glass of beer with me?'"[30]

The tenement home, too, presented a problem to parents who wished to maintain control over their daughters' sexuality. Typical tenement apartments offered limited opportunities for family activities or chaperoned socializing. Courtship proved difficult in homes where families and boarders crowded into a few small rooms, and the "parlor" served as kitchen, dining room, and bedroom. Instead, many working-class daughters socialized on streetcorners, rendezvoused in cafes, and courted on trolley cars. As one settlement worker observed, "Boys and girls and young men and women of respectable families are almost obliged to carry on many of their friendships, and perhaps their lovemaking, on tenement stoops or on street corners."[31] Another reformer found that girls whose parents forbade men's visits to the home managed to escape into the streets and dance halls to meet them. Such young women demanded greater independence in the realm of "personal life" in exchange for their financial contribution to the family. For some, this new freedom spilled over into their sexual practices.[32]

The extent of the sexual culture described here is particularly difficult to establish, since the evidence is too meager to permit conclusions about specific groups of working women, their beliefs about sexuality, and their behavior. Scattered evidence does suggest a range of possible responses, the parameters within which most women would choose to act and define their behavior as socially acceptable. Within this range, there existed a subculture of working women who fully bought into the system of treating and sexual exchange, by trading sexual favors of varying degrees for gifts, treats, and a good time. These women were known in underworld slang as "charity girls," a term that differentiated them from prostitutes because they did not accept money in their sexual encounters with men. As vice reformer George Kneeland found, they "offer themselves to strangers, not for money, but for presents, attention, and pleasure, and most important, a yielding to sex desire."[33] Only a thin line divided these women and "occasional prostitutes," women who slipped in and out of prostitution when unemployed or in need of extra income. Such behavior did not result in the stigma of the "fallen woman." Many working women apparently acted like Dottie: "When she needed a pair of shoes she had found it easy to 'earn' them in the way that other girls did." Dottie, the investigator reported, was now known as a respectable married woman.[34]

Such women were frequent patrons of the city's dance halls. Vice investigators note a preponderant number of women at dances who clearly were not prostitutes, but were "game" and "lively"; these charity girls often comprised half or more of the dancers in a hall. One dance hall investigator distinguished them with the observation, "Some of the women ... are out for the coin, but there is a lot that come in here that are charity."[35] One waiter at La Kuenstler Klause, a restaurant with music and dancing, noted that "girls could be gotten here, but they don't go with men for money, only for good time." The investigator continued in his report, "Most of the girls are working girls, not prostitutes, they smoke cigarettes, drink liquers and dance dis.[orderly] dances, stay out late and stay with any man, that pick them up first."[36] Meeting two women at a bar, another investigator re-marked, "They are both supposed to be working girls but go out for a good time and go the limit."[37]

Some women obviously relished the game of extracting treats from men. One vice investigator offered to take a Kitty Graham, who apparently worked both as a department store clerk and occasional prostitute, to the Central Opera House at 3 A.M.; he noted that "she was willing to go if I'd take a taxi; I finally coaxed her to come with me in a street car."[38] Similarly, Frances Donovan observed waitresses "talking about their engagements which they had for the evening or for the night and quite frankly saying what they expected to get from this or that fellow in the line of money, amusement, or clothes."[39] Working women's manipulation of treating is also suggested by this unguarded conversation overheard by a journalist at Co-ney Island:

> "What sort of a time did you have?"
> "Great. He blew in $5 on the blow-out."
> "You beat me again. My chump only spent $2.50."[40]

These women had clearly accepted the full implications of the system of treating and the sexual culture surrounding it.

While this evidence points to the existence of charity girls—working women defined as respectable, but who engaged in sexual activity—it tells us little about their numbers, social background, working lives, or relation-ships to family and community. The vice reports indicate that they were generally young women, many of whom lived at home with their families. One man in a dance hall remarked, for example, that "he sometimes takes them to the hotels, but sometimes the girls won't go to [a] hotel to stay for the night, they are afraid of their mothers, so he gets away with it in the hallway."[41] While community sanctions may have prevented such activity within the neighborhood, the growth of large public dance halls, cabarets, and metropolitan amusement resorts provided an anonymous space in which the subculture of treating could flourish.

The charity girl's activities form only one response in a wide spectrum of social and sexual behavior. Many young women defined themselves sharply against the freer sexuality of their pleasure-seeking sisters, associating "respectability" firmly with premarital chastity and circumspect behavior. One working woman carefully explained her adherence to propriety: "I never go out in the evenings except to my relatives because if I did, I should lose my reputation and that is all I have left." Similarly, shop girls guarded against sexual advances from co-workers and male customers by spurning the temptations of popular amusements. "I keep myself to myself," said one saleswoman. "I don't make friends in the stores very easily because you can't be sure what any one is like."[42] Settlement workers also noted that women who freely attended "dubious resorts" or bore illegitimate children were often stigmatized by neighbors and workmates. Lillian Betts, for example, cites the case of working women who refused to labor until their employer dismissed a co-worker who had born a baby out of wedlock. To Betts, however, their adherence to the standard of virginity seemed instrumental, and not a reflection of moral absolutism: "The hardness with which even the suggestion of looseness is treated in any group of working girls is simply an expression of self-preservation."[43]

Other observers noted an ambivalence in the attitudes of young working women toward sexual relations. Social workers reported that the critical stance toward premarital pregnancy was "not always unmixed with a certain degree of admiration for the success with the other sex which the difficulty implies." According to this study, many women increasingly found premarital intercourse acceptable in particular situations: "'A girl can have many friends,' explained one of them, 'but when she gets a "steady," there's only one way to have him and to keep him; I mean to keep him long.'"[44] Such women shared with charity girls the assumption that respectability was not predicated solely on chastity.

Perhaps few women were charity girls or occasional prostitutes, but many more must have been conscious of the need to negotiate sexual encounters in the workplace or in their leisure time. Women would have had to weigh their desire for social participation against traditional sanctions regarding sexual behavior, and charity girls offered to some a model for resolving this conflict. This process is exemplified in Clara Laughlin's report of an attractive but "proper" working woman who could not understand why men friends dropped her after a few dates. Finally she receives the wordly advice of a co-worker that social participation involves an exchange relationship: "Don't yeh know there ain't no feller goin' t'spend coin on yeh fer nothin'? Yeh gotta be a good Indian, Kid—we all gotta!"[45]

For others, charity girls represented a yardstick against which they might measure their own ideas of respectability. The nuances of that measurement were expressed, for example, in a dialogue between a vice investigator and the hat girl at Semprini's dance hall. Answering his proposal for a date, the investigator noted, she "said she'd be glad to go out with me but told me there was nothing doing [i.e., sexually]. Said she didn't like to see a man spend money on her and then get disappointed." Commenting on the charity girls that frequented the dance hall, she remarked that "these women get her sick, she can't see why a woman should lay down for a man the first time they take her out. She said it wouldn't be so bad if they went out with the men 3 or 4 times and then went to bed with them but not the first time."[46]

For this hat girl and other young working women, respectability was not defined by the strict measurement of chastity employed by many middle-class observers and reformers. Instead, they adopted a more instrumental and flexible approach to sexual behavior. Premarital sex *could* be labeled respectable in particular social contexts. Thus charity girls distinguished their sexual activity from prostitution, a less acceptable practice, because they did not receive money from men. Other women, who might view charity girls as promiscuous, were untroubled by premarital intimacy with a steady boyfriend.

This fluid definition of sexual respectability was embedded within the social relation of class and gender, as experienced by women in their daily round of work, leisure, and family life. Women's wage labor and the demands of the working-class household offered daughters few resources for entertainment. At the same time, new commercial amusements offered a tempting world of pleasure and companionship beyond parental control. Within this context, some young women sought to exchange sexual goods for access to that world and its seeming independence, choosing not to defer sexual relations until marriage. Their notions of legitimate premarital behavior contrast markedly with the dominant middle-class view, which placed female sexuality within a dichotomous and rigid framework. Whether a hazard at work, fun and adventure at night, or an opportunity to be exploited, sexual expression and intimacy comprised an integral part of these working women's lives.

## NOTES

1. See, for example, Carroll D. Wright, *The Working Girls of Boston* (1889; New York: Arno Press, 1969).

2. "Influences in Street Life," University Settlement Society *Report* (1900), p. 30.

3. Marie S. Orenstein, "How the Working Girl of New York Lives," New York State, Factory Investigating Commission, *Fourth Report Transmitted to Legislature*, February 15, 1915, Senate Doc. 43, vol. 4, app. 2 (Albany: J. B. Lyon Co., 1915), p. 1697.

4. William T. Elsing, "Life in New York Tenement-Houses as Seen by a City Missionary," *Scribner's* 11 (June 1892): 716.

5. For a more detailed discussion of these women, and further documentation of their social relations and leisure activities, see my dissertation, "Cheap Amusements: Gender Relations and the Use of Leisure Time in New York City, 1880 to 1920," Ph.D. diss., Brown University, 1982.

6. Investigator's Report, Remey's, 917 Eighth Ave., February 11, 1917, Committee of Fourteen Papers, New York Public Library Manuscript Division, New York.

7. George Kneeland, *Commercialized Prostitution in New York City* (New York: The Century Co., 1913), p. 68; Louise de Koven Bowen, "Dance Halls," *Survey* 26 (3 July 1911): 384.

8. Committee on Amusements and Vacation Resources of Working Girls, two-page circular, in Box 28, "Parks and Playgrounds Correspondence," Lillian Wald Collection, Rare Book and Manuscripts Library, Columbia University, New York.

9. See, for example, Investigator's Report, Princess Cafe, 1206 Broadway, January 1, 1917; and Excelsior Cafe, 306 Eighth Ave., December 21, 1916, Committee of Fourteen Papers.

10. "Social Life in the Streets," University Settlement Society *Report* (1899), p. 32.

11. Paul Klapper, "The Yiddish Music Hall," *University Settlement Studies* 2, no. 4 (1905): 22.

12. For a description of Coney Island amusements, see Edo McCullough, *Good Old Coney Island; A Sentimental Journey into the Past* (New York: Charles Scribner's Sons, 1957), pp. 309–13; and Oliver Pilot and Jo Ransom, *Sodom by the Sea: An Affectionate History of Coney Island* (Garden City, N.J.: Doubleday, 1941).

13. Belle Lindner Israels, "The Way of the Girl," *Survey* 22 (3 July 1909): 486.

14. Investigator's Report, La Kuenstler Klause, 1490 Third Ave., January 19, 1917, Committee of Fourteen Papers.

15. Hutchins Hapgood, *Types from City Streets* (New York: Funk and Wagnalls, 1910), p. 131.

16. Clara Laughlin, *The Work-A-Day Girl: A Study of Some Present Conditions* (1913; New York: Arno Press, 1974), pp. 47, 145. On working women's clothing, see Helen Campbell, *Prisoners of Poverty: Women Wage Earners, Their Trades and Their Lives* (1887; Westport, Conn.: Greenwood Press, 1970), p. 175; "What It Means to Be a Department Store Girl as Told by the Girl Herself," *Ladies Home Journal* 30 (June 1913): 8; "A Salesgirl's Story," *Independent* 54 (July 1902): 1821. Drinking is discussed in Kneeland, *Commercialized Prostitution,* p. 70; and Belle Israels, "Diverting a Pastime," *Leslie's Weekly* 113 (27 July 1911): 100.

17. Investigator's Report, Weimann's, 1422 St. Nicholas Ave., February 11, 1917, Committee of Fourteen Papers.

18. Israels, "Way of the Girl," p. 489; Ruth True, *The Neglected Girl* (New York: Russell Sage Foundation, 1914), p. 59.

19. "A Salesgirl's Story," p. 1821; Lillian Betts, *Leaven in a Great City* (New York: Dodd, Mead, 1902), pp. 251–52.

20. New York State, Factory Investigating Commission, *Fourth Report,* vol. 4, pp. 1585–86; Robert Woods and Albert Kennedy, *Young Working-Girls: A Summary of Evidence from Two Thousand Social Workers* (Boston: Houghton Mifflin, 1913), p. 105.

21. New York State, Factory Investigating Commission, *Fourth Report,* vol. 5, p. 2809; see also Sue Ainslie Clark and Edith Wyatt, *Making Both Ends Meet: The Income and Outlay of New York Working Girls* (New York: Macmillan, 1911), p. 28.

22. Consumers' League of New York, *Behind the Scenes in a Restaurant: A Study of 1017 Women Restaurant Employees* (n.p., n.p., 1916), p. 24; Frances Donovan, *The Woman Who Waits* (1920; New York: Arno Press, 1974), p. 42.

23. New York Bureau of Labor Statistics, *Second Annual Report* (1884), pp. 153, 158; *Third Annual Report* (1885), pp. 150–51.

24. Report of Commission on Social Morality from the Christian Standpoint, Made to the 4th Biennial Convention of the Young Women's Christian Associations of the U.S.A., 1913, Records File Collection, Archives of the National Board of the YWCA of the United States of America, New York, N.Y.

25. Clark and Wyatt, *Making Both Ends Meet,* pp. 187–88; see also Dorothy Richardson, *The Long Day,* in *Women at Work,* ed. William L. O'Neill (New York: Quadrangle, 1972); Amy E. Tanner, "Glimpses at the Mind of a Waitress," *American Journal of Sociology* 13 (July 1907): 52.

26. Committee of Fourteen in New York City, *Annual Report for 1914,* p. 40; Clark and Wyatt, *Making Both Ends Meet,* p. 188; Donovan, *The Woman Who Waits,* pp. 26, 80–81.

27. Esther Packard, "Living on Six Dollars a Week," New York State, Factory Investigating Commission, *Fourth Report,* vol. 4, pp. 1677–78. For a discussion of women's wages in New York, see ibid., vol. 1, p. 35; and vol. 4, pp. 1081, 1509.

28. Packard, "Living on Six Dollars a Week," p. 1685.

29. New York State, Factory Investigating Commission, *Fourth Report,* vol. 4, pp. 1512–13, 1581–83; True, *Neglected Girl,* p. 59.

30. Marie Orenstein, "How the Working Girl of New York Lives," p. 1702. See also Esther Packard, *A Study of Living Conditions of Self-Supporting Women in New York City* (New York: Metropolitan Board of the YWCA, 1915).

31. "Influences in Street Life," p. 30; see also Samuel Chotzinoff, *A Lost Paradise* (New York: Knopf, 1955), p. 81.

32. On the rejection of parental controls by young women, see Leslie Woodcock Tentler, *Wage-Earning Women: Industrial Work and Family Life in the United States, 1900–1930* (New York: Oxford University Press, 1979), pp. 110–13. For contemporary accounts, see True, *Neglected Girl,* pp. 54–55, 62–63. 162–63; Lillian Betts, "Tenement House Life and Recreation," *Outlook* (11 February 1899): 365.

33. "Memoranda on Vice Problem: IV. Statement of George J. Kneeland," New York State, Factory Investigating Commission, *Fourth Report,* v.1, p. 403. See also Committee of Fourteen, *Annual Report* (1917), p. 15, and *Annual Report* (1918), p. 32; Woods and Kennedy, *Young Working-Girls,* p. 85.

34. Donovan, *The Woman Who Waits,* p. 71; on occasional prostitution, see U.S. Senate, *Report on the Condition of Women and Child Wage-Earners in the United States,* U.S. Sen. Doc. 645, 61st Cong., 2nd Sess. (Washington, D.C.: GPO), vol. 15, p. 83; Laughlin, *The Work-A-Day Girl,* pp. 51–52.

35. Investigator's Report, 2150 Eighth Ave., January 12, 1917, Committee of Fourteen Papers.

36. Investigator's Report, La Kuenstler Klause, 1490 Third Ave., January 19, 1917, Committee of Fourteen Papers.

37. Investigator's Report, Bobby More's, 252 W. 31 Street, February 3, 1917, Committee of Fourteen Papers.

38. Investigator's Report, Remey's, 917 Eighth Ave., December 23, 1916, Committee of Fourteen Papers.

39. Donovan, *The Woman Who Waits,* p. 55.

40. Edwin Slosson, "The Amusement Business," *Independent* 57 (21 July 1904): 139.

41. Investigator's Report, Clare Hotel and Palm Gardens/McNamara's, 2150 Eighth Ave., January 12, 1917, Committee of Fourteen Papers.

42. Marie Orenstein, "How the Working Girl of New York Lives," p. 1703; Clark and Wyatt, *Making Both Ends Meet,* pp. 28–29.

43. Betts, *Leaven in a Great City,* pp. 81, 219.

44. Woods and Kennedy, *Young Working-Girls,* pp. 87, 85.

45. Laughlin, *The Work-A-Day Girl,* p. 50.

46. Investigator's Report, Semprini's, 145 W. 50 Street, October 5, 1918, Committee of Fourteen Papers.

# 7

## Housewives, Socialists, and the Politics of Food: The 1917 New York Cost-of-Living Protests

### Dana Frank

*World War I engulfed Europe beginning in August 1914, and although the United States did not officially enter the war until April 1917, the nation felt its impact earlier. Employment expanded, union organizing gave workers a newfound voice, and suffragists and socialists grew in strength. The dislocations of war spawned varied protests. Dana Frank highlights a little-studied protest in this period—that of working-class housewives in New York City against the escalating cost of basic necessities. In a remarkable series of demonstrations, working-class women in the city mobilized to boycott chicken, fish, and vegetables. Reminiscent of bread riots in European cities in earlier periods, the cost-of-living protests in New York City revealed the value systems within which working-class women operated and the contradictions between these values and those of a capitalist market economy.*

In mid-February 1917, an independent working-class housewives' movement erupted right in the heart of the Socialist party of America's great stronghold, New York City. Thousands of immigrant Jewish women burst into violent street protests against the high cost of living. They instituted a boycott on chicken, fish, and vegetables which shut down much of the city's foodstuffs marketing for two weeks, riveting public attention on the food price issue and sending public officials scurrying to and fro in panic.

New York Socialists seized the opportunity for agitational work presented by this women's uprising. They jumped quickly into the food protest fray of February 1917 and themselves organized an extensive series of cost-of-living protests designed to direct the movement toward Socialist goals. . . . Their activities climaxed in a Madison Square demonstration of over 5,000 women, which spilled over into an attack on the Waldorf-Astoria hotel. Socialist-organized protest continued for over a month and a half, eclipsed finally by the entrance of the country into World War One and the imposition of federal food controls.

This wave of cost-of-living protests offers us a wonderful example of working-class housewives' political activism. In protesting high food prices, through their own traditional modes of organizing, New York's Jewish

This article is excerpted from *Feminist Studies*, Volume 11, Number 2 (Summer, 1985): 255–85 by permission of the publisher, FEMINIST STUDIES, Inc., c/o Women's Studies Program, University of Maryland, College Park, MD 20742.

*Food boycotter flanked by New York City policemen.* Independent, *March 5, 1917.*

housewives took up political action on their own terms. For them, consumer issues were paramount: married women, charged with converting wages into food and shelter by expending rather than earning wages, experienced their primary contact with the capitalist economy in the neighborhood marketplace, where from 40 to 60 percent of the family's income was spent on food.[1] When they protested against rising food prices, New York's immigrant Jewish women demonstrated their own perceptions of political economy: who they believed was in power; what they thought should be done to alleviate their distress, and, most importantly, how they believed they as women could affect the economic system in which they were enmeshed. Through their boycott, demonstrations, and neighborhood solidarity, the city's Jewish women acted upon their own model for political action.

U.S. food prices began to rise rapidly in late 1915, after creeping up very gradually since the 1890s. The causes were complex: as World War One progressed, increasing food exports to Europe decreased the overall supply available in the United States, just as high domestic employment rates simultaneously increased demand; food brokers, meanwhile, took advantage of these new market conditions and manipulated the price and availability of key commodities. Poor grain crops in 1916 and an anticipated poor crop for 1917 further exacerbated the situation. Over the course of 1916 prices rose still more sharply than they had the previous year.[2] Although average wages also rose (under pressure from the greatest waves of strikes the country had yet seen), the benefits of unionization were by no means evenly distributed across all workers; and even in relatively highly unionized industries such as the garment trade, prices consistently outstripped wages.[3]

In February 1917 retail food costs in New York City, after rising inexorably for months, leapt dramatically to new heights. Basic commodities increased 20 or 30 percent in price over the course of a few days; many individual foods reached prices two and three times those of the year before. Eggs, for example, rose from $0.32 a dozen in 1916, to $0.80 a year later; beets from $0.02 to $0.05 a pound; and cabbages from $0.02 a pound to $0.12.[4] Making matters worse, noncash food sources—with which the poor traditionally compensated for too-low wages—dried up. In an interview with Dorothy Day for the socialist daily *New York Call* in late 1916, an Irish woman with three children bemoaned, "Before, when I was short, I used to go around to the bakeries in the good neighborhoods, and they'd give me the bread two for five when it was one day old, and sometimes for nothing. But I can't get a roll, even ... because flour has gone up from $3.50 to $11.00 a barrel.[5]

The price crunch brought disaster to many of New York's Jewish immigrants. Almost overnight the rising food costs depleted savings families might have accumulated over the course of decades. To avert starvation, the city's immigrant Jewish families adopted two basic strategies: on the one hand, increasing the aggregate amount of money available to the family for expenditure on food, by selling the family's possessions or adding to the number of wage earners in the family—or both.[6] One "East Side Mother" told of how, as prices rose and her husband, who worked only seasonally as a presser, took ill, she herself, then her daughter and son, successively took jobs.[7] On the other hand, families attempted to reduce food expenditures, by purchasing foods of increasingly inferior quality in smaller and smaller quantities, and by changing their menus drastically, replacing food to which they had become accustomed with cheaper items. One of Day's interviewees gave up flour for very cheap grade cornmeal; investigators for the city's charity department found poor people eating "decayed" onions and potatoes. Ultimately, the hardest-hit families found themselves simply eating less food. Several sources reported mothers placating their children with water colored with milk.[8]

But for these women a third strategy for dealing with the high cost of living was to protest. In the third week of February when prices began their steepest climb yet, and Jewish women's "last resort," potatoes and onions, leapt from $0.05 to $0.10 and $0.14 to $0.18 a pound, respectively, New York's Jewish women responding by calling for a citywide boycott of the two vegetables. Violent street protests enforcing their boycott broke out in Jewish neighborhoods throughout the city, beginning in the Williamsburg district of Brooklyn and spreading by 19 and 20 February throughout greater New York. Although sources are sketchy, it appears that the boycott movement had gathered momentum over the course of the two weeks prior to 20 February. One source reported protests beginning on the East Side "several days" before the twenty-first; another reported a boycott in the Claremont district of the Bronx beginning on the eighteenth. New York City Commissioner of Weights and Measures Joseph Hartigan admitted on the twenty-first that what he termed "incipient riots" had been reported by grocers in the Bronx, Brownsville, the East Side, and at 102nd Street and Second Avenue, for fifteen days previous.[9]

By Wednesday, 21 February, women in these neighborhoods banned the sale not only of onions and potatoes but also of vegetables altogether. The next day—Thursday the twenty-second—they angrily added chicken to the list, when they set out to buy their weekly sabbath chickens and found that the price had risen from the previous week's $0.20 a pound to $0.32. And, because they believed that its preparation required purchase of boycotted onions, that same day the women also banned the sale of fish.[10] Marie Ganz, an anarchist who played a briefly prominent role in the demonstrations which grew out of the boycott, claimed in her 1920 autobiography that women were allowed to buy "only certain foods in which there seemed to be the least profiteering. They could buy bread, butter, milk and cereals ... and any person caught buying anything else was mobbed."[11]

The boycott succeeded almost immediately in halting sales of chickens, fish, and many vegetables in Jewish neighborhoods. By Thursday the twenty-second, newspapers reported "no customers" even for those vendors who slashed prices to save their stocks from spoilage. Peddlers deserted their pushcarts or removed them from the streets altogether. Onion shipments accumulated unsold at wholesalers' wharves. In general, food prices held stable for a few days, although retail chicken prices did fall that same Thursday. But by Monday the twenty-sixth, wholesalers cut their rates sharply, and retail prices on a wide range of foods plummeted for the next two weeks, as the boycott remained in effect. By 11 March, potato prices, for example, had fallen from their preboycott high of $0.10 or $0.11 a pound to $0.06.[12]

During the last week of February and the first week of March, while this boycott was so successfully maintained, New York's Jewish women's struggle rapidly escalated; it became a broad movement including demonstrations, marches, pleas before the governor and mayor, and even an outright "riot." But before we examine those expanded forms of protest, the boycott movement itself calls for more detailed scrutiny.

For the women involved, the mild-sounding phrase "establishing a boycott" meant both violence and great vigilance. It meant forcing members of their neighborhood community to publicly demonstrate their observance of the collective ban. The protesting women primarily concentrated their violence and crowd persuasion on convincing peddlers, butchers, and grocers not to sell the boycotted foods. One hundred women gathered on the East Side's Rivington Street, for example, overturned pushcarts, scattered their goods, and threatened to light the kerosene which they poured over other peddlers' vegetables. In many cases infuriated women did totally demolish pushcarts along with their contents. Women surrounded grocers', butcher shops, or fish sellers', and "dared the owners to come out"; on East Fourth Street, forty women poured into a butcher shop and threatened the butcher with his own cleavers.[13] Ganz recalled that "the women used their black shopping bags as clubs, striking at the men. . . . Onions, potatoes and cabbages flew through the air."[14]

Structurally, the boycott movement entailed three key elements: (1) mass meetings, such as that in Williamsburg on 19 February at which 2,000 women collectively pledged to enforce their boycott the next morning; (2) roving inspections, ensuring the advertisement and thoroughness of the movement; and (3) permanently posted pickets at key marketing sites. Several hundred women on the East Side, for example, "surged" through their local shopping districts, "waving the head and wings and mutilated bodies of chickens," "passing from one shop to another, but always leaving a sufficient number of pickets at each poultry market to prevent business."[15]

When the city's police attempted to restrain and arrest protesters, they quickly became a second object of the women's wrath.[16] In the Bronx, for example, after a patrolman "remonstrated" a woman on picket duty who had snatched a bag of just-purchased onions from an old man, the policeman was set upon by the infuriated women, and so was Patrolman Rehn, who responded to the whistle's call for aid. When Mrs. Kiffel was finally put under arrest, volunteers from half a score of houses ran to her assistance and the two policemen were in the centre of a screaming mob of women when Captain Kinsler with the reserves rushed upon the mob.

Caps were smashed, buttons and insignia torn from uniforms, hair was pulled, and it was 15 minutes before Mrs. Kiffel and six of her attendants had been put under arrest.[17]

As this example illustrates, women were quick to act in solidarity when one of their number was set upon by the police. Repeatedly, crowds of women attempted rescue operations, first as their fellow protester was being arrested, and then at the police station.[18] Citywide arrests mounted nonetheless—to sixty on the twenty-third—although Police Inspector Sweeney issued instructions dictating gentle treatment. Despite his order that "no women be arrested except those whose conduct could not be overlooked," arrests increased to 100 on 1 March.[19]

Finally, the protesters reacted equally furiously to shoppers, female and male, who did not observe their boycott. Pickets approached shoppers and informed them of the boycott, cautioning them against purchase of forbidden goods. If they persisted in buying, the women seized and destroyed the shoppers' purchases. On 23 February, for example, an Orchard Street picket guard of "two hundred irate women" stood guard all day, and when a woman bought fish against their will, wrested it from her and threw it into the street.[20] These acts often involved pulling hair, tearing clothes, and scratching faces. "A man who bought a chicken at Waalch's poultry in Wales avenue was pursued by 200 women into a saloon two blocks away. After the crowd had threatened to wreck the place, the proprietor induced the man to throw his purchase to the mob, who destroyed it."[21]

Aside from the obvious reason that prices were skyrocketing, why exactly did these women choose to rebel, and so fiercely? A closer look at individual protesters and the characteristics they shared suggests a partial explanation. With few exceptions, the women on whom information is available—through newspaper interviews and statistics reported on those arrested—were married and in their mid- or late thirties. Each was the mother of several children, usually four or five, and so had reached the point in women's life cycle at which responsibilities for food were greatest. ... Many of the women who engaged in the protests were not the poorest of the poor. They did have husbands still living, and their husbands were employed, albeit seasonally, earning from $10.00 to $15.00 a week, on the average—one as a cigarmaker, another as a shoemaker, many in the garment industry. Although such wages were not high, it appears that until the most recent price leaps, families could live on these wages reasonably comfortably, and in a few cases even save.[22]

Rather than absolute poverty, a shared experience of swiftly declining living standards, caused by rising prices, drove these women to protest. The women's own words expressed this experience. Mrs. Ida Markowitz, for example, an East Side protester who supported her five children on the $10.00 a week her husband brought in as a cloakmaker, voiced her refusal to lower her standard of living: "We don't want their oleomargarine. I could buy butter once on my husband's wages—I don't see why I shouldn't have the same to-day."[23] Mrs. Yetta Stillman, whose husband earned $10.00 as a shoemaker, complained to a reporter who wrote "two years ago this income was enough to feed their six children and buy them shoes and clothing. But to-day—not even potatoes." "Even two months ago it wasn't as hard as it is today." By protesting, these women expressed a limit to redefining their lives beyond which they would not be pushed. As one woman explained in the middle of a demonstration, "With $14 a week we used to just make a living. With prices as they are now, we could not even live on $2 a day. We would just exist."[24] In that distinction between existing and living lay the women's motivation to protest. . . .

In protesting so vehemently, many of New York's Jewish women may also have been motivated by their knowledge that the end of the garment trade's winter season rapidly approached. The New York City clothing industry employed workers in two seasons, shutting down from April to July and again in the late fall. The protesters certainly knew that their budgetary situation would only worsen as the spring progressed.[25]

When the women spoke in their own words of their reasons for protesting, they presented very simple arguments. Almost always, they simply described the sheer enormity of the task of feeding their families under such conditions, and above all, their frustration with the impossibility of performing that task. "I keep my house clean, I keep my windows open, I keep my children clean," one woman declared. "But I can't get the things they must have to eat. I can do nothing more." Another protester voiced identical exasperation: "What am I going to do today? I have my man; he's a tailor, out of work, and two children to feed."[26] Often, protesting women simply pointed to price changes of different foods to explain their acts, or just described their worsening situation. One protester's response epitomized the women's arguments. "Today I went to buy a quart of milk. I paid ten cents for it. The woman who followed me had to pay twelve cents for the same thing. . . . Lima beans have gone up eight cents in four days. And yesterday I found out I couldn't buy a penny's worth of salt any more. No wonder we started rioting. We can't starve without a protest of some kind."[27]

But clearly these women, in choosing their "protest of some kind," also acted out of a Jewish tradition of women's activism, and consumer activism in particular, transplanted from Europe. Jewish women in the New World protested unacceptable prices in almost precisely the same manner on several previous occasions. Toronto's Jewish women boycotted their city's kosher butchers in 1908 and again in 1914, for example.[28] Paula E.

Hyman has investigated one particular earlier outbreak in detail, a New York City kosher meat boycott in 1902. In May of that year, when meat prices jumped 50 percent, middle-aged Jewish women (Hyman found that the medium age of boycott leaders was thirty-nine), averaging 4.3 children each, formed neighborhood bands to enforce a boycott of kosher butchers. Mass meetings complemented a door-to-door canvass informing women of the movement and collecting funds. The women invaded offending butchers' shops and seized and destroyed the purchases of shoppers who violated their pact. Meticulously organized, their movement succeeded at least temporarily in bringing the prices of meat down from $0.18 to $0.14 a pound.[29] Although the precise ways in which New York's Jewish women remembered and learned from this protest fifteen years earlier remain obscure, we can at least imagine that the 1902 boycott, along with other similar boycotts known to the women of New York, suggested the tactical form which their 1917 protest would take. This protest tradition clearly deserves further attention—for food protests identical in basic form to New York's broke out in Philadelphia, Boston, Chicago, and many other cities during early 1917.

But to the working-class Jewish women who protested in New York, the idea of a neighborhood-based, consumer-enforced boycott must also have quite simply made sense. The women boycotters designed their movement around pressuring the marketplace at the point at which they were accustomed to encountering it. They knew from experience in haggling with local grocers that prices were not absolute; they knew that purchasing power could affect prices, if apply craftily; and they knew that grocers' stocks were extremely perishable.[30] The neighborhood market, moreover, was familiar to them. Produce and poultry dealers were known at least by face, if not by name and family ties. The familiarity which nurtured New York's Jewish boycott movement grew out of the neighborhood setting itself: women could join with their neighbors in militant protest without even leaving the streets that were well-known to them. They could act in close proximity to their homes and to their children—recall the incident above when "volunteers from half a dozen houses" ran to a sister's assistance in her battle with police.[31]

Equally important, women engaged in a local consumer boycott movement could carve out an activist place for themselves within their roles as wives and mothers outside of the paid labor force. They could act out of what Temma Kaplan identifies as "female consciousness" shared by many women who accept the sexual division of labor and the responsibilities it assigns to women, but who take those responsibilities seriously enough to rebel, if necessary, to fulfill them. "Women with female consciousness demand the rights that their obligations entail," Kaplan argues. "The collective drive to serve those rights has revolutionary consequences insofar as it politicizes the networks of everyday life."[32] Kaplan's model suggests that the sexual division of labor, as New York's Jewish women experienced it in 1917, both motivated them to rise up in protest, and set the framework within which their uprising would fit. Thus the protesting women demanded their rights to feed their children, demanded that the market yield up a "living" to their families, and also protested in ways that enabled them to continue to fulfill childcare responsibilities, staying close to home or bringing children along to demonstrations.

In voicing their demands as consumers, New York's immigrant Jewish mothers displayed no complex theory of the political economy of food. Although they did say prices were too high and set about lowering them, the women's analysis was neither abstract nor structural. Yet with their actions they expressed a belief that, through carefully orchestrated solidarity, ordinary people *could* affect the market from below. They believed in this enough to beat up their neighbors, go without the cheapest and most desirable foods for over two weeks, and risk arrest involving fines they couldn't pay, or even jail. At home in their neighborhoods, together and assertive, they felt powerful.

Comfortable as they were with protesting in their own front yards, New York's Jewish women also proved willing to venture into unfamiliar areas of the city to pursue their demands. As they did so, their movement rapidly escalated into a citywide struggle against the high cost of living, involving anarchists, Socialists, Progressives, and city officials, each offering their own solution to the crisis. . . .

On 20 February, as boycott-enforcing street actions spread across New York's Jewish section, a crowd of over 1,000 women gathered in the East Side's Rutgers Square. They had been drawn by an announcement in the morning's *Forward* placed by five women the night before. When after speeches and much shouting someone in the crowd suggested a march on City Hall, two women, Ida Harris and Marie Ganz, led the crowd to City Hall Park, where the women demanded to see the mayor, John Purroy Mitchel. In Yiddish and English, many of them in tears, the protesters held their babies up as testimony and demanded food, screaming, "You see them—they are starving. We want bread"; "Feed our children.". . .

This City Hall demonstration marked a transition in the Jewish women's protest movement: the women left their traditional neighborhood realm of protest and expanded their demands to call for direct grants of food. Moreover, in marching to the mayor's seat of power they now held city officials as well as grocers and peddlers responsible for the crisis. Their movement, however, in its tactics, remained largely spontaneously organized and characterized by highly emotional crowd actions.

The Socialists' agitational efforts climaxed on Saturday the twenty-fourth with a massive price protest demonstration in Madison Square. . . . By midafternoon on the twenty-fourth approximately 5,000 protesters had amassed in the square. Observers estimated the crowd at 90 percent foreign-born and 80 percent female, with many of the women accompanied by children or baby carriages. Overall, "The whole affair ... was powerful in its chaos, its disorganization, its freedom from personal dominance," one observer reported. "Anybody who had anything to say mounted a soap box or a curb and said it. There were as many as 15 speakers ... at any one time."[33]

Several of the signs carried by demonstrators displayed a ... blend of socialist analysis of the cost-of-living issue with demands growing out of the boycott movement. Slogans like "Uncle Sam, Why Feed Murderers? Feed Your Children," and "Feed America first! Our children are starving. Come down with prices," for example, incorporated the socialist critique that war profiteering and exports had caused the crisis. Other banners and signs displayed a rough class-consciousness of more ambiguous origin: "Protest. The East New York and Brounsville [*sic*] Organisation of Working people. We want cheaper the high cost of food," and, "Mr. Mayor, never mind Riverside Drive. We want onions, potatoes, chickens too!" A third group of signs simply asked for food—though they did also implicitly hold government officials responsible: "Open the warehouses. We demand food for our children." "Bread! Bread! Give us enough bread to eat."[34]

Later in the day ... the protesters found something more active to do. And their actions diverged sharply from the Socialists' plan for the afternoon. When Socialist speaker Bella Zilberman asked only rhetorically how many of her listeners would march to the Waldorf-Astoria where Governor Whitman was rumored to be stopping, and "show him that you are hungry," more than a thousand women and children surged to the hotel and tried desperately to get in. A scene ensued which in its chaos and violence approached the classic meaning of "riot." Crying and screaming women beat upon the quickly barricaded doors of the hotel for two hours. One group of protesters stopped a passing car and dragged out its drivers, shouting "Yah! Yah! You ride in comfort while we walk and starve." The women's cries in this protest reiterated their desperation, their confusion, and their desire for help. "Give us bread." "We are starving." "Why can't we see the Governor?" When mounted police arrived and began to club the women, they fought back fiercely but also expressed a wish to avoid confrontation. "Don't touch us!" they cried. "Don't kill us. We are hungry. We came here to get help, not to fight the police." As the evening progressed, many of the women began to realize that they had become separated from their children and began a loud "wailing" of distress. "The policemen seemed to be at a loss how to handle them. They declared they could have cleared the streets in a quarter of an hour had there been men to deal with. But the harder they pushed and the louder they bellowed the wilder the women became." Ultimately the women retreated to their neighborhoods, many of them by way of the police station either under arrest or in search of lost children. . . .[35]

In participating in Socialist-sponsored demonstrations, in small "mass meetings" organized by independent consumer groups, and in more informal small-scale demonstrations, the boycotting women added to their protest design a new tactic. They expanded both their modes of protest and the spatial dimension of their movement. Simultaneously, they expanded their demands beyond those of lowered retail prices: they cried "give us food," demanding outright grants of food from the city. In so doing, however, they diverged from the Socialists, who on no occasion called for direct distribution of free food, preferring, rather, to demand the purchase and sale of food at cost.

Nor did the protesting women heed the Socialists' admonitions against violence. They continued unabated to enforce their boycott using traditional coercive methods. The women's acts of violence in fact reached their greatest intensity after the Socialists had been preaching against violence for several days. Using boycott-related arrests as a very crude measure, in combination with press assessments of the relative extent of each day's street activities, it appears that protests reached their greatest ferocity on 1 March, when 100 people were arrested.[36] Overall, in the two weeks between 19 February and 5 March, street protests followed a weekly cycle, reaching their greatest intensity on Thursday (Jewish women's traditional marketing day for the sabbath), subsiding somewhat on Friday, ceasing altogether for the sabbath and the next day because of newly strict police enforcement of a law closing grocers' on Sundays, and breaking out with renewed vigor upon the women's return to the market on Monday. . . .

The women's design for protests . . . continued to follow the dictates of their traditional views about the morality of food. A final development in the boycotters' story indicates that many of them not only refused to pay outrageous prices, but also specifically refused to too radically change their families' diets. . . . Many women initially joined the movement less out of actual starvation than out of a sense of limits reached, as in the case of the woman who asserted her continuing right to butter. Those limits boiled down to an unwillingness to altogether abandon traditional foods. Potatoes, onions, and chickens were dietary staples to which they believed they had a basic right if they were to fulfill their responsibility to truly sustain their families. More importantly, the rituals of preparing kosher foods played a crucial role in the religious and cultural self-definition of New York's immigrant Jewish people. Following the exact rules prescribing the foods to be served on the sabbath or the precise way to butcher a chicken was antithetical to adapting the family diet according to the vagaries of the market. Women bought and served traditional foods not only out of mere habit, but also because those foods expressed their commitment to a religious life.[37]

The women's boycott . . . eventually came to an end. Although Theresa Malkiel, speaking for the Socialists, proclaimed the boycott still in effect on 8 March, by Wednesday the seventh potatoes and other vegetables began to reappear on pushcarts. The next day, Thursday, the previous peak day in the protest cycle, no street actions were reported, and Friday purchases were reported back to normal, although one small protest broke out in the

Bronx. The situation as a whole suggests that while Socialist organizers sought to continue the boycott, albeit nonviolently, and denied reports that it was over, the Jewish women in the neighborhoods who had successfully initiated and prosecuted it chose to relax their vigilance and resume buying.[38]

Although the exact reasons why the women decided to end their boycott remain unclear, their boycott tactic may have been inherently self-limiting. After all, the women who protested had renounced their favorite foods in order, ultimately, to obtain those very same foods. Just as they were unwilling to too drastically change their eating habits under pressure from rising prices, they must also have been unwilling to adapt to the exigencies of a boycott situation too indefinitely.

But the women's decision to resume buying must have also been motivated by the ostensible success of their movement. By the second week in March, prices of boycotted items did drop sharply. Onions plummeted from $0.18 a pound retail to $0.11 and $0.12; potatoes from $0.10 to $0.07 and $0.08; and chickens from $0.32 a pound to around $0.22.[39] However, the protest's long-term effect on prices was only temporary: statistics show that retail food costs in New York City rose continuously over the course of 1917, decreasing their rate of rise somewhat during the winter of 1917–18 but resuming their sharp claimb in 1918.[40]

Although New York's Socialists saw the cost-of-living issue as at best secondary or tertiary to the real task at hand, the boycotters, by sharp contrast, joined the price protest movement precisely out of an urgent and deeply felt commitment to the cost-of-living issue. Consumer organizing spoke directly to their daily lives and concerns; they saw cheaper food as a valuable end in itself. Indeed, for these housewives, prices must have taken on a significance equivalent to, or perhaps surpassing, the importance of wages to those who work for pay. Not only did prices translate wages into goods and services, but also price levels determined these women's working conditions. High prices made women's work harder. Scouting the streets for bargains, overhauling menus, satisfying finicky family members, planning to the last penny—all these consequences of rising prices could multiply a housewife's work immensely. Food price protests were these women's way of organizing at their own workplace, as workers whose occupation was shopping, preparing food, and keeping their families content.

### NOTES

The original version of this article also explored the relationship between food protestors and the organizational activities of the New York Socialist parties. Space considerations have required abridging the article to one that is more narrowly focused.

1. Winifred Stuart Gibbs, *The Minimum Cost of Living: A Study of Families of Limited Income in New York City* (New York: Macmillan, 1917); National Industrial Conference Board, *The Cost of Living in the United States* (New York: National Industrial Conference Board, 1925).

2. David Kennedy, *Over Here: The First World War and American Society* (New York: Oxford University Press, 1980), 117; Wesley Clair Mitchell, *History of Prices during the War* (Washington, D.C.: GPO, 1919), 38–39.

3. Paul Douglas, *Real Wages in the United States, 1890–1926* (Boston: Houghton Mifflin, 1930), 19–60; National Industrial Conference Board, 4–7; *Historical Statistics of the United States: Colonial Times to 1970,* 2 vols. (Washington, D.C.: GPO, 1975), 2: 212; David Montgomery, *Workers' Control in America: Studies in the History of Work, Technology, and Labor Struggles* (Cambridge: Cambridge University Press, 1979), 95–97; Mitchell, 47; Marie Ganz, *Rebels: Into Anarchy—And Out Again* (New York: Dodd, Mead & Co., 1920), 247.

4. *New York American,* 21 Feb. 1917; Mitchell; National Industrial Conference Board; *Historical Statistics of the United States.*

5. *New York Call,* 30, 15 Nov. 1916.

6. Ibid., 21 Apr. 1917.

7. Donald Wilhelm "I Don't Know: An East Side Mother's Story of the Food Riots," *Independent,* 12 Mar. 1917, 452–53.

8. *New York Call,* 1 Oct., 15, 26 Nov. 1916; 23 Feb. 1917; *New York American* 21, 23 Feb. 1917.

9. *New York Call,* 20, 21 Feb. 1917; *New York American,* 21 Feb. 1917; *New York Times,* 23 Feb. 1917; Bruno Lasker, "The Food Riots," *Survey,* 3 Mar. 1917, 639.

10. *New York Times,* 23 Feb. 1917; *New York American,* 23 Feb. 1917.

11. Ganz, 260.

12. *New York American,* 22, 23, 24, 27 Feb. 1917; *New York Call,* 27, 28 Feb., 1, 2, 4, 8, 13 Mar. 1917; *New York Times,* 22, 25 Feb. 1917; *New York World,* 23, 24 Feb. 1917; "To Control The Cost of Living," *Survey,* 10 Mar. 1917, 661.

13. *New York American,* 21, 23 Feb. 1917; *New York Call,* 23, 28 Feb. 1917; *New York World,* 20 Feb. 1917.

14. Ganz, 251.

15. *New York Call,* 20 Feb. 1917; *New York Times,* 21 Feb. 1917.

16. *New York Call,* 27 Feb. 1917; *New York American,* 27 Feb. 1917.

17. *New York American,* 21 Feb. 1917.

18. *New York Evening Journal,* 21 Feb. 1917; *New York Call,* 27 Feb., 2 Mar. 1917.

19. *New York American,* 24 Feb. 1917; *New York Call,* 28 Feb. 1917.

20. *New York Call,* 24 Feb. 1917.

21. Ibid., 23 Feb., 1, 2 Mar. 1917; *New York American,* 23 Feb. 1917.

22. *New York American,* 24 Feb. 1917; Lewis Lorwin, *The Women's Garment Workers: A History of the International Ladies Garment Workers' Union* (New York: B.W. Huebsch, 1924), 531–42; Irving Howe, *World of Our Fathers* (New York: Simon & Schuster, 1976), 145–46.

23. *New York American,* 27 Feb. 1917.

24. *New York American,* 24 Feb. 1917; *New York Call,* 4 Mar. 1917.

25. Jack Hardy, *The Clothing Workers* (New York: International Publishers, 1935), 68; Joel Seidman, *The Needle Trades* (New York: Farrah & Rinehart, 1942), 205.

26. *New York Call,* 7, 4 Mar. 1917.

27. *New York American,* 23 Feb. 1917; see also 24 Feb. 1917.

28. Wayne Roberts, *Honest Womanhood: Feminism, Femininity, and Class Consciousness among Toronto Working Women, 1893–1914* (Toronto: New Hogtown Press, 1976), 41.

29. Paula E. Hyman, "Immigrant Women and Consumer Protest: The New York City Kosher Meat Boycott of 1902," *American Jewish History* 70 (1980): 91–105.

30. Along similar lines, Hyman (97) argues that the 1902 boycott participants, "recognizing that prices were set by the operation of the laws of supply and demand, as modified, in this case, by the concentration of the wholesale meat industry, ... hit upon a boycott of meat as the most effective way to dramatically curtail demand." For an example of similar protests in the eighteenth century, see Olwen Hufton, *Bayeux in the Late Eighteenth Century* (Oxford, England: Oxford University Press, 1967), 231–35.

31. *New York American,* 21 Feb. 1917.

32. Temma Kaplan, "Female Consciousness and Collective Action: The Case of Barcelona, 1910–1918," *Signs* 7 (Spring 1982): 545–66.

33. *New York American,* 23, 25 Feb. 1917; *New York Call,* 23, 24, 25 Feb. 1917; *New York Times,* 25 Feb. 1917; *New York World,* 23, 25 Feb. 1917.

34. *New York American,* 25 Feb. 1917; *New York Call,* 25 Feb. 1917.

35. *New York Call*, 25 Feb. 1917; *New York American, New York World*, 25 Feb. 1917.
36. *New York Call*, 2 Mar. 1917.
37. Howe, 13.
38. *New York Call*, 8, 9 Mar. 1917.
39. *New York American*, 27 Feb. 1917; *New York Call*, 27, 28 Feb., 1, 2, 8, 11 Mar. 1917; "To Control the Cost of Living," *New York World*.
40. National Industrial Conference Board.

# 8

## Organized Voluntarism: The Catholic Sisters in Massachusetts, 1870–1940

### Mary J. Oates

*Catholic women have been relatively neglected by historians of American women, but their ability to live in separate communities of women as an alternative to marriage was greater than for any other group. Mary J. Oates describes the erosion of the autonomy and power of those communities after 1880 when, although the communities enjoyed phenomenal growth, Catholic sisters' work as teachers in the expanding system of parochial schools came under the closer scrutiny of a church hierarchy increasingly focused on considerations of cost.*

The labor force which historically has staffed most charitable and educational institutions of the Catholic Church in the United States has come from religious communities of women. Yet the sisters' role has rarely been studied. Literature dealing with them has ranged from anti-Catholic tracts of the nineteenth and early twentieth centuries to community histories and biographies of foundresses. Both have tended to reinforce the view of sisters as socially peripheral women, aloof from society, its needs and concerns.[1]

Official Catholic publications, while recording the activities and accomplishments of churchmen, have neglected full-time female church workers. For example, priests were enumerated by name, location, and work in every issue of the *Official Catholic Directory* over 1870–1940. In the case of sisters, the directory provided the name of the superior of the local convent and usually the number of sisters. Church histories remain oriented toward the decisions of hierarchy and clergy.[2] Fortunately communities of women have preserved documents and annals of their members and work, although the quality and completeness of these records vary. This archival material, together with directory data and scattered contemporary sources, allows us to investigate the experience of the sisters in Massachusetts.

Though similar to that of their counterparts in other states, this experience is uniquely grounded in the history of the church in Boston. The Catholic Church remained a central social as well as religious institution in the lives of Massachusetts citizens between 1870 and 1940. In 1870, the diocese of Boston encompassed the state of Massachusetts. By 1880 and throughout the rest of the period, it included the counties of Essex, Middle-

Excerpted from "Organized Voluntarism: The Catholic Sisters in Massachusetts, 1870–1940," by Mary J. Oates in *American Quarterly* 30 (Winter 1978): 652–80. Copyright 1978 American Studies Association.

The Boston School for the Deaf
Randolph - June 1911

*Sisters of St. Joseph with schoolchildren: Boston School for the Deaf, 1911. Archives, Sisters of St. Joseph, Brighton, Mass.*

sex, Suffolk, Norfolk, and Plymouth, with the exception of the towns of Mattapoisett, Marion, and Wareham. Our discussion of Massachusetts in this paper deals, unless otherwise noted, with the archdiocese of Boston. Although tensions between Irish Catholics and native New Englanders had eased in the years following the Civil War, they never disappeared, and church organizations served as supportive and unifying forces for a working-class population.[3]

Although in 1870 fewer Catholic women than men engaged in full-time church work in Massachusetts, the picture changed over succeeding decades. Table 1 indicates the extent of this change. By 1890 there were almost twice as many women as men, and in the twentieth century the female/male ratio climbed even higher, so that by 1940 more than two-thirds of church workers were women. . . . This change in proportions is peculiar. Other things equal, one might expect the propensity for church service to be similar for both sexes. Or, if the higher prestige attached to church work for men is considered, the totals might be higher for them. If, as some have suggested, the women's early socialization leads to their being more attracted than men to church work, it is difficult to account for the near parity in numbers of men and women church workers before 1890.

TABLE 1 Distribution of Full-Time Catholic Church Workers, by Occupation and Sex, Archdiocese of Boston, 1870–1940

| | Members of Religious Communities of Women | | | | | | |
|---|---|---|---|---|---|---|---|
| Year | Hospital Work[a] (%) | Social Work[b] (%) | Academies and Boarding Schools[c] (%) | Parochial Schools[d] (%) | Other Work[e] (%) | Total Number of Sisters[f] | Female/ Male Ratio |
| 1870 | 12.2 | 24.4 | 11.3 | 46.2 | 5.9 | 221 | 0.80 |
| 1880 | 10.0 | 28.4 | 4.9 | 42.4 | 14.3 | 370 | 1.19 |
| 1890 | 5.0 | 17.3 | 4.5 | 53.0 | 20.3 | 942 | 1.99 |
| 1900 | 5.1 | 14.0 | 6.2 | 54.7 | 20.0 | 1,457 | 1.98 |
| 1910 | 4.4 | 15.2 | 6.8 | 55.3 | 18.2 | 1,699 | 1.85 |
| 1920 | 4.0 | 11.6 | 7.8 | 59.6 | 16.9 | 2,649 | 2.48 |
| 1930 | 2.8 | 9.3 | 6.5 | 63.6 | 17.7 | 3,605 | 2.21 |
| 1940 | 3.1 | 9.2 | 8.2 | 62.6 | 16.9 | 4,164 | 2.16 |

[a]Nursing and administrative work.
[b]With women, orphans, the elderly, the handicapped, the poor in asylums and homes.
[c]Teaching and support services.
[d]Teaching and support services.
[e]This column includes sisters whose work is unspecified. Such work would include community administration, housekeeping, cooking, laundry work. Novices, postulants, sick and retired sisters who are not engaged in full-time work are included here. Also included are cloistered nuns, sisters in retreat work, missionaries.
[f]Includes professed sisters, novices, and postulants.

Religious brothers (members of religious communities, but not ordained priests) never accounted for even one-fifth of churchmen throughout the period, and for the most part they taught boys in parochial schools and private academies. Most men belonged to the diocesan clergy and engaged in pastoral work in local parishes. Priests who belonged to religious orders taught men and boys, conducted retreats and missions, and assisted in parish work. Although an expanding Catholic population stimulated demand for more men to serve growing needs, the nature of the work they were expected to accomplish remained the same. In this sense the growth rate of male church workers may be considered natural. The difference between male and female growth rates suggests the presence of exogenous factors which affected the supply of women workers differently.

In 1870 Massachusetts sisters worked in the traditionally female professions, but within this category there was diversity: teaching, nursing, or social work with the poor, the handicapped, the elderly, or orphans. After 1880 (see Table 1) this variation disappeared as sisters moved into education, particularly into parochial school teaching.... By 1940 two-thirds of all sisters in Boston were found in parochial schools. While in 1880 nearly 40 percent of all sisters undertook hospital and social work, by 1940 only

12 percent were found in these occupations. Instead of expanding, women's options narrowed.

Since women's communities specialized in a single occupation, it is unlikely that much of the increase of sisters in parochial schools can be accounted for by direct shifts of personnel out of nonteaching occupations into schools. Over the period, Catholic services expanded in all the areas in which sisters were involved. . . . The number of sisters per thousand Catholics in the archdiocese increased more than six-fold over the 70-year period, allowing the sisters to staff these many institutions. Evidently the service which sisters elected to provide to the Catholic population was the education of their children in parochial schools. The growing number of young women interested in convent life selected the teaching orders.

The major explanation for this shift in sisters' occupational tastes is that after 1880 the development of a system of parochial schools was defined as the "critical need" of the church in Massachusetts. Young women entering church service were encouraged to join teaching communities in order to meet this need. These communities grew rapidly, and were remarkably youthful. Of the 536 living members of one diocesan teaching community in 1919, for example, more than 60 percent had not yet made perpetual vows. Most of these sisters would be well under 30 years of age.[4] Although communities outside Massachusetts were recruited for faculty (Canadian sisters were often invited to teach in parish schools in factory towns with French-speaking populations), the two major teaching groups, the Sisters of Notre Dame de Namur and the Sisters of St. Joseph, drew their members for the most part from the local population.

By 1870 parochial schools had become characteristic of many dioceses, but not in Massachusetts. In 1873, for example, 68 percent of parishes in the archdiocese of New York had schools attached; as late as 1900, the corresponding figure for the archdiocese of Boston was only 42 percent. In that year Boston ranked seventeenth among 20 chief dioceses in the country in this regard, only Portland, San Francisco, and Springfield ranking lower, although Boston was the third largest diocese in the nation.[5]

The concept of a large school system was never popular with Archbishop John J. Williams, leader of the Boston church from 1866 to 1907. Once a public school student himself, he was unconvinced of the need for separate schools for Catholic children. If parish priest and people proposed to build a school, he approved, but unlike many of his fellow bishops, he did not promote a school network. When questioned by Rome about the Boston school situation, Williams was casual in his reply. His 1879 report noted that "the schools are public. . . . Even in the smallest town they are set up according to law, and . . . this is defended as doing nothing contrary to the children's religion."[6] Not all his priests agreed with Williams' position and the school issue occasioned some divisiveness within the diocese.[7]

In 1884 the situation changed. The Third Plenary Council of Baltimore, composed of the hierarchy of the United States, commanded that parochial school systems be developed in every diocese in the country. . . . The decree of the Council of Baltimore brought about not only rapid construction of schools in Massachusetts, but also a demand for a teaching force. Sisters rather than priests, brothers, or laypersons became the group in demand. Their response was most evident in the increase in their numbers and in the slower expansion of their work in other areas, but the rise in demand for teachers had other effects on women. After 1884 the history of the Massachusetts sisters became linked to that of the parochial schools.

The recruitment of female labor can be understood only in the context of the roles defined by church and society as acceptable for women. To have sisters for the schools, increasing numbers had to view membership in a religious community as a desirable lifestyle, and teaching as an attractive career. Throughout the period under study, long-term careers for women were the exception rather than the norm; their options remained centered around marriage and family. Liberal Catholic writers and intellectuals frequently argued for a wider choice, but official spokesmen did not.[8] Sermons, press editorials, and literature were consistent. In 1928 the leader of the Boston church stated unequivocally that "the home is woman's normal sphere—maidenhood, wifehood, motherhood and home. . . ." Such passive "virtues" as self-effacement and submission to authority he viewed as peculiarly female. "You must put yourselves in the background. . . . That is precisely the discipline which women even more than men need every day."[9] Ambition was not encouraged, and feminists advocating careers, independence, and equality for women were looked upon with suspicion and apprehension.

> And if, after graduating with highest honors, she insists on keeping up her study of—well, let us say astronomy, we doubt not but the telescope will not bother her husband half as much as it will the baby on her lap; and we venture to predict that she will find more delight in its twinkling eyes than in all the planets of the solar system.[10]

A 1910 survey found that nearly two-thirds (64 percent) of all females in Boston ten years of age and over were not employed. This figure does not include the 2 percent who were still enrolled in school. Only 34 percent were wage earners. Single women were in the labor force in this period but usually left it at marriage, and the average woman's working experience outside the home was short. The majority of Boston women were housewives, precluded from working outside their homes except in cases of necessity. Of females who were gainfully employed, 38 percent were engaged in domestic and personal service, work similar to that done in the home. Clerking in stores and office work occupied another 28 percent and factory work 24 percent. Only 9 percent were to be found in the professions. Within this category, teaching and nursing ranked first and second, accounting for 4 percent and 2 percent respectively of all employed women. The professions of women were fewer and less varied than those of Boston men.[11] Teaching had long provided attractive and accessible employment to women; a study of the period before 1860 found that 20 percent of Massachusetts women had been teachers at some time in their lives, even though in any given year the schools employed less than 2 percent of women in the 15–60 age bracket.[12] . . .

For a number of Catholic women wishing to undertake socially important and professional work, a life of church service as a member of a religious community appeared at least competitive with its major alternative. Such a choice was socially acceptable; the sisters, drawn from and serving the Catholic population, were held in high regard. ". . . Woman was created to be a wife and mother; that is, after a special religious calling to the service of God."[13] Bound by vows of poverty, celibacy, and obedience, they were expected to epitomize the womanly virtues and to serve the church with little concern for recompense. We have seen that increasingly larger numbers of women than men undertook church work in the archdiocese of Boston between 1870 and 1940. Austere though convent life appeared, the prospect of banding together with other women to respond to pressing needs appealed to youthful idealism. The community would train the young woman for her life's work, and she could choose among a number of professions, expressing her preference through her selection of an order. . . .

It is often assumed that parents enrolled their sons as often as their daughters in the parochial schools, since this was true in public schools. Such was not the case in Massachusetts. Only in the later years of the period did the number of boys enrolled approach that of girls. In 1870 just two of every ten students were boys, and the ratio was slow to change. (See Table 2.)

One might suspect that the different proportions meant that boys left school earlier to take jobs. . . . If boys were leaving parochial schools more often than girls, we should observe similar proportions in kindergarten and primary grades, and a lower representation of boys at the grammar and high school levels. Table 2 shows the percentages of girl students by grade level in 1900. High school enrollments were heavily female, but fewer than two percent of all parochial school children were found in these grades. In both kindergarten and primary grades, the proportion of girls is above 50 percent, and the enrollment of boys in grammar grades is not notably lower than that in kindergartens. If boys were not leaving school earlier, we must conclude that parents were enrolling daughters more often than sons in these schools.

During the nineteenth century, Massachusetts sisters were identified with the education of girls. A large number of parochial schools in the state were staffed by a single community, the Sisters of Notre Dame de Namur, whose work was the education of girls and whose rule forbade the teaching

*TABLE 2 A.   Enrollment of Girls in Parochial Schools, 1870–1940*

| Year | Percent of Girls in Total Parochial School Enrollment | Total School Population |
|------|-------------------------------------------------------|-------------------------|
| 1870 | 79.9 | 6,110 |
| 1880 | 79.3 | 9,478 |
| 1890 | 65.6 | 24,966 |
| 1900 | 59.3 | 37,543 |
| 1910 | 56.4 | 51,237 |
| 1920 | 54.9 | 73,133 |
| 1930 | 53.1 | 95,346 |
| 1940 | 52.4 | 93,569 |

*Source:* Compiled from data in *Official Catholic Directories,* 1870–1940

*B.   Enrollment of Girls by Grade Level In Parochial Schools, 1900*

| Grade Level | Percent of Girls In Grade Enrollment |
|-------------|--------------------------------------|
| Ungraded[a] | 52.8 |
| Kindergarten | 57.1 |
| Primary (Grades 1–4) | 56.0 |
| Grammar (Grades 5–9) | 59.0 |
| High (Grades 10–12) | 83.4 |

[a]These were students of several grade levels taught in one class by one teacher. See *Catholic Educational Review,* 1 (Mar. 1911), 266.

*Source:* Louis S. Walsh, *Historical Sketch of the Growth of the Catholic Schools in the Archdiocese of Boston* (Newton: St. John's Industrial School, 1901), Appendix 11. Data are for school year 1899–1900.

of boys. In 1872 "there were thirteen Catholic Parochial Schools [in the Boston diocese] eleven for girls. . . . The Sisters of Notre Dame . . . did not wish to teach the larger boys."[14] If a parish were to undertake the education of boys, additional costs could be expected since brothers or laypersons had to be found to instruct them. A number of parishes did open boys' schools, but these were usually opened latest and closed first if costs proved prohibitive. In a Chicopee parish, for example, the Christian Brothers were dismissed after 25 years of teaching in the school ". . . as the expense of two communities was too heavy on our little parish. . . ."[15] In public school systems, separate schools for girls and boys were not uncommon; of 23 Boston grammar schools in 1866, nine were solely for boys and eight for girls.[16] The problem peculiar to the parochial schools at this time was that, unlike women teachers in public schools, the sisters available to teach would not instruct boys.

Two changes brought about the greater enrollment of boys in the

Catholic schools of the twentieth century. The Sisters of Notre Dame, in response to pressure, agreed by the 1880s to teach boys through the second grade, or up to about age eight.[17] This concession alleviated the problem somewhat. In 1873, however, an economy-minded pastor, eager to enroll both boys and girls in his school in Jamaica Plain, had invited Sisters of St. Joseph from Brooklyn, New York, to staff it. The rule of this community did not prohibit the teaching of boys at any grade level, and the Jamaica Plain school became the first in New England to have both boys and girls taught by sisters through the elementary grades. . . . Teaching the young children, both boys and girls, became the work of women, a trend paralleling developments in the local public schools half a century earlier.[18] For the most part the sisters worked under the supervision of pastors and bishops.

In maintaining a parochial school system financed by working class parishes the cost of teaching services was paramount. In local public schools in late nineteenth- and early twentieth-century Massachusetts, instructional expenses averaged 60 percent of annual school expenditures.[19] Paying a faculty at public school scales was out of the question, and the teaching communities of men and women were identified as an attractive source of low-cost labor. These groups were willing to subsidize the schools by contributing their services, receiving only a salary for living expenses. Soon sisters were sought in preference to brothers since their salary levels were lower. . . .

Actual salaries paid sisters for full-time work over the 1870–1940 period varied little over time, location, or occupation. A comparison of the sister's salary with the salary of the woman teaching in a Boston public school can be made by examining Tables 3 and 4. Public school salaries were not adjusted annually. In fact, they were practically unchanged between 1866 and 1877 and between 1889 and 1896. Adjustments, when made, were not always favorable to the teachers. In 1877, for example, salaries were cut $7\frac{1}{2}$ percent.[20] Nevertheless, salaries did increase, and a Boston Public School Teachers' Retirement Fund was established in 1900.

This comparison indicates how women were subsidizing the parochial schools. But another question remains: Was the salary paid the sister-teacher sufficient for her to live on? A 1911 study of 450 wage-earning women in Boston concluded that "annual earnings of approximately $500 a year, or $10 a week, may be taken as the amount of a living wage for women workers in Boston."[21] Using the data presented in Table 4, let us estimate the sister's average income for 1911 as $300, a cash stipend of $250 plus a $50 payment in kind in the form of housing. If we view the sister as a single working woman, then it is clear she was not receiving a salary even approaching the minimum standard. Her income was only 43 percent of the average income received by other professional women, and 32 percent of the salary paid public elementary school teachers.

Even though the sisters received only about three-fifths of the esti-

TABLE 3 *Maximum Annual Salaries of Women Teachers in Public Elementary Schools, Boston, Massachusetts, Selected Years, 1867–1919*

| Year | Salaries of Regular Teachers[a] | Salaries After Adjusting for Cost of Living (1913 = 100)[f] |
|------|------|------|
| 1867 | $ 650 | $ 628 |
| 1873 | 800[b] | 945 |
| 1878 | 1,080[c] | 1,552 |
| 1880 | 1,080 | 1,515 |
| 1896 | 1,146[d] | 1,822 |
| 1899 | 936 | 1,416 |
| 1911 | 936 | 1,023 |
| 1916 | 1,176[e] | 1,037 |
| 1919 | 1,368 | 725 |

[a]Teachers without executive or administrative duties.

[b]Primary grades only.

[c]Grammar grades only.

[d]Average of maximum primary ($1,080) and maximum grammar ($1,212) salaries. After 1906, the distinction between grammar and primary grades was eliminated.

[e]Median salary.

[f]Burgess Cost-of-Living Index, Series E 184, *Historical Statistics of the United States, Colonial Times to 1970* (Washington: U.S. Department of Commerce, 1975), Part I, 212.

mated living wage, their salaries did allow them to subsist, although not in any degree of comfort. Since they lived communally their situation resembled that of a family more than a number of independent single women. Funds were held in common, with all stipends paid to the local superior. After deducting the local group's contribution to central community expenses, the superior had discretion over the remaining funds. The sisters cooked for themselves, so their food expenditures were lower than if they had had to purchase meals in restaurants, cafeterias, or lodging houses. Similarly, in 1915, the estimated cost of rent, light, and heat for an individual in a normal family was $44.72 for a year. The $50 per sister per year for housing is consistent with this interpretation. "Living costs more for a woman 'adrift' than for a member of a family group."[22]

Clothing for sisters was not so great an expense as for the average working woman. With the exception of such items as shoes or gloves, sisters rarely purchased ready-made clothing. Cloth for their habits was purchased in bulk and the clothing was made by the sisters themselves. These habits never varied and were not replaced until worn out. Ordinary health costs may have been lower than might be expected since physicians and dentists often cared for the sisters at little or no charge. Extraordinary or lengthy medical care was paid for by the motherhouse from central funds.

The proportion of sisters' salaries allocated to "savings" was higher

TABLE 4  Annual Salaries Paid to Sisters Working Full-Time in Church Institutions,
Selected Years, 1860–1937

| Year | Cash Payment Per Sister | Payment in Kind per Sister | Type of Work | Location |
|---|---|---|---|---|
| 1860 | no fixed sum | housing,[a] board | teaching | elementary school, South Boston[1] |
| 1898 | $ 50 | housing, board | nursing | hospital, Springfield, Mass.[2] |
| 1902 | 325 | housing | teaching | school for deaf,[b] Jamaica Plain, Mass.[3] |
| 1908 | 300 | housing probably | teaching | parochial school, New York City[4] |
| 1910 | 300 | housing | teaching | parish high school, U.S. average[5] |
| 1912 | 200 | housing | teaching | elementary school, U.S. average[6] |
| 1912 | 250 | none | teaching | elementary school, U.S. average[6] |
| 1919 | 300 | housing probably | teaching | parochial school, Chicago[7] |
| 1924 | under $300 | housing | teaching | parochial school, Boston[8] |
| 1937 | 335 | housing | teaching | parochial school, U.S. average[9] |

[a]Utilities, simple furnishings, and maintenance were included in all cases.

[b]This school, opened in 1899 by the Sisters of St. Joseph, received state aid a year later. It remained under Catholic auspices, but was open to all and inspected by the state. The state aid explains the relatively higher reimbursement of the sisters teaching there.

Sources: (1) A Member of the Congregation, The American Foundations of the Sisters of Notre Dame de Namur, Compiled from the Annals of Their Convents (Philadelphia: Dolphin, 1928), 339; (2) Rev. John J. McCoy, History of the Catholic Church in the Diocese of Springfield (n.p.p.: Hurd and Everts, 1900), 27–28; (3) Letter of Rev. Thomas Magennis to Mother Genevieve, Feb. 15, 1902 (Archives, Sisters of St. Joseph, Brighton, Mass.); (4) J. A. Burns, The Growth and Development of the Catholic School System in the United States (New York: Benziger, 1912), 280. In 1909, this salary was raised to $400 for the diocesan teaching order; (5) "Report of the Committee on High Schools," Catholic Educational Review, 2 (June 1911), 605–26; (6) Burns, The Growth and Development, 280; (7) James W. Sanders, The Education of an Urban Minority, Catholics in Chicago, 1833–1965 (New York: Oxford Univ. Press, 1977), 159; (8) Motherhouse Annals, Sept. 4, 1924, Archives, Sisters of St. Joseph; (9) Clarence Elwell, "The Financing of Teacher Education," Catholic Educational Review, 38 (Feb. 1940), 152–53. This figure is the average salary per year per sister for 53 communities.

than that of other working women. These salaries were the major source of revenue for central community needs, including the provision of food, housing, clothing, and all personal needs of the novices and postulants, the retired, and sick sisters. All educational costs incurred in preparing the young sisters for their work in the schools had to be borne by the communities, since no regular assistance in this area was given by either the diocese or the parish. The communities also met retirement and long-term medical costs. Land had to be purchased and buildings erected to house and maintain the young, the sick, and the elderly. With such limited income, substantial debt was often incurred. Although sympathetic pastors and wealthy Catholics helped in meeting these costs, for the most part they were assumed by the communities. . . .

Sisters supplemented the stipends from the schools by giving art and music lessons and, when possible, by opening tuition-charging academies for girls. Although the number of such schools increased from four to eighteen between 1870 and 1940, the proportion of all sisters teaching in academies, boarding schools, and colleges remained constant. (See Table 1.) The communities in demand for parochial school work opened the smallest number of academies, since the permission of the bishop had to be obtained. But these sources of income remained minor, and pressures on the stipends from the parishes increased as payments remained stable while the communities expanded and matured. . . .

Despite increasing costs, requests by women's communities for larger stipends were sometimes considered unreasonable. One community appealed for a salary of at least $300 for the sisters in 1924, since "they can hardly live on the present one. . . ." Ironically, a local pastor refused to consider it because he was building a school.[23] Others expected the sisters to contribute toward parish expenses, and diocesan officials had to assure the sisters that the "pastor is to supply whatever is necessary for school and convent."[24] . . .

The movement of men away from parish school teaching and the increasing concentration of Massachusetts sisters in education strengthened the already substantial segregation by sex in church work. The teaching of parish school students was left to the sisters, who had no real control over either the schools or the convents attached to them. The degree to which women's communities subsidized the parochial school system makes all the more surprising the dearth of literature on this aspect of the schools' financing.

Since historians have given much attention to Protestant disapproval of parochial schools in Massachusetts, especially after 1884,[25] it is sometimes assumed that local Catholics received the Council decree of a school in every parish with unanimous enthusiasm. On the contrary, there is evidence of "great lukewarmness" among the laity. . . . The objection of Catholics to parochial schools was not their cost but their inferiority to public schools. "Now what is the motive that prompts these disobedient Catholics in preferring the public to their parish schools? Why it is that their children will be better taught in the former. . . ."[26]

> The present generation have nearly all been educated in the public schools and we have become so accustomed to consider them better than any other, that now that Catholic schools are being established in many parishes, there is found a strange reluctance on the part of many to send their children to them.[27]

Pressures on parents in the post-1884 period to enroll their sons as well as their daughters in schools taught by sisters raised questions about the kind of education the boys would receive. Although public school faculties had long been female, the public had never associated them primarily with the education of girls. Contemporary descriptions of parochial schools suggest that they emphasized moral development and manners. . . .

> The parochial school is a reflection from the convent mirror, and the good nuns, besides teaching and enforcing the domestic virtues, especially correct whatever is rude or unbecoming in the manners of their scholars. Hence, even to the smallest points, such as the position of the feet in standing and walking, etc., they pay strict attention.[28]. . .

Not all Catholic parents approved of such training for daughters, many of whom were attending public schools. An editor chastised "those misguided Catholic parents and guardians who keep their girls out of the sisters' schools, asserting that they learn more in other schools."[29] . . .

Inadequate facilities and large class size also supported the view that the burgeoning schools were inferior. A not uncommon situation prevailed in St. Thomas School in Jamaica Plain, where classes were conducted in the basement of the church for 17 years before a school building was erected.[30] An average class size of 48.6 pupils in parochial schools in 1899 compares favorably with 51.5 in Boston elementary schools. If all classes (kindergarten, elementary, high, Latin, and normal) are included, the Boston figure would be 44 for 1897. The grades for this comparison, however, are the elementary ones, since few parochial schools went beyond this level. . . .

Another concern was the training of parochial school teachers. Young sisters, without normal school preparation, were expected to acquire their skills on the job. In average level of schooling these young women were like their contemporaries in the nation's normal schools, 88 percent of whose students as late as 1890 were not yet high school graduates.[31] In this era, the small number of sisters who had graduated from high school before joining a community were assigned to teach older students.[32] The bishops at the Council of Baltimore, sensitive to criticism on this point, sought to ensure a minimum training for sisters by requiring an examination of all new teachers. They urged the women's communities to open normal schools for their members and also requested that sufficient time be allotted for teacher training.[33] But the mandate of a school in every parish slowed progress toward better preparation. The local parish was more concerned about the number of sisters available than their quality.

Religious superiors of the women's communities had little choice but to acquiesce in the wishes of bishops and pastors, many of whom were not convinced of the necessity of pre-job training for elementary teaching. Mother Mary Regis, first superior of the Sisters of St. Joseph, wished to delay opening a school in 1879 until the sisters were better trained. The bishop's representative informed her that novices, with no pre-service training, could learn by apprenticeship. The superiors provided what assistance they could to their new teachers, but this was necessarily sporadic and informal.

"For a few months we have had Professor Dunton of the training school in the city, to give the sisters instruction in the methods of teaching."[34] During the school year, better educated sisters were sent from convent to convent to instruct the others. Young, inexperienced teachers were assigned to the lower grades. . . .

As the number of parish schools increased late in the century, Archbishop Williams lent support to the women's communities in their efforts to reconcile conflicting pressures from pastors and parents. In 1889 he ordered them not to send novices into the schools. Again in 1901, they were instructed to refuse pastors seeking teachers for new schools "unless the number of Sisters who have made their novitiate is sufficient to supply the demand."[35]. . .

Despite lack of formal training, especially in the pre-1920 period, the sisters had an advantage not shared by many public school colleagues in their commitment to a lifetime career. The young teacher started out "learning by doing," but she had the guidance and counsel of older, more experienced sisters. Her own experience in the teaching of young children became an increasing asset. . . .

Though the inability of women's communities to give their members professional education was related to the demand after 1884 for sisters in the classroom, there was little recognition of the cost either to sisters or to their students. Sometimes it was acknowledged obliquely; Cardinal O'Connell, for example, in 1923 ordered that one community omit some daily prayers "so as to give the Sisters more time for study."[36] But assistance was not provided at the expense of the sisters' presence in the schools, and short normal training in novitiates and extension courses remained the ordinary means of educating parochial school faculties.

A related issue is the effect of low incomes on the sisters' professional and social lives. Extra-convent activities permitted to sisters had traditionally been fewer than those considered acceptable for priests and brothers. In this, church authorities reflected, in a more extreme way, society's strictures on women's activities and behavior, always more circumscribed than men's. But in the 70 years between 1870 and 1940 social and professional options for American women had broadened. Higher education and economic independence were becoming realities for many, and the goals of countless others. At the same time, the sphere of action allowed to members of women's communities not only did not widen, but in some areas appears to have become more restricted.

Limitation of extra-convent activities served to minimize the financial needs of sisters above subsistence, and the greater scope of action viewed as appropriate for male church workers was used to justify wage differentials between men and women. The economic constraints facing women's communities no doubt contributed to the stringency of the rules regulating their members' behavior. Aware of increasing costs, inflexible salary scales, and falling real incomes, community superiors were unable to press for modification of regulations inhibiting sisters' activities. Thus occurred a widening of differences between norms of behavior acceptable for sisters and laywomen. The clearest evidence of the importance of financial considerations is the imposition by Church authorities from without of many regulations with little observable "religious" significance. In the early years of the period, to take but one example, travel among convents and to the homes of relatives was not uncommon in some communities. But by 1890, an ecclesiastical authority was on record as disapproving of sisters' leaving the convent for visiting or shopping. A decade later, social visiting and visits to the sick were curtailed. By the close of the period, social visits of any kind by sisters were enjoined by the cardinal unless specific permission were obtained for each visit.[37] By 1940, therefore, sisters were limited in mobility to convent, church, and school, while their lay counterparts were moving into new arenas.

In their professional activities, sisters were even more restricted. Anonymity and self-effacement, rarely demanded of their male colleagues in church service, were carried to extremes. At the July 1909 convention of the Catholic Education Association in Boston, for example, a paper written by a Sister of Notre Dame was read for her by a priest.[38] Such restrictions abounded and discouraged professional participation.

Although the activities of sisters were generally restricted, Massachusetts sisters were particularly affected after 1907. William O'Connell's views on women's place, set forth earlier, were evident in his dealings with communities of sisters. In his analysis, their financial straits resulted from inept and inefficient management by women. As an example of the problems these groups presented for him on his arrival in Boston, he cited the motherhouse and convents of the Sisters of St. Joseph which, he maintained, were "floundering about in a very precarious moral and financial condition."[39] Yet most members of this community were employed in parochial schools, lived in parish-owned convents, and had no control over their salaries. O'Connell never conceded that low salaries might have occasioned some of the financial difficulties faced by sisters. Rather, the charge of incompetence was used repeatedly to justify tighter control over communities of women. Consultation was required on minor as well as major matters throughout his 36-year tenure. His approach was described with pride in his autobiography:

> After removal of the old Superior, the new one who took her place received the clearest and minutest instructions which to this day she has carefully and docilely executed. . . . The whole management and control . . . was put under close supervision and direction, with the result that the institution today, once nearly swamped in debt, is financially perfectly sound, while the real work of the institution . . . is incomparably more capably and efficiently accomplished.[40]

While there were instances of mismanagement in women's as in other communities, the methods of rectifying it showed little regard for the sisters. Under canon law, the bishop had the right to intervene in a range of areas affecting women. But the exercise of heavy control over their internal as well as external affairs prevented any steps toward self-determination for decades. Although churchmen did not escape his paternalistic approach,[41] O'Connell viewed women's communities as especially needing clerical supervision and direction.

The expansion of the parochial schools in Boston after the Council of 1884 had little effect on the numbers of churchmen, their rate of increase, or their choice of work. But it had dramatic implications for the lives of the labor force that staffed the schools. After that date, the control of women's communities over their work and the institutions in which they worked eroded. The sudden and exogenously ordered expansion in a major occupation of sisters created serious problems, especially in Massachusetts, a state which prior to 1884 had moved slowly in response to directives in the matter of church schools. Responding to a special need of the church, young women joined teaching communities. At the same time, these communities were gradually losing much of the moderate control they possessed over the professional and social lives of their members.

If the school campaign had not occurred, parishes wanting church schools for their children would have opened them when they could afford them, and sisters could have expected to receive reasonable recompense. With adequate salary levels and enlightened leadership the communities would presumably have allowed their members to take advantage of professional opportunities and to move, as laywomen and male members of religious communities were doing, into a wider range of activities. Altogether, the quality of the sisters' work would have been enhanced.

The 1870–1940 period ended with Massachusetts sisters still concentrated in "women's work." Occupational segregation had even deepened in these years. While women in full-time church work in 1870 were well distributed over a range of occupations, by 1940 that variation and flexibility of choice were gone. Within women's occupations, the majority of sisters by 1940 were engaged in the teaching of young children.

## NOTES

1. See, for example, Maria Monk, *Awful Disclosures of Maria Monk* (New York: D. M. Bennett, 1878, originally written in 1836); Theodore Dwight, *Open Convents* (New York: Van Nostrand and Dwight, 1836); Edith O'Gorman, *Trials and Persecutions of Miss Edith O'Gorman* (Hartford: Connecticut Publishing, 1881); and Fred Hendrickson, *The "Black Convent" Slave or Nunnery Life Unveiled* (Toledo: Protestant Missionary Publishing, 1914).
2. The most complete history of the Catholic church in Boston is a good example: Robert H. Lord, John E. Sexton, and Edward T. Harrington, *History of the Archdiocese of Boston, in the Various Stages of its Development, 1604 to 1943,* 3 vols. (New York: Sheed and Ward, 1944).

3. Oscar Handlin, *Boston's Immigrants* (New York: Atheneum, 1968), 215–16; Barbara Miller Solomon, *Ancestors and Immigrants: A Changing New England Tradition* (Chicago: Univ. of Chicago Press, 1972).

4. Archives, Sisters of St. Joseph, Brighton, Mass., *Motherhouse Annals*, Aug. 10, 1919.

5. Jay P. Dolan, *The Immigrant Church* (Baltimore: Johns Hopkins Univ. Press, 1975), Table 3, 106; and Louis S. Walsh, *Historical Sketch of the Growth of Catholic Parochial Schools in the Archdiocese of Boston* (Newton: St. John's Industrial School, 1901), Appendix 6. It should be noted that parochial schools were rarely large enough to accommodate all the parish childen.

6. *Special Report of the Diocese to the Office of the Propaganda*, Jan. 11, 1879, in answer to a letter of June 1878. Cited by Donna Merwick, *Boston Priests, 1848–1910* (Cambridge: Harvard Univ. Press, 1973), 102.

7. Merwick, *Boston Priests*, 111–16.

8. Mary A. Dowd, "The Public Rights of Women," *Catholic World*, 59 (June 1894), 312–20.

9. *Sermons and Addresses of His Eminence William Cardinal O'Connell* (Boston: Pilot Publishing, 1931), Vol. 10:226, and Vol. 5:126.

10. William Seton, "The Higher Education of Woman and Posterity," *Catholic World*, 73 (Apr. 1901), 149.

11. Document No. 87, *Report of A Study of Certain Phases of the Public School System of Boston, Mass.* (Boston Finance Commission, 1916), from Table 2, 129, Table 3, 130–31, and Table 7, 137–38.

12. Richard M. Bernard and Maris A. Vinovskis, "The Female School Teacher in Ante-Bellum Massachusetts," *Journal of Social History*, 10 (Spring 1977), 333.

13. John Paul MacCorrie, "The War of the Sexes," *Catholic World*, 63 (Aug. 1896), 614.

14. Walsh, *Historical Sketch*, 3–4.

15. A Member of the Congregation, *The American Foundations of the Sisters of Notre Dame de Namur, Compiled from the Annals of Their Convents* (Philadelphia: Dolphin, 1928), 363.

16. *General Regulations of the Public Schools*, Boston, Jan. 1869, 61.

17. Sisters Helen Nugent, *Sister Louise: American Foundress of the Sisters of Notre Dame* (Washington: Catholic University of America Studies in American Church History, Vol. 10, Diss. 1931), 193.

18. Bernard and Vinovskis, "Female School Teacher," 337.

19. Charles Phillips Huse, *The Financial History of Boston, 1822–1909* (Cambridge: Harvard Univ. Press, 1916), Appendix 1, 365; and School Document No. 1, 1920, *Annual Report for the Financial Year Ending January 31, 1920*, School Committee of the City of Boston, 60–61.

20. School Document No. 7, 1929, *Annual Report of the Superintendent, 1929*, 86; School Document No. 15, 1909, *Annual Report of the School Committee of the City of Boston, 1909*, 39; and John Koren, *Boston, 1822 to 1922* (Boston: Printing Dept., 1922), 107.

21. Louise Marion Bosworth, *The Living Wage of Women Workers*, Supplement to the *Annals of the American Academy of Political and Social Science* (May 1911), 11. A similar estimate was provided for 1915 by Lucile Eaves, *The Food of Working Women in Boston*, Massachusetts State Department of Health (Boston: Wright and Potter, 1917), 99.

22. Eaves, *Food of Working Women*, 80.

23. Archives of the Sisters of St. Joseph, *Motherhouse Annals*, Sept. 4 and Sept. 16, 1924. This was an appeal for a *cash* stipend of $300.

24. Archives of the Sisters of St. Joseph, *Motherhouse Annals*, June 15, 1929.

25. Solomon, *Ancestors and Immigrants*, 48–55, provides a good survey of the varied reactions of Protestants to the schools. See also *Address of Archbishop Williams to the Catholic Union of Boston*, Mar. 12, 1891.

26. *The Sacred Heart Review*, Sept. 6, 1890, 1.

27. *The Sacred Heart Review*, Sept. 3, 1892, 9.

28. Ibid., Feb. 22, 1890, 5.

29. Ibid., Oct. 4, 1890, 14.

30. O'Hara, *Educational Contribution*, 8. Walsh, *Historical Sketch*, Appendix 4, 11, reports that in 1900, 17 percent of parochial schools were located in convents and church basements.

31. W. W. Parsons, "The Normal School Curriculum," *National Educational Association Proceedings, 1890* (Topeka: Kansas Publishing, 1890), 718–24.

32. For example, an 1899 graduate of Mt. St. Joseph Academy in Brighton returned to her alma mater as a sister and a faculty member two years later. Sister Mary Catherine, *History of*

*the Sisters of St. Joseph,* unpublished manuscript, Archives of the Sisters of St. Joseph, no date, 102, 118. The period covered by this manuscript is 1873–1914.

33. The new teachers who were, in fact, subject to the examination requirement included only lay teachers and sisters in diocesan communities. James A. Burns, "The Development of Parish School Organization," *Catholic Educational Review,* 3 (May 1912), 424.

34. Letter of Sister M. Regis to Rt. Rev. J. Laughlin, Dec. 31, 1879, Archives of the Sisters of St. Joseph. The instructor referred to was Professor Larkin Dunton, Headmaster of the Boston Normal School. See also *Just Passing Through,* 34–35.

35. Letter of Rev. William Byrne, Vicar General, to Mother M. Regis, Nov. 30, 1889, and Letter of Father Magennis to Mother Mary Genevieve, Aug. 24, 1901, Archives of the Sisters of St. Joseph.

36. *Motherhouse Annals,* Jan. 29, 1923, Archives of the Sisters of St. Joseph.

37. *Motherhouse Annals,* various years in the 1880s; July 21, 1890; Apr. 10, 1903; Sept. 21, 1935, Archives of the Sisters of St. Joseph.

38. *The American Foundations of the Sisters of Notre Dame de Namur,* 218.

39. William Cardinal O'Connell, *Recollections of Seventy Years* (Boston: Houghton Mifflin, 1934), 270.

40. O'Connell, *Recollections,* 279, referring to the Sisters of the Good Shepherd, Roxbury, Mass.

41. See O'Connell, *Recollections,* 273, and Merwick, *Boston Priests,* 188–96.

# 9

# Discontented Black Feminists: Prelude and Postscript to the Passage of the Nineteenth Amendment

## Rosalyn Terborg-Penn

*Although numerous black leaders and organizations were counted among the supporters of woman suffrage, Rosalyn Terborg-Penn describes widespread discontent among black feminists at the suffrage movement's accommodation to racism among white voters. With the achievement of suffrage, black women found their right to vote frequently denied in southern states with little response on the part of white suffragists. As a result of continuing racial discrimination, black feminists increasingly focused on race issues in the 1920s and after. A predominantly white feminist movement that turned a blind eye to racial discrimination had little appeal for black feminists. These women organized primarily on behalf of their race, a stance that reflected a reasonable appraisal of the realities of power in the United States in the interwar years.*

A significant number of black women and black women's organizations not only supported woman suffrage on the eve of the passage of the Nineteenth Amendment but attempted to exercise their rights to vote immediately after the amendment's passage in 1920. Unfortunately for them, black women confronted racial discrimination in their efforts to support the amendment and to win the vote. Consequently, discontented black feminists anticipated the disillusionment that their white counterparts encountered after 1920. An examination of the problems black women faced on the eve of the passage of the woman suffrage amendment and the hostility black women voters endured after the amendment passed serves as a preview of their political status from 1920 to 1945.

The way in which black women leaders dealt with these problems reveals the unique nature of feminism among Afro-American women. Black feminists could not overlook the reality of racism and class conflict as determining factors in the lives of women of their race. Hence, black feminists of the post-World War I era exhibited characteristics similar to those of black feminists of the woman suffrage era and of the late nineteenth-century black women's club movement. During each era, these feminists could not afford to dismiss class or race in favor of sex as the major cause of oppression among black women.

This material originally appeared in *DECADES OF DISCONTENT: The Women's Movement, 1920–1940*, Lois Scharf and Joan M. Jensen, eds. (Contributions in Women's Studies, No. 28, Greenwood Press, Westport, CT, 1983), pp. 261–78. Copyright © 1983 by Lois Scharf & Joan M. Jensen. Abridged and reprinted with permission.

PRELUDE TO PASSAGE
OF THE NINETEENTH AMENDMENT

On the eve of the passage of the Nineteenth Amendment, black women leaders could be counted among other groups of women who had worked diligently for woman suffrage. At least ninety black women leaders endorsed woman suffrage, with two-thirds of these women giving support during the decade immediately before passage of the amendment. Afro-American women organized suffrage clubs, participated in rallies and demonstrations, spoke on behalf of the amendment, and wrote essays in support of the cause. These things they had done since the inception of the nineteenth-century woman's rights movement. However, the largest woman suffrage effort among black women's groups occurred during the second decade of the twentieth century. Organizations such as the National Federation of Afro-American Women, the National Association of Colored Women (NACW), the Northeastern Federation of Colored Women's Clubs, the Alpha Kappa Alpha Sorority, and the Delta Sigma Theta Sorority actively supported woman suffrage. These organizations were national or regional in scope and represented thousands of Afro-American women. Some of the women were from the working class, but most of them were of middle-class status. Across the nation, at least twenty black women suffrage organizations or groups that strongly endorsed woman suffrage existed during the period.[1] . . .

The enthusiastic responses of black women to woman suffrage may seem astonishing when one realizes that woman suffrage was a predominantly middle-class movement among native born white women and that the black middle class was very small during the early twentieth century. Furthermore, the heyday of the woman suffrage movement embraced an era that historian Rayford Logan called "the nadir" in Afro-American history, characterized by racial segregation, defamation of the character of black women, and lynching of black Americans, both men and women. It is a wonder that Afro-American women dared to dream a white man's dream—the right to enfranchisement—especially at a time when white women attempted to exclude them from that dream.[2] . . .

The existence of a double standard for black and white women among white woman suffragists was apparent to black women on the eve of Nineteenth Amendment passage. Apprehensions from discontented black leaders about the inclusion of black women as voters, especially in the South, were evident throughout the second decade of the twentieth century. During the early years of the decade, black suffragists such as Adella Hunt Logan, a club leader and suffragist from Tuskegee, Alabama; Mary B. Talbert, president of the National Association of Colored Women; and Josephine St. Pierre Ruffin, a suffragist since the 1880s from Boston and the editor of the *Woman's Era*, a black women's newspaper, complained about the double standard in the woman suffrage movement and insisted that white suffragists set aside their prejudices to allow black women, burdened by both sexism and racism, to gain political equality.[3]

Unfortunately, with little influence among white women, the black suffragists were powerless and their words went unheeded. By 1916 Carrie Catt, president of the NAWSA, concluded that the South had to be conciliated if woman suffrage was to become a reality. Thus, in order to avoid antagonizing southern white women who resented participating in the association with black women, she urged southern white delegates not to attend the NAWSA convention in Chicago that year because the Chicago delegation would be mostly black.[4]

The trend to discriminate against black women as voters continued, and in 1917 the *Crisis*, the official organ of the National Association for the Advancement of Colored People (NAACP), noted that blacks feared white female voters because of their antiblack woman suffrage and antiblack male sentiments. Afro-American fears went beyond misgivings about white women. In 1918 the editors of the *Houston Observer* responded to black disillusionment when they called upon the men and women of the race to register to vote in spite of the poll tax, which was designed especially to exclude black voters.[5]

Skepticism about equality of woman suffrage among blacks continued. Mrs. A. W. Blackwell, an African Methodist Episcopal Church leader in Atlanta, estimated that about 3 million black women were of voting age. She warned, however, that a "grandmother clause" would be introduced after passage of a suffrage amendment to prevent black women, 90 percent of whom lived in the South, from voting.[6]

Disillusionment among black suffragists became so apparent that several national suffrage leaders attempted to appease them with reassurances about their commitment to black woman suffrage. In 1917 Carrie Catt and Anna Shaw wooed black female support through the pages of the *Crisis*. In the District of Columbia, the same year, Congresswoman Jeanette Rankin of Montana addressed an enthusiastic group of Alpha Kappa Alpha Sorority women at Howard University. There she assured the group that she wanted all women to be given the ballot regardless of race.[7]

However, in 1917 while the New York state woman suffrage referendum was pending in the legislature, black suffragists in the state complained of discrimination against their organizations by white suffragists during the statewide woman suffrage convention at Saratoga. White leaders assured black women that they were welcomed in the movement. Although the majority of the black delegates were conciliated, a vocal minority remained disillusioned.[8]

By 1919, the year before the Nineteenth Amendment was adopted by Congress, antiblack woman suffrage sentiments continued to plague the movement. Shortly before the amendment was adopted, several incidents occurred to further disillusion black feminists. Mary Church Terrell, a

Washington, D.C., educator and national leader among black club women, reported that white suffragists in Florida discriminated against black women in their attempts to recruit support for the campaign. In addition, the NAACP, whose policy officially endorsed woman suffrage, clashed with Alice Paul, president of the NWP because she allegedly said "that all this talk of Negro women voting in South Carolina was nonsense."[9] Later, Walter White, the NAACP's assistant to the executive secretary, complained to Mary Church Terrell about Alice Paul and agreed with Terrell that white suffrage leaders would be willing to accept the suffrage amendment even if it did not enfranchise black women.[10]

Within a week after receiving Walter White's letter, Mary Church Terrell received a letter from Ida Husted Harper, a leader in the suffrage movement and the editor of the last two volumes of the *History of Woman Suffrage*, asking Terrell to use her influence to persuade the Northeastern Federation of Colored Women's Clubs to withdraw their application seeking cooperative membership in the NAWSA. Echoing sentiments expressed earlier by NAWSA president Carrie Catt, Harper explained that accepting the membership of a black organization was inexpedient for NAWSA at a time when white suffragists sought the cooperation of white southern women. Harper noted that the major obstacle to the amendment in the South was fear among whites of the black woman's vote. She therefore asked federation president Elizabeth Carter to resubmit the membership application after the passage of the Nineteenth Amendment.[11] ...

During the last months before the passage of the Susan B. Anthony amendment, black suffragists had been rebuffed by both the conservative wing of the suffrage movement, the NAWSA, and by the more radical wing, the NWP. Why then did Afro-American women continue to push for woman suffrage? Since the 1880s, most black women who supported woman suffrage did so because they believed that political equality among the races would raise the status of blacks, both male and female. Increasing the black electorate, they felt, would not only uplift the women of the race, but help the children and the men as well. The majority of the black suffragists were not radical feminists. They were reformers, or what William H. Chafe calls social feminists, who believed that the system could be amended to work for them. Like their white counterparts, these black suffragists assumed that the enfranchised held the key to ameliorating social ills. But unlike white social feminists, many black suffragists called for social and political measures that were specifically tied to race issues. Among these issues were antimiscegenation legislation, jim crow legislation, and "lynch law." Prominent black feminists combined the fight against sexism with the fight against racism by continuously calling the public's attention to these issues.[12] ...

Blacks understood the potential political influence, if not political power, that they could harness with woman suffrage, especially in the South. White supremacists realized it too. Although there were several reasons for southern opposition to the Nineteenth Amendment, the one common to all states was fear of black female suffrage. This fear had been stimulated by the way in which Afro-American women responded to suffrage in states that had achieved woman suffrage before the passage of the federal amendment. In northern states with large black populations, such as Illinois and New York, the black female electorate was significant. Chicago elected its first black alderman, Oscar De Priest, in 1915, the year after women won the right to vote. In 1917, the year the woman suffrage referendum passed the New York state legislature, New York City elected its first black state assemblyperson, Edward A. Jonson. In both cities the black female vote was decisive in the election. In the South, Texas Afro-American women mobilized in 1918 to effectively educate the women of their race in order to combat white opposition to their voting.[13]

By 1920 white southern apprehensions of a viable black female electorate were not illusionary. "Colored women voter's leagues" were growing throughout the South, where the task of the leagues was to give black women seeking to qualify to vote instructions for countering white opposition. Leagues could be found in Alabama, Georgia, Tennessee, and Texas. These groups were feared also by white supremacists because the women sought to qualify black men as voters as well.[14]

Whites widely believed that black women wanted the ballot more than white women in the South. Black women were expected to register and to vote in larger numbers than white women. If this happened, the ballot would soon be returned to black men. Black suffrage, it was believed, would also result in the return of the two-party system in the South, because blacks would consistently vote Republican. These apprehensions were realized in Florida after the passage of the Nineteenth Amendment. Black women in Jacksonville registered in greater numbers than white women. In reaction, the Woman Suffrage League of Jacksonville was reorganized into the Duval County League of Democratic Women Voters. The members were dedicated to maintain white supremacy and pledged to register white women voters.[15]

In Texas, where women could vote before the passage of the Nineteenth Amendment, black women, nevertheless, were discriminated against. In 1918 six black women had been refused the right to register at Fort Worth on the ground that the primaries were open to white Democrats only. Efforts to disfranchise black women in Houston failed, however, when the women took legal action against the registrars who attempted to apply the Texas woman suffrage law to white women only. A similar attempt to disqualify Afro-American women in Waxahachie, Texas, failed also.[16]

Subterfuge and trickery such as the kind used in Texas was being used throughout the South by 1920. In North Carolina, the predictions of Mrs. A. W. Blackwell came true when the state legislature introduced a bill known as the "grandmother clause" for women voters. The bill attempted to protect illiterate white women from disfranchisement, but the legislators had not taken into account that "grandfather clauses" had been nullified by the Supreme Court. Nonetheless, black leaders called to the women of the race to stand up and fight. This they did.[17]

In 1920 black women registered in large numbers throughout the South, especially in Georgia and Louisiana, despite major obstacles placed against them by the white supremacists. In defense, Afro-American women often turned to the NAACP for assistance. Field Secretary William Pickens was sent to investigate the numerous charges and recorded several incidents which he either witnessed personally or about which he received reports. In Columbia, South Carolina, during the first day of registration black women apparently took the registrars by surprise. No plan to disqualify them had been put into effect. Many black women reported to the office and had to wait for hours while the white women were registered first. Some women waited up to twelve hours to register. The next day, a $300 tax requirement was made mandatory for black women. If they passed that test, the women were required to read from and to interpret the state or the federal constitutions. No such tests were required of white women. In addition, white lawyers were on hand to quiz and harass black women. Although the *Columbia State*, a local newspaper, reported disinterest in registering among black women, Pickens testified to the contrary. By the end of the registration period, twenty Columbia black women had signed an affidavit against the registrars who had disqualified them. In the surrounding Richland County, Afro-American women were disqualified when they attempted to register to vote. As a result, several of them made plans to appeal the ruling.[18]

Similar reports came from Richmond, Virginia, where registrars attempted to deny or successfully denied black women the right to register. A black woman of Newburn, North Carolina, signed an affidavit testifying to the difficulty she had in attempting to register. First she was asked to read and to write the entire state constitution. After successfully reading the document, she was informed that no matter what else she did, the registrar would disqualify her because she was black. Many cases like this one were handled by the NAACP, and after the registration periods ended in the South, its board of directors presented the evidence to Congress. NAACP officials and others testified at a congressional hearing in support of the proposed enactment of the Tinkham Bill to reduce representation in Congress from states where there was restriction of woman suffrage. White supremacy prevailed, however, as southern congressmen successfully claimed that blacks were not disfranchised, just disinterested in voting. Hence, despite the massive evidence produced by the NAACP, the Tinkham Bill failed to pass.[19]

The inability of the NAACP to protect the rights of black women voters led the women to seek help from national woman suffrage leaders. However, these attempts failed also. The NWP leadership felt that since black women were discriminated against in the same ways as black men, their problems were not woman's rights issues, but race issues. Therefore, the woman's party felt no obligation to defend the rights of black women.[20]

That they would be abandoned by white female suffragists in 1920 came as no surprise to most black women leaders. The preceding decade of woman suffrage politics had reminded them of the assertions of black woman suffrage supporters of the past. Frederick Douglass declared in 1868 that black women were victimized mainly because they were blacks, not because they were women. Frances Ellen Watkins Harper answered in 1869 that for white women the priorities in the struggle for human rights were sex, not race. By 1920 the situation had changed very little, and many black suffragists had been thoroughly disillusioned by the machinations of the white feminists they had encountered.[21]

## POSTSCRIPT—BLACK FEMINISTS, 1920–1945

Afro-American Women continued to be involved in local and national politics during the post-World War I years. However, few organized feminist activities were apparent among the disillusioned black feminists of the period. Afro-American women leaders and their organizations began to focus on issues that continued to plague both the men and women of the race, rather than upon issues that concerned white feminists. The economic plight of black women kept most of them in poverty and among the lowest of the working classes. Middle-class black women were still relatively few in number. They were more concerned about uplifting the downtrodden of the race or in representing people of color throughout the world than in issues that were limited to middle-class feminists. Hence, during the 1920s there was little concern among black women over the Equal Rights Amendment debate between the more conservative League of Women Voters (LWV) and the more radical NWP. Although the economic roles of many white American women were expanding, the status of black women remained basically static between the wars. As a result, black feminists identified more with the plight of third world people who found themselves in similar oppressed situations. Former black suffragists were more likely to participate in the Women's International League for Peace and Freedom (WILPF) or the International Council of Women of the Darker Races than in the LWV or the NWP.

A look at the 1920s reveals that most of the black women's organizations that were prominent during the woman suffrage era remained so. Nonetheless, new groups were organized as well. Elizabeth Carter remained president of the Northeastern Federation of Colored Women's Clubs, which celebrated its twenty-fifth anniversary in 1921. The leadership of the NACW was in transition during the 1920s. Mary B. Talbert retired as president and was succeeded by a former suffragist, Hallie Q. Brown, in 1922. In the middle of the decade Mary McLeod Bethune assumed the presidency. In 1922 several NACW leaders organized the International Council of Women of the Darker Races. Margaret Murray Washington, the wife of the late Booker T. Washington and the first president of the National Federation of Afro-American Women, was elected president.[22]

In addition to these established black women's organizations, there was the women's arm of Marcus Garvey's United Negro Improvement Association (UNIA). At its peak, in 1925, the UNIA had an estimated membership of 2 million and can be considered the first mass movement among working-class black people in the nation. Amy Jacques Garvey, Marcus Garvey's wife, was the articulate leader of the women's division and the editor of the women's department of the UNIA official newspaper, *Negro World*. A feminist in the international sense, Amy Jacques Garvey's feminist views embraced the class struggle as well as the problems of Third World women. . . . Garvey called for black women's dedication to social justice and to national liberation, abroad as well as at home.[23]

Garvey was a radical who happened to be a feminist as well. Her views were ahead of her time; thus, she would have fit in well with the midtwentieth century radical feminists. However, the demise of the UNIA and the deportation of Marcus Garvey in 1927 shattered much of Amy Jacques Garvey's influence in the United States and she returned to Jamaica. In the meantime, the majority of black feminists of the 1920s either joined the white social feminists, such as Jane Addams and the WILPF, or bypassed the feminists altogether to deal with race issues within black organizations.

The leadership of the WILPF was old-line and can be characterized as former progressives, woman suffragists, and social feminists. Jane Addams presided over the organization before U.S. entry into World War I and brought black women such as Mary Church Terrell, Mary B. Talbert, Charlotte Atwood, Mary F. Waring, and Addie W. Hunton into the fold. Terrell had been a member of the executive committee since 1915. As a league representative, she was elected a delegate to the International Congress of Women held in Paris in 1919. Upon her arrival, Terrell was impressed with the conference delegates but noticed that there were none from nonwestern countries and that she was the only delegate of color in the group. As a result, she felt obliged to represent the women of all the nonwhite countries in the world, and this she attempted to do. . . . Terrell's position and thinking were in keeping with the growing awareness among black women leaders in the United States that Third World people needed to fight oppression together.[24]

Although Mary Church Terrell remained an active social feminist, her public as well as her private views reflected the disillusionment of black feminists of the woman suffrage era. In 1921 she was asked by members of the WILFP executive committee to sign a petition requesting the removal of black troops from occupied German territory, where they were alleged to be violating German women. Terrell refused to sign the petition because she felt the motives behind it were racist. In a long letter to Jane Addams, the executive committee chairman, Terrell explained why she would not sign the petition. She noted that Carrie Catt had investigated the charges against the black troops and found them to be unfounded. The troops, from French colonies in Africa, were victims, Terrell contended, of American propaganda against black people. Making a dramatic choice between the feminist organization position and her own loyalty to her race, Terrell offered to resign from the executive committee. Addams wrote her back, agreeing with Terrell's position and asking her not to resign.[25] In this case, when given the choice between the politics of feminism and race pride, Terrell felt that her energies were needed most to combat racism, and she chose to take a nationalist position in the controversy....

[In the 1920s] most black women's organizations had turned from attempts to establish coalitions with white women's groups to concentrate upon pressing race problems. Lynching was one of the major American problems, and black women organized to fight it. On the national front, black women's groups used political strategies and concentrated their efforts toward passage of the Dyer Anti-Lynching Bill. In 1922 the Northeastern Federation of Colored Women's Clubs appointed a delegation to call on Senator Lodge of Massachusetts to urge passage of the Dyer bill. In addition, the Alpha Kappa Alpha Sorority held its national convention in Indianapolis and sent a telegram to President Warren Harding urging the support of his administration in the passage of the bill. Also that year, the NACW met in Richmond and appointed an antilynching delegation to make contact with key states needed for the passage of the Dyer bill in Congress. In addition, the delegation was authorized to meet with President Harding. Among the black women in the delegation were veteran antilynching crusader Ida B. Wells-Barnett, NACW president Hallie Q. Brown, and Rhode Island suffragist Mary B. Jackson.[26]

Perhaps the most renowned antilynching crusader of the 1920s was Spingarn Medal winner Mary B. Talbert. In 1922 she organized an executive committee of 15 black women, who supervised over 700 state workers across the nation in what Talbert called the Anti-Lynching Crusade. Her aim was to "unite a million women to stop lynching," by arousing the consciences of both black and white women. One of Talbert's strategies was to provide statistics that showed that victims of lynching were not what propagandists called sex-hungry black men who preyed upon innocent white women. The crusaders revealed that eighty-three women had been lynched in the United States since Ida B. Wells-Barnett had compiled the first comprehensive annual report in 1892. The Anti-Lynching Crusade was truly an example of woman power, for the crusaders believed that they could not wait for the men of America to stop the problem. It was perhaps the most influential link in the drive for interracial cooperation among women's groups. As a result of its efforts, the 1922 National Council of Women, representing 13 million American women, resolved to "endorse the Anti-Lynching Crusade recently launched by colored women of this country."[27]

Although the Dyer bill was defeated, it was revised by the NAACP and introduced again in the House of Representatives by Congressman Leonidas C. Dyer of Missouri and in the Senate by William B. McKinley of Illinois in 1926. That year the bill failed again, as did similar bills in 1935, 1940, and 1942. However, it was the effort of blacks and white women organized against lynching that pressed for legislation throughout the period. Without a doubt, it was the leadership of black women, many of whom had been active in the late nineteenth-century women's club movement and in the woman suffrage movement, who motivated white women in 1930 to organize the Association of Southern Women for the Prevention of Lynching. Although a federal antilynching bill never passed the Congress, by the end of the 1940s public opinion had been sufficiently convinced by the efforts of various women's groups that lynching was barbarous and criminal. Recorded incidents of lynching ceased by 1950.

Even though interracial cooperation in the antilynching campaign was a positive factor among black and white women, discrimination against black women by white women continued to plague feminists. In 1925, for example, the Quinquennial of the International Council of Women met at the Washington Auditorium in the District of Columbia. The council sought the cooperation of NACW president Mary McLeod Bethune and arrangements were made to have a mass choir of black women perform. The night of the concert, black guests were placed in a segregated section of the auditorium. Mary Church Terrell reported that when the singers learned of what was happening, they refused to perform.[28] ...

National recognition of black women did not really come until 1936, when Mary McLeod Bethune was appointed director of the Division of Negro Affairs, National Youth Administration, under the Franklin D. Roosevelt administration. The founder of Bethune-Cookman Institute in Daytona, Florida, Bethune had been a leader in the black women's club movement since the early 1920s. NACW president from 1924 to 1928, she founded the National Council of Negro Women (NCNW) in 1935. What feminist consciousness Bethune acquired was thrust upon her in the mid-1930s because for the first time, a black woman had the ear of the president of the United States and the cooperation of the first lady, who was concerned not only about women's issues, but about black issues. In 1936 Bethune took advantage of her new status and presented the concerns of the NCNW to Eleanor Roosevelt. As a result, sixty-five black women leaders attended a meeting with Eleanor Roosevelt to argue the case for their greater representation and appointments to federal bureaus. They called for appointments of professional black women to the Children's Bureau, the Women's Bureau, and each department of the Bureau of Education that dealt with the welfare of women and children. The NCNW also wanted the appointment of black women to administrative positions in the Federal Housing Administration and Social Security Board. In addition, they called for enlarging the black staff of the Bureau of Public Health and for President Roosevelt to suggest to the American Red Cross that they hire a black administrator.[29]

The NCNW requests reflect two trends among middle-class women in the mid-1930s. First, they were calling for positions that black women had never held, nor would achieve until a generation later; consequently, their ideas were revolutionary ones in terms of federal policies. Second, they were calling for policies to benefit not only their sex, but their race; hence, the NCNW reflected the position established by black feminists a generation before.

Middle-class black women clearly reflected their dedication to uplifting the race at a time when most Afro-Americans were thwarted not only by race prejudice but also by economic depression. Although activities that involved race uplift were not feminist in orientation, many black feminists took an active role in them. In an interview with Mary McLeod Bethune in 1939, Lillian B. Huff of the *New Jersey Herald News* asked her about the role of black women leaders and how Bethune related to her leadership position. Bethune, who had come from humble origins, felt that black women had room in their lives to be wives and mothers as well as to have careers. But most importantly, she thought, black women should think of their duty to the race.[30]

Bethune's feelings were not unique to black women, for most black feminists and leaders had been wives and mothers who worked yet found time not only to struggle for the good of their sex, but for their race. Until the 1970s, however, this threefold commitment—to family and to career and to one or more social movements—was not common among white women. The key to the uniqueness among black feminists of this period appears to be their link with the past. The generation of the woman suffrage era had learned from their late nineteenth-century foremothers in the black women's club movement, just as the generation of the post-World War I era had learned and accepted the experiences of the preceding generation. Theirs was a sense of continuity, a sense of group consciousness that transcended class. Racial uplift, fighting segregation and mob violence, contending with poverty, as well as demanding rights for black women were long-standing issues of concern to black feminists. . . .

By 1940 Mary Church Terrell had written her autobiography. At the age of seventy-seven, she was one of the few living links with three generations of black feminists. In her introduction, Terrell established her own interpretation of her life story, which in many ways reflected the lives of other black feminists. "This is the story of a colored woman living in a white world. It cannot possibly be like a story written by a white woman. A white woman has only one handicap to overcome—that of sex. I have two—both sex and race. I belong to the only group in this country which has two such huge obstacles to surmount. Colored men have only one—that of race."[31]

Terrell's reference to her status as an Afro-American woman applied throughout United States history to most black women, regardless of class. In view of this, it is not surprising that black women struggled, often in vain, to keep the right to vote from 1920 to 1940. A brief reference to this struggle, a story in itself, reveals that they fought to keep the little influence they had although black feminists anticipated that many of them would lose. Nonetheless, black female enthusiasm was great immediately following passage of the Nineteenth Amendment. In Baltimore alone, the black electorate increased from 16,800 to over 37,400 in 1921, indicating that the number of black women voters surpassed the number of black men registered to vote. By 1922, however, attempts to thwart the influence of black women voters were spreading across the South. As a result, the NACW recommended that all of its clubs lobby for the enforcement of the Nineteenth Amendment.[32]

By 1924 feminist Nannie Burroughs had assessed the status of black women of voting age and their relationship to white feminists. Burroughs noted that white women continued to overlook or to undervalue the worth of black women as a political force in the nation. She warned white female politicians to tap the potential black female electorate before white men exploited it.[33] With the exception of Ruth Hanna McCormick, who recruited Mary Church Terrell to head her 1929 Illinois campaign for the United States Senate, warnings such as Burrough's did not seem to influence white female leaders. For example, disillusioned members of the Republican Colored Women State Committee of Wilmington, Delaware, protested unsuccessfully when they lost their representation on the state Republican committee. A merger of the Women's Advisory Committee, a white group, with the State Central Committee had caused the elimination of black women representatives. The decline in black women's participation in Republican party politics was evident by 1928, when only 8 out of 104 black delegates to the Republican National Convention were women. The same year, the NACW program did not even bother to include suffrage among its priorities for women of the race.[34]

Although President Roosevelt made good his promise to Mary McLeod Bethune, so that by 1945 four black women had received outstanding federal appointments, the political viability of black women in the early 1940s was bleak. The list of black elected officials from 1940 to 1946 included no women.[35] Agents of white supremacy continued to subvert what vestiges of political influence blacks held. For example, in 1942 Congressman Martin Dies, chairman of the congressional committee investigating un-American activities, attempted to link several national black leaders to the Communist party. Among the group was Mary McLeod Bethune, who remained the only black woman prominent in national politics.[36]

Hence, over twenty years after the passage of the Nineteenth Amendment racial discrimination festered in most areas of American life, even among feminists and women in political life. Prejudice did not distinguish between middle-class and working-class black women, nor between feminists and nonfeminists who were black. Although black women continued to use what political rights they maintained, the small number of those politically viable made little impact upon public policies.

## NOTES

1. See Rosalyn Terborg-Penn, "Nineteenth Century Black Women and Woman Suffrage," *Potomac Review* 7 (Spring-Summer 1977): 13–24; and Rosalyn M. Terborg-Penn, "Afro-Americans in the Struggle for Woman Suffrage" (Ph.D. dissertation, Howard University, 1977), pp. 180–85.

2. See Rayford W. Logan, *The Negro in the United States* (Princeton, N.J.: Van Nostrand, 1957); and Terborg-Penn, "Discrimination Against Afro-American Women," pp. 17–27.

3. Terborg-Penn, "Afro-Americans in the Struggle for Woman Suffrage," chapter 4.

4. David Morgan, *Suffragists and Democrats: The Politics of Woman Suffrage in America* (East Lansing, Mich.: Michigan State University Press, 1972), pp. 106–07.

5. *Crisis* 15 (November 1917): 18; *Negro Year Book, 1918–1919*, p. 60.

6. Mrs. A. W. Blackwell, *The Responsibility and Opportunity of the Twentieth Century Woman* (n.p., n.d.), pp. 1–5. This pamphlet is housed in the Trevor Arnett Library, Atlanta University.

7. *The Crisis* 15 (November 1917): 19–20; *New York Age*, 10 May 1917.

8. *New York Age*, September 20, 1917.

9. Walter White to Mary Church Terrell, 14 March 1919, Mary Church Terrell Papers, Box no. 3, Library of Congress, Washington, D.C. (hereafter cited as MCT Papers); Charles Flint Kellogg, *NAACP: A History of the National Association for the Advancement of Colored People, 1909–1920* (Baltimore: Johns Hopkins Press, 1967), p. 208.

10. Walter White to Mary Church Terrell, 14 March 1919, MCT Papers, Box no. 3.

11. Ida Husted Harper to Mary Church Terrell, 18 March 1919, and Ida Harper to Elizabeth Carter, 18 March 1919, MCT Papers, Box no. 3.

12. Terborg-Penn, "Afro-Americans in the Struggle for Woman Suffrage," chapters 4 and 5.

13. *Ibid.*, pp. 207, 217–18, 225.

14. *Crisis* 19 (November 1920): 23–25; *Negro Year Book, 1921*, p. 40.

15. Kenneth R. Johnson, "White Racial Attitudes as a Factor in the Arguments Against the Nineteenth Amendment," *Phylon* 31 (Spring 1970): 31–32, 35–37.

16. Terborg-Penn, "Afro-Americans in the Struggle for Woman Suffrage," pp. 301–02.

17. *Ibid.*, pp. 303–04.

18. William Pickens, "The Woman Voter Hits the Color Line," *Nation* 3 (October 6, 1920): 372–73.

19. *Ibid.*, p. 373; NAACP, *Eleventh Annual Report of the NAACP for the Year 1920* (New York: NAACP, 1921), pp. 15, 25–30.

20. William L. O'Neill, *Everybody Was Brave* (Chicago: Quadrangle Press, 1969), p. 275.

21. Terborg-Penn, "Afro-Americans in the Struggle for Woman Suffrage," p. 311.

22. *Negro Year Book, 1922–24*, p. 37.

23. *The Negro World*, 24 October 1925, 5 March 1927. See Mark D. Matthews, " 'Our Women and What They Think,' Amy Jacques Garvey and *The Negro World*," *Black Scholar* 10 (May–June 1979): 2–13.

24. Mary Church Terrell, *A Colored Woman in a White World* (Washington, D.C.: Randsdell, Inc., 1940), pp. 330–33.

25. *Ibid.*, pp. 360–64.

26. *Ibid.*, pp. 37–38; *Crisis* 23 (March 1922): 218; *Crisis* 24 (October 1922): 260.

27. *Crisis* 24 (November 1922): 8.

28. Terrell, *A Colored Woman in a White World*, pp. 370–71.

29. Mary McLeod Bethune, Vertical File, Howard University, Washington, D.C., Clippings

Folder, 1930, *Black Dispatch*, 16 April 1936 (hereafter cited as Bethune Vertical File and the source).

30. Bethune Vertical File, *New Jersey Herald News*, 14 October 1939.

31. Terrell, *A Colored Woman in a White World*, first page of the introduction.

32. *Crisis* 23 (December 1921): 83; *Negro Year Book, 1922–24*, p. 37.

33. *Negro Year Book, 1922–24*, p. 70.

34. Terrell, *A Colored Woman in a White World*, pp. 355–56; *Negro Year Book, 1922–24*, p. 70; *Negro Year Book, 1931–32*, pp. 13, 92–93. Blacks did not vote the Democratic party on a large scale until the second Franklin D. Roosevelt administration.

35. *Negro Year Book, 1947*, pp. 286–87, 289–91.

36. Bethune Vertical File, *Black Dispatch*, 10 October 1942.

# 10
## The Professionalization of Birth Control
### Linda Gordon

*Reproductive rights have emerged as one of the most contested arenas of twentieth-century politi-*
*cal activity. Linda Gordon's account of Margaret Sanger's place in that struggle between 1914*
*and 1940 helps us understand the origin of many features of women's reproductive struggles*
*in the 1990s. Chief among these is the difficulty of advocating change through cross-class alli-*
*ances. In this chapter Gordon shows us how, through Sanger's support of the "Doctors-Only*
*Bill" in 1926, the medical profession gained the power it enjoys today in shaping the nation's*
*reproductive policies. Sanger's alliance with physicians and the medical profession's definition*
*of reproductive rights as the right to privacy set the stage for today's debate. In that debate the*
*rights of middle-class women to the privacy of their personal choice are rarely linked with the*
*rights of poor women to publicly funded reproductive choice.*

The socialists and sex radicals who began the birth-control movement
before the First World War were amateurs. With few exceptions, mostly
men, they had no professional or socially recognized expertise in sexology,
public health, demography, or any related fields. (If they were professionals
at anything, it was radical agitation!) They fought for birth control because
it was self-evidently in their own interest as women. The intellectual work
that had influenced them most in their birth-control views was philosophy,
radical ethics sometimes grounded in political appraisals of social problems. Birth control was, for them, pre-eminently a political and moral issue.

But after the war, the birth-control movement changed. The local birth-
control leagues with radical and socialist leadership lost their momentum.
Birth control became an increasingly centralized cause, dominated from
New York City by Sanger's American Birth Control League and Dennett's
Voluntary Parenthood League. The strategies that dominated—opening
clinics and lobbying for legislation—required large sums of money, and the
power of the wealthy in the organizations increased accordingly. People
accustomed to working in respectable, even elegant, charity organizations
joined the movement. Birth-control leagues began to sponsor balls and expensive white-tie dinners. Simultaneously the weakening of the organized
Left deprived the birth-control movement of leadership that might have
created alternative tactics and strategies. Respectable legal tactics produced
different results from militant law-defying ones. The latter attracted radicals
and angry, poor people; the former attracted more prosperous people,
those eager for reform but not desperately in need of fundamental social

Excerpted from Chapter 10 of *Woman's Body, Woman's Right: A Social History of Birth Control*
*in America* (New York: Grossman Publishers, 1976). Reprinted by permission of the author.
Notes have been renumbered.

*Margaret Sanger awaiting trial, 1916. Sophia Smith Collection, Smith College.*

change. It was not always possible for more conservative reformers to for-give birth control's early associations with bohemianism, radicalism, and illegality. In efforts to break those associations, birth-control organizers in the 1920s often condemned and publicly disassociated themselves from rad-icals.

The main factor behind this new conservatism of the birth-control movement was the entrance of professionals into the cause on a large scale. Professionalization was not the only important development in the birth-control cause in the 1920s, but it was the single most influential one. The professionals took over birth-control groups less often by driving out the radicals (though this did happen in a few places), than by joining a cause that radicals had deserted. For most socialists, the war itself, then the Rus-sian Revolution and the defense of the American Left against repression seemed more pressing issues from 1918 on.

The reason the radicals thought it politically correct to change their causes so quickly was that most of them had seen birth control as a reform issue rather than a revolutionary demand, something requiring less than fundamental change in the society. The tendency to distinguish between fundamental and superficial change, between revolution and reform, was characteristic of those influenced by a Marxist analysis of society. These Marxists argued that certain aspects of social reality determined others, and the prevalent Marxist interpretation had placed matters of sexual and re-productive relations in the "superstructure," among other cultural phenom-ena determined ultimately by the "base" (economic relations). In the post-war development of Marxism, rejection of the absolute distinction between "base" and "superstructure" has been an important theme. Contemporary Marxist feminism is reviving that critique of "vulgar," simplistic Marxism. In the World War I reform era it was already clear to many feminists that changes in sexual and reproduction patterns would produce far-reaching changes in daily life, class consciousness, and even class composition that could not be dismissed as "superstructure" and therefore not primary or urgent. But they could not, in that historical era, integrate this into a Marx-ism that then saw the world exclusively through the eyes of men.

Thus it was partly due to the flatness of the existing Marxism that many feminists were attracted to liberal reformers, who perceived birth con-trol as fundamental. Doctors saw it as a health measure, and naturally doc-tors viewed human health as a fundamental, not a superficial, condition of social progress. Eugenists' hereditarian views led them to consider repro-duction the fundamental condition of social progress. Therefore, members of both groups, once converted to the birth-control cause, devoted them-selves to it with passion and perseverance.

The leadership of Margaret Sanger was an important factor in facilitat-ing, even encouraging, the professionalization of the birth-control move-ment. Despite a tactical radicalism, which she learned from and shared with other socialists, Sanger's approach to birth control was distinguished by her willingness to make it her full-time, single cause. From her return from Europe to face trial for *The Woman Rebel* in 1915, until her trial for the illegal Brownsville clinic in 1917, an ambivalent political posture helped her to retain the support of many disparate political groups. She simultaneously pursued direct action and defiance of the law and, with a "low profile" on her radical ideas, organized financial and public-relations support from conservative and wealthy reformers. At the same time Sanger was preparing an organizational structure to give her ongoing power.

In the fall of 1916—even while she had been working on the Brownsville clinic—she founded the *Birth Control Review*. She recruited Frederick Blossom, a professional charity fund-raiser from Cleveland, to come to New York as its paid editor and manager.[1] In December she founded the New York Birth Control League (NYBCL) as an alternative to the National Birth Control League (NBCL), organized by Mary Ware Dennett, and Blossom also worked for Sanger's organization. An ugly disagreement and then split between Sanger and Blossom exploded in 1917. Whoever was in the right— and it seems likely both of them acted badly—the quarrel demonstrated Sanger's rigid need for personal control and separated her still further from the radical movement. Blossom quit when he could not have his way and took the records and small bank account of the *Review*. Sanger brought formal charges against him. Blossom had been a member of the Socialist party, and other socialists in the NYBCL were infuriated at Sanger's turning to the capitalist state to solve her quarrel; they formed an investigation committee which condemned Sanger and exonerated Blossom. Ironically, Blossom's subsequent behavior led the IWW to conduct another investigation in 1922 which condemned him for the break with Sanger.[2]

Whatever the actual issues involved, Sanger did not quail before the disapproval of her former socialist comrades. Ironically, some of them had defended Sanger's need for personal control on the grounds that she was trying to create a movement with radical politics. Dennett's NBCL had always excluded people identified with the far Left and avoided radical tactics like civil disobedience, and Sanger's radical reputation had arisen partly in being distinguished from Dennett. But even before the break with Blossom and his socialist supporters, Sanger had begun to move in another equally conservative direction, though it was not widely perceived as such at the time.

From the beginning of planning for her Brownsville clinic she had sought a doctor to prescribe and fit contraceptives. New York state law at the time would have permitted her to legalize the clinic by putting it under a physician's supervision, and this was an important part of her motivation. Section 1142 of the New York State Penal Code made it a misdemeanor to give out any contraceptive information, but section 1145 allowed lawfully practicing physicians to prescribe devices for the cure and prevention of disease. Sanger believed that this provision intended to allow only the pre-scription of prophylactic measures against venereal disease, and wanted to challenge and broaden its interpretation. But Sanger's conviction that con-traception required the attendance of a physician was based on a belief deeper then mere legal tactics. Since she was a nurse herself, it seems odd that she should have doubted that a nurse could fit a diaphragm as well as a doctor. Her earliest medical tutor, Dr. Johannes Rutgers of Holland, had taught her to fit a diaphragm; she herself fitted some of his patients while in The Hague. While she was there, Rutgers was training midwives in con-traceptive technique so that they could start birth-control clinics elsewhere.[3] Nevertheless, Sanger argued to the end of her career—even after laws no longer stood in her way—that every applicant for birth control should see a doctor. After the forcible closure of the clinic, Sanger quickly returned to the search for medical support for her work. As early as January 11, 1917, a year before Sanger was brought to trial for the Brownsville Clinic, her New York Birth Control League was urging modification of the laws to per-mit physicians only to give out birth-control information.[4] Dennett's NBCL, with its more respectable image, was nevertheless fighting for a more thor-oughgoing legislative reform—a bill simply removing birth control from any definition of obscenity.

Margaret Sanger's leadership was particularly responsible for making birth control a medical issue in the United States. In the 1920s she also courted recognition and support from another group of professionals—the demographers, geneticists, and other academics who led the eugenics movement. But in promoting professionals to increasing importance in the birth-control movement, Sanger just helped along a trend that would have happened without her. She was not responsible for the decline of the femi-nist movement, although her individualist and dominating style of working did not help to build solidarity with surviving feminist groups. She was not responsible for the repression, division, and shrinking of the socialist move-ment; her opportunist alliances with antisocialists and conservatives for the cause of birth control were partly necessitated by the refusal of male-dominated socialism to incorporate birth-control and women's liberation issues into their programs. All these factors plus the economic weakening of the working class created a political power vacuum where the socialists had been. Sanger did not wish to give up her birth-control campaign, nor could she fill that vacuum by herself; she had to find support. Sanger has often been criticized for her urge to dominate and her liking for power, weaknesses she clearly had. But not even she had the personal influence to substitute for a movement, or to articulate the needs of masses of American women when the masses were silent and depoliticized.

## DOCTORS

Despite the efforts made by pro-birth-control doctors in attacking sex-ual continence, most physicians remained opposed to contraception in the early 1920s. The predominant position among prestigious doctors was not merely disapproval but revulsion so hysterical that it prevented them from accepting facts. As late as 1925 Morris Fishbein, editor of the *Journal of the American Medical Association*, asserted that there were no safe and effective birth-control methods.[5] In 1926 Frederick McCann wrote that birth control had an insidious influence on the female, causing many ailments; and that although "biology teaches" that the primary purpose of the sexual act is to reproduce, the seminal fluid also has a necessary and healthful effect on the female.[6] Many doctors believed that they had a social and moral responsibility to fight the social degeneration that birth control represented. The social values underlying their opposition were often extremely conservative. ". . . fear of conception has been an important factor in the virtue of many unmarried girls, and . . . many boys are likewise kept straight by this means . . . the freedom with which this matter is now discussed . . . must have an unfortunate effect on the morals of our young people. It is particularly important . . . to keep such knowledge from our girls and boys, whose minds and bodies are not in a receptive frame for such information."[7] George Kosmak, a prominent gynecologist, attacked the birth controllers for their affiliations with anarchism and quackery. Although he acknowledged that physicians should have the right to prescribe contraception in those extraordinary cases in which it was necessary to save life, he reasserted that sexual abstinence ought to be the means of avoiding not only unwanted children but also deleterious sexual excess.

Physicians arguing for a higher valuation of human sexuality as an activity in itself had gained support by 1920, not only among radicals. A leading spokesman for this point of view among prestigious physicians was gynecologist Robert Latou Dickinson. He had used his medical expertise to comment on social problems for several decades previously. In 1902 he had written on masturbation, urging a less hysterical view of its dangers,[8] in 1895 he had defended women's bicycling against those who argued that it might foster the masturbation habit.[9] He believed that mutual sexual satisfaction was essential to happy marriage. As early as 1908 he was giving instruction in contraception as premarital advice to his private patients.[10]

Dickinson encouraged his Ob/Gyn colleagues to take greater initiatives as marriage and sex counselors. In his 1920 address as president of the American Gynecological Society he recommended that the group take an interest in sociological problems. He too disliked the radical and unscientific associations of the birth-control movement. But unlike Kosmak he preferred to respond not by ignoring the movement but by taking it over, and he urged his colleagues to that strategy as early as 1916.[11]

At first Dickinson and his physician supporters were hostile to the Sanger clinic. They tried to get Sanger and Dr. Dorothy Bocker, head of the Clinical Research Bureau, to accept the supervision of a panel of medical men, but failed. In 1925 Dickinson wrote a report scathingly critical of the value of Bocker's scientific work.[12] But several factors intervened to lessen this hostility and even bridge the gap between Sanger and the Committee on Maternal Health. One was the fact that the CMH clinic found it difficult to get enough patients with medical indications for contraception. The CMH insistence on avoiding publicity and open endorsement of birth control made women reluctant to try the clinic, anticipating rejection and/or moralistic condemnation of their desire for birth control. Furthermore, it was still extremely difficult to obtain diaphragms, which had to be smuggled into the country. By 1926 three years of work had produced only 124 incomplete case histories. Meanwhile Sanger's clinic saw 1655 patients in 1925 alone, with an average of three visits each.[13]

Another factor leading toward unity between the two clinics was Sanger's conciliatory, even humble, attitude toward Dickinson and other influential doctors. Her organization, the American Birth Control League, had been courting medical endorsement since its establishment in 1921. The League accumulated massive medical mailing lists, for example, and sent out reprints of pro-birth-control articles from medical journals.[14] Sanger's wealthy second husband paid a $10,000 yearly salary to a doctor, James F. Cooper, to tour the country speaking to medical groups for the ABCL.[15] Although even he was not immune from attacks as a quack,[16] he commanded the attention of male physicians as no woman agitator could ever have done. And Cooper's prestige was enhanced by his sharing the speakers' platform with prestigious European physicians at the International Birth Control Conference held in New York in 1925 under ABCL auspices. Indeed, the prestige of the Europeans—whose medical establishment was far more enlightened on the birth-control question than the American— was sufficient to entice the president of the AMA, William A. Pusey, to offer a lukewarm endorsement of birth control at that conference.[17] The ABCL kept exhaustive files, not only of letters but also from their clipping service, on every physician who appeared even mildly favorable to birth control. By 1927 they had 5484 names.[18] These were collected from the thousands all over the country who wrote asking the ABCL for help. The writers were asked for the names of doctors near them; the ABCL then wrote the doctors asking whether "it is your custom to give contraceptive advice in your regular course of practice, to those patients who in your judgment need it." The names of those who responded positively were then sent to applicants from their vicinity.[19]

In response to criticism of her clinic from the Dickinson group in 1925, Sanger, avoiding any defensive reaction, asked the Committee on Maternal Health to take over and run the clinic, hoping in return to be able to get licensing from the State Board of Charities. Dickinson demanded in return the removal of all propagandistic literature and posters, to which Sanger agreed. The scheme failed anyway, because Sanger's radical reputation and opposition from the Catholic Church led the State Board to refuse a license.[20] Dickinson, on the other hand, made his professional influence clear and useful to Sanger by procuring for her a $10,000 grant from the Rockefeller-backed Bureau of Social Hygiene.

Undoubtedly, the largest single factor drawing doctors into the birth-control movement, however, was Sanger's support for a "doctors-only" type of birth-control legislation. Sanger had apparently been strongly influenced by Judge Crane's 1918 decision in her trial for the Brownsville clinic. In it he had upheld her conviction under the New York State law on obscenity but suggested the possibility of a broad interpretation of section 1145 of the act which made an exception for physicians prescribing contraception for the cure or prevention of disease, by defining disease broadly, as any pathological bodily change. Since then Sanger and her ABCL had worked, both on a state and a federal level, for legislation that would simply strike out all restrictions on doctors' rights to prescribe contraception, giving them unlimited discretion. The ABCL also proposed an amendment to section 211 of the U.S. Penal Code exemption from Post Office restriction on all medical and scientific journals, all items prescribed by physicians, and all items imported by manufacturers, wholesalers, or retail druggists doing business with licensed physicians.[21]

Mary Ware Dennett and her colleagues in the Voluntary Parenthood League, meanwhile, continued to campaign for an open bill, exempting discussion of contraception from all restrictions for anyone. VPL arguments against the doctors-only bill were substantial. "Yes, of course we believe in medical advice for the individual, but again how about the large mass of women who cannot reach even a clinic? . . . Mrs. Sanger's own pamphlet on methods finds its way through the American mails . . . and *it is not a physician's compilation.* . . . Mrs. Sanger herself testified 'that the Clinical Research Department of the American Birth Control League teaches methods so simple that once learned, any mother who is intelligent enough to keep a nursing bottle clean, can use them.'"[22] Furthermore, Dennett argued, the doctors-only bill left "the whole subject . . . still in the category of crime and indecency."[23] Not only did it accept the definition of sexuality without reproduction as obscene, but it also removed the technique of birth control from a woman's own control. If women could not have direct access to birth-control information, they would have to get their information from doctors along with censorship at worst and moral guidance at best. . . .

Many doctors, of course, believed that they had an ethical duty to oppose an "open bill." Sharing the views expressed by Kosmak in 1917, their sense of professional responsibility and importance led them to anticipate all sorts of moral and physiological disasters should contraceptive information and devices be generally available. Strategically, Dickinson feared that an open bill would increase religious opposition to birth-control legalization.[24] Sanger's opposition to Dennett's bill combined condescension, conservatism, and compromising practicality. "I have come to realize," she wrote to Dennett supporter James Field in 1923, "that the more ignorant classes, with whom we are chiefly concerned, are so liable to misunderstand any written instruction that the Cause of Birth Control would be harmed rather than helped, by spreading abroad unauthoritative literature." To Dennett Sanger wrote that "clean repeal" was impossible because it would have to mean removing abortion from the obscenity category as well, something which Sanger knew could never win and which she probably did not personally accept. "You," she wrote to Dennett, ". . . are interested in an abstract idea . . . I am interested in women, in their lives. . . ."[25]

. . . Doctors-only bills were defeated in every state in which they were proposed, even in states without large Catholic populations.[26] Indeed, the pattern of development of the Birth Control Leage of Massachusetts (BCLM) was echoed in many local birth-control leagues. After the radical originators of the movements left for other causes that seemed to them more pressing (or in a few instances were pushed out by professionals and conservatives), the birth-control leagues sunk into lower levels of activity and energy. The impact of professionals—particularly doctors—on birth control as a social movement was to depress it, to take it out of the mass consciousness as a social issue, even as contraceptive information continued to be disseminated. Furthermore, the doctors did not prove successful in the 1920s in winning even the legislative and legal gains they had defined as their goals. Although some birth-control organizers, such as Cerise Jack of the BCLM, felt that they were torn between radical demands and effectiveness, in fact there is reason to question whether the surrender of radical demands produced any greater effectiveness at all.

. . . By 1930 there were fifty-five clinics in twenty-three cities in twelve states.[27] In Chicago a birth-control clinic was denied a license by the City Health Commissioner, but the League secured a court order overruling him and granting a license. Judge Fisher's 1924 decision in this case marked out important legal precedents. His opinion held that the project was a clinic under the meaning of the law; that there existed contraceptive methods not injurious to health; that the actions of the Health Commissioner (who had cited biblical passages in his letter of refusal to license!) amounted to enforcing religious doctrines, an illegal use of power; that the obscenity statutes only sought to repress "promiscuous" distribution of contraceptive information; that "where reasonable minds differ courts should hesitate to condemn."[28]

As the clinic movement mushroomed around the country, however, conflict continued about how and by whom the clinics should be controlled. In New York Sanger still resisted relinquishing personal control of her clinic to the medical profession. No doubt part of her resistance came from a desire to control things herself, especially since she had lost control of the ABCL and the *Birth Control Review* by 1929.[29] But part of her resistance, too, came from disagreement with the doctors' insistence on requiring medical indications for the prescription of contraceptive devices. Her Clinical Re-

search Bureau had consistently stretched the definition of appropriate indications; and if an appropriate medical problem that justified contraception
could not be found, a patient was often referred to private doctors, for
whom prescribing contraceptives would be less dangerous.[30] Sanger was
willing to avoid an open challenge to the law on the question of indications,
but she was not willing to allow close medical supervision to deprive physically healthy women of access to contraception. Sanger always retained a
critical view of medical control. As late as 1940 she wrote to Dr. Clarence
Gamble, "I am absolutely against our educational or propaganda or organizational work being in the hands of the medicos. . . . Being a medico yourself
you will know exactly what I mean because you are not strictly medical."[31]
Yet nationally her work had the objective impact of supporting medical control. The only birth-control help the ABCL ever offered individuals was directing them to sympathetic physicians. At ABCL-sponsored birth-control
conferences nonmedical people were excluded from the sessions that discussed contraceptive technique.[32] The VPL protested against this policy; but
the VPL was also excluded from these conference programs.[33] There was
resistance to these policies in some local birth-control groups. Caroline Nelson, for example, the IWW birth controller of the prewar period, still active
in California, complained in 1930 of

> nothing more nor less than an effort to get the laymen out of the field to leave
> it to the doctors. Now we have this Conference called by Margaret Sanger, who
> wants the dissemination of the information limited to doctors, which means
> that every doctor can demand the arrest and prosecution of every layman who
> hands it on. Fine! The whole proposition has been evolved outside the medi-
> cal profession. They have tried with all their professional sneers to hold it
> back, and refused to include it in their medical curriculum. Now when they
> find that they can't hold it back, they want to appropriate it and police the
> layman.[34]

But Sanger's control over the national conferences, lobbying efforts, and
publicity was complete, and the increasing medical control was not checked.

Sanger faced a serious problem: without medical approval her clinics
were illegal and vulnerable. In New York she continued to seek a license to
guarantee the safety and stability of her clinic. When she withdrew the clinic
from the auspices of the ABCL in 1928, Sanger once again approached
Dickinson requesting that he find her a medical director whose prestige
might help obtain a license. Dickinson in reply demanded that the clinic be
entirely turned over to a medical authority, suggesting New York Hospital.
Sanger was convinced that such an affiliation would hamstring her work
and refused it. Then, in April 1929, the clinic was raided by the police. As
at Brownsville thirteen years before, a plainclothes policewoman asked for
and was supplied with contraceptives. She even came for her second
checkup to make sure her diaphragm was fitting her well—then returned
five days later with a detachment of police, arrested three nurses and two

physicians, and confiscated the medical records. The last action was a mistake on the part of the police, for it united the medical profession behind Sanger and in defense of confidential medical records. Furthermore, the policewoman had been a poor choice because the clinic doctors had indeed found that she had pelvic abnormalities that provided a proper medical indication for giving her a diaphragm. The case was thrown out of court. (Some time later the policewoman returned to the clinic, off duty, to seek treatment for her pelvic disorders!)[35]

... Increasingly, the clinics were operated by groups of professional and well-to-do people for the poor. They were charities, not self-help organizations. Eugenic logic had convinced many of these educated people that this particular charity was very much in their own interest; that without population limitation the poor and the unwashed could become a political threat. The members of the ABCL were not the main clients of the clinics they had sparked, but went to private doctors. The attitude of many doctors toward their private patients continued, well into the mid-twentieth century, to parallel that of many elite nineteenth-century doctors: although they opposed the "promiscuous," "indiscriminate" dissemination of contraception, they did not question their own discrimination and even thought it important that private doctors should be able to make exceptions to the policies they supported as general rules. Well-to-do women were able to secure diaphragms without medical indications from doctors who may themselves have opposed making it possible for clinics to use the same principles. The discretionary right of the individual doctor was a privilege as cherished by the profession as that of privacy—and the latter, of course, protected the former.

The new respectability of the birth-control movement shaped the constituency of the ABCL. In 1927 questionnaires were mailed to a random fifth (7800) of ABCL members and of these 964 were completed.[36] This sample may have tended to raise the apparent class level of the members as more educated people were more likely to reply, but even allowing for some degree of distortion the results are significant. Politically the membership was slightly more Republican than the whole country, the men more inclined to be Republican than the women. (Fifty-five per cent of men were Republicans, 19 per cent Democrats; the women's figures were 46 per cent and 25 per cent.) One-third of the members were from cities of more than fifty thousand people; 43 per cent of the members were within five hundred miles of New York City, although this proportion had declined from 60 per cent in 1922, suggesting increasing penetration of the whole country with birth-control interest and knowledge. The organization seemed not to be dominated by big cities, with half the membership from population centers of less than twenty-five hundred. ABCL techniques in procuring members, however, require a reinterpretation of this phenomenon. Throughout the 1920s ABCL responses to letters of inquiry about birth control either explicitly or implicitly told writers that they could not receive information unless they joined the League. "The information that you desire can only be given to League members," said a form letter signed by Sanger.[37] Thus big-city dwellers, more likely to have access to clinics or local birth-control organizations, had less incentive to join the national organization; ABCL membership could not, therefore, be said to be representative of the over-all distribution of people interested in birth control as a cause.

The only check on professional influence would have been a broader-based, popular birth-control movement. No social group of equal size could contest the power of the professionals; only a much larger group could have done that, either a working-class movement or a feminist one. The former was unimaginable by 1920. Even the union movement lost ground in the 1920s; working-class movements demanding larger social change had been severely beaten in the repressive period that followed World War I. Furthermore, the men who dominated all forms of working-class organization at that time were hostile to and/or uninterested in birth control.

The source of the feminist failure in birth control is complex. In addition to many external factors, a contradiction within the feminist movement itself was sharply debilitating; that is, the vision of a new sexual order which this feminism contained was threatening to many of its advocates. . . . In the nineteenth century contraception—the severing of sex from reproduction and hence from family control—was not in the interest of the majority of women. In the 1920s that situation had changed. Sex outside of marriage had been incorporated into a relatively stabilized new family structure, and contraception itself was accepted by most women. But the potential volatility of a continued social movement frightened the relatively privileged women who became reformers in the 1920s. Whether themselves "career women" or, more commonly, leisured wives able to do volunteer work, they were a generation reaping the benefits of a relative social emancipation, one that applied only to their class. They could have "help" with the housework or at least with the children; they could get effective contraceptives to reduce the number of their children; they enjoyed social acceptance for their work in the public arena, including public speaking, traveling alone, supervising others. On the other hand, they had not experienced the raising of expectations which was to influence their daughters and granddaughters, expectations which made the continued inequality with men of their class frustrating and galling. Perhaps even more than their nineteenth-century suffragist predecessors, they felt enormously different from the working-class poor whom they tried to help.

The problem was that their very estrangement from the less privileged majority of women cost them their own coherence as feminists. The essence of feminism has always been a view of all women as united by certain problems and strengths, the "bonds of womanhood."[38] When class distinctions make this vision of a common womanhood impossible, they dissolve the basis for any feminist analysis or strategy. Taking advantage of their class privileges for their own personal advancement, the prosperous reformers of the 1920s lost the mass base that could have made them a powerful influence. Without a constituency demanding change, they became merely a group of individuals, whereas their male professional rivals in the birth-control organizations had the power of the capitalist class behind them. Their inability to spark a mass movement made them simultaneously unable to create even a coherent militance among a small group, for they had no larger goals that distinguished them from their male colleagues.

## NOTES

1. Frederick Blossom to Rose Pastor Stokes, November 11, 1916. Stokes mss., Tamiment Library.
2. Henry Fruchter to Elizabeth Gurley Flynn, report on Blossom, September 16, 1922; Margaret Sanger to Flynn, November 3, 1922, both in Sanger, Library of Congress (hereafter LC).
3. Margaret Sanger, *Autobiography* (New York: W. W. Norton, 1938), pp. 211–12, and *My Fight for Birth Control* (New York: Farrar & Rinehart, 1931), p. 110; Mary Ware Dennett, *Birth Control Laws* (New York: F. H. Hitchcock, 1926), p. 11.
4. Letter to members of NBCL from its Executive Committee, January 11, 1917, Stokes mss.; statement by Dennett, November 18, 1921, Sanger, LC.
5. Morris Fishbein, *Medical Follies* (New York: Boni & Liveright, 1925), p. 142.
6. Frederick McCann, Presidential Address to League of National Life, printed in *Medical Press and Circular*, November 3, 1926, p. 359.
7. See George Kosmak in *Bulletin, Lying-in Hospital of the City of New York*, August 1917, pp. 181–92. For similar views among other doctors, see, for example, Edward C. Podvin, "Birth Control," *New York Medical Journal*, February 10, 1917, pp. 258–60; C. Henry Davis, "Birth Control and Sterility," *Surgery, Gynecology and Obstetrics*, March 1923, pp. 435–39; B. S. Talmey, in *New York Medical Journal*, June 23, 1917, pp. 1187–91.
8. Robert L. Dickinson, "Hypertrophies of the Labia Minora and Their Significance," *American Gynecology* 1 (1902): 225–54, quoted in James Reed, "Birth Control and the Americans," Harvard dissertation, 1974.
9. Robert L. Dickinson, "Bicycling for Women from the Standpoint of the Gynecologist," *American Journal of Obstetrics* 31 (1895): 24–37, quoted in Reed thesis, pp. 51–52.
10. Robert L. Dickinson, "Marital Maladjustment: The Business of Preventive Gynecology," *Long Island Medical Journal* (1908): 1–5, quoted in Reed thesis, p. 58.
11. David M. Kennedy, *Birth Control in America:* The Career of Margaret Sanger (New Haven: Yale University Press, 1970), p. 179.
12. Kennedy, *Birth Control in America*, p. 191.
13. James W. Reed, "Birth Control and the Americans, 1830–1970," Ph.D. dissertation, Harvard University, 1974, pp. 77–82; Kennedy, *Birth Control in America*, p. 190; Lawrence Lader, *The Margaret Sanger Story and the Fight for Birth Control* (Garden City, NY: Doubleday, 1955), p. 216.
14. ABCL files, quoted in F. M. Vreeland, "The Process of Reform Groups in the Field of Population," Ph.D. dissertation, University of Michigan, 1929, p. 280.
15. Sanger to J. Noah Slee, February 22, 1925, Sanger, LC; see also ABCL Papers, Boxes 4, 5, 6, Houghton Library, Harvard University.
16. W. N. Wishard, Sr., "Contraception. Are Our County Societies Being Used for the American Birth Control League Propaganda?," *Journal of the Indiana Medical Association*, May 1929, pp. 187–89.
17. *Proceedings, Sixth International Birth Control Conference*, 3:19–30, 49–60.
18. Vreeland, "Process of Reform," p. 280.
19. Form letters in ABCL.

20. Kennedy, *Birth Control in America*, p. 196.

21. ABCL, *An Amendment to the Federal Law Dealing with Contraception*, pamphlet, n.d., in ABCL.

22. Mimeographed letter to VPL members from President Myra P. Gallert, December 2, 1925, Alice Park mss., Stanford University.

23. Dennett, *Birth Control Laws*, p. 88.

24. Kennedy, *Birth Control in America*, pp. 222–23.

25. Sanger to James Field, June 5, 1923, ABCL, Box 2; Sanger to Dennett, March 4, 1930 and unmailed draft of same February 25, 1930, in Sanger mss., Sophia Smith Collection, Smith College [hereinafter given as Sanger, Smith]; see also *Journal of the American Medical Association* 85 (1925): 1153–54; and Sanger to Dennett, [1929], Park mss.

26. Dennett, *Birth Control Laws*, pp. 72–93.

27. There were six in New York, seven in Los Angeles, three in San Francisco, four in Alameda County in California, three in Chicago, and others in Baltimore, Detroit, Cleveland, Buffalo, Philadelphia, Denver, Atlanta, Minneapolis, Newark, Cincinnati, San Antonio, Charlottesville. See Lader, *Margaret Sanger Story*, p. 219; and Appendix B, pp. 358–59.

28. *Birth Control and Public Policy, Decision of Judge Harry M. Fisher of the Circuit Court of Cook County, November 1923*, pamphlet, Illinois Birth Control League, 1924.

29. Sanger was undoubtedly a difficult person who did not thrive on cooperative work. Her personal struggles within the birth-control movement are well described in Kennedy's *Birth Control in America*.

30. For example, see minutes of advisory council, Harlem Clinical Research Bureau, May 20, 1931, in Sanger, Smith.

31. Sanger to Dr. Clarence Gamble, February 4, 1940, in Sanger, Smith.

32. Conference program, Sanger, LC.

33. Letter to VPL from Gallert; for Sanger's justification of this exclusion, see, for example, Sanger to Prof. James Field, August 13, 1923, BCLM.

34. Caroline Nelson to Alice Park, February 3, 1930, Park mss.

35. Sanger, *Autobiography*, pp. 402–408.

36. The findings of this survey are presented in Vreeland, "Process of Reform," pp. 154 ff., and all the following information is taken from that source.

37. Sanger form letter and many responses are in ABCL.

38. Sarah Grimke signed her 1838 letters, an early statement of American feminism, with this *double entendre* on the word "bonds."

# 11

# The Black Community
# and the Birth Control Movement

## Jessie M. Rodrique

*Agency is a fundamental element of an understanding of power, and Jessie M. Rodrique argues that the declining black birthrate in the twentieth century was a function of self-conscious black effort. This decline was not simply the result of conservative, elitist programs aimed at controlling reproduction within the black community. Rodrique demonstrates considerable evidence of the practice of "deliberate family limitation" among African Americans between 1920 and 1945. As in Terborg-Penn's analysis of black feminists and the suffrage movement, here, too, we see black supporters of birth control staking out their own positions within the movement and demanding that the larger movement take into account the needs and concerns of African Americans. Once again, a view of cultural diffusion from middle class to working class, or from white to black, is an inadequate framework within which to explore cultural change among women in the twentieth century.*

The decline in black fertility rates from the late nineteenth century to World War II has been well documented. In these years the growth rate of the black population was more than cut in half. By 1945 the average number of children per woman was 2.5, and the degree of childlessness, especially among urban blacks, had reached unprecedented proportions. Researchers who explain this phenomenon insist that contraception played a minimal role, believing that blacks had no interest in the control of their own fertility. This belief also affects the interpretation of blacks' involvement in the birth control movement, which has been understood as a movement that was thrust upon an unwilling black population.

This essay seeks to understand these two related issues differently. First, I maintain that black women were, in fact, interested in controlling their fertility and that the low birth rates reflect in part a conscious use of birth control. Second, by exploring the birth control movement among blacks at the grassroots level, I show that despite the racist ideology that operated at the national level, blacks were active and effective participants in the establishment of local clinics and in the birth control debate, as they related birth control to issues of race and gender. Third, I show that despite black cooperation with white birth control groups, blacks maintained a degree of independence that allowed the organization for birth control in their communities to take a qualitatively different form.

Excerpted from "The Black Community and the Birth Control Movement," by Jessie M. Rodrique, in Kathy Peiss and Christina Simmons, eds., *Passion and Power: Sexuality in History* (Philadelphia, Temple University Press, 1989). Copyright MARHO: The Radical Historians Organization.

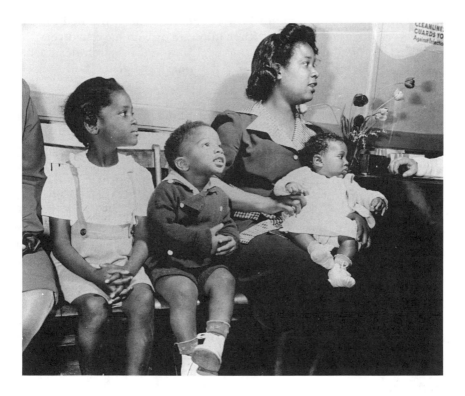

*Woman and children in waiting room of Harlem birth control clinic, c. 1940. Sophia Smith Collection, Smith College.*

Demographers in the post–World War I years accounted for the remarkable decline in black fertility in terms of biological factors. Fears of "dysgenic" population trends coupled with low birth rates among native, white Americans underlay their investigations of black fertility. Population scholars ignored contraception as a factor in the birth decline even as late as 1938. Instead, they focused upon the "health hypothesis," arguing that the fertility drop resulted from general poor health, especially sterility caused by venereal disease. While health conditions seem likely to have had some effect, there is no reason to exclude contraceptive use as an additional cause, especially when evidence of contraceptive knowledge and practice is abundant.[1]

In drawing their conclusions, researchers also made many questionable and unfounded assumptions about the sexuality of blacks. In one large study of family limitation, for example, black women's lower contraceptive use was attributed to the belief that "the negro generally exercises less prudence and foresight than white people do in all sexual matters."[2] Nor is the entire black population represented in many of these studies. Typically their sample consists of women whose economic status is defined as either poor or very poor and who are either illiterate or who have had very little education. Population experts' ideological bias and research design have tended to foreclose the possibility of Afro-American agency, and thus conscious use of contraception.[3]

Historians who have chronicled the birth control movement have focused largely on the activities and evolution of the major birth control organizations and leading birth control figures, usually at the national level. None have interpreted the interests of the movement as particularly beneficial to blacks. Linda Gordon, in her pathbreaking book, *Woman's Body, Woman's Right*, focused on the 1939 "Negro Project," established by the Birth Control Federation of America (BCFA) as a conservative, elitist effort designed "to stabilize existing social relations." Gordon claims that the birth control movement in the south was removed from socially progressive politics and unconnected to any analysis of women's rights, civil rights, or poverty, exemplifying the movement's male domination and professionalization over the course of the twentieth century. Other historians concur, asserting that birth control was "genocidal" and "anathema" to black women's interests, and that the movement degenerated into a campaign to "keep the unfit from reproducing themselves." Those who note its presence within the black community in a slightly more positive light, qualify their statements by adding the disclaimer that support and information for its dissemination came only from the black elite and were not part of a grassroots movement.[4]

There is, however, an ample body of evidence that suggests the importance of birth control use among blacks. Contraceptive methods and customs among Africans as well as nineteenth-century slaves have been well documented. For example, folklorists and others have discovered "alum water" as one of the many birth control measures in early twentieth-century southern rural communities. The author of a study of two rural counties of Georgia noted the use of birth control practices there and linked it to a growing race pride. In urban areas a "very common" and distinctive practice among blacks was to place Vaseline and quinine over the mouth of the uterus. It was widely available and purchased very cheaply in drugstores.[5]

The black press was also an abundant source of birth control information. The *Pittsburgh Courier*, for example, carried numerous mail order advertisements for douche powder, suppositories, preventative antiseptics, and vaginal jellies that "destroyed foreign germs."[6] A particularly interesting mail order ad was for a product called "Puf," a medicated douche powder and applicator that claimed to be a "new guaranteed method of administering marriage hygiene." It had a sketch of a calendar with the words "End Calendar Worries Now!" written across it and a similar sketch that read "Tear-Up Your Calendar, Do Not Worry, Use Puf." The instructions for its use indicate euphemistically that Puf should be used "first," meaning before intercourse, and that it was good for hours, leaving little doubt that this product was fully intended to be used as a birth control device.[7]

Advertisements for mail order douches are significant since they appear to reflect a practice that was widespread and well documented among black women. Studies conducted in the mid-thirties overwhelmingly concluded that douching was the preferred method of contraception used by black couples. Yet contemporary researchers neglected to integrate this observation into their understanding of the fertility decline since they insisted that douching was an "ineffective contraceptive." However ineffective the means, the desire for birth control in the black community was readily apparent, as George Schuyler, editor of the *National Negro News*, explained: "If anyone should doubt the desire on the part of Negro women and men to limit their families it is only necessary to note the large sale of preventive devices sold in every drug store in various Black Belts."[8]

Within the black community the practice of abortion was commonly cited by black leaders and professionals as contributing to the low birth rates. Throughout the twenties and thirties the black press reported many cases of abortions that had ended in death or the arrest of doctors who had performed them. Abortion was discussed in the *Pittsburgh Courier* in 1930 in a fictionalized series entitled "Bad Girl," which dealt with a range of attitudes toward childbearing among Harlem blacks. When Dot, the main character, discovers she is pregnant, she goes to a friend who works in a drugstore. The author writes:

> Pat's wonderful remedy didn't help. Religiously Dot took it and each night when Eddie came home she sadly admitted that success had not crowned her efforts. "All that rotten tasting stuff just to keep a little crib out of the bedroom." After a week she was tired of medicine and of baths so hot that they burned her skin.[9]

Next, she sought the advice of a friend who told her that she would have to have "an operation" and knew of a doctor who would do it for fifty dollars.

The *Baltimore Afro-American* observed that pencils, nails, and hat pins were the instruments commonly used for self-induced abortions and the *Birth Control Review* write in 1936 that rural black women in Georgia drank turpentine for the same purpose. The use of turpentine as an abortifacient is significant since it is derived from evergreens, a source similar to rue and camphor, both of which were reported by a medical authority in 1860 to have been used with some success by southern slaves. Although statistics for abortions among black women are scarce, a 1938 medical study reported that twenty-eight percent or 211 of 730 black women interviewed said that they had had one or more abortions. A black doctor from Nashville in 1940 asserted in the *Baltimore Afro-American* that abortions among black women were deliberate, not only the result of syphilis and other diseases: "In the majority of cases it is used as a means of getting rid of unwanted children."[10]

These data, while somewhat impressionistic, indicate that a number of contraceptive methods were available to blacks. Many were, and still are, discounted as ineffective "folk methods."[11] There was, however, a discernible consciousness that guided the fertility decline. A discourse on birth control emerged in the years from 1915 to 1945. As blacks migrated within and out of the south to northern cities, they began to articulate the reasons for limiting fertility. It is here that one begins to see how interconnected the issue of birth control was to many facets of black life. For women, it was linked to changes in their status, gender roles within the family, attitudes toward motherhood and sexuality, and, at times, feminism. Birth control was also integral to issues of economics, health, race relations, and racial progress.

In these years blacks contributed to the "official" nationwide debate concerning birth control while also voicing their particular concerns. Frequent coverage was given to birth control in the black press. Newspapers championed the cause of birth control when doctors were arrested for performing abortions. They also carried editorials in favor of birth control, speeches of noted personalities who favored its use, and occasionally sensationalized stories on the desperate need for birth control. Often, the topic of birth control as well as explicit birth control information was transmitted orally, through public lectures and debates. It was also explored in fiction, black periodicals, and several issues of the *Birth Control Review* dedicated to blacks.[12]

Economic themes emerged in the birth control discourse as it related to issues of black family survival. Contraceptive use was one of a few economic strategies available to blacks, providing a degree of control within the context of the family economy. Migrating families who left behind the economy of the rural south used birth control to "preserve their new economic independence," as did poor families who were "compelled" to limit their numbers of children. A 1935 study of Harlem reiterated this same point, adding that the low birth rates of urban blacks reflected a "deliberate limitation of families." Another strategy used by black couples for the same purpose was postponing marriage. Especially in the years of the Depression, birth control was seen as a way to improve general living conditions by allowing more opportunities for economic gain.[13]

Birth control was also linked to the changing status of black women and the role they were expected to play in the survival of the race. On this issue a degree of opposition to birth control surfaced. Some, most notably black nationalist leader Marcus Garvey, believed that the future of the black race was contingent upon increasing numbers and warned that birth control would lead to racial extinction. Both Garveyites and Catholic church officials warned that birth control interfered with the "course of nature" and God's will.[14]

These issues were evident in an exchange between the journalist J. A.

Rogers and Dean Kelly Miller of Howard University in 1925. Writing in *The Messenger*, Rogers took Miller to task for his statements concerning the emancipation of black women. Miller is quoted as saying that black women had strayed too far from children, kitchen, clothes, and the church. Miller, very aware that black women had been having fewer children, cautioned against race suicide. Using the "nature" argument of Garvey and the Catholic church, he argued that the biological function of women was to bear and rear children. He stated, "The liberalization of women must always be kept within the boundary fixed by nature." Rogers strongly disagreed with Miller, saying that the move of black women away from domesticity and childbearing was a positive sign. Rogers wrote, "I give the Negro woman credit if she endeavors to be something other than a mere breeding machine. Having children is by no means the sole reason for being."[15]

Other black leaders supported this progressive viewpoint. In his 1919 essay "The Damnation of Women," W. E. B. Du Bois wrote that "the future woman must have a life work and future independence. . . . She must have knowledge . . . and she must have the right of motherhood at her own discretion."[16] In a later essay he described those who would confine women to childbearing as "reactionary barbarians."[17] Doctor Charles Garvin, writing in 1932, believed that it was the "inalienable right of every married woman to use any physiologically sound precaution against reproduction she deems justifiable."[18]

Black women also expressed the need for contraception as they articulated their feelings about motherhood and sexuality. Black women's fiction and poetry in the years from 1916 to the early thirties frequently depicted women who refused to bring children into a racist world and expressed their outrage at laws that prevented access to birth control information. Nella Larsen, for example, in her 1928 novella *Quicksand*, explored the debilitating physical and emotional problems resulting from excessive childbearing in a society that demanded that women's sexual expression be inextricably linked to marriage and procreation.[19]

Others spoke of the right not to have children in terms that were distinctly feminist. For example, a character in the *Courier* serial "Bad Girl" put it this way: "The hospitals are wide open to the woman who wants to have a baby, but to a woman who doesn't want one—that's a different thing. High prices, fresh doctors. It's a man's world, Dot. The woman who wants to keep her body from pain and her mind from worry is an object of contempt."[20] The changing status of women and its relation to childbearing were also addressed in Jessie Fauset's 1931 novel, *The Chinaberry Tree*. Fauset's male characters asserted the need for large families and a "definite place" for women in the home. The female character, however, remained unconvinced by this opinion. She had "the modern girl's own clear ideas on birth control."[21]

Other writers stressed the need for birth control in terms of racial

issues and how birth control could be used to alleviate the oppressive circumstances of the black community. For example, Chandler Owen, editor
of *The Messenger*, wrote a piece for the 1919 edition of the *Birth Control Review*
entitled "Women and Children of the South." He advocated birth control
because he believed that general improvements in material conditions
would follow from fewer children. Observing that young black women in
peonage camps were frequently raped and impregnated by their white over-
seers, Owen also linked involuntary maternity to racial crimes.[22]

The advocacy of birth control for racial progress occurred most frequently during the Depression, and it helped to mobilize community support for clinics. Newell Sims of Oberlin College, for example, urged that
birth control for blacks would be a "step toward independence and greater
power" in his 1931 essay "A New Technique in Race Relations." In his opinion a controlled birth rate would free more resources for advancement. The
black press hailed the essay as "revolutionary."[23] Other advocates insisted
that all blacks, but especially poor blacks, become involved in the legislative
process to legalize birth control. It was imperative that the poor be included
in the movement since they were the ones most injured by its prohibition.
One black newspaper, the *San Francisco Spokesman*, promoted a very direct
and activist role for blacks on this issue. "To legalize birth control, you and I
should make expressed attitudes on this question a test of every candidate's
fitness for legislative office," it argued in 1934. "And those who refuse or
express a reactionary opinion should be flatly and uncompromisingly rejected."[24]

For many blacks birth control was not a panacea but one aspect of a
larger political agenda. Unlike some members of the white community who
myopically looked to birth control as a cure-all for the problems of blacks,
most blacks instead described it as a program that would "modify one cause
of their unfavorable situation."[25] They stressed that true improvement could
come only through the "equalization of economic and social opportunities."[26] Newell L. Sims summed up this position most eloquently in his 1932
essay "Hostages to the White Man." It was a viewpoint stressed well into
the forties by numerous and leading members of the black community. He
wrote:

> The negro in America is a suppressed class and as such must struggle for
> existence under every disadvantage and handicap. Although in three genera-
> tions since slavery he has in many ways greatly improved his condition, his
> economic, social and political status still remain that of a dominated ex-
> ploited minority. His problem is, therefore, just what it has been for three
> quarters of a century, i.e., how to better his position in the social order. Natu-
> rally in all his strivings he has found no panacea for his difficulties, for there
> is none. The remedies must be as numerous and varied as the problem is
> complex. Obviously he needs to employ every device that will advance his
> cause. I wish briefly to urge the merits of birth control as one means.[27]

Many also insisted that birth control be integrated into other health care provisions and not be treated as a separate "problem." E. S. Jamison, for example, writing in the *Birth Control Review* in 1938 on the "Future of Negro Health," exhorted blacks to "present an organized front" so that birth control and other needed health services could be made available to them. Yet he too, like Sims, emphasized independence from the white community. He wrote that "the Negro must do for himself. Charity will not better his condition in the long run."[28]

Blacks also took an important stand against sterilization, especially in the thirties. Scholars have not sufficiently recognized this point: that blacks could endorse a program of birth control but reject the extreme views of eugenicists, whose programs for birth control and sterilization often did not distinguish between the two. The *Pittsburgh Courier*, for example, whose editorial policy clearly favored birth control, was also active in the anti-sterilization movement. It asserted in several editorials that blacks should oppose the sterilization programs being advanced by eugenicists and so-called scientists because they were being waged against the weak, the oppressed, and the disfranchised. Candidates for sterilization were likely to be those on relief, the unemployed, and the homeless, all victims of a vicious system of economic exploitation. Du Bois shared this viewpoint. In his column in the *Courier* in 1936 he wrote, "the thing we want to watch is the so-called eugenic sterilization." He added that the burden of such programs would "fall upon colored people and it behooves us to watch the law and the courts and stop the spread of the habit." The *San Francisco Spokesman* in 1934 called upon black clubwomen to become active in the anti-sterilization movement.[29]

Participation in the birth control debate was only one aspect of the black community's involvement; black women and men also were active in the establishment of birth control clinics. From 1925 to 1945 clinics for blacks appeared nationwide, many of which were at least partly directed and sponsored by local black community organizations. Many of the organizations had a prior concern with health matters, creating an established network of social welfare centers, health councils, and agencies. Thus, birth control services were often integrated into a community through familiar channels.[30]

In Harlem the black community showed an early and sustained interest in the debate over birth control, taking a vanguard role in agitation for birth control clinics. In 1918 the Women's Political Association of Harlem, calling upon black women to "assume the reins of leadership in the political, social and economic life of their people," announced that its lecture series would include birth control among the topics for discussion.[31] In March of 1923 the Harlem Community Forum invited Margaret Sanger to speak to them at the Library Building in the Bronx, and in 1925 the Urban

League made a request to the American Birth Control League that a clinic be established in the Columbus Hill section of the city.

Although this clinic proved unsuccessful, another clinic, supported by the Urban League and the Birth Control Clinical Research Bureau, opened a Harlem branch in 1929. This particular clinic, affiliated with Margaret Sanger, had an advisory board of approximately fifteen members, including Harlem-based journalists, physicians, social workers, and ministers. There was apparently very little opposition to the work of this clinic, even among the clergy. One minister on the advisory board, William Lloyd Imes of the St. James Presbyterian Church, reported that he had held discussions on birth control at his church; at another meeting he announced that if a birth control pamphlet were printed, he would place it in the church vestibule. Another clergyman, the Reverend Shelton Hale Bishop, wrote to Sanger in 1931 that he believed birth control to be "one of the boons of the age to human welfare."[32] The Reverend Adam Clayton Powell of the Abyssinian Baptist Church both endorsed birth control and spoke at public meetings where he denounced the "false modesty" surrounding questions of sex. Ignorance, he believed, led to unwanted pregnancies among young girls.[33]

Support for birth control clinics by black community organizations was also apparent in other locations throughout the country. Their activism took various forms. In Baltimore, for example, a white birth control clinic had begun to see blacks in 1928. In 1935 the black community began organizing and by 1938 the Northwest Health Center was established, sponsored and staffed by blacks. The Baltimore Urban League played a key role in its initial organization, and the sponsoring committee of the clinic was composed of numerous members of Baltimore's black community, including ministers, physicians, nurses, social workers, teachers, housewives, and labor leaders.[34]

In Richmond, Fredericksburg, and Lynchburg, Virginia, local maternal welfare groups raised funds for expenses and supplies for the birth control clinics at the Virginia Medical College and the Hampton Institute, and publicized birth control services at city health departments. And in West Virginia, the Maternal and Child Health Council, formed in 1938, was the first statewide birth control organization sponsored by blacks.[35] . . .

Clinics in other cities were located in black community centers and churches. For example, the Kentucky Birth Control League in 1936 reported that one of the clinics in Louisville was located in the Episcopal Church for Colored People and was operated by a Negro staff. The Cincinnati Committee on Maternal Health reported in 1939 the opening of a second black clinic where a black physician and nurse would work.[36]

Community centers and settlement houses were also part of the referral network directing blacks to birth control services. The Mother's Health Office in Boston received clients from the Urgan League, the Robert Gould Shaw House, and the Harriet Tubman House. The Henry Street Settlement sent women to the Harlem clinic, and the Booker T. Washington Community Center in San Francisco directed black women to the birth control clinic in that city. In 1935 the Indiana Birth Control League reported that black clients were directed to them from the Flanner House Settlement for Colored People.[37]

In 1939 the Birth Control Federation of America (BCFA) established a Division of Negro Service and sponsored pilot clinics in Nashville, Tennessee, and Berkeley County, South Carolina. The Division consisted of a national advisory council of thirty-five black leaders, a national sponsoring committee of 500 members who coordinated state and local efforts, and administrative and field personnel. The project in Nashville was integrated into the public health services and located in the Bethlehem center, a black social service settlement, and the Fisk University Settlement House. Both clinics were under the direction of black doctors and nurses. The program was also supplemented by nine black public health nurses who made home visits and performed general health services including birth control. The home visits served the large numbers of women who worked as domestics and could not attend the clinics during the day; 5,000 home visits were made in Nashville in a two-year period. In South Carolina, clinic sessions providing both medical care and birth control services were held eleven times each month at different locations in the county for rural women, seventy percent of whom were black.[38]

Simultaneously with the development of these two projects, the BCFA launched an educational campaign to inform and enlist the services of black health professionals, civil groups, and women's clubs. While professional groups are often credited with being the sole source of birth control agitation, the minutes and newsletters of the Division of Negro Service reveal an enthusiastic desire among a broad cross-section of the black community to lend its support for birth control. In fact, black professional groups often worked closely with community groups and other "non-professionals" to make birth control information widely available. . . .

The participation of Negro Home Demonstration Clubs in birth control work is significant because it is an entirely overlooked and potentially rich source for the grassroots spread of birth control information in the rural South. Home Demonstration Clubs grew out of the provisions of the Smith-Lever Cooperative Extension Act of 1914 and had, by the early twenties, evolved into clubs whose programs stressed health and sanitation. The newsletter of the Division of Negro Service in 1941 reported that five rural State Negro Agricultural and Home Demonstration Agents offered full cooperation with the division. The newsletter included the response of H. C. Ray of Little Rock, Arkansas. He wrote, "We have more than 13,000 rural women working in home demonstration clubs . . . it is in this connection that I feel our organization might work hand in hand with you in bringing about some very definite and desirable results in your phase of community improvement work. We will be glad to distribute any literature." Also involved with rural birth control education were several tuberculosis associations and the Jeanes Teachers, educators funded by the Anna T. Jeanes foundation for improving rural black schools.[39]

Other groups showed interest in the programs of the Division of Negro Service either by requesting birth control speakers for their conventions or by distributing literature to their members. Similar activities were conducted by the Virginia Federation of Colored Women's Clubs, which represented 400 women's clubs, the Negro Organization Society of Virginia, the National Negro Business League, the National Negro Housewives League, the Pullman Porters, the Elks, the Harlem Citizens City-Wide Committee, and the Social Action Committee of Boston's South End. In 1944, for example, the NAACP and a black boilermakers' union distributed Planned Parenthood clinic cards in their mailings to their California members. Twenty-one Urban Leagues in sixteen states as of 1943 actively cooperated with the BCFA in the display of exhibits, distribution of literature, the promotion of local clinical service, and adult community education programs. These national and local black organizations advocated birth control as one aspect of a general program of health, education, and economic development in the late thirties and early forties.[40]

Even in their cooperation with the BCFA, leading members of the black community stressed their own concerns and disagreements with the overall structure of the birth control movement. Their comments reveal important differences in orientation. At a meeting of the National Advisory Council of the Division of Negro Service in 1942, members of the council made it clear that birth control services and information must be distributed to the community as a community. . . . This approach to birth control diverged significantly from the conservative strategy of the white BCFA leadership, which insisted that birth control services be dispensed by private, individual physicians. Black physicians, it seems, were more sensitive to the general health needs of their population and more willing to experiment with the delivery of birth control services. They favored the integration of birth control into public health services while many white physicians were opposed.[41]

Others on the council stated that black women could be reached only through community organizations that they trusted, and they stressed again the necessity of not isolating birth control as a special interest to the neglect of other important health needs. Still others pointed to the need for birth control representatives who recognized social differences among urban blacks.

At the level of clinic attendance, clinicians also observed a difference between white and black patrons. Black women, they noted, were much more likely to spread the word about birth control services and bring their relatives and friends to the clinics. Some rural women even thought of "joining" the clinic as they might join a community organization. A white woman, however, was more likely to keep the information to herself and attend the clinic alone. A statistician from the Census Bureau supported this observation when he speculated in 1931 that "grapevine dissemination" of birth control information contributed to low black birth rates. These reports are a testimony to the effectiveness of working-class black women's networks.[42] . . .

In the past scholars have interpreted the birth control movement as a racist and elitist set of programs imposed on the black population. While this may describe the intentions of the national white leadership, it is important to recognize that the black community had its own agenda in the creation of programs to include and reach wide segments of the black population.

As this essay demonstrates, black women used their knowledge of "folk methods" and other available methods to limit their childbearing. The dramatic fertility decline from 1880 to 1945 is evidence of their success. Moreover, the use of birth control was pivotal to many pressing issues within the black community. The right to control one's own fertility emerged simultaneously with changing attitudes toward women in both the black and white communities that recognized their rights as individuals and not only their roles as mothers. And these changing attitudes contributed to the dialogue within the black community about the future of the family and strategies for black survival. Birth control also emerged as part of a growing race consciousness, as blacks saw birth control as one means of freeing themselves from the oppression and exploitation of white society through the improvement of their health and their economic and social status. Birth control was also part of a growing process of politicization. Blacks sought to make it a legislative issue, they opposed the sterilization movement, and they took an active and often independent role in supporting their clinics, educating their communities, and tailoring programs to fit their own needs. In their ideology and practice blacks were indeed a vital and assertive part of the larger birth control movement. What appears to some scholars of the birth control movement as the waning of the movement's original purposes during the 1920s and 1930s was within the black community a period of growing ferment and support for birth control. The history of the birth control movement, and the participation of black Americans in it, must be reexamined in this light.

## NOTES

1. Reynolds Farley, *Growth of the Black Population* (Chicago: 1970), 3, 75; Stanley Engerman, "Changes in Black Fertility, 1880–1940," in *Family and Population in Nineteenth Century America,* ed. Tamara K. Hareven and Maris A. Vinovskis (Princeton: 1978), ch. 3.

2. Raymond Pearl, "Contraception and Fertility in 2,000 Women," *Human Biology* 4 (1932): 395.

3. Joseph McFalls and George Masnick, "Birth Control and the Fertility of the U.S. Black Population, 1880 to 1980," *Journal of Family History,* Vol. 6 (1981): 89–106.

4. Linda Gordon, *Woman's Body, Woman's Right* (New York: 1976), 332–35; Paula Giddings, *When and Where I Enter: The Impact of Black Women on Race and Sex in America* (New York: 1984), 183; Robert G. Weisbord, *Genocide? Birth Control and the Black American* (Westport, Conn.: 1975); William G. Harris, "Family Planning, Socio-Political Ideology and Black Americans: A Comparative Study of Leaders and a General Population Sample" (Ph.D. dissertation, University of Massachusetts, 1980), 69.

A brief chronology of early birth control organizations is as follows: the American Birth Control League was founded in 1921 and operated by Margaret Sanger until 1927. In 1923 Sanger had organized the Clinical Research Bureau and after 1927 controlled only that facility. In 1939 the Clinical Research Bureau and the American Birth Control League merged to form the Birth Control Federation of America. In 1942 the name was changed to the Planned Parenthood Federation of America (hereafter cited as ABCL, BCFA, and PPFA).

5. For contraceptive use among Africans, see Norman E. Himes, *Medical History of Contraception* (New York: 1936). For statements concerning birth control use among black Americans, see W. E. B. Du Bois, "Black Folks and Birth Control," *Birth Control Review* 16 ( June 1932): 166–67 (hereafter cited as *BCR*); Herbert Gutman, *The Black Family in Slavery and Freedom 1750–1925* (New York: 1976). Du Bois had first observed the trend toward a steadily decreasing birth rate in *The Philadelphia Negro: A Social Study* (Philadelphia: 1899). For folk methods see Elizabeth Rauh Bethel, *Promiseland: A Century of Life in a Negro Community* (Philadelphia: 1981), 156–57; Newbell Niles Puckett, *Folk Beliefs of the Southern Negro* (New York: 1926); Arthur Raper, *Preface to Peasantry: A Tale of Two Black Belt Counties* (Chapel Hill, N.C.: 1936), 71; "Report of the Special Evening Medical Session of the First American Birth Control Conference" (1921), Box 99, Folder 1017, Margaret Sanger Papers, Sophia Smith Collection, Smith College, Northampton, Mass.

6. *Pittsburgh Courier,* 25 April 1931, n.p. (hereafter cited as *Courier*).

7. *Courier,* 1 December 1934, 7.

8. McFalls and Masnick, "Birth Control," 103; George Schuyler, "Quantity or Quality," *BCR* 16 ( June 1932): 165–66.

9. See, for example, *Courier,* 9 March 1935, 2; and *San Francisco Spokesman,* 1 March 1934, 1 (hereafter cited as *Spokesman*); Vina Delmar, "Bad Girl," *Courier,* 3 January 1931, 2.

10. *Baltimore Afro-American,* 3 August 1940, n.p. (hereafter cited as *Afro-American*); "A Clinic for Tobacco Road," *BCR* 3 [New Series] ( January 1936): 6; Gutman, *The Black Family,* 80–85; John Gaston, "A Review of 2,422 Cases of Contraception," *Texas State Journal of Medicine* 35 (September 1938): 365–68; *Afro-American,* 3 August 1940, n.p. On abortion see also "Birth Control: The Case for the State," *Reader's Digest*  (November 1939).

11. McFalls and Masnick, "Birth Control," 103.

12. "Magazine Publishes Negro Number on Birth Control," *San Francisco Spokesman,* 11 June 1932, 3; "Birth Control Slayer Held Without Bail," *Courier,* 11 January 1936, 4.

13. Alice Dunbar Nelson, "Women's Most Serious Problem," *The Messenger* (March 1927): 73; Clyde Kiser, "Fertility of Harlem Negroes," *Milbank Memorial Fund Quarterly* 13 (1935): 273–85; Caroline Robinson, *Seventy Birth Control Clinics* (Baltimore, 1930), 246–51.

14. Weisbord, *Genocide?,* 43.

15. J. A. Rogers, "The Critic," *The Messenger* (April 1925).

16. W. E. B. Du Bois, "The Damnation of Women," in *Darkwater: Voices from Within the Veil,* ed. Herbert Aptheker (1921; rpt. Millwood, N.Y.: 1975).

17. W. E. B. Du Bois, "Birth," *The Crisis* 24 (October 1922): 248–50.

18. Charles H. Garvin, "The Negro's Doctor's Task," *BCR* 16 (November 1921): 269–70.

19. For an excellent discussion of the theme of sexuality in black women's fiction, see the introduction to Nella Larsen, *Quicksand and Passing,* ed. Deborah E. McDowell (New Brunswick, N.J.: 1986). See also Mary Burrill, "They That Sit in Darkness," and Angelina Grimké, "The Closing Door," *BCR* 3 (September 1919); Jessie Fauset, *The Chinaberry Tree* (New York: 1931); Angelina Grimké, *Rachel* (n.p., 1920); Georgia Douglas Johnson, *Bronze: A Book of Verse* (1922; rpt. Freeport, N.Y.: 1971).

20. Delmar, "Bad Girl," *Courier,* 3 January 1931, 2.

21. Fauset, *The Chinaberry Tree,* 131–32, 187.

22. Chandler Owen, "Women and Children of the South," *BCR* 3 (September 1919): 9, 20.

23. Quoted in *Courier*, 28 March 1931, 3, and *Norfolk Journal and Guide*, 28 March 1931, 1.

24. J. A. Ghent, "Urges Legalization of Birth Control: Law Against Contraception Unjust to the Poor," *Spokesman*, 9 July 1932, 3; "The Case of Dr. Devaughn, or Anti-Birth Control on Trial," *Spokesman*, 22 February 1934, 6.

25. W. G. Alexander, "Birth Control for the Negro: Fad or Necessity?" *Journal of the National Medical Association* 24 (August 1932): 39.

26. Charles S. Johnson, "A Question of Negro Health," *BCR* 16 (June 1932): 167–69.

27. Newell L. Sims, "Hostages to the White Man," *BCR* 16 (July–Auguat 1932): 214–15.

28. E. S. Jamison, "The Future of Negro Health," *BCR* 22 (May 1938): 94–95.

29. "Sterilization," *Courier*, 30 March 1935, 10; "The Sterilization Menace," *Courier*, 18 Jan. 1936, 10; W. E. B. Du Bois, "Sterilization," *Courier*, 27 June 1936, 1; "Are Women Interested Only in Meet and Eat Kind of Club?" *Spokesman*, 29 March 1934, 4.

30. For examples of black social welfare organizations see, for example, William L. Pollard, *A Study of Black Self-Help* (San Francisco: 1978); Edyth L. Ross, *Black Heritage in Social Welfare, 1860–1930* (London: 1978); Lenwood G. Davis, "The Politics of Black Self-Help in the United States: A Historical Overview," in *Black Organizations: Issues on Survival Techniques*, ed. Lennox S. Yearwood (Lanham, Md.: 1980). This statement is also based on extensive reading of the *Pittsburgh Courier, Norfolk Journal and Guide, Baltimore Afro-American, San Francisco Spokesman,* and *New York Age* for the 1920s and 1930s.

31. *The Messenger* (July 1918): n.p.

32. "Report of executive secretary" (March 1923), Series I, Box 4, Planned Parenthood Federation of America Papers, American Birth Control League Records, Sophia Smith Collection, Smith College, Northampton, Mass.; Hannah Stone, "Report of the Clinical Research Department of the ABCL" (1925), Series I, Box 4, PPFA Papers; "Urban League Real Asset, Clinic an Example of How it Assists," *Courier*, 2 November 1935, 1; William Lloyd Imes to Margaret Sanger, 16 May 1931 and 23 November 1932, Box 122b, Folders 1333 and 1336, Sanger Papers; Shelton Hale Bishop to Margaret Sanger, 18 May 1931, Box 122b, Folder 1333, Sanger Papers.

33. "Minutes of the first meeting of 1932, Board of Managers, Harlem Branch" (25 March 1932), Box 122b, Folder 1336; Sanger Papers; "Companionate Marriage Discussed at Forum," *New York Age*, 12 May 1928, n.p.

34. E. S. Lewis and N. Louise Young, "Baltimore's Negro Maternal Health Center: How It Was Organized," *BCR* 22 (May 1938): 93–94.

35. "West Virginia," *BCR* 23 (October 1938): 121; "Birth Control for the Negro," Report of Hazel Moore (1937), Box 22, Folder 10, Florence Rose Papers, Sophia Smith Collection, Smith College; "Negro Demonstration Project Possibilities" (1 December 1939), Box 121, Folder 1309, Sanger Papers.

36. "Annual Reports of the State Member Leagues for 1936, the Kentucky Birth Control League," Series I, Box 4, PPFA Papers; "Annual Report 1938–39, Cincinnati Committee on Maternal Health," Box 119A, Folder 1256, Sanger Papers.

37. "Mother's Health Office Referrals" (5 January 1933), Massachusetts Mother's Health Office, Central Administrative Records, Box 35 and 36, Planned Parenthood League of Massachusetts, Sophia Smith Collection, Smith College; "PPFA field report for California, 1944," Box 119, Folder 1215, Sanger Papers; "Annual Meeting of the BCFA, Indiana Birth Control League, 1935," Series I, Box 4, PPFA Papers.

38. "Chart of the Special Negro Project Demonstration Project," Box 22, Folders 8 and 2, Rose Papers; John Overton and Ivah Uffelman, "A Birth Control Service Among Urban Negroes," *Human Fertility* 7 (August 1942): 97–101; E. Mae McCarroll, "A Condensed Report on the Two Year Negro Demonstration Health Program of PPFA, Inc.," presented at the Annual Convention of the National Medical Association, Cleveland, 17 August 1942, Box 22, Folder 11, Rose Papers; Mabel K. Staupers, "Family Planning and Negro Health," *National News Bulletin of the National Association of Colored Graduate Nurses* 14 (May 1941): 1–10.

39. "Preliminary Annual Report, Division of Negro Service" (7 January 1942), Box 121, Folder 1309, Sanger Papers; "Doctors' Annual Meeting Marked by Fine Program; Local Committee Involved in Planning Meeting," *New York Age*, 7 September 1929, 8; "National Medical Association Meeting Held in Washington," *New York Age*, 27 August 1921, 4. For information on the Smith-Lever Extension Act, see Alfred True, *A History of Agricultural Extension Work in the United States 1785–1923* (Washington, D.C.: 1928).

40. Information on organizations is based on numerous reports and newsletters from the years 1940–42, in Box 22, Rose Papers; see also "Newsletter from Division of Negro Service, December, 1941," Box 121, Folder 1309, and "PPFA Field Report for California, 1944," Box 119, Folder 1215, Sanger Papers.

41. "Activities Report, January 1, 1942–February 6, 1942" and "Progress Outline 1940–42," Box 22, Folder 4, Rose Papers; *Family Guardian* (Massachusetts Mother's Health Council) 5 (December 1939): 3, and 10 (July 1940): 3; "Minutes of the National Advisory Council Meeting, Division of Negro Service," 11 December 1942, Box 121, Folder 1310, Sanger Papers; Peter Murray, *BCR* 16 (July–August 1932): 216; M. O. Bousefield, *BCR* 22 (May 1938): 92. James Reed notes the opposition of the American Medical Association to alternative forms of health care systems in *From Private Vice to Public Virtue,* Part IV and 254.

42. "Notes on the Mother's Clinic, Tucson, Arizona," Box 119, Folder 1212, Sanger Papers; "A Clinic for Tobacco Road," *BCR* 3 [New Series] (January 1936): 6–7; Leonore G. Guttmacher, "Securing Patients for a Rural Center," *BCR* 23 (November 1938): 130–131; "Chas E Hall [*sic*] Census Bureau Expert, Gives Figures for Ten States in Which Number of Children Under Five Shows Decrease," *New York Age,* 7 November 1931, 1.

# 12

## Why Were Most Politically Active Women Opposed to the ERA in the 1920s?

### Kathryn Kish Sklar

*The dispute over whether to pursue strategies for women's advancement based on women's difference from men or on women's similarities to men, accentuated by the Equal Rights Amendment proposed in 1922, debilitated the "women's movement" during the interwar years. Reflecting its nineteenth-century origins, the suffrage movement's mainstream continued to support notions of difference to justify women's political goals and unique contributions to the nation's welfare. Expressing new notions of sexual equality that emerged shortly before the 1920s, however, the National Woman's Party threatened a wide range of legislation that had been carefully constructed on gender differences, including a path-breaking 1921 statute benefiting infant and maternal health. Thus, the strategy whereby "social feminists" had emphasized gender differences as a means of obtaining legislation to enhance the lives of poor people generally conflicted with the strategy of ERA proponents to advance the interests of professional women. Fueled by this fundamental class distinction in their goals, these groups formed two warring camps until the 1970s, one advocating the interests of working women through such institutions as the U.S. Women's Bureau, the other advocating the interests of professional women.*

Students of the history of American women are often surprised to discover that the vast majority of suffrage supporters were opposed to the Equal Rights Amendment when it was first proposed in the 1920s. Why were groups as diverse as the National Women's Trade Union League, the General Federation of Women's Clubs, and the League of Women Voters initially hostile to the ERA? Why did some of them remain hostile for decades thereafter? Why did most women reformers view the amendment's proponents as traitors to the cause of "organized womanhood?" Answers to these questions are important to a complete understanding of the history of the Equal Rights Amendment. They help explain not only why most politically active women opposed the ERA in the 1920s, but why they continued to do so until the 1970s, long after the conditions that generated their initial hostility had ceased to exist. As a strategy for understanding that hostility, this essay focuses on Florence Kelley, the amendment's chief opponent.

Opposition to the amendment had many sources within the ranks of those who supported woman suffrage. Some championed a more conservative approach to the advancement of women's rights, preferring piecemeal or gradual changes to the "blanket" approach of a constitutional amendment. Others objected to the cult of personality that developed within the National Woman's Party around the amendment's originator, Alice Paul. But by far the chief origin of resistance to the early ERA was the fear generated among opponents that the amendment would invalidate a wide range of labor and health legislation that women reformers during the past thirty years had struggled to obtain for American working and poor women.[1]

Such legislative efforts peaked in 1921 with the passage of the Sheppard-Towner Maternity and Infancy Protection Act, which sought to reduce the nation's high rates of infant and maternal mortality through the allocation of federal funds for health education at the county level. The Sheppard-Towner Act exemplified a four stage pattern of action that was well established within women's political culture by 1920: "investigate, educate, legislate, and enforce."

The U.S. Children's Bureau—itself the creation of women reformers in 1911, and staffed by them thereafter—undertook rigorous and extensive investigations of infant mortality rates. They found that the United States ranked seventeenth in maternal and eleventh in infant mortality. Poor babies were at greater risk. One baby in six died in families with annual incomes of less than $450; one in ten died among those earning $650–$850; while only one in sixteen died in families enjoying incomes of $1,250. Meanwhile, nations like New Zealand with public clinics for infant health achieved an infant death rate of one in twenty-one. Many women's organizations, including the National Consumers' League and the newly founded League of Women Voters, joined the Children's Bureau in educating the public about the need for a program of nationally funded clinics to stem the tide of unnecessary infant deaths. Mass-circulation magazines like *Good Housekeeping* and *Woman's Home Companion* fueled the publicity campaign. Bowing to the effectiveness of this campaign, Congress passed the Act and placed the Children's Bureau in charge of the allocation of its funds. In Sheppard-Towner women not only obtained the passage of path-breaking legislation; they also oversaw its enforcement.[2]

Nowhere else in the western world did women's political culture exercise such power. Their achievement was partly due to the success of the Women's Joint Congressional Committee, a coalition of nearly two dozen national women's organizations, in claiming to speak for 20,000,000 members. Partly it was due to the desperate need for infant and maternal health care, which was not forthcoming from any other source. Other industrial nations provided for infant and maternal health through governmental programs run by male doctors and bureaucrats. The absence of such programs in the United States opened unprecedented opportunities for women's political culture. In this as in many other examples, women's political culture used gender-specific legislation as a means of meeting the needs of poor people.[3]

The American Medical Association strenuously opposed the Sheppard-Towner Act, calling it an "imported socialistic scheme."[4] The American Public Health Association opposed it on the grounds that it empowered women bureaucrats rather than (male) professionals. The supporters of the ERA seemed to play into the hands of the enemies of the most popular legislation ever advanced by American women. The amendment was doomed from the start, since only a tiny minority of women activists (primarily from elite backgrounds) were willing to jeopardize what most women saw as essential protections for female workers and for mothers.[5]

Although scholars have only begun to study the history of early opposition to the Equal Rights Amendment, it seems clear that many active opponents viewed themselves as participants in a class struggle to alleviate the oppression of poor women and children. Florence Kelley (1859–1932) typified and led this source of ERA opposition. Whereas most hostility toward the ERA in the 1980s tended to come from the political right, in the 1920s it was located primarily on the political left. Kelley herself was a lifelong socialist. As secretary general of the National Consumers' League from its founding in 1899 until her death in 1932, she was the single most powerful force behind the passage of child-labor legislation and hours and wages laws for working women.[6]

In 1953, U.S. Supreme Court Justice Felix Frankfurter wrote that Kelley "had probably the largest single share in shaping the social history of the United States during the first thirty years of this century," owing to her powerful role "in securing legislation for the removal of the most glaring abuses of our hectic industrialization following the Civil War." Even more important than the legislation itself, Frankfurter thought, was "the continuing process she so largely helped to initiate, by which social legislation is promoted and eventually gets on the statute books."[7]

The passage of social legislation was more difficult in the United States than in Great Britain and elsewhere. That was in part because of the power invested in the judicial branch of government, especially the U.S. Supreme Court, which in the late nineteenth and early twentieth centuries was very conservative. A fateful court decision in 1905 defined the vexatious terms under which American reformers had to lobby for social legislation in ensuing decades. In *Lochner* v. *New York*, the court ruled unconstitutional a state law limiting to ten hours the working day for those employed in bakeries. The rationale behind the law was that longer hours were unhealthy, tending to promote tuberculosis and other diseases, which were then passed on to customers. The court's opinion held, however, that hours could be regulated only when the worker himself was exposed to unhealthy conditions, such as in mines. Otherwise the terms of the contract between employers and employees could not be regulated.[8]

Eventually the court reversed this stand, ruling in *Bunting* v. *Oregon* in 1917 that state laws limiting working hours in manufacturing to ten a day were constitutional. The precedent for the court's 1917 ruling came in 1908, when in response to the *Lochner* decision, Florence Kelley and her allies successfully argued in *Muller* v. *Oregon* that the hours of women working in manufacturing could constitutionally be limited to ten a day, since sociologial evidence demonstrated that women's health was injured when they labored longer than ten hours daily.[9]

Historians of labor legislation in the United States have noted that men tended to "fight the battle from behind the women's petticoats," since men benefited from laws passed to protect women, and since men's laws tended to follow the legal precedent set by women's.[10] That was true in other countries, as well, but nowhere so emphatically as in the United States, since in no other Western nation was it so difficult to obtain such regulations. In the 1920s, one-half of those employed in the steel industry worked twelve hours a day—longer than in any other nation except Japan.[11] Even though the eight-hour day was the single most popular goal of the labor movement in the United States as early as the 1880s, it was not established for all workers by federal legislation until the Fair Labor Standards Act of 1938—an act upheld by the U.S. Supreme Court in 1941. Thus, in response to the 1905 *Lochner* decision, Kelley and her associates in the National Consumers' League pursued a strategy of obtaining court approval of minimum-hour legislation for women and then extending that approval to cover men. She and her allies were almost as instrumental in the 1917 *Bunting* decision as in the 1908 *Muller* decision.[12] They used gender-specific legislation as a means of advancing class-specific goals.

Florence Kelley was extremely effective in organizing middle-class women consumers into groups that undertook political action on behalf of what they saw as the rights and interests of working women and children. By 1912 some sixty local chapters of the National Consumers' League had successfully agitated for legislation governing the labor of children in almost every state, and that of women in most states.[13]

Kelley's personal charisma and moral indignation over the oppression of women and children workers fueled much of this activity. During a 1908 visit to the United States, the German sociologist Max Weber found Kelley "by far the most outstanding figure" he and his wife had met; he learned from her "a great deal more about the radically evil things in this world."[14] In part Kelley's moral fervor came from her Quaker family background. As early as 1882, the year she graduated from Cornell, she published an article on the oppression of women workers, "Need Our Working Women Despair?"[15] In part her fervor was due to her knowledge of the "scientific materialistic" writings of Karl Marx and Friedrich Engels, which she translated in the 1880s. She developed a lifelong commitment to socialism in the 1880s and saw class struggle behind the exploitative practices of the sweatshop conditions in which women and children toiled long hours for pitifully small wages.

As a socialist, Kelley saw the power of the state as the logical means of ending such oppression. And as the daughter of one of the most influential congressmen in the nineteenth century (William "Pig Iron" Kelley, who was elected to fifteen consecutive terms in the U.S. House of Representatives between 1860 and 1890), Florence Kelley knew that government was respon-sive to organized groups, especially those that represented the interests of capital. As she saw it, her contribution to the political process was to make government more responsive to the interests of laboring women and chil-dren.

Florence Kelley's success was based on more than her own personal charisma and background, however, for she was born into a generation of middle- and upper-middle-class women who constituted the first generation of college-educated women, many of whom did not marry and instead de-voted their lives to much-needed social reforms. In the 1890s, a significant number of these college graduates joined forces in the social settlement movement. Living together in houses in the midst of urban slums, these reformers formed lifelong communities, providing one another with mu-tual support and supplying their society with an ongoing critique of the causes and consequences of urban poverty. In 1891 there were only six set-tlements in the United States; by 1900 over a hundred had been founded, and by 1910 there were more than four hundred. Thereby talented women were recruited into social reform in every American city.[16]

Jane Addams, cofounder in 1889 of America's most famous social set-tlement, Hull House of Chicago, was the best known of this group of college-educated women, but it also included many other activists who organized themselves and others to advance enlightened public policy. Hull House residents included, for example, Julia Lathrop, first director of the U.S. Children's Bureau from 1911 to 1920; Dr. Alice Hamilton, founder of the field of industrial medicine; and Grace Abbott, founder in 1907 of the Im-migrants Protective League. In New York at the Henry Street Settlement, which she founded in 1895, Lillian Wald pioneered in the organization of public-health nursing. Florence Kelley was a bridge between the settlements of Chicago and New York, since she lived with Addams in the 1890s and with the Henry Street group from 1899 until 1926. More than at any time before or since, settlements made possible the consolidation of the energies of women activists, vastly increasing their social and political effectiveness.[17]

Thus, when the suffrage movement modernized its tactics under the direction of Carrie Chapman Catt in 1910 and embarked on the last stage of its protracted struggle to bring women into the mainstream of American political life, other women were already well established in that mainstream. Viewing their causes as mutually beneficial, social reformers and suffragists joined forces during the decade before the passage of the Nineteenth Amendment in 1920. Votes for women would enhance the power of social reformers, while the reformers' social agenda strengthened the suffrage cause by providing concrete examples of the good that would flow from women's votes.[18]

Nevertheless, any coalition as diverse as the one supporting woman suffrage in 1920 was likely to break up when the single issue that tied it together was accomplished. Thus, even more surprising than the divergence of the National Woman's Party from the rest of the suffrage movement in 1921 was the solidarity that persisted among other elements of the suffrage coalition after the vote was won.

That solidarity was nowhere more visible than in the movement's opposition to what they called the "blanket amendment." By January 1923, the *New York Times* listed the following organizations in the amendment's "counterlobby": "the League of Women Voters, the National Consumers' League, the Women's Trade Union League, the Charity Organization Society, the Girls' Friendly Society, the National Council of Catholic Women, the Council of Jewish Women, the National Association for Labor Legislation, the Women's Christian Temperance Union, the American Association for Organizing Family Social Work, the National League of Girls' Clubs, the Parent Teachers' Association, the National Federation of Federal Employees, and the National Congress of Mothers."[19] Also opposed were the American Association of University Women, the YWCA, and the General Federation of Women's Clubs. Only the National Federation of Business and Professional Women's Clubs did not openly oppose the proposed amendment.[20]

This remarkable unanimity among women's groups was partly due to their reluctance to venture into new and more radical solutions to women's inequality. To a considerable degree, however, it was also due to the momentum of social reform within the suffrage movement that supported the enactment of special protective legislation for working and for poor women. The Sheppard-Towner Act was passed in 1921 as a result of effective lobbying efforts of some twenty women's organizations combined under the umbrella organization of the Women's Joint Congressional Committee. Many believed that such special legislation, as well as state mothers' pension laws and other protective measures, would be invalidated by the Equal Rights Amendment.

A solution to this dilemma was tried in the state of Wisconsin,[21] where in 1921 a version of the ERA was passed with a clause that exempted all legislation designed to protect women. The Wisconsin example failed to resolve the debate, however, because the Wisconsin judiciary was noted for its political liberalism and thus could not provide an adequate test of how the amendment might be interpreted by the more conservative federal judiciary.[22]

Meanwhile, the antagonism to the amendment by reform leaders such as Florence Kelley was vastly increased in the early 1920s by the U.S. Supreme Court's consideration of the constitutionality of minimum-wage laws for women. By 1923, fifteen states and territories, beginning with Massachusetts in 1912, had passed minimum-wage statutes for women. Florence Kelley and the National Consumers' League were the chief proponents of this reform. In *Adkins* v. *Children's Hospital*, the U.S. Supreme Court ruled the Washington, D.C. minimum-wage law unconstitutional, saying that the Nineteenth Amendment demonstrated that men and women were equal, and therefore women did not need special legislation. Revealing the antilabor and procapital bias of the decision, the court wrote that "it should be remembered that of the three fundamental principles which underlie government, and for which government exists—life, liberty, and property—the chief of these is property."[23] Minimum-wage laws were crippled by this decision until the Supreme Court began to face an avalanche of New Deal labor legislation in the 1930s. In 1937 it reversed itself on minimum wages for women in *West Coast Hotel* v. *Parrish*, and in 1941 it finally unambiguously approved minimum wages for all workers producing goods intended for interstate commerce in *United States* v. *Darby*, thus upholding the constitutionality of the 1938 Fair Labor Standards Act.

The struggle over the ERA in the 1920s took place in a context in which women's organizations endorsed special legislation for women as part of a general reform effort to improve working conditions for women and men alike. The strategy worked with hours legislation, but it failed with wage legislation. In 1923 the National Woman's Party heralded the Supreme Court's decision in the Adkins case, allying itself with what the National Consumers' League considered reactionary political forces. The politics of gender and the politics of class were inextricably combined. At issue was not only what was best for women but what was best for American society as a whole. This clash of social visions was intensified in the late 1920s, when, reflecting the more conservative temper of the times, the Sheppard-Towner Act was allowed to die for lack of funding. The forces of progressive reform no longer could command legislative majorities at the state or federal level, but there was one thing they could and did continue to do long after the conditions that initially had generated their animosity had passed—oppose the Equal Rights Amendment. Support for the amendment on the political left and within the ranks of organized labor came in the 1970s from a new generation that had not experienced "the women's war" of the 1920s.

## NOTES

1. The best study of ERA opposition is J. Stanley Lemon's chapter "Feminists against Feminists" in his book *The Woman Citizen: Social Feminism in the 1920's* (Urbana: University of Illinois Press, 1973), pp. 181–208.
2. See Lemons, *Woman Citizen*, pp. 153–80.
3. Lemons, *Woman Citizen*, p. 157. For a comparative perspective on infant health care, see Alisa C. Klaus, "Babies All the Rage: The Movement to Prevent Infant Mortality in the United States and France, 1890–1920," (Ph.D. Diss., University of Pennsylvania, 1986).
4. Lemons, "The Sheppard-Towner Act: Progressivism in the 1920s," *Journal of American History*, 55 (1969), 776–86.
5. See Lemons, *Woman Citizen*, pp. 153–80.

6. For biographical information on Florence Kelley, see Louise Wade on Kelley in *Notable American Women*, 3 vols, ed. Edward T. James, Janet Wilson James, and Paul S. Boyer (Cambridge: Harvard University Press, 1971).

7. Felix Frankfurter's "Foreword," in Josephine Goldmark, *Impatient Crusader: Florence Kelley's Life Story* (Urbana: University of Illinois Press, 1953).

8. See Stanley Kutler, ed., *The Supreme Court and the Constitution, Readings in American Constitutional History* (New York: W. W. Norton, 1977, 2d ed.), pp. 282–89.

9. Ibid., pp. 291–92.

10. Elizabeth Brandeis, "Labor Legislation," in John R. Commons, *History of Labor in the United States, 1896–1932*, 4 vols. (New York: Macmillan Co., 1935), vol. 3, p. 462. See also Anne Corinne Hill, "Protection of Women Workers and the Courts: A Legal History," *Feminist Studies* 5, no. 2 (Summer 1979): 247–73.

11. David Brody, *Steelworkers in America: The Nonunion Era* (Cambridge: Harvard University Press, 1960), pp. 271–73.

12. See Louis L. Athey, "The Consumer's Leagues and Social Reform, 1890–1923" (Ph.D. diss., University of Delaware, 1965), p. 221.

13. Ibid., p. 270.

14. Marianne Weber, *Max Weber: A Biography* (New York: Wiley and Sons 1975), p. 302.

15. Florence Kelley, "Need Our Working Women Despair?" *International Review* (Nov. 1882), pp. 517–26.

16. See Allen F. Davis, *Spearheads for Reform: The Social Settlements and the Progressive Movement, 1890–1914* (New York: Oxford University Press, 1967), p. 12 and passim.

17. For a list of eighteen women reform leaders in the social settlement movement, see "Settlement House Leaders" in the "Classified Index," vol. 3 of *Notable American Women*.

18. See William O'Neill, *Everyone Was Brave: A History of Feminism in America* (New York: Quadrangle, 1969). This title was taken from a eulogy of Kelley at her memorial service, where Newton Baker said, "Everybody was brave from the moment she came into the room."

19. "The Woman's War," *New York Times*, Jan. 14, 1922. Clipping from Mary Van Kleek Collection, box 96, folder 1519, Sophia Smith Collection, Smith College.

20. See Lemons, *Woman Citizen*, p. 190.

21. Ibid., pp. 181–208.

22. Ibid., pp. 187–189.

23. See Athey, "Consumer's Leagues," pp. 171–204; quote from Lemons, *The Woman Citizen*, p. 239.

# 13

## Companionate Marriage and the Lesbian Threat

### Christina Simmons

*With the advent of woman suffrage and a more forthright acceptance of women in the public sphere, the 1920s saw a new emphasis on "companionate marriage" in contrast to the Victorian view of the separation of women's and men's responsibilities within marriage. Increasingly, commentators acknowledged women's sexuality and the importance of mutual sexual satisfaction. The price for this new view of marital relations was a marked denigration of homosocial or homosexual relations among women. What once was viewed as a natural expression of affection among women was now viewed as deviant. Christina Simmons makes clear the interrelationship between these two developments and the implications of the "lesbian threat" in terms of power considerations between the sexes.*

> Back in the dim ages when I was a schoolgirl we were not so well informed about the proper names for things. . . . If, now, Miss Barnes' school is representative at all, we have indications of a growth in half-knowledge which makes all girlish fondnesses suspect, so that the door is shut on these minor "innocent" outlets which have done so much to preserve woman's purity, or else it is opened wide on the horrendous and fascinating.
>
> Lorine Pruette, "The Flapper"[1]

Citing Carman Barnes' story about a girls' boarding school, psychologist Lorine Pruette reflected in 1930 that sharpened public awareness of sexuality was creating a new kind of moral rigidity in American culture. Affection and friendship between young women which had seemed innocent in the nineteenth century might arouse disapproval in the twentieth.[2] A girl might either be pushed ever earlier into "the frankness of a heterosexual relation" or be exposed to homosexual possibilities newly made "horrendous and fascinating" by the flapper's modish but superficial sexual knowledge.[3] Pruette commented that the older women in Katharine B. Davis' famous study had moved easily "between homosexual and heterosexual relations without necessarily evil consequences," but they had been raised "before our present era of frankness was well under way."[4] Pruette's reflection raises an important historical question—why fear of lesbianism constituted such a significant problem in the dominant heterosexual ideology of the 1920's and 1930's.

"Companionate Marriage and the Lesbian Threat," by Christina Simmons, from *Frontiers*, IV:3 (1979): 54–59.

Molly Dewson and Polly Porter on the dairy farm where they lived together in western Massachusetts, c. 1912. David Hall, Castine, Maine.

As much of the "sexual revolution" of the 1920's took place in words as in actions.[5] A spate of literature outlining the new "companionate" marriage, one based on friendship and sexual satisfaction, appeared in the 1920's, followed by more technical marriage manuals and popular medical advice in the next decade.[6] These works represented the cultural definition of changes in gender relations which had been stirring in social life since the late nineteenth century.[7] Those who wrote books and articles on sex were educators, social workers, psychologists, physicians, and others in a rising class of trained professional people, mostly male. In the 1910's and 1920's radical voices among them spoke for feminism and/or for sexual liberation.[8] Many more, however, acknowledged social changes but feared conflict between the sexes might result. They sought harmony between the sexes by reforming what seemed the most oppressive elements of Victorian marriage. This latter group articulated a new sexual ideology which achieved cultural hegemony by the 1930's and which represented a morality more suited to the social needs of the corporate liberal state than its Victorian predecessor.[9]

Proponents of the new companionate marriage gave great attention to women because they attributed the need for sexual reform primarily to historical changes in women's lives. The nineteenth-century sex-segregation of leisure among the respectable classes began dissolving in the 1890's; by the 1910's a small but noticeable group of elite urban women were going to restaurants and cabarets in male company. Middle-class couples joined working-class men and women at the new movie theatres. Already in the 1910's a few women adopted boyish "flapper" clothing and male habits like smoking and drinking in public. They turned against styles which emphasized women's distance and differentiation from men.[10] The expansion of women's education and of their paid employment in the higher social classes by 1900 generated a less exclusively domestic image of women in the culture. The professional work of some college women, the political activity of the suffrage movement, even the social and charitable activity of club women gave women a more salient presence outside the home.[11] Women of the upper-middle and upper classes were the implicit concern because they were the most immediate subjects of the dominant sexual morality and were expected to exemplify it to the women of other classes.[12]

As women discarded Victorian delicacy they seemed more like men, that is, as individuals with a right to personal fulfillment rather than a duty to sacrifice self for men and children. For example, in one 1919 novel an aspiring young social researcher exclaims, when asked if she would disobey her father, "Certainly! First of all I am a human being. That is what Ibsen's Nora said."[13] Being drawn into the public sphere made them more sexual, too: "By the very act of working, something has happened to her . . . she has become in important psychological elements, a man . . . more significantly they absorb, with their jobs, the masculine attitude toward sex."[14] Recognition of women's individuality and sexuality was a way of acknowledging a

new kind of energy and social power, which pertained to more than reproduction and the domestic sphere. Companionate marriage represented the
attempt of mainstream marriage ideology to adapt to women's perceived
new social and sexual power.

This power was manifested, as one man observed, in "the increasing
subordination of . . . maternity to sexuality . . . of love to passion, or procreation to recreation." The "vast reservoirs of erotic energy resident in women," freed from purely domestic and reproductive activities, were over-
flowing.[15] Many sexual reformers cited Freudian concepts to justify belief in
the strength and universality of sexual drives. They argued that suppressing
sexual desire was psychologically and even physically unhealthy.

Companionate marriage directed female sexual energies toward men
and marriage. Judge Ben Lindsey popularized the essential elements in his
1927 book *Companionate Marriage:* 1) easier divorce, especially for childless
marriages; 2) legalization of birth control; 3) provision of sex education for
youth. These concrete reforms relied on two assumptions: that intense psychological companionship, or friendship, should characterize relations between husband and wife and that the sexual aspect of this intimacy was
particularly important.[16] This form of marriage was said to provide the
equality women deserved and to be a bond of "creative companionship and
interdependent cooperation." "Does the husband really want a mere permanent housekeeper, a faithful drudge, an unpaid servant, or does he desire a real life companion and a friend . . . ?"[17] The wife was to be included
in the budget planning and was to have access to money without asking for
it; the husband might help a little with dishes and housework. Women were
to receive their rights to sexual pleasure as well; sexual literature warned
men to abandon the stereotypical Victorian sexual aggression in favor of
sensitivity, gentleness, and a slower pace.[18] Divorce, birth control, and sex
education all helped women to exercise greater control over the conditions
of the marital bond.

The new model compared favorably with reformers' exaggerated image of Victorian marriage—its duty-bound separate male and female
spheres and its emotional and sexual repression. One sociologist concluded
"there is every reason to suppose that asceticism has received in this generation a death blow from which it can never recover. It has passed forever
from the category of ideals into that of mental abnormalities, and its morbid
significance is being generally recognized."[19] By deprecating nineteenth-
century marriage, advocates of companionate marriage in effect showed
how enlightened and fair the new form was.

But what happened if women did not wholly reject Victorian gender
relations but rather kept their distance from men and preferred each other's company? The ponderous traditions and social structures separating
and differentiating the sexes now appeared as obstacles to heterosexual
comradeship and romance. And conversely, women's segregation and soli-

darity with each other took on a menacing aspect unknown in earlier generations.[20] If women's sexual desires exhibited the urgency long attributed to men's, and if an intense love relationship seemed vital for personal happiness, then lesbian relationships were the logical result of the absence or failure of heterosexuality. "We do not blame anyone for seeking normal affection and love; we all need it to be happy. How can we blame a woman, who, through no fault of her own, has been deprived of such affection from a man, and turns to another woman for it?"[21] In these writings the specter of lesbianism arose in association with perceptions of the persisting differences and distance between men and women. But as is so clear in racial segregation, such separation meant inequality as well and consequently resistance from the oppressed group. Whether female resistance to heterosexual relationships actually occurred or not, the recognition of sexual inequality engendered in the culture a male *fear* of resistance, often expressed as a fear of lesbianism.

Within the voluminous literature of this new sexual ideology a conception of homosexuality was developing which made it into a very significant, if not the major, "deviation" from the dominant heterosexual pattern, especially for women. Historian Carroll Smith-Rosenberg has argued that early nineteenth-century American culture did not define lesbianism as a distinct sexual pattern.[22] Such innocence was gone by 1920. Accompanying the reformulation of heterosexual ideology during this period was a surprisingly extensive commentary on female homosexuality. The critical point about this literature is that it treated homosexuality as a condition which developed in specific relation to heterosexuality, namely through the failure or deprivation or rejection of the latter. Consequently, such writings denigrated not only exclusive lesbians but also women who might once have moved easily between homosexuality and heterosexuality and women experiencing conflict in relationships with men.[23]

By the 1920's discussion of homosexuality was expanding a little beyond strictly medical and scientific circles and was using popular Freudian concepts.

Older theories of homosexuality as a congenital abnormality still appeared, and some researchers pursued hormone theories, but environmental explanations were taking precedence.[24] The ascendancy of psychodynamic explanations focused attention on the process whereby young people "acquired" homosexuality and strengthened efforts to control it by changing the predisposing environmental factors. Both lay and medical writers loosely included factors from social as well as from family life among possible causes.

Whether homosexuality was actually increasing or not, some commentators said that is it was, owing to the disruptions of the Great War and the changing sexual morality of the 1920's. "The rhythm of the jazz age has infected our sex life. . . . The modern mad quest for stimulation is driving men and women into the arms of abnormality."[25] Such beliefs can be understood as expressions of cultural anxiety about the supposed social sources of homosexuality, as discussions of the "social" causes of homosexuality were a constituent element of the dominant heterosexual ideology. Often, homosexuality was turned into a threatening, oppositional alternative to the heterosexual pattern, especially in the case of women, thus presenting a cultural meaning that homosexuality had not carried in the nineteenth century.

Inherited rules governing social interaction between the sexes were premised on a fear of heterosexual contact for respectable women outside of marriage. But some marriage reformers began to feel that the spirit of the rules was so directed against heterosexuality that to some women romantic involvement with other women appeared socially safer than involvement with men: "Paradoxically many women believe, long after they have grown up, that an emotional relationship with a member of their own sex is no such breach of the conventions as an intimate relationship with a man."[26] Several authors noted that the hazards of adolescent heterosexual adventures were much exaggerated compared to the failure of heterosexuality altogether: "The anxious parental and social attempts to insure against such accidents, by repression and segregation, can produce homosexuality, perversions of all sorts, and sexual and emotional incapacities which can in the long run produce more individual unhappiness and more social ills than a boy's gonorrhea or a girl's illegitimate baby."[27]

Sex-segregated institutions, particularly schools, were said to be keeping young women and men from learning to know and live with each other. Sexual theorists' emphasis on individual fulfillment and romantic intimacy made marriage an arena for compromise and adjustment between two personalities. As the marriage manifestoes of the 1920's faded into the more technical advice works of the 1930's, problems of psychological adjustment within marriage received much attention.[28] Concerned about sources of marital instability, reformers scrutinized single-sex education: "The unwholesome fashionable practice of sex-segregated schools brings young people into a homosexual atmosphere." Deprived of male contact, young girls might not learn to love men. They would develop an "unconscious homosexuality" which would operate "to make mating so difficult as to be almost impossible, and to make matings unsatisfactory and unstable when they ... [were] formally achieved."[29]

Failure to "achieve" heterosexual union was labeled immaturity. Critical of women's "emotional debauchery," one pair of researchers said of a lesbian college student: "she was so much of a child that she needed the complete understanding which only a person of her own sex could give her."[30] From another perspective, one might say the defenders of marriage were afraid that if psychological compatibility had become a major criterion for good relationships, then two women might sometimes find happiness more easily than a woman and a man.

The many single graduates of the women's colleges as well as independent young reformers and professional women, made notorious when Theodore Roosevelt accused them of causing race suicide, were widely known to live with other women when they did not live with their families.[31] Suspicion accumulated that these relationships were "unhealthy" at least. The mother of a young statistician portrayed in one novel asked, "'Have you never met a man you fancied?' . . . 'I shall never love romantically,' was the forcible answer. 'What time have I for love?'" Yet the daughter "spoke with more enthusiasm" of her roommate: "'She is studying to be a librarian. We met each other last year and we've been rooming together since this fall; she means everything to me, mummy.'" The novelist judges the daughter's bohemian existence unnatural, the result of feminist disdain for domesticity and absorption in work and social causes.[32]

Despite overwhelming male economic advantages and social and political power, some women, especially in the higher social classes, were better able than their mothers and grandmothers had been to decline marriage if they chose.[33] One psychologist attributed female homosexuality in part to a feminist desire for life work besides motherhood and an unwillingness to marry the average man.[34] Another author speculated, not unreasonably, that women's ability not to marry had raised public awareness of lesbianism: "For thousands of years moralists and legalists have denounced homosexuality between men, but no code has ever forbidden physical relationship between women ... since it did not necessarily prevent child-bearing, or cause children to be born illegitimately. . . . When feminism ... increased, and women began to be increasingly celibate, the question of 'mannish' women began finding its way into popular novels (*The Well of Loneliness*) into plays (*The Children's Hour*) and into parlor conversations."[35]

Suspicions of lesbianism often centered on women of higher status because they were perceived to have significant power. One critic noted that employment made all women more sexually receptive but that working-class women became heterosexually promiscuous while professional women became lesbians.[36] Upper-middle-class and upper-class women were the ones who worked for suffrage and Progressive reforms and lived in social settlements, but they were still needed to support, comfort, and provide children for men of their class. Roosevelt had criticized their childlessness, but dominant-class ideologues of the 1920's and 1930's showed fear and disapproval of these women's independence by insinuating their lesbianism.[37] What marriage reformers were doing in effect was to perceive women's autonomy and resistance to male domination in sexual terms and to deprecate the legitimacy of their social and economic aspirations.

Remnants of Victorian gender relations, then, acted as social causes of homosexuality according to many architects of the new marriage. Influenced by rules of propriety and sex-segregated institutions, women with education and financial resources established domestic arrangements that were free of male support or control and which were possibly lesbian.[38] Some critics found lesbianism an unfortunate but understandable result of such conditions, to be pitied, even tolerated. As companionate marriage gained legitimacy, however, others began to see a "psychologically sick" lesbianism as the cause rather than the effect of women's resistance to heterosexuality. They became defensive, trying to reduce women's protests to narrowly sexual motivation: "The driving force in many agitators and militant women who are always after their rights, is often an unsatisfied sex impulse, with a homosexual aim. Married women with a completely satisfied libido rarely take an active interest in militant movements."[39] Such a reversal occurred among reformers concerned about the persistence of sexual conflict even in the new marriage. Claiming that companionate marriage had ended Victorian inequities, they found in lesbianism an "irrational" psychological cause for behavior which subtly challenged male sexual dominance within marriage.

Lesbianism was blamed for both aggressive and inhibited female sexuality. Despite the alleged equality of partners in companionate marriage, male sexual leadership remained the norm. Women who flouted feminine decorum in intercourse drew harsh disapproval. The male superior position in coitus, for example, symbolized the man's dominance in the relationship, and a women who wished to usurp it risked censure. One physician claimed, "A homosexual woman often wants to possess the male and not to be possessed by him. . . . With them orgasm is often only possible in the superior position."[40] He associated lesbianism with a rejection of women's natural, subordinate role within heterosexual activity.

The complete absence of female sexual participation, however, also indicated lesbianism to these modern defenders of marriage. Women had to walk a fine line between appropriate modesty and neurotic prudery. The latter became problematic when women internalized sexual conventions so thoroughly as to resist heterosexuality in disgust or fear. Because sexual harmony was so sought after in companionate marriage, too much female naivete or embarrassment was counterproductive and seemed old-fashioned by the 1920's.[41] Purity, too, began to arouse suspicions of lesbianism. An upbringing of "excessive repressions" or "morbid or silly warnings against the opposite sex" might encourage lesbian tendencies. Alternatively, a person characterized by "'prudishness' and 'stiffness,' or more favorably . . . 'unapproachable purity' or 'high ideals,'" might be influenced by "unconscious homosexuality."[42]

More specifically, prudery caused frigidity, the leading female problem in marital adjustment according to most proponents of companionate marriage. Many writers expressed sympathy for women with the problem and saw them as victims of a sexually repressive socialization. In that sense frigidity provided an argument for sex education and women's sexual rights in companionate marriage.[43] At the same time, certain reformers, including some who also expressed sympathy, feared or resented female frigidity. They interpreted it as a sign of "man-hating," or rejection of the female role.

Mixed with words of encouragement to women to accept and express their sexuality were warnings of what might happen if they did not: "women will have to be bluntly reminded that one main source of prostitution and unfaithfulness is the selfish and unsurrendered wife."[44] Losing a husband was what women risked when they failed in heterosexual "adjustment."

As the cultural definition of marriage shifted to include greater emphasis on mutual sexual pleasure, women's dissatisfaction grew proportionately more alarming. "The woman who gets no pleasure at all in coitus cannot truly love her husband. Love demands more than respect or admiration." Respect or admiration might have been sufficient for the Victorians, but no more. Defensive sexual advisers turned to attack. "Some married women thought to dislike coitus only because of a superior modesty, in reality are deceiving themselves and others. Their frigidity is on a homosexual basis, all their real interests being feminine."[45] Another man described the "nightmare" of marriage to a lesbian: After intercourse, "they feel cold, and do not experience the normal glow; they talk *as though nothing important had happened*. These women often despise their husbands in various ways" (my italics).[46] In normal heterosexual intercourse "something important" did happen—when a woman expressed or feigned love and desire for a man in spite of the socially determined inequality between them, she symbolized some acceptance of her position, whether from having achieved an individually satisfactory relationship or from the need to please him. Overt sexual coldness destroyed the illusion of harmony.

Thus in cultural terms lesbianism represented women's autonomy in various forms—feminism, careers, refusal to marry, failure to adjust to marital sexuality.[47] It became a symbol in a cultural context of increased expectation and evaluation of sexual activity for women as well as for men in the new form of companionate marriage. How well this new ideology of marriage described the typical patterns of people's sexual lives requires investigation, but no one could have remained totally isolated from its power. Directives about gender relations were expressed not only in articles and books of advice but directly by health care and social work professionals, clergy, radio, movies, advertising, and government policies.[48] We cannot know how many people were influenced by arguments for co-education, earlier dating and marriage, and breaking up friendships between adolescent girls. The intention was clear—"to train young people for—we need not hesitate to use the phrase—living happily ever after in heterosexual matehood."[49]

The ebullient atmosphere of sexual liberation which characterized the 1910's and 1920's allowed room for more open discussion of lesbianism than had ever existed in the United States before. Trying to explain what most of them could not accept as legitimate, sexual theorists found social causes of lesbianism in clashes between an anachronistic morality and a perceived new female power in social and sexual life. As the ideology of companionate marriage became established, however, attitudes toward female resistance, and thus toward lesbianism, hardened among many marriage theorists and counselors. Creators of the new ideology had hoped to modify some extreme features of male dominance but were far from ready to institute what feminists would have defined as equality. The decline of organized feminism after 1920 must certainly have been one factor allowing dissemination of such an intensely heterosexual vision of personal life. In the absence of a powerful feminist voice, exponents of companionate marriage tempered the liberating potential of new sexual ideas and judged women's sexuality acceptable only insofar as its energy was channeled into marriage and the service of men.

## NOTES

Thanks to Linda Kealey and Bruce Tucker for their comments on this essay.

1. Lorine Pruette, "The Flapper," in V. F. Calverton and S. D. Schmalhausen, *The New Generation: The Intimate Problems of Modern Parents and Children* (New York: Macaulay, 1930), pp. 574–75.

2. Diana Frederics [pseud.], *Diana: A Strange Autobiography* (1939; rpt. New York: Arno, 1975), p. 222.

3. Pruette, p. 577.

4. Ibid., p. 585. Katharine B. Davis did one of the earliest sociological studies of sexual behavior. She used written questionnaires to survey college graduates and club women in the early 1920's and published the results in 1929 in *Factors in the Sex Life of Twenty-Two Hundred Women* (New York: Harper & Bros.).

5. Maurice A. Bigelow, *Sex-Education: A Series of Lectures Concerning Knowledge of Sex in Its Relation to Human Life* (New York: Macmillan, 1916), p. 254; Ernest R. Groves, *The Marriage Crisis* (New York: Longmans, Green, 1928), pp. 165–68.

6. For example, Ben Lindsey and Wainwright Evans, *The Companionate Marriage* (New York: Boni and Liveright, 1927); Floyd Dell, *Love in the Machine Age: A Psychological Study of the Transition from Patriarchal Society* (New York: Farrar, 1930); LeMon Clark, *Emotional Adjustment in Marriage* (St. Louis: C. V. Mosby, 1937); *Sexology*, 1933+; *Popular Medicine*, 1934+.

7. Christopher Lasch, *Haven in the Heartless World: The Family Beseiged* (New York: Basic Books, 1977), p. 9; V. F. Calverton, *The Bankruptcy of Marriage* (New York: Macaulay, 1928), p. 146.

8. Grete Meisel-Hess, *The Sexual Crisis: A Critique of Our Sex Life,* trans. Eden and Cedar Paul (New York: Critic and Guide, 1917), pp. 20–24, 74; V. F. Calverton, "Sex and Social Struggle," in *Sex in Civilization,* ed. V. F. Calverton and S. D. Schmalhausen (New York: Macauley, 1929), p. 271; J. William Lloyd, "Sex Jealousy and Civilization," in *Sex in Civilization,* pp. 233–46; Calverton, *Bankruptcy,* p. 215.

9. Dell, p. 68; Stuart Ewen, *Captains of Consciousness: Advertising and the Social Roots of the Consumer Culture* (New York: McGraw-Hill, 1976), especially Part III, chapters 1, 5, 6.

10. Lewis Allan Erenberg, "Urban Night Life and the Decline of Victorianism: New York City's Restaurants and Cabarets, 1890–1918," Diss. University of Michigan 1974, p. 131; Lary Linden May, "Reforming Leisure: The Birth of Mass Culture and the Motion Picture Industry,

1896–1920," Diss. University of California, Los Angeles 1977, p. 110; James R. McGovern, "The American Woman's Pre-World War I Freedom in Manners and Morals," *Journal of American History,* 55 (1968), 322; Floyd Dell, *Looking at Life* (New York: Knopf, 1924), pp. 23–24.

11. Phyllis Blanchard and Carlyn Manasses, *New Girls for Old* (New York: Macaulay, 1930), pp. 231, 235, 241–46; C. Gasquoine Hartley, *Women's Wild Oats: Essays on the Re-Fixing of Moral Standards* (New York: Stokes, 1920), pp. 38, 43; S. D. Schmalhausen, "The Sexual Revolution," in *Sex in Civilization,* p. 359–60.

12. Daniel Scott Smith has argued that working-class sexual behavior was beginning to leave behind Victorian styles after 1875 and that the "sexual revolution" of the 1920's was middle-class, "The Dating of the American Sexual Revolution: Evidence and Interpretation," in *The American Family in Social-Historical Perspective,* ed. Michael Gordon (New York: St. Martin's, 1973), pp. 321–35. Floyd Dell also explicitly proclaims sexual changes as a "middle-class revolution," *Love in the Machine Age,* p. 201.

13. Nalbro Bartley, *A Woman's Woman* (Boston: Small, Maynard, 1919), p. 46.

14. Horace Coon, *Coquetry for Men* (New York: Amour Press, 1932), pp. 110–11; Clark, p. 51.

15. Schmalhausen, "The Sexual Revolution," pp. 379, 402. Younger feminists of the period differed from their predecessors in embracing sexuality more enthusiastically. See Elaine Showalter, ed., *These Modern Women: Autobiographical Essays from the Twenties* (Old Westbury, N.Y.: Feminist Press, 1978), p. 15.

16. Lindsey and Evans, pp. 175–76; Coon, pp. 184–88; Ira S. Wile and Mary Day Winn, *Marriages in the Modern Manner* (New York: Century, 1929), pp. 12–13, 263–64.

17. Sherwood Eddy, *Sex and Youth* (Garden City, N.Y.: Doubleday, Doran, 1929), pp. 140, 149; Wile and Winn, p. 178; Beatrice Forbes-Robertson Hale, "Women in Transition," in *Sex in Civilization,* p. 75.

18. Eddy, pp. 151, 154; Margaret Sanger, *Happiness in Marriage* (New York: Blue Ribbon, 1926), pp. 122–24, 225; Groves, p. 100.

19. Groves, p. 214.

20. Carroll Smith-Rosenberg, "The Female World of Love and Ritual: Relations between Women in Nineteenth-Century America," *Signs,* 1, 1 (Autumn 1975), 27.

21. Ralph Hay, "Mannish Women or Old Maids?" *Know Yourself,* 1 ( July 1938), 78; also, Lindsey and Evans, p. 187; Eleanor Bertine, M.D., "Health and Morality in the Light of the New Psychology," *Proceedings of the International Conference of Women Physicians* (New York: The Woman's Press, 1919), IV, pp. 10, 11.

22. Smith-Rosenberg, 8, 27; Jonathan Katz, *Gay American History* (New York: Thomas Y. Crowell, 1976), p. 449.

23. Katz includes a good example of such doubt in excerpts from the diary of Dorothy Thompson, 1932, p. 558.

24. Arno Karlen, *Sexuality and Homosexuality: A New View* (New York: Norton, 1971), pp. 324, 330; John F. W. Meagher, M.D., "Homosexuality: Its Psychobiological and Psychopathological Significance," *The Urologic and Cutaneous Review,* 33 (1929), 510.

25. S. D. Schmalhausen, "The Freudian Emphasis on Sex," in *The Sex Problem in Modern Society,* ed. John Francis McDermott (New York: Modern Library, 1931), p. 64; also, Olga Knopf, *Women on Their Own* (Boston: Little, Brown, 1935), p. 157.

26. Dorothy Dunbar Bromley and Florence Haxton Britten, *Youth and Sex: A Study of 1300 College Students* (New York: Harper, 1938), p. 129; also Hay, 77; Noah E. Aronstam, M.D., "The Well of Loneliness—An Impression," *The Urologic and Cutaneous Review,* 33 (1929), 543.

27. Floyd Dell, "Sex in Adolescence," in *Sex Education: Facts and Attitudes* (New York: Child Study Association of America, 1934), p. 49; Norman Himes, *Your Marriage: A Guide to Happiness* (New York: Farrar & Rinehart, 1940), p. 24. One of the authors more tolerant of homosexuality argued that homosexuality was indeed less serious than illegitimacy or venereal disease and that people should not be so upset about it. Aaron J. Rosanoff, M.D., "Human Sexuality, Normal and Abnormal, From a Psychiatric Standpoint," *Urologic and Cutaneous Review,* 33 (1929), 530. The novel *A Woman's Woman* (above, note 13) contrasts a celibate sister who lives with another woman and the other sister in the family, a flirtatious girl who falls for a worthless man. The latter's failings are much better accepted by the family.

28. For example, Blanchard and Manasses, pp. 186–87; Clark, p. 7.

29. Dell, *Love in the Machine Age,* pp. 238, 308; also Bromley and Britten, p. 118. The proportion of American colleges confined to one sex or the other declined continuously from 1870

on, mostly because the majority of new schools were co-educational. Very few women's colleges opened after 1930; I have not discovered whether fears of lesbianism played any direct role in this phenomenon. See Mabel Newcomer, *A Century of Higher Education for American Women* (New York: Harper, 1959), pp. 37–40.

30. Bromley and Britten, p. 129; also, Himes, p. 22.

31. Linda Gordon, *Woman's Body, Woman's Right* (New York: Grossman, 1976), p. 136; Eleanor Rowland Wembridge, "The Professional Education of Women and the Family Problem," *Social Hygiene*, 6 (1920), 183.

32. Bartley, pp. 27–29.

33. Peter Filene, *Him/Her/Self: Sex Roles in Modern America* (New York: Harcourt, Brace, Jovanovich, 1974), pp. 29–30. Filene cites figures showing that in 1915, for instance, only 39 percent of all living alumnae of eight women's colleges and Cornell were married, p. 27. Actually the proportion of ever-married people in the population was rising, and the age of marriage was declining, from 1890 on. Because the reality differed from reformers' impressions, it seems even more likely that the more visible single women of higher classes were the primary concern. See Donald J. Bogue, *The Population of the United States* (Glencoe, Ill.: The Free Press, 1959), p. 216.

34. Phyllis Blanchard, *The Adolescent Girl: A Study From the Psychoanalytic Viewpoint* (New York: Moffat, Yard, 1920), pp. 170–71.

35. Hay, 77.

36. Coon, pp. 112–15; also Maurice Chideckel, M.D., *Female Sex Perversion* (New York: Eugenics, 1935), p. vii. In practice, accusations were not restricted by class. In the film, *With Babies and Banners: Story of the Women's Emergency Brigade*, Women's Labor History Film Project, 1978, about women's participation in the 1937 autoworkers' strike in Flint, Michigan, one participant recalls that male unionists called women "queers" when they wanted to do more than traditional support work for the union.

37. Blanche Wiesen Cook has described these women's relationships with each other and with men in "Female Support Networks and Political Activism: Lillian Wald, Crystal Eastman, Emma Goldman," *Chrysalis*, No. 3 (1977), pp. 43–61.

38. Katz, p. 449. Katz notes the historical change from the assumption of asexual friendships to "vulgarizations of Freudianism" which found sex everywhere.

39. Meagher, 511.

40. Meagher, 513; see also George K. Pratt, M.D., "Accepting One's Sexual Role," in *Sex Education: Facts and Attitudes*, p. 39; Ernest R. Groves, Gladys Hoagland Groves, and Catherine Groves, *Sex Fulfillment in Marriage* (New York: Emerson, 1942) suggested for instance, that other positions were useful in exceptional circumstances such as when the man was weak or lacking in sexual control, pp. 163, 179–80.

41. Eddy, p. 127; Dell, *Love in the Machine Age*, p. 311; Sanger, p. 100.

42. In order, Meagher, 508; Edward Podolsky, M.D., "'Homosexual Love' in Women," *Popular Medicine*, 1 (February 1935), 375; Dell, *Love in the Machine Age*, p. 308. See also Blanchard, p. 169.

43. Groves, *Marriage Crisis*, p. 100; Wile and Winn, p. 54; Clark, p. 96; Joseph Collins, M.D., *The Doctor Looks at Love and Life* (Garden City, N.Y.: Doubleday, Doran, 1926), pp. 36, 43.

44. Eddy, p. 316; also Clark, pp. 31, 97; Lindsey and Evans, pp. 119, 199; Groves et al., *Sex Fulfillment*, p. 186.

45. Meagher, 512.

46. Podolsky, 375.

47. Blanche Wiesen Cook has argued similarly in her essay, "'Women Alone Stir My Imagination': Lesbianism and the Cultural Tradition," *Signs*, 4, 4 (Summer 1979), 739.

48. Robert S. Lynd and Helen Merrell Lynd, *Middletown: A Study in Modern American Culture* (New York: Harcourt, Brace, and World, 1929), pp. 266–71; May, pp. 212–31; Ewen; Lasch, pp. 20–21; U.S. Public Health Service, *Sex Education: A Symposium for Educators* (Washington, D.C.: 1927), pp. v–vi.

49. Dell, *Love in the Machine Age*, p. 364; also Himes, p. 26; Lindsey and Evans, p. 134; Edwood L. Fantis, M.D., "Homosexuality in Growing Girls," *Sexology*, 2 (February 1935), 349.

# 14

## "This Work Had an End": African-American Domestic Workers in Washington, D.C., 1910–1940

### Elizabeth Clark-Lewis

*Power relations between white mistresses and black domestic servants provide the focus of Eliza-beth Clark-Lewis's study of African-American domestic servants in Washington, D.C., in the early twentieth century. Drawing upon oral history interviews with elderly former servants, Clark-Lewis shows how black migrants from the South relied upon their churches and penny savers clubs to achieve a modicum of independence. Their desire to develop lives of their own was aided by their shift from work as live-in servants to household day work. In this process they gained a new sense of identity, self-respect, and freedom. The increasing personal autonomy of black servants contributed, in turn, to the growth of black community institutions, which further reinforced independent black political culture in the nation's capital.*

The living-in jobs just
kept you running; never stopped.
Day or night you'd be getting
something for somebody. You'd
serve them. It was never a
minute of peace. . . .

But when I went out
days on my jobs, I'd get my
work done and be gone. I guess
that's it. This work had a
end.[1]

When African-American women migrated from the rural South to the urban centers of the North to work as live-in servants, few imagined they were beginning an escape from restraints imposed by race, gender, and class. But escape they did, and this essay examines the transition of twenty-three such women as they moved beyond live-in household servitude to self-employment during the first three decades of this century. It also dem-onstrates that as their roles changed, they experienced a new freedom to

*Tuskegee Institute class in domestic science, c. 1904. Library of Congress.*

exercise control over their own lives, and their perceptions about themselves and their relationships to others underwent a significant change. It
is important to recognize, however, that these changes occurred within a
restrictive cultural environment.[2]

An urban scholar noted in the last decade of the nineteenth century
that "household service now drew the despised race to the despised calling."[3] A variety of historical circumstances were responsible for the household employment revolution this scholar perceived during the years between 1900 and 1930, a revolution that has received very little scholarly
attention because service work is outside the market and has historically
been poor women's work. Few social scientists have asked why, in the twentieth century, this employment has gone from a white "golden age" to an
African- American "problem era," from the age of the white "servant girl"
to the African-American "cleaning woman."[4]

National census employment data for the years between 1900 and
1930 reveal the largest employment increases for white women in clerical,
sales, and factory occupations. Simultaneously, the number of native-born
white women in household service work *fell* by 40 percent. Poor migrants,

from abroad or from rural areas, had historically provided servants for urban households unable to acquire native-born white women servants. When foreign immigration slowed to a trickle after World War I, an important source of new white servants was eliminated. Within the first two decades of the twentieth century, household work lost its importance as an occupation for white women. By contrast, the number of African-American female household workers *increased* by 43 percent. Nationally, during the 1900–1930 period, the southern exploitive system triumphed: African-American women were forced into a "servant caste."[5]

Surveys of specific northern urban centers found that the sharp rise in the number of African-American household workers had three sources: the new, large-scale migration of African-Americans to urban centers outside the South; the face that African-American women were twice as likely as white women to be employed; and discriminatory policies that barred African-American women from 86 percent of employment categories. By 1926 the predominance of African-American migrant women in household service in Washington, D.C., was well established. During the early twentieth century, the District of Columbia experienced the largest percentage increase in African-American population in the eastern United States. More important, in 1900, 54 percent of the employed African-American women in the District were working in domestic service; by 1930, that figure had risen to 78 percent.[6]

Expanded employment opportunities lured a stream of migrants to the urban North, where they moved into segregated communities that coalesced around churches, schools, philanthropic institutions, and businesses. But because of antimigrant biases in the established African-American communities, only rarely could the newcomers find work in businesses owned by African-Americans or in the segregated schools of the communities where they settled. Disproportionately young, female, and poorly educated, they found themselves in urban centers where the pattern of racial segregation combined with class and gender restrictions to limit the jobs available to them. In overwhelming numbers the female migrants became household workers.[7]

Early social scientists enumerated the statistical (but none of the qualitative) changes that household work underwent as a result of the large influx of African-American women seeking this employment in areas outside the rural South. In recent studies, social historians have analyzed the forces that have shaped household work, described the reasons why different groups entered household work, and observed the change in the character of this employment with the advent of each group. The hypotheses developed by these historians are important, but they need to be tested at the local level; moreover, they do not emphasize the impact of this employment on the lives of the workers themselves.[8]

Washington, D.C., is an excellent locus for a case study of African-

American household workers. Large numbers of migrants were attracted to Washington, a burgeoning commercial center with a demand for unskilled labor and a benign racial image reinforced by articles in nationally distributed African-American newspapers. In 1883 one paper asserted that "Washington has become a town with very free negro and white mixing at social activities. The two also live in racially integrated areas."[9]

In order to understand Dolethia Otis's statement, "This work had a end," it is necessary to examine the context from which these women emerged and the manner in which the shift from "servant" to "employee" was made. Using an interdisciplinary cultural approach, I have attempted to explore important dimensions of their occupations, learning directly from them their attitudes concerning the sociology of work. The conditions under which they were reared and the system of meanings, values, and aspirations they developed before their employment as household workers provides a background against which their adult lives can be more fully appreciated and understood.

In the South, during the late nineteenth century, girls were quickly incorporated into the work routine of their households. "By four you'd do field work; by six you'd be doing small pieces in a tub every washday and bring all the clear water for rinsing the clothes. By eight, you'd be able to mind children, do cooking, and wash. By ten you'd be trained up. Really, every girl I know was working-out by ten. No play, 'cause they told you: life was to be hardest on you—always."[10] This brief statement by an eighty-six-year-old migrant worker from Virginia reveals much about the early lives of African-American women born in the rural southeastern United States during the late nineteenth and early twentieth centuries.

Fourteen of the twenty-three women I interviewed grew up on farms owned by their parents; nine lived on share-tenant farms. Nearly all were reared in extended family households, consisting of mothers, fathers, grandparents, siblings, and other relatives. They were all born between 1884 and 1911. Each household included at least one former slave; thus every woman in the study vividly recalled hearing firsthand descriptions of the degrading conditions of slavery. Further, the women were able to cite beliefs held by those former slaves regarding patterns and practices that enabled slaves families to survive under the harshest of circumstances.

Family support, according to all of the women interviewed, was a focal point of rural churches. In addition to religious instruction, churches provided the only mutual aid, educational, and recreational activities available to African-American families in the rural South. After the family, the church was the most important means of individual and community expression.[11]

The education of all of the women in the study had been severely limited by the need to help support the family, which they recognized as their primary responsibility by the age of seven. They worked first on the family farm, caring for the youngest children and serving as apprentices to older girls and women. Each of the twenty-three women recalled her mother's leaving home for residential (live-in) employment in white households in the surrounding area and recognized that independently employed children were an important part of the family's survival strategy.[12] "Like everybody, by eight years old I went in to work with Mama," said Bernice Reeder in discussing the short period of outside tutelage which preceded a girl's first employment as live-in servant to a white family. She was alone on her first job, "at just nine years old! I was so scared," she continued. "Nobody cared you were a child. . . . You was a worker to them."[13] The economic constraints faced by African-Americans in the rural South in the late nineteenth and early twentieth centuries made such early labor an unavoidable and accepted part of family and community life.

It was essential that girls learn young to meet the three-part training criteria developed by African-Americans in rural areas of the South. Each girl child was first required to become proficient in child care and housekeeping duties for her extended family. She then learned to perform household duties, under the supervision of adult kin, in the homes of whites in the surrounding communities. Finally, following this period of tutelage, she undertook housekeeping tasks alone in the homes of local southern white employers. By the age of ten, the women in this study told me, they also had to show clearly that they had the maturity to take another step: to travel to Washington, D.C., where sisters and aunts who worked as live-in servants (and sent money home) needed support in the form of child care and housekeeping by younger family members.

These girls made the journey north by train. None had ever been out of her home state before. Twenty were taken to the train station by a male relative; all left their places of birth in the early morning, traveled alone, and were met by other relatives upon arrival in Washington.

When sharing reminiscences of their northbound journey, the women always described the feeling of freedom they experienced. "When you got on the train," Velma Davis exclaimed, "you felt different! Seem like you'd been bound up, but now this train untied you. It's funny . . . like being untied and tickled at the same time!"[14] The girls understood that their first obligation was to carry on the rural-based family survival strategy in the homes of kin who served Washington's white households as live-in workers. The only significant change in their lives, initially, was the move to the North.

Many studies that investigate the importance of the northern migration emphasize only the contribution southern women made to the child care and the financial stability of the northern household. Other studies suggest that the real benefits of migration went to the rural southern families in the form of money sent home monthly by kin residing in the North. These arguments tend to polarize the rural–urban relationship; neither acknowledges the dual/multiple roles played by both northern and southern relatives. When rural families (lacking financial resources) permitted their young women to migrate out of the South to assist relatives residing in the North, migration was seen as a continuation of the survival/support culture developed in the South. All segments of the African-American family operated under the assumption that older members of the kin group assisted younger ones for the very basic purpose of ensuring the survival of the family's young people and of the family as a whole in both North and South.

Urban kin gave support to the migrant in several ways, if we may judge from information provided by the women interviewed. They paid all of her travel expenses to Washington, helped her adjust to urban life, and found employment for her within twelve months. In all the cases studied, the women were hired where their kin had contacts; in twenty-one of twenty-three cases, the coresident kin acquired employment for the migrants in households where they themselves were currently living. The girls migrated originally to provide support only to their urban kin; once they themselves became employed, however (after an average of one year), they were expected to assume responsibility for meeting the needs of both the urban and rural segments of the family.

As newly hired live-in servants, these female migrants learned that their primary role was to serve the mistress of the house, not just to complete the assigned tasks—a departure from the way they had worked in southern households. In the South, these African-American household workers had received daily task assignments from the white male head of the household. Migrants stressed that in Washington they slowly learned a new employment reality. Through trial and error, and with the advice of the more experienced earlier migrants, they learned to act in response to the needs of the wife rather than the husband.[15]

Each of the twenty-three women was dismayed to learn that uniforms were mandatory in the District of Columbia. The wearing of uniforms was perceived by all as the major difference between their servant *work* in the South and their servant *role* in Washington.[16] For these women, the uniform objectified the live-in servant and determined her fate in the workplace. The home was the white mistress's stage and major realm of influence, and the uniform legitimized her power. Ophilia Simpson recalled that "them uniforms just seemed to make them know you was theirs. Some say you wore them to show different jobs you was doing. Time in grey. Other times serving in black. But mostly them things just showed you was always at their beck and call. Really that's all them things means!"[17]

Tasks assigned and directions given to the household staff were perceived by the migrant woman as the white woman's means of expressing her power, which she exercised principally on migrants. When Velma Davis lived in with a Chevy Chase family, the treatment she experienced differed from that accorded servants not born in the South. "She knew you was from down home, working to help them survive, so, that woman just plain ran us to death! People from up here could leave, so she'd be more careful with all them 'cause they'd quit on her. But for me it was a job that kept me up here . . . it wasn't hard like the field jobs . . . and I could keep money going home. It was a for sure help—a blessing."[18]

Despite the fact that each woman (and her family in the rural South) desperately needed the income her labor generated, within seven years these women were actively trying to leave the "servant life." There were several aspects of live-in employment that they all disliked. The uniform formalized the serving of the family for long hours, which they could not control. The wife as the authority figure had little respect for their needs. Worse still, they were forced to live in small quarters completely isolated from the African-American community.[19]

But it was the question of church participation that first stimulated more than half of those interviewed to seek a change. Not being able to attend regular services on Sundays and generally feeling left out of the continuing life of their churches became for these women a potent symbol of the restrictions of live-in labor. "Even working-out down home, you'd go to church," Costella Harris explained, bedridden at eighty-six after a lifetime of household employment in Georgetown. "Everybody did," she continued slowly. "Now, most came just to hear the Word. But some came to keep from being in a kitchen somewhere. . . . Church gave you six, not seven days of work. But up here you never saw inside any church on Sunday, living-in."[20]

Painful as all these restrictions were, however, they were probably not sufficient by themselves to lead the women to reject live-in servant work. The *ability* to make the change emanated from the phenomenon known as "penny savers clubs." Twenty-one of the twenty-three women actively associated themselves with such mutual benefit associations, which sponsored social gatherings and provided sickness and death benefits to members. The organizations—begun by poor migrant working women who barely sustained themselves economically—were citywide, but active membership in each one was restricted to persons from specific states (or regions of a state) in the South. Although rarely mentioned in the literature, the penny savers clubs served as a vital economic base for the female migrant.[21] After an average of six years of saving, the women were able to develop the important economic leverage they needed to leave servant life.

The role of the church and of the penny savers clubs in first awakening the desire for change and then facilitating the process of that change cannot be overestimated. The clubs permitted the women, during the transition from live-in service to household day work, to maintain financial security for themselves and their kin in the rural South. No woman left live-in work until she had saved enough money to maintain herself and send money monthly to rural kin. The concern all these women had about the continuity of support to their southern families equaled or exceeded the concern they had for their own circumstances. They sought to find a less circumscribed economic and employment environment without abandoning one of the original motivations for leaving their rural families—relief of the family's economic distress.

The women soon identified laundresses as critical figures in their search for autonomy. Laundresses served as role models: unlike the other staff members, they did not belittle the migrant woman's desire to gain household work on a nonresidential basis, and they alone knew the categories and rules related to operating within several households simultaneously. The laundress also brought information about households that were seeking the services of women on a live-out basis for one or two days a week.[22] All but two women in the study acted upon the advice of a laundress when they located and acquired their first jobs as household day workers, and even those two had found the laundress to be the *only* staff member who supported their ambition to escape live-in work.

The women saw six major benefits to the shift from live-in servant to household day worker. First, as indicated by the language they used to describe their experiences, their work seemed more their own. They spoke of their earlier jobs in depersonalized language because they sought detachment from their employers and a buffer against the employers' insensitivity to them as workers and African-Americans. References to their lives as live-in servants were characterized by the frequent use of "you." Here, for example, are some of Virginia Lacey's comments: "You was brought up here . . . you better never blink," and "You was worked to death."[23] Velma Davis recalled, "When I say 'my job,' I mean a job I got and I'd keep if they acted decent. 'They job' is for them; a job that you did and did, more and more— from one thing to another, early to late, and you worked! It's hard to tell what I mean."[24]

Second, the previously isolated African-American women began to make contact with one another amid their newly flexible working conditions, encountering many others like themselves. The structure that had created social marginality among African-Americans in Washington was slowly being dismantled; the women's isolated and restrictive living circumstances were relegated to an oppressive past. Bernice Reeder said that during twelve years as a live-in servant she had always believed that eventually she would have an opportunity for a better life. "Every working day," she said, "I knew in myself me living in it wouldn't be for long. And it wasn't just me. *All* us came here to do better!"[25]

Third, as the women changed jobs, they moved to rooms in boardinghouses and began to adopt a sharply different lifestyle. The other girls in the house where Velma Davis became a boarder "was all doing day-work, too," and "soon I was doing just about everything with them. I just like being with these girls [who] was single, nice."[26] After the move from live-in servant work, Velma Davis said that she did not see her family for long periods of time. She said that it was when she moved to the boardinghouse that she began to feel she had finally left home. In 1919, Beulah Nelson took a room in a house where there were other boarders like herself. She said, "I lived there for three years, and I didn't see my brother much at all." She described the parties she and the other female boarders were allowed to host, and told me, "Them was my best days, and that's how I met my husband!"[27] ...

Fourth, their places of work changed. Employers usually hired someone other than their former live-in servants to work as daily household employees. The women acknowledged this policy; thus, in communicating their new plans to their employers, they understood that future employment in that household would not be considered. "People who had a full staff only wanted full-time live-in workers," contributed eighty-one-year-old Helen Venable, whose roots were in Alabama. "When you said you wanted to work days, you left there. She told you, you'd not be able to come back. It was okay, 'cause you'd got all set."[28]

Fifth, each women indicated that turning to day work produced a subtle change in her relationship to the white women for whom she worked. Virginia Lacey described the new experience with an employer this way: "She'd meet you at the door, tell you how she wanted her house done, and she'd be gone. You did the work without her in the way, slowing you up. On a day job we all knew how to get everything done—but, in your own way. Having anybody around will make you work slower."[29] The household day worker was able to dictate her own pace, set her own priorities for tasks, and organize the process by which she completed designated chores. ...

Finally, all of the women stressed that as they moved out of live-in work, they shed their uniforms and other symbols of their identities as live-in servants. Each had felt locked into a narrow and constricted role by the need to wear uniforms of "black for this" and "gray for that." Discarding that badge of their station in life clearly disaffiliated them from their previous work. Octavia Crockett, though very ill and weak, was eager to tell me that "when I got my first day job, I told them right off that I wasn't wearing a uniform. Them things are what really makes you a live-in ... I had my own work dresses and all. They is just as nice."[30] ...

Some scholars and artists who are sensitive to the problems of domestic service have tended to view negatively the bags in which day workers carried their clothes.[31] But these women took pride in the fact that they "carried work clothes" to their jobs; they felt that the bags were symbols of personal freedom and in that sense were positive. In fact, Marie Davis reported that workers often called them "freedom bags"; she observed, "When I got to carry clothes, I was finally working in what I wanted to. No black or gray uniforms or castoffs from the whites down home. I was proud to put my stuff in a bag at home. I guess I wanted to finally show I didn't wear a uniform. I wasn't a servant."[32]

A new identity was gained. Gone was the identity to which they were born or which had been ascribed to them; this new one they had *achieved* on their own, and their newly acquired friends and associates validated this achieved status.[33] As Bernice Reeder explained, "Once you got some work by the day and got around people who did it, you'd see how you could get ahead, get better things. You'd see how to get more and more days, some party work, extra sewing, staff like that."[34] Velma Davis agreed: "When I started working days, other people [other household day workers] would show you how to get a few extra dollars. In this town you could make more money, and they'd sure show you how."[35]

The women's transformed identities and modified employment modes led to several other changes in the African-American community. For one, the women's interest in the penny savers clubs waned. . . . Although the associations continued to exist after the fall of the stock market, household day workers perceived them as institutions serving the needs of live-in servants. The day workers transferred their money to banks, in part because their new jobs gave them the opportunity to do so.[36] As Eula Montgomery remarked, "I'd have used them [banks] earlier, but with that woman you never got time to go to a place like that. I know I didn't."[37] Minnie Barnes verified this point: "I used a bank as a day worker because it was on my streetcar line home."[38]

"Most of the women," explained Helen Venable, "felt them clubs wasn't for workers; it wasn't for . . . people getting their money on payday or getting paid every week."[39] The savings clubs, like uniforms, were viewed as symbols of the servant role. Marie Davis said, "The banks was better than clubs. They was for servants; banks was for people with jobs."[40] The women wanted to deal with established savings institutions, as other salaried employees did, and using a bank was a public acknowledgment of their new status as independent workers.

The waning of the mutual benefit associations did not, however, mean the decline of support for rural kin. On the contrary, economic assistance typically increased after the transition to household day work. In speaking of the support she provided her relatives still living in the South, Velma Davis said, "I didn't miss a month. . . . That's why I got myself set before I left live-in. I never missed sending my share home."[41] If anything, the women adhered even more strongly to their premigration beliefs concerning kinship obligations. . . .

The level of these women's participation in the African-American churches of Washington also changed significantly. Live-in servant work had greatly restricted their attendance and involvement in church activities. Velma Davis recalled, "Living in? You never dreamed of going to day service. Sundays, you'd be out of there [the live-in household], if you was good, by four or five."[42] Regular participation in daytime church services was also an indication of status. "Big people, like government messengers, or people working in a colored business office, that's who'd be regular at Sunday day services," Eula Montgomery said. Individuals who worked in those types of jobs, she pointed out, had their Sundays free; they could also, therefore, "be on the church's special committees."[43]

Live-in service had limited all aspects of interactions with other church members. Eula Montgomery went on: "If you lived in a room in the attic, how could you be in any of them clubs? You couldn't bring nobody over there. . . . You never got to be in a fellowship. That was for people who got off on Saturday and Sunday. They had a nice place to have people over to—not no kitchen." She also explained the contrast between the professed religious beliefs of employers and their practices in relationship to live-in servants: "Now, they'd get up and go out to Sunday morning church. . . . He'd act like Sunday was such a holy day around there. He made it clear Sundays was a day of rest. But us? We'd work like dogs just the same. We didn't get no rest on that day."[44] . . .

Regular church attendance, achieved through less confining employment, was accompanied by more leisure-time activity. A married couple could go to morning church services, and in summer they could go out for picnics, Dolethia Otis pointed out.[45]

Participation in church and leisure activities was viewed, not surprisingly, as representative of the attainment of *better* work; according to Nellie Willoughby, a migrant from Virginia, "it showed you had work you didn't live at."[46] It did not mean that these women did *easier* work. The point was that the work they did—even if more strenuous—permitted some previously unavailable free time. Bernice Reeder cited the laundress as an example: "She'd have four washes to do. Then she'd have them heavy irons for ironing time. She worked, but she'd still be able to get to church. She was on so many boards. . . . She worked real hard for six days, but every Sunday she was off. Then, too, she had evenings to herself."[47] The washing and ironing constituted backbreaking labor; the live-in servants recognized this fact. But as live-out work it offered a number of advantages, the most often stated of which was that it allowed the worker to develop new social roles.

All of the women interviewed asserted that household day work was directly responsible for their ability to participate in the churches. The result of this change was wider church membership. Previously, working-class women had not been well represented in the African-American churches. "Most women down at Mason Street Baptist who were real active," said Helen Venable, "were educated good and had jobs like teaching. As people got more away from live-in you saw a lotta different people in all the things that church has. Then more and more people got in the church's clubs or work."[48]

The growth of African-American churches in Washington, then, was a direct consequence of the steady influx of these working-class (former live-in) women.[49] They strongly supported church expansion because their participation in the church activities further separated them from the stigma of servitude. . . .

Live-in servant work imposed countless burdens upon African-American female migrants to the District of Columbia before the Depression, yet "service-class" women developed and controlled philanthropic organizations that allowed them eventually to escape the boundaries of live-in servant employment. Although the African-American women quoted here remained in household service work all their lives, they restructured its salient features and created more freedom for themselves.

Reformers who rely only on archival records may view household service work as "a dead end."[50] Scholars all too often see household workers as merely products of change, never as its causes; as objects of events, not as their subjects; as passive reactors, not as active forces in history.[51] The words and lives of these women refute such views. Orra Fisher's response sums up best what the women expressed when asked about the progress and the success they have seen in their lives:

> I worked hard to serve God and to see that my three girls didn't have to serve nobody else like I did except God. I satisfied to know I came a long way. From a kitchen down home to a kitchen up here, and then able to earn money, but live with my children and grands. Now Jesus took me every step—that's real.
>
> But look at me, with more than I ever dreamed I'd have. And my three, with houses, and jobs. My girls in an office, and the baby—my son—over twenty years in the Army. I get full thinking about it. I had it bad, but look at them.[52]

## NOTES

1. Dolethia Otis, interviewed by author, September 1982. All names used are pseudonyms.

2. For a full discussion of this employment transformation, see Elizabeth Clark-Lewis, *This Work Had a End: The Transition From Live-in to Day Work* (Memphis, 1985). For the purposes of this paper, females employed on a daily basis primarily to clean private family homes will be referred to as household workers. However, no adjustments will be made to any terms within direct quotes.

3. Isabel Eaton, "Special Report on Negro Domestic Service," in W. E. B. Du Bois, *The Philadelphia Negro* (New York, 1899), 136–37.

4. Bettina Aptheker, *Woman's Legacy: Essays on Race, Sex, and Class in American History* (Amherst, Mass., 1982), 112; Ann Oakley, *The Sociology of Work* (London, 1974), 96; Evelyn Nakano Glenn, "The Dialectics of Wage Work: Japanese-American Women and Domestic Service, 1905–1940," *Feminist Studies* 6 (1980): 432–71; Susan Strasser, "Mistress and Maid, Employer and Employee: Domestic Service Reform in the United States, 1897–1920," *Marxist Perspectives* 1 (Winter 1978): 52–67; Daniel Sutherland, *Americans and Their Servants* (Baton Rouge, 1981), 6.

5. U.S. Department of Commerce, Bureau of the Census, *Negro Workers in the United States, 1920–1932* (Washington, D.C., 1935), 294, 297, 300, 303–4, and *Fifteenth Census of the United States, 1930—Population Bulletin and Summary* (Washington, D.C., 1934), 6; Joseph Hill, *Women in Gainful Occupations, 1870–1920* (Washington, D.C., 1929), 38, 59, 90, 96, 105, 117; Du Bois, *Philadelphia Negro*, 434.

6. Records of the Government of the District of Columbia—General Files and Records of the National Council of Negro Women, RG 351, National Archives; Records of the Bureau of Human Nutrition and Home Economics—Servant Living Needs (Colored), RG 176, National Archives; National Committee on Household Employment, *There Must Be a Code of Standards* (Washington, D.C., 1974); Mary Waggoman, "Wartime Job Opportunities for Women Household Workers in Washington, D.C.," *Monthly Labor Review* 60 (March 1945): 575–84; Grace Fox,

"Women Domestic Workers in Washington, D.C.," *Monthly Labor Review* 54 (February 1942): 338–45.

7. George E. Haynes, *Negro Migration* (Washington, D.C., 1919); Ray S. Baker, "The Negro Goes North," *World's Work* 34 (July 1917): 315; Florette Henri, *Black Migration* (Garden City, N.Y., 1976), 53–60.

8. David Katzman, *Seven Days a Week* (New York, 1978), ix; Alba Edwards, "Comparative Occupational Statistics for the United States, 1870–1940," in the Sixteenth U.S. Census, 1940, *Population* (Washington, D.C., 1943); Allyson Grossman, "Women in Domestic Work," *Monthly Labor Review* 103 (August 1980):18; "Women and Child Labor," *Monthly Labor Review* 15 (July 1922): 116–17.

9. Constance Green, *Washington: A History of the Capitol* (Princeton, N.J., 1962), and *The Secret City* (Princeton, N.J., 1967); Waggoman, "Wartime Job Opportunities"; "Notes from Washington," *National Negro Register* 3 (June 1883).

10. Naomi Yates, interviewed by author, 15 September 1982; Stewart Tolnan, "Black Family Formation and Tenancy in the Farm South, 1900," *American Journal of Sociology* 90 (September 1984): 305–25; Lawrence Levine, *Black Culture and Black Consciousness* (New York, 1977).

11. Melvin Williams, *Community in a Black Pentecostal Church: An Anthropological Study* (Pittsburgh, Pa., 1974), 8–10; Carter G. Woodson, *The Rural Negro* (Washington, D.C., 1930), 150–78.

12. Christine E. Bose, "Household Resources and U.S. Women's Work: Factors Affecting Gainful Employment at the Turn of the Century," *American Sociological Review* 49 (August 1984): 474–77.

13. Bernice Reeder, interviewed by author, 18 March 1981.

14. Velma Davis, interviewed by author, 20 July 1982.

15. Katzman, *Seven Days a Week*, 155, 214–15.

16. Peter Berger and Thomas Luckman, *The Social Construction of Reality* (Garden City, N.Y., 1966), 89–92.

17. Ophilia Simpson, interviewed by author, 12 July 1982.

18. Velma Davis interview.

19. Aptheker, *Woman's Legacy*, 122; E. R. Haynes, "Negroes in Domestic Service in the United States," *Journal of Negro History*, October 1923, 384–442.

20. Costella Harris, interviewed by author, 15 November 1982.

21. One Mississippi penny savers club is documented in Records of the Government of the District of Columbia—Blue Plains Industrial School (Colored), 1927, RG 351, National Archives.

22. "A Washerwoman," *Independent* 57 (November 1904): 1073–76; Katzman, *Seven Days a Week*, 84–86.

23. Virginia Lacey, interviewed by author, 27 July 1982.

24. Velma Davis interview.

25. Bernice Reeder interview.

26. Velma Davis interview.

27. Beulah Nelson, interviewed by author, 14 August 1982.

28. Helen Venable, interviewed by author, 21 July 1982 and 9 September 1982.

29. Virginia Lacey interview.

30. Octavia Crockett, interviewed by author, 3 May 1984.

31. Turner Brown, *Black Is . . .* (New York, 1969), 68–69; Louise Mitchell, "Slave Markets Typify Exploitation of Domestics," *Daily Worker*, 5 May 1940; Carter G. Woodson and Lorenzo Greene, *The Negro Wage Earner* (New York, 1969), 230–31.

32. Marie Davies, interviewed by author, 3 August 1982.

33. Ward Goodenough, "Rethinking 'Status' and 'Role': Toward a General Model of the Cultural Organization of Social Relationships," in *Cognitive Anthropology*, ed. Stephen Tyler (New York, 1969), 314.

34. Bernice Reeder interview.

35. Velma Davis interview.

36. Edward Denison, *Economic Growth in the United States* (New York, 1961), 2–4; Jessie Blayton, "The Negro in Banking," *Bankers Magazine* 4 (December 1936): 511–14; Gunnar Myrdal, *An American Dilemma* (New York, 1944), 316–17.

37. Eula Montgomery, interviewed by author, 15 September 1982.

38. Minnie Barnes, interviewed by author, 12 July 1982.

39. Helen Venable interview.

40. Marie Davies interview.

41. Velma Davis interview.

42. Velma Davis interview.

43. Eula Montgomery interview. See Williams, *Community,* 33–47, for an excellent analysis of Afro-American women in urban churches.

44. Eula Montgomery interview.

45. Dolethia Otis interview.

46. Nellie Willougby, interviewed by author, 28 July 1982.

47. Bernice Reeder interview. Women migrants and lighter work are discussed in Kelly Miller, *Race Adjustment* (Miami, Fla., 1969), 171.

48. Helen Venable interview.

49. E. Franklin Frazier, *The Negro Church in America* (New York, 1971); A. H. Fauset, *Black Gods of the Metropolis* (Philadelphia, 1971); "The Black Church," *Black Scholar* 2 (December 1970): 3–49.

50. Katzman, *Seven Days a Week,* 11; Lucy Maynard Salmon, *Domestic Service* (New York, 1897), 141–42n.

51. Henri, *Black Migration,* x.

52. Orra Fisher, interviewed by author, 2 August 1982.

# 15
## Redefining "Women's Work": The Sexual Division of Labor in the Auto Industry During World War II
### Ruth Milkman

*An overly rosy view of "Rosie the Riveter" is the object of Ruth Milkman's revisionist analysis of women's work in the automobile industry during World War II. She marshals an impressive array of evidence to argue for a short-term, wartime shift in the boundaries between men's and women's work. Ultimately, she shows, women's wartime experience included the persistence of job segregation by sex even in the face of dramatic economic growth and change. The emergence in the postwar years of what Betty Friedan called the "Feminine Mystique" provides further evidence that the wartime experience of women did not pose any enduring challenge to power relations across the gender divide.*

Feminists have deliberately idealized the experience of women workers during World War II, challenging the ideology of "woman's place" which obliterated women's wartime contribution to industrial production from public memory. The stunning imagery of female strength and versatility captured in photographs of women industrial workers in the 1940s has become a mainstay of contemporary "feminist realism." Ultimately, our vision of social change encompasses more than securing equal access for women to alienating jobs in capitalist industry: work itself must be fundamentally transformed—for both women and men. But in the meantime, so long as women workers are excluded from basic industry and ghettoized in low-status, poorly paid jobs, the woman war worker will remain a resonant symbol.

A closer look at the actual experience of women industrial workers during the war years, however, suggests that the retrospective feminist construction of their place in history is apocryphal. Women were hired to do "men's jobs" during the war on a scale unparalleled before or since, but this was in no way the result of a feminist campaign. In basic industries like auto, employers were initially quite resistant to the idea of hiring women for war work. They did so only when the supply of male labor had been completely exhausted because of military conscription on the one hand and the rapid expansion of demand for labor to produce military hardware on

This article is excerpted from FEMINIST STUDIES, Volume 8 (1982): 336–72, by permission of the publisher, FEMINIST STUDIES, Inc., c/o Women's Studies Program, University of Maryland, College Park, MD 20742.

*Cover of UAW publication,* Ammunition, *August, 1944. The Archives of Labor and Urban Affairs, Wayne State University.*

the other. It was not a change in management beliefs about women's capabilities in industry that led to their incorporation into jobs previously considered suitable only for men, but rather the male labor shortage during the war years which led to the change in management's beliefs.

Once women were drawn upon to meet the need for labor in war-bloated "heavy" industries, moreover, they were not randomly incorporated into "men's jobs" as vacancies occurred. Instead, *new* patterns of occupational segregation by sex were established "for the duration" within sectors of the economy previously monopolized by men. So Rosie the Riveter did a "man's job," but more often than not she worked in a predominantly female department or job classification.[1]

The wartime experience of women in industry is a fruitful object of feminist analysis, then, but for reasons opposite to those generally presumed. The economic mobilization led to a shift in the location of the boundaries between "men's" and "women's" work, not the elimination of those boundaries. The persistence of segregation during the war, in the face of a massive influx of women into the labor force and a dramatic upheaval in the previously established sexual division of labor, poses quite starkly the fundamental problem of explaining how and why job segregation by sex is maintained and reproduced over and over again throughout the history of capitalist development.[2]

The underlying forces that continually reproduce segregation within the supposedly "impersonal" wage labor market remain obscure if the problem is approached at the level of the individual employer or firm. Once women have been introduced into the paid labor force at a lower cost than men, one would expect that the relentless efforts of capital to maximize profits would lead employers to substitute women for men whenever possible, at least until the costs of female and male labor power are equalized. It appears quite irrational for management to differentiate rigidly between women and men workers, as if they were truly noninterchangeable sources of labor power. But the ideology of sex typing and the job segregation it legitimates do serve the *class* interest of capital, despite the countervailing pressures impinging on individual capital.

Collectively, capital benefits from the existence of gender divisions within the working class in that they—like racial and other intraclass cleavages—foster political disunity within what might otherwise be a stronger source of opposition to capital.[3] In addition, and crucially, segregation by sex within the wage labor market helps to secure the daily and generational reproduction of the working class through the unpaid household labor of women, by denying female workers a living wage and maintaining their economic dependence on men and on families. At the same time, the sexual division of labor in the household is exactly what constitutes women as a source of "cheap" and expendable labor to begin with.[4]

Of course, not only collective capital but also male workers benefit from job segregation by sex, at least in the short term. Not only do men receive higher wages than women within the wage labor market, but the concentration of women in poorly paid, insecure jobs ensures that women will perform personal services for men in the household even if they also work for pay. While capital, not the male work force, generally controls the process of job definition and allocation, insofar as men mobilize themselves to maintain the subordination of women within the wage labor market, the interest of collective capital in a gender-segregated labor market is reinforced.[5]

But if male workers pursued their *class* interest, rather than seek to maintain their position as a privileged gender, they would mobilize *against* job segregation by sex. Male workers have a class interest in working-class unity. Job segregation by sex, even as it reinforces male power over women, threatens at the same time to undercut the bargaining power of male labor vis-à-vis capital, precisely because of the "cheapness" of female labor. In short, the class interest and what might be called the gender interest of male workers directly conflict with one another. Historically, the apparent domination of men's gender interest over their class interest in shaping their relationship to job segregation by sex must be explained, not presumed from the outset as inevitable or "given." It is crucial for feminists to understand the specific historical conditions under which male workers' class interests might predominate over their gender interests, if we are to have any hope of successfully eliminating job segregation.

Unions, which historically have been disproportionately controlled by men, have often served to maintain the gender privileges of their male members. But there are also historical instances in which the class interest of male workers instead has prevailed in the policy and practice of unions. For example, fear of female substitution, jeopardizing the labor market position of male workers, may lead male-dominated unions to struggle for equality between women and men in the labor market, in spite of the immediate benefits the male gender enjoys as a result of job segregation.

For the class interest of male workers to prevail over their gender interest in a sustained way, however, an oppositional ideology must be generated which challenges the legitimacy of the elaborate and deeply rooted ideology of gender division. The most thoroughgoing such oppositional ideology, namely, feminism, has had remarkably *little* influence on the American labor movement. But there have been moments in the history of industrial unionism when an ideological commitment to nondiscrimination and class unity has galvanized male workers and their organizations to struggle against rather than for job segregation.

Failing this, the interest of collective capital is reinforced by the gender interest of male workers in job segregation by sex and its rationalizing ideology of occupational sex typing. Both these interests are served by the maintenance of the family as an institution of social reproduction based on unpaid female labor. Women's participation in wage labor on equal terms with men would ultimately undermine the unequal sexual division of labor in the household. Access to an individual wage, even on terms unequal to men, erodes the structure of women's economic dependence on men and on families. This is precisely why, rather than disappearing as women's labor force participation increases, occupational sex typing persists and indeed becomes ever more important: it constructs women's "primary" commitment as devotion to home and family, whether or not they also work for pay.

This interdependence between the circumscribed roles of women in the family and in the labor market, which has been observed in a wide range of circumstances by feminist scholars, helps explain the particular case of the reconstruction of job segregation by sex within the mobilized economy of the early 1940s. During the World War II years, married women and mothers poured into the labor force in massive numbers for the first time, posing an unprecedented threat to family stability.[6] Thus, far from being rendered unnecessary by the exigencies of the war emergency, job segregation was more crucial than ever before at this juncture. The sex typing of the jobs newly opened to women "for the duration" reconciled women's new economic situation with their traditional position as guardians of the hearth. This was manifested in the pervasive wartime propaganda image of "woman's place" on the nation's production lines, which portrayed women's war work in industry as a temporary extension of domesticity.

The World War II experience not only reveals the resilience of the structure of job segregation by sex and of the *general* ideology of sexual division which legitimates it, but it also renders completely transparent the specific *idiom* of sex typing, which is flexibly applied to whatever jobs women and men happen to be doing. Jobs which had previously been cast in terms suggestive of the very quintessence of masculinity were suddenly endowed with femininity and glamour "for the duration." The propaganda newsreel *Glamour Girls of '43*, for example, suggested:

> Instead of cutting the lines of a dress, this woman cuts the pattern of aircraft parts. Instead of baking cakes, this woman is cooking gears to reduce the tension in the gears after use. . . . They are taking to welding as if the rod were a needle and the metal a length of cloth to be sewn. After a short apprenticeship, this woman can operate a drill press just as easily as a juice extractor in her own kitchen. And a lathe will hold no more terrors for her than an electric washing machine.[7]

Virtually any job could be labeled as "woman's work" in this way.

Idioms of sex typing are unified in the global presumption that "men's work" and "women's work" are fundamentally distinct, but they also vary among sectors of the economy, specific industries, and even individual firms. In "pink collar" service and clerical sector jobs, the skills and capacities presumed to be developed by wives and mothers, such as nurturance, solicitousness to emotional and sexual needs, and skill in providing personal services, are the central reference point of the idiom of sex typing. Sex segregation in the manufacturing sector speaks a different language, rooted less in women's family role than in their real or imagined biological characteristics. No one pretends that being nurturant or knowing how to make a good cup of coffee are important qualifications for "female" factory jobs. Here the idiom centers on such qualities as manual dexterity, attention to detail, ability to tolerate monotony, and, of course, women's relative lack of physical strength. Analogies to domestic labor are present in both the pink collar and blue collar idioms, but the physical tasks comprising house-work are paramount in descriptions of women's manual labor outside the home, rather than the psychological tasks stressed in relation to women's paid "mental" work.

If the underlying logic of job segregation by sex is rooted in the collec-tive interest of capital, reinforced by the gender interest of male workers, in preserving the sexual division of labor within the family, this still does not adequately explain the *specific* location of women in the wage labor force at a given point in time. Once established, idioms linking women's paid and unpaid work tend to acquire a certain ideological stability, in the form of "tradition." In practice, such "traditions" often guide the actual hiring and placement policies pursued by management. Yet, as suggested by the flexibility with which the idiom was readjusted during the war, the ideological construction of the sexual division of labor obscures the eco-nomic and political forces that help shape the particular configurations of sex-specific employment.

Employers must take account of a range of economic considerations in their hiring decisions: not only the available supplies of female and male labor and their relative costs, but also such factors as the proportion of a firm's capital outlays made up by wages, and the ease with which labor costs can be passed on to consumers. There are also political constraints which limit, or potentially limit, management's freedom in allocating jobs to women and men. For example, the greater the actual or anticipated male resistance to feminization, the less likely an employer may be to attempt it. Managerial initiatives affecting the sexual division of labor may become objects of political struggle for women and/or men workers, especially when the sex-specific supply-and-demand equilibrium in a labor market is dis-rupted—which occurs quite regularly in a dynamic capitalist economy. Usually these struggles are over marginal changes in the sexual division of labor, but there are times when more dramatic shifts in the structure of the labor market take place, presenting political opportunities for a broader challenge to the sexual division of wage labor as a whole. The large-scale economic dislocations associated with the mobilization for World War II and the subsequent postwar reconversion presented one such historical opportunity. . . .

## "WOMEN'S WORK"
## IN THE PREWAR AUTO INDUSTRY

Automotive manufacturing relied on an overwhelmingly male work force in the years before World War II, with women accounting for less than one-tenth of its labor force throughout that period. The revolutionary organization of production around the moving assembly line laid the basis for auto's development as a high-wage, capital-intensive industry, in which employers had relatively little incentive to substitute female labor for its more expensive male equivalent. While the representation of women in the industry was abnormally low, women auto workers were concentrated in a relatively small number of jobs and in particular branches of the industry, consistent with the broader pattern of job segregation by sex found throughout the nation's economy. Although small numbers of women could be found scattered through many departments of the plants, they were clustered primarily in the upholstery or "cut-and-sew" divisions of body plants, and in small parts assembly.[8]

Although women auto workers earned wages higher than those available in most other fields of female employment, throughout the industry women's wages were far below men's. In 1925, the average hourly earnings of female workers in the auto industry were forty-seven cents, compared with a seventy-three cent average for men.[9] ...

The idiom in which the sexual division of labor in the prewar auto industry was cast stressed the suitability of women for "light" or "delicate" work in accounting for their concentration in particular job classifications. "In finishing, polishing, and upholstery, where much hand work is required," wrote one observer in 1929, "they [women] are considered fast workers." In another typical rendition, it was suggested that women were especially well represented in the parts branch of this industry "since they are adept at assembly of light units."[10] These were the characteristics associated with "women's work" in the manufacturing sector generally, in the prevailing idiom of sex typing: "light," "repetitive" work, demanding manual "dexterity."

Yet the actual sexual division of labor in the prewar auto industry bore at best a limited relationship to such factors. The majority of jobs done by both women and men in the industry were repetitive operations, and most required some degree of manual "dexterity." There were also some "women's jobs" which required substantial physical exertion. ...

Once firmly established, the sexual division of labor in the auto industry remained remarkably stable during the years before the war. Even during the economic depression of the 1930s, when the auto industry underwent a severe profitability crisis, there was surprisingly little change in the sexual division of labor. ...

During the 1930s, then, the auto industry remained predominantly male with a clearly demarcated "women's place" in its various divisions, essentially unchanged in this respect from the nonunion era. It was not the political forces unleashed with unionization, but the economic impact of World War II that exploded the traditional sexual division of labor in the auto industry.

REDEFINING "WOMEN'S WORK"
IN THE WARTIME AUTO INDUSTRY

The immediate impact of U.S. entry into World War II on the auto industry was a complete shutdown of production. Consumer production of cars and trucks was banned shortly after Pearl Harbor, and in February 1942 the last car rolled off the assembly line. There followed massive layoffs of auto workers, as the industry retooled for war production, and "conversion unemployment" was particularly pronounced among women auto workers. The number and proportion of women in the industry therefore dropped in the first part of 1942, but this was followed by a sudden rise in the representation of women as demand for labor outstripped the available supply of men. In April 1942, only one of every twenty auto production workers was a woman; eighteen months later, one out of four workers in the industry's plants was female.[11]

Initially, women war workers in the auto industry were employed only in jobs that had long before been established within the industry as "women's work." Although a U.S. Employment Service survey of war work in early 1942 found that women could capably perform the tasks required in 80 percent of job classifications, UAW woman-employing plants showed women in only 28 percent of the classifications, on average, in July of that year. "The chief classifications on which they were employed," the UAW reported, "were assembly, inspection, drill press, punch press, sewing machines, filing, and packing."[12] Such positions had long before been associated with women. . . .

The government pressured the auto firms to hire women, but made no effort whatsoever to influence their placement within the industry once management let them into the factory gates. The U.S. Employment Service routinely filled employer job openings which called for specific numbers of women and men, and while ceilings were imposed on the number of men who could be allocated to each plant, employers had a free hand in placing women and men in particular jobs within this constraint.[13] Although the UAW sometimes contested the sexual division of labor after the fact, the initial decisions about where to place women within the plant job structure were left entirely to management.

Women were not evenly distributed through the various jobs available in the war plants, but were hired into specific classifications which management deemed "suitable" for women and were excluded from other kinds of jobs. . . . A 1943 government survey of the industry's Detroit plants, for example, found over one-half of the women workers clustered in only five of seventy-two job classifications. Only 11 percent of the men were employed in these five occupations.[14]

Job segregation by sex was explicitly acknowledged in many automotive plants during the war. . . . Management was quick to offer a rationale for the concentration of women in certain kinds of jobs and their exclusion from others, just as it had done in the prewar period. "Womanpower differs from manpower as oil fuel differs from coal," proclaimed the trade journal *Automotive War Production* in October 1943, "and an understanding of the characteristics of the energy involved was needed for obtaining best results." ...

Repeatedly stressed was the lesser physical strength of the average woman worker.... This emphasis on the physical limitations of women workers had a dual character. Not only did it provide a justification for the sexual division of labor, but it also served as the basis for increased mechanization and work simplification. "To adjust women's jobs to such [physical] differences, automotive plants have added more mechanical aids such as conveyors, chain hoists and load lifters." Although production technology was already quite advanced in auto relative to other industries, the pace of change accelerated during the war period. This was due at least as much to the combined impact of the labor shortage and the opportunity to introduce new technology at government expense as to the desire to make jobs easier for female workers, but the latter was particularly stressed by the industry's spokespersons.[15]

There was a contradiction in the management literature on women's war work. It simultaneously stressed the fact that "women are being trained in skills that were considered exclusively in man's domain" and their special suitability for "delicate war jobs."[16] The link between these two seemingly conflicting kinds of statements was made primarily through analogies between "women's work" in the home and in the war plants. "Why should men, who from childhood on never so much as sewed on buttons," inquired one manager, "be expected to handle delicate instruments better than women who have plied embroidery needles, knitting needles and darning needles all their lives?"[17]

Glamour was a related theme in the idiom through which women's war work was demarcated as female. As if calculated to assure women—and men—that war work need not involve a loss of femininity, depictions of women's new work roles were constantly overlaid with allusions to their stylish dress and attractive appearance. ...

Ultimately, what lay behind the mixed message that war jobs were at once "men's" and "women's" jobs was unambiguous point: women *could* do "men's work," but they were only expected to do it temporarily. ...

The wartime idiom of job segregation by sex combined such familiar prewar themes as women's dexterity and lack of physical strength with a new emphasis on the value of women's multivaried experience doing housework and an unrelenting glamourization of their new work roles. That the construction of a "women's place" in the wartime auto industry was achieved so quickly and effectively owed much to the power of this elaborate ideology of occupational sex labeling. Although the initiative came from management, neither unions nor rank-and-file workers—of either gen-der—offered much resistance to the *general* principle of differentiation of jobs into "female" and "male" categories. Nor was the idiom of "woman's place" in the war effort ever frontally challenged. There was a great deal of conflict, however, over the location of the boundaries between the female and male labor markets within the wartime auto industry, and over wage differentials between these newly constituted markets.

## AMBIGUITY AND LABOR-MANAGEMENT CONFLICT OVER "WOMEN'S WORK"

... A dilemma pervaded the auto industry, and other war industries as well, in the aftermath of conversion. How to go about classifying the new sets of jobs which had come into existence "for the duration" was ambigu-ous not only for management, but also for workers themselves—both fe-male and male. There was of course some resemblance between many of the new war jobs and their predecessors in the peacetime auto industry, but the conversion process with its attendant technological changes and the dramatic shifts in the composition of the labor force combined to create tremendous disarray in what had before the war been a relatively stable system of job organization. Although in this example the issue of gender was not explicitly broached, distinctions like "heavy" and "light," or "ma-jor" and "minor" more often than not coincided with the sexual division of labor in this period. The problem of ambiguity in job classifications was not limited to the dilemma of where to assign sex labels, but this issue was central to the more general case illustrated here. . . .

It was the union's official policy to leave initial decisions on such mat-ters to management, and then to negotiate any necessary adjustments. None of the women at the [United Automobile Workers (UAW) Women's Confer-ence in 1942] conference objected to the idea of using some system of job classification arrived at in this way—on the contrary, they hoped it might protect them from assignment to overly strenuous jobs. Evidence that such abuses had occurred in the prewar period only served to reinforce the wom-en's support for a more systematic classification of jobs.

This view, however, was soon proven naive. The union historically had developed other principles of job assignment which conflicted with the no-tion that women should be placed on the lighter jobs. There were numerous charges that management was manipulating the sexual division of labor in the mobilization period in ways calculated to undermine the seniority-based job preference rights of the prewar (that is, predominantly male) labor force. . . .

There were also numerous grievances . . . filed by the UAW against General Motors (GM) in late 1943 and early 1944. "When female employees were brought into the plant and assigned to various jobs," according to the Umpire's summary of one set of such grievances concerning the Chevrolet Gear and Axle Plant,

> complaints arose from the male employees who were on the so-called "waiting lists" pending possible promotion to higher rated classifications. These male employees complained that the placing of women in the jobs above them in rate prevented the male employees from gaining the promotions to which they would ordinarily have been entitled.[18]

What provoked these union challenges was not a belief that the idiom of sex typing (on which all parties seemed to agree) had been incorrectly applied. Rather, the central concern was that management was undercutting the seniority principle as a factor in job placement. Thus the evolution of the sexual division of labor in the war years became entangled with political and economic conflicts which involved a range of other issues. The ways in which management, the union, and rank-and-file workers defined and sought to advance their respective interests in relation to the sexual division of labor were determined in the larger context of labor relations and shop floor politics.

What was the role in these struggles of the women workers whose position in the auto industry was directly affected by their outcomes? Many of the key wartime conflicts over the sexual division of labor took place before many women had even entered the auto industry and were essentially fought out between male workers and management. The new women workers, most of whom had no factory or union experience, scarcely had time to get their bearings, much less develop the political resources they needed to participate effectively in struggles over job classification, during the short period when the wartime sexual division of labor was established. . . .

For the majority of the new women auto workers, the chance to work in a unionized basic industry, in virtually any job category, meant an enormous improvement in their economic circumstances. . . . Under such circumstances, it is not surprising that most women were relatively indifferent to their placement within what was in any case a completely new and unfamiliar system of job classification. . . .

The explicit struggles waged by the UAW (generally on behalf of its prewar, predominantly male, membership), in opposition to managerial initiatives affecting the sexual division of labor, effectively incorporated the interests of men into the process of defining boundaries between "women's work" and "men's work." In addition, the way in which management initially constructed the wartime sexual division of labor reflected the differential in political power between the sexes, and the anticipation that any opposition to the specific pattern of job placement by sex would come from men rather than from women. Thus, beneath the idiomatic construction of the sexual division of labor in terms of "heavy" and "light" jobs, and so forth, a set of political principles can be discerned according to which the allocation of jobs by gender was organized. In the wartime auto industry, women were excluded from positions where they supervised men or directly proceded them in the flow of work. Indeed, this was the case throughout the economy, and not only during the war: *job segregation* coincides with a *gender hierarchy* within the labor market.[19] ...

## CONCLUSION

The changes in the sexual division of labor in the auto industry during the mobilization for World War II illustrate the way in which job segregation by sex can be reproduced in the face of dramatic changes in the economic setting. Although neither the war period nor the auto experience is typical in women's labor history, that job segregation was reconstituted under such extreme circumstances—in a high-wage industry and in a situation in which women's incorporation into basic industry's work force was construed as temporary—suggests the resilience of the ideology of sex typing and the job segregation it enforces. The auto experience during this period reveals the way in which that ideology, as constrained by a particular set of economic exigencies and political forces, provided the basis for automotive management to construct a new sexual division of labor "for the duration."

In the absence of an organized feminist movement or consciousness, the only vehicle for political struggle over the sexual division of labor in this period was the labor movement. The UAW did challenge managerial initiatives in this area during the mobilization, most importantly in the form of demands for "equal pay for equal work." Here the conflict was essentially between male auto workers and management, as women were new to both the industry and the union and were not yet a politically effective force. In addition, just securing access to "men's jobs" in the auto plants brought such a dramatic improvement in women workers' status and pay that the sexual division of labor *within* the wartime industry understandably did not preoccupy them.

During the postwar reconversion, when these gains were threatened and when women had accumulated some political experience, they would mobilize in opposition to management's effort to return to the prewar sexual division of labor in the auto industry. In the mobilization period, however, women and men alike generally accepted as legitimate the overall idiom of the sexual division of labor in that industry. The struggles which took place focused on where the boundaries between women's and men's work should be drawn, without questioning the existence of such boundaries, as the equal pay example well illustrates. Ultimately, then, despite the dramatic upheaval in women's position in the work force during the war, the ideology of sex typing retained its power for both workers and management in the auto industry. In the absence of either a more fully developed class consciousness or a feminist movement, there was really no political basis for a sustained challenge to job segregation and the ideology of gender division which underpins it. Rather than romanticizing the wartime experience of women workers, we need to specify the kind of consciousness, of both class and gender, that might make it possible to dismantle the sexual division of paid labor and to transform work itself.

## NOTES

1. Karen Skold, "The Job He Left Behind: Women and Shipyard Workers in Portland, Oregon During World War II," in *Women, War, and Revolution,* ed. Carol R. Berkin and Clara M. Lovett (New York: Holmes, Meier, 1980). For a more detailed account of the situation in the auto industry, see Ruth Milkman, *Gender at Work: The Dynamics of Job Segregation by Sex during World War II* (Urbana: University of Illinois Press, 1987).

2. To be sure, the existence of a clearly defined sexual division of labor is not peculiar to capitalist societies—quite the contrary. Yet the persistence and reproduction of job segregation within capitalist relations of production presents a distinct theoretical problem—and an especially paradoxical one. . . . An adequate theoretical account of the continuous reproduction of job segregation by sex in capitalist societies has yet to be developed. The perspective frequently put forward by Marxist feminist theorists—that male domination exists as a "system," usually called "patriarchy," which is separate from and preceded capitalism, and is theoretically irreducible to it—while a possible starting point for such a theory, by itself offers no way out. This simply *presumes* the persistence of gender inequality within capitalism in general, and the capitalist labor market in particular, rather than *explaining why* it persists, which is hardly self-evident.

3. This consideration is stressed in the literature on "labor market segmentation" developed by Marxist economists. See, for example, Richard Edwards, Michael Reich, and David Gordon, eds., *Labor Market Segmentation* (Lexington, Mass.: D.C. Heath and Co., 1975), especially the Introduction. However, this literature fails to distinguish between the class interests of capital and the interests of individual capital, missing a critical aspect of the problem altogether.

4. This dynamic has been discussed extensively in Marxist feminist literature. See especially Veronica Beechey, "Some Notes on Female Wage Labour in Capitalist Production," *Capital and Class,* no. 3 (Autumn 1977), pp. 45–66; and Heidi Hartmann, "Capitalism, Patriarchy, and Job Segregation by Sex" in *Women and the Workplace: The Implications of Occupational Segregation,* ed. Martha Blaxall and Barbara Reagan (Chicago: University of Chicago Press, 1976).

5. This is the main emphasis in Hartmann, "Capitalism, Patriarchy, and Job Segregation."

6. The war years produced a "family crisis" with many parallels to that of our own time and aroused many of the same concerns among contemporaries. This is discussed indirectly in Karen Anderson, *Wartime Women: Sex Roles, Family Relations and the Status of Women in World War II* (Westport, Conn.: Greenwood Press, 1981), chap. 3.

7. The transcript of this newsreel was made available to me by the Rosie the Riveter Film Project, Emeryville, California. Additional examples of the wartime idiom are cited below.

8. Statistics on the representation of women in the auto industry for this period are scattered and not entirely consistent. The 1930 Census reported that women were 7 percent of all workers employed by the industry, and the 1940 Census enumeration produced a figure of 9 percent. U.S. Department of Commerce, Bureau of the Census, *Fifteenth Census of the United States, 1930: Population,* 5:468; and *Sixteenth Census of the United States 1940; Population,* 3:180. William McPherson reported in 1940 that women made up about 5 percent of the wage earners in auto assembly plants, about 10 percent of those in body plants, and about 20 percent of

those in parts plants. See his *Labor Relations in the Automobile Industry* (Washington: Brookings Institute, 1940), pp. 8–9.

9. U.S. Department of Labor, Bureau of Labor Statistics, *Wages and Hours of Labor in the Motor Vehicle Industry: 1925*, Bulletin No. 438 (1927), pp. 2–3.

10. Robert W. Dunn, *Labor and Automobiles* (New York: International Publishers, 1929), p. 74; William McPherson, "Automobiles," in *How Collective Bargaining Works*, ed. Harry A. Millis (New York: Twentieth Century Fund, 1942), p. 576.

11. On conversion, see Barton J. Bernstein, "The Automobile Industry and the Coming of the Second World War," *Southwestern Social Science Quarterly* 47 ( June 1966): 22–33; and Alan Clive, *State of War: Michigan in World War II* (Ann Arbor: University of Michigan Press, 1979), pp. 18–42.

12. "Women in War Industries, *"UAW Research Report,* 2 (September 1942), p. 1.

13. U.S. Congress, Senate, *Manpower Problems in Detroit,* Hearings before a Special Committee Investigating the National Defense Program, 79th Cong., 1st Session, March 9–13, 1945, pp. 13534, 13638.

14. Computed from data in U.S. Department of Labor, Bureau of Labor Statistics, Division of Wage Analysis, Regional Office No. 8-A, Detroit, Michigan, 3 December 1943, Serial No. 8-A-16, "Metalworking Establishments, Detroit, Michigan, Labor Market Area, Straight-Time Average Hourly Earnings, Selected Occupations, July 1943," Mimeographed copy in UAW Research Department Collection, WSUA, Box 28, Folder: "Wage Rates (Detroit) Bureau of Labor Statistics, 1943–5." Women were 22 percent of the labor force surveyed here. If these data are compared to those in the 1940 Bureau of Labor Statistics survey cited in note 8, the degree of segregation by sex in the auto industry during the war is put into better perspective. In 1940, women were only 2.5 percent of the labor force, and two occupational groups accounted for one-half of the women in the industry. In 1943, five groups accounted for 51 percent of the women, which, given the much greater representation of women in the auto work force, does not indicate a significant decline in the degree of segregation.

15. "Provisions in Plants for Physical Differences Enable Women to Handle Variety of War Jobs," *Automotive War Production* 2 (September 1943): 7. Also see "Technological Advances in Automotive Plants Help to Combat Growing Manpower Crisis," *Automotive War Production* 2 (September 1943): 3; and "Automotive Industry Reducing War Costs Through Improved Production Techniques, *Automotive War Production* 2 (March 1943): 3.

16. "Women Work for Victory," *Automotive War Production* 1, (November 1942): 4; "Engineers of Womanpower," *Automotive War Production* 2 (October 1943): 4–5.

17. "Engineers of Womanpower," p. 4.

18. Umpire Decision No. C-139, 29 November 1943, "Hiring of Women," *Decisions of the Impartial Umpire Under the October 19, 1942 Agreement between General Motors Corporation and the International Union, United Automobile, Aircraft and Agricultural Implement Workers of America—Congress of Industrial Organizations,* vol. 1 (privately published, Detroit: General Motors Corporation and United Automobile Workers), pp. 465–67.

19. I have not uncovered evidence of this specific to the auto industry, but the wartime literature on managerial policy toward women war workers generally is replete with insistences that women make "poor supervisors" and the like. See for example, American Management Association, *Supervision of Women on Production Jobs: A Study of Management's Problems and Practices in Handling Female Personnel,* Special Research Report No. 2 (New York: AMA, 1943). For a general discussion of this issue, see also Joan Acker and Donald R. Van Houten, "Differential Recruitment and Control: The Sex Structuring of Organizations," *Administrative Science Quarterly,* 19 ( June 1974): 152–63.

# 16

## White Women Volunteers in the Freedom Summers: Their Life and Work in a Movement for Social Change

### Mary Logan Rothschild

*The Civil Rights Movement of the 1950s and 1960s served as crucible for the creation of the twentieth century's "second wave" of feminism. Not since the emergence of feminism in the antislavery movement of the 1830s had white women participated in a social movement that so effectively challenged the fundamental structures of their society's racial inequality. As in the 1830s, women's experience in that movement clarified their understanding of their society's structure of gender inequalities and generated a vanguard for a new feminist movement in the subsequent decade. Mary Logan Rothschild explores the development of the growing consciousness of gender issues among white and black women active in this social movement. She also explains why they sometimes perceived those issues differently.*

In the Freedom Summers of 1964 and 1965, 650 northern white women left their comfortable communities to work in the southern direct action civil rights movement. They went with the hope that their work would in some way make life better for black people in the South. Their experience in the South stands as a case study of institutional sexism in an integrated movement dedicated to racial equality and social change. The institutional sexism they encountered was, for the most part, unconscious and unanalyzed. It was also analogous to the institutional racism they carried with them as part of their own northern white upbringing. To the extent that this is foremost an analysis of problems and failures within what was an exciting and dynamic movement, it tends to obscure the joy, optimism, and humanism which infused a great deal of movement life and work. This examination stands, however, as a case study of women's roles in a movement that saw inequality in terms of race and class and not in terms of sex.

... My interpretation is based upon an examination of archival sources, such as letters and application forms, transcripts of interviews of the volunteers conducted in 1964 and 1965, my own interviews of fifty volunteers two to eight years later, and the analyses of such other scholars as Michael Aiken and Sara Evans.[1]

The Freedom Summers of 1964 and 1965 represented a turning point

This article is excerpted from *FEMINIST STUDIES*, Volume 5, Number 3 (Fall 1979): 466–495, by permission of the publisher, FEMINIST STUDIES, Inc., c/o Women's Studies Program, University of Maryland, College Park, MD 20742.

*Civil Rights March. World Wide Photos.*

in the ideological development of the student branch of the civil rights movement.[2] From the first lunch counter sit-in by black students in Greensboro, which began the sixties' rebirth of nonviolent direct action campaigns, the student movement sought the integration of blacks into the mainstream of American society. Although many tactics evolved after the sit-ins, including among others Freedom Rides, Voter Registration Campaigns, and Freedom Votes, the goals of most movement workers remained attaining integration and political rights for blacks. Only after the experiment of bringing hundreds of northern white student volunteers to the South during the Freedom Summers to work in direct action projects did the staff of the major organizations shift their ideology from purposeful integration to a form of separatism which in 1965 was called "self-determination."

Throughout the South from 1960 through 1965, students, mainly southern and northern blacks and a handful of whites, worked in nonviolent direct action projects under the auspices of three major civil rights organizations. The Congress of Racial Equality (CORE) was the oldest of the direct action groups, having begun in the North in 1942. Though in 1960 CORE was primarily a northern civil rights group, its sponsorship of the

Freedom Rides thrust it into the forefront of the burgeoning southern direct action movement. The primary southern direct action group in 1960 was the Southern Christian Leadership Conference (SCLC) headed by the charismatic young leader of the Montgomery bus boycott, the Reverend Martin Luther King. The third group, the Student Nonviolent Coordinating Committee (SNCC) was founded in 1960 by students who had participated in direct action campaigns.... SNCC continually initiated new tactics and programs, and SNCC staff members became famous for their raw courage in the face of severe white violence.

While CORE, SCLC, and SNCC all held similar goals, they generally sponsored separate projects in different places in the South.... Only in the state of Mississippi did all of the civil rights groups in the South—CORE, SCLC, SNCC, and the National Association for the Advancement of Colored People (NAACP), which did not generally engage in direct action work—come together to form an umbrella organization called the Council of Federated Organizations (COFO). Because Mississippi was legendary as the purest stronghold of white resistance to equality for blacks, the civil rights groups there were more disposed to band together for strength and ignore their sometimes very real differences....

The Mississippi Summer Project ... was born of desperation: the southern movement was stymied by the winter of 1964. Four years after direct action campaigns began in the South, white repression of blacks continued almost unabated. In the deep South, blacks had made painfully few gains in integration, voter registration, or community organization. Beatings, bombings and less violent forms of economic intimidation kept the movement small, edgy, and dangerous. Worse yet, the northern media was losing interest in showing beating after beating on television. Southern work was becoming bereft of "news value." ...

The students who answered the call to be volunteers came South usually for two months. At a minimum, they had to pay for their transportation, have $150 to support themselves, and be able to raise a $500 bond. In 1964 about 650 young people went to Mississippi, and a year later about 750 fanned throughout the entire South. Although the sponsoring groups differed in style and political perceptions and there were changes in the political climate between 1964 and 1965, it is possible to draw a general profile of the volunteers, for there was a remarkable underlying similarity among the people who went South to work in the Freedom Summer projects.

Although the application forms were not standardized and it is impossible to say precisely how many volunteers were white, Asian American, or black, the overwhelming majority were white. A random sample of 220 Mississippi volunteers' files showed 88 percent of the volunteers were white, 11 percent were black, and 1 percent were Asian Americans. CORE had a fairly equal division of blacks and whites, but only dealt with approximately forty people and most of the twenty blacks were from the South. A complete count of the 282 Mississippi Federal Democratic Party (FDP) applications for 1965 that mentioned race found 94 percent of the volunteers were white, 4 percent were black, and 2 percent were Asian Americans.[3] ...

The overwhelming majority of volunteers were students and teachers. Although volunteers who went South were from all types of colleges, there was a very high proportion from the most prestigious private and public schools, especially Harvard, Stanford, the University of Wisconsin, and the University of California at Berkeley.[4]

Even in comparison with other students, the volunteers held high educational aspirations. In 1965, 25 percent of the FDP-SNCC workers had more than sixteen years of schooling,[5] and Summer Community Organizing the Political Education (SCOPE) volunteers indicated that 73 percent planned postgraduate study in liberal arts fields.[6] Many volunteers valued education for its intrinsic importance to their personal development, in contrast to students who saw education as a career path. The study of SCOPE volunteers by Aiken, Demareth, and Marwell indicated, moreover, that while students who remained in the North preferred careers as business executives, lawyers, physicians, engineers, and "housewives," the volunteers preferred careers as professors, social workers, and clergy.[7]

The civil rights movement was a national concern, and the Freedom Summers attracted volunteers from every state in the Union. They were overwhelmingly urbanites. More than 90 percent in 1964 and 1965 came from towns classified as urban by the United States Census Bureau, whereas only 70 percent of the total population were urban dwellers. Two out of five volunteers came from the northeastern states; of those states, New York sent by far the largest number. The midwestern and west coast states sent the next largest group: if their numbers were combined, they formed just under half of the total group. A very few volunteers came from the mountain and southwestern states. In both 1964 and 1965, the southern states produced more white volunteers than both the mountain and southwestern states combined.[8]

Most student volunteers came from families with a secure economic standing. One FDP women volunteer remarked in 1965, "My father's money has been able to buy my idealism."[9] Indeed, the SCOPE study found that two-thirds of its subjects belonged in the upper and upper-middle classes.[10] ... For a minority of the volunteers, however, work in the South constituted a definite financial handicap and a few noted they would have to forego college temporarily, due to their loss of summer earnings. In some cases, church groups and northern civil rights affiliates sponsored individual volunteers. These groups paid the volunteers' expenses, enabling them to go South without financial aid from their parents.

In addition to their relatively high economic standing, the volunteers' parents had attained a very high educational level for their generation. Three out of four had finished at least twelve years of school, and a substantial number had more than sixteen years of schooling. Most of them held high status jobs as doctors, lawyers, professors, teachers, business executives and civil servants, and they were highly represented in service occupations. They were also in the political mainstream; more considered themselves Democrats than Republicans, but very few deviated from America's two major parties.[11]

In their stated political philosophy, the volunteers differed from their fellow students, but not on the issue of racial equality because most northern college students favored full equality for southern blacks.[12] The volunteers veered to the left of their colleagues in their broad range of social concern, and they more often believed that the federal government should spend a larger portion of the budget on antipoverty, medicare, and educational programs. Perhaps most important to the future of the movement, the SCOPE study found in 1965 that volunteers were more worried about the prospect of nuclear war than other college students. Fully three times as many volunteers as others wanted the United States to initiate negotiations to end the Vietnam War.[13]

In their activities, the volunteers mirrored their spoken concern. In 1964, 92 percent of the volunteers had participated in at least some civil rights activities in the North. In 1965, 95 percent of the FDP volunteers and 78 percent of the SCOPE volunteers had worked in the civil rights movement before the summer. Over half of the volunteers participated in their communities in tutoring programs, settlement work, and voter registration. ... Even in 1964, 15 percent of the volunteers indicated activity in peace groups, and more than 10 percent had previously worked with the American Friends Service Committee in work camps outside their communities.[14]

The overwhelming majority of the volunteers considered themselves "Liberal Democrats," "Liberals" or nonaffiliated "Socialists." They thought the existing political institutions could accomplish their desire for a more just society and saw their wishes as consistently American in orientation. They were, in fact, not far to the left of the stated goals of the Johnson Administration in its search for the Great Society.[15] For example, of those 1965 FDP volunteers who indicated membership in Students for a Democratic Society (SDS), 37 percent also indicated membership in the Democratic Party. Even in 1965 fewer than 10 percent identified themselves as radicals.[16]

These white volunteers were children of the American Dream. They came South enormously naive about the black community and the terrible pressures that civil rights direct action brought with it. Although clearly there were many motivating factors, some more noble than others, almost all of the volunteers passionately believed in the justice of their cause: it was truly a case of black and white. For ivory-tower college students, there was also charisma in the act of confrontation itself. ...

In 1964, approximately 300 white women went to Mississippi as volunteers, and in 1965 around 350 white women fanned throughout the entire South. Women were nearly half of all the volunteers. Unlike the vanguard of strong southern black and white women who early joined the movement, often at great personal cost, and who were experienced staff workers by 1964, these northern women represent a relatively anonymous group who lived the daily lives of women's work in a social movement. Many of the dynamics of their participation are similar to the early abolition and temperance movements, but there are some obvious twentieth-century differences, particularly the experience of living together in racially integrated groups.

While women volunteers sometimes seemed to have the same experiences as their male colleagues, more often their life in the South was different in both quality and texture, and they had to contend with many problems not shared by their fellow male volunteers. In fact, there were differences between men and women volunteers from the beginning of their involvement in the movement.

Even before the volunteers went to orientation, recruiting material inferred that men were more desirable than women, ostensibly because of the danger and the need to act in the community. In 1965, when CORE staff recruited volunteers, they made formal priorities and sought, in order, black men, black women, white men, and lastly, white women. David Dennis, the director of CORE's Southern Office, explained their policy:

> We had low on the list the white females, because they cause problems usually, you know. That's one thing that infuriates a white male in the South especially, but just about anywhere, any place, you know ... it's that whole interracial ... sex problem, you see ... white people can usually, in the South especially, can usually stomach to see a white male and a Negro male walking down the street, or a white male and a Negro female, you know, it's accepted, to some extent. But it infuriates people, it causes tremendous reactions, when there's a white female and Negro male involved, walking down the street.... So to somewhat get out of that we decided that maybe the best thing to do would be to use that priority system.[17] ...

Also, it was more common for northern organizations to provide men, rather than women, with financial support to reduce the financial hardships of volunteering.

Most volunteers' parents were at least initially somewhat reluctant for their children to participate in the Summer Projects; they feared for their children's safety and often wondered why they had to go South. Most parents recovered quickly, however, and supported their children emotionally and financially. . . .

Despite this general pattern, however, many more women than men spoke of difficulties in obtaining parental approval to go South and, unlike men volunteers, women were not allowed to work on any COFO or FDP project without parental approval if they were under 21 years old.[18] This held true, also, for the more conservative, and therefore perhaps less threatening, SCLC-sponsored SCOPE projects. . . .

As a result of these obstacles, women often had to be more motivated than men and felt they particularly had to prove their political worth. In the main, they were more qualified in terms of previous social-action work and tended to have more direct political expertise than their male counterparts. When divided according to sex, 1965 FDP volunteers show a significantly different pattern of previous political activity. Four out of five FDP women had been "very active" in the movement, which is defined as having affiliation with a civil rights group and participating in direct action demonstrations. By contrast only three out of five men fit that category. . . . Women volunteers . . . consistently had substantially more civil rights experience, which also, generally, was of more radical nature than their male colleagues' experience.[19] . . .

Additionally, some women indicated their motivation to go South for these projects lay partially in their realization that, as women, they had only a short time to . . . act on their political beliefs. In America in 1964, it was assumed that middle-class women would be "settled" before their early twenties were past. Women of this class could certainly go to college and they could even work for a while; but there was a clear expectation that these were but phases in a woman's life, filling in the blanks before her true vocation of marriage and raising a family began. . . . Women volunteers saw their lack of family ties as something unique about them which enabled them to act on their beliefs and differentiated them from other women their age. . . . Women volunteers often saw themselves as very different from their old friends who were locked into a traditional female role. At the time, however, none voiced a radical challenge to, or seemed to discard, the ultimate inevitability of the traditional wife-mother role. Instead, many of the women appeared confused and ambivalent about what they would ultimately do, expressing with great pain their alienation from what they considered the norm. . . .

When the volunteers, both male and female, arrived in the South, they found themselves in projects in which the social structure of American society was turned on its head. In general, young black men and then black women held the power and status in the project and, in most cases, considerably below them were white men and then white women. In a few projects, due to the individuals involved, the black women shared some of the men's status, though they rarely shared their power, unless they ran their own projects without male staff members.[20] The racial dynamics changed only very infrequently when, in response to some particular project tension, the men would bond—black and white together—in a controlling position over the women, who remained divided.

The black-white divisions in the projects became more pronounced as southern civil rights work continued. Particularly in 1965, the concepts of local control and self-determination assured the extension of the racial divisions within the project staff and in turn depended upon the expansion of black-controlled organizing in the community. Working in projects with the usual structure of black men and black women in control was an education in itself, particularly for the male volunteers. Although most volunteers at the time saw the black and white positions in the structure, few identified the male and female dynamics.

In both summers, women volunteers did all kinds of work, but in 1964 in Mississippi, when the projects tended to be more structured, women were generally cast in traditional women's jobs. They were most often Freedom School teachers, or project office workers, and they were dedicated to their work.... Unlike Freedom School teaching, which most women enjoyed, office assignments often disappointed women volunteers because field work was where the action was and it held a higher status. Nevertheless, unromantic office work was crucial to the running of the projects and many women performed tirelessly in those jobs....

In a kind of middle ground between teaching and full-time office work, community center positions, especially librarian-cum-social workers, tended to be solely a woman's prerogative. In sharp distinction, relatively few women in 1964 were assigned full time to voter registration, although many occasionally canvassed part-time after their other jobs were finished for the day. During the 1964 summer, no women were assigned to canvass sharecroppers who lived on plantations, for instance, because plantation canvassing was viewed as an almost paramilitary venture. Each episode was seen as an assault on a prominent and powerful white citizen's "land and people." Because often only one dirt road led in and out of the plantation, all plantation canvassing was planned down to the last detail. Usually a local movement worker would "infiltrate" the plantation and draw a detailed map to minimize the inherent danger, and only the best drivers were allowed to go. White women volunteers were also not sent to especially dangerous towns, like McComb, Mississippi.... When integrated teams were needed in particularly dangerous areas to show the movement's dedication to "black and white together," those teams were always male.[21]

There were at least two reasons for these job assignments: teaching, office, and community center work were deemed less dangerous and therefore more suitable for women, and the COFO staff did not question sexual stereotypes in job assignments.[22] By 1965 in the FDP project, there were many more women canvassers and even some women union organizers of women laundry workers. This seeming enlargement of roles for women was due mainly to the concept of local control, coupled with the logistics of running smaller projects which meant most volunteers did several tasks. It did not represent a conscious expansion of women's work in the movement....

In those projects located in homes in the black community, rented to house groups of civil rights workers (Freedom Houses), women volunteers usually did the housework, too. Women particularly resented their role in the Freedom House, as one volunteer explained, "working with fifteen people, it takes one person almost all day just to cook and clean up, and do laundry, which is difficult. Especially the girls, we wound up doing much more work than the fellows did. We didn't come down here to work as a maid this summer, we came down to work in the field of civil rights."[23]

While women performed the menial work of the offices and Freedom Houses, they rarely made policy decisions, although decision making differed greatly from project to project. When time permitted, policy decisions seemed, in general, to be made by higher level staff, who were mainly men. . . .

All the northern volunteers arrived in the South besieged by many strange and difficult new experiences. The extreme poverty, established community racism, black staff suspicion, and power construct of the offices combined to make the volunteers' first days and weeks a continual test. But women volunteers had an additional problem many simply did not know how to handle. They faced what two volunteer professors described as a "sexual test" which became a sort of "rite of passage" before women could be considered serious workers.[24] This test was whether or not women volunteers could deal with sexual advances from black men in the movement. Women and men volunteers generally accepted premarital sex, reflecting the attitude of their college colleagues. Yet out of a desire to please the black community and to lessen the chances that projects would be attacked by southern racists, in every orientation session project leaders counseled volunteers to be discreet in their sex lives, if not to forego sexual activity for the duration.[25]

There were obviously several ways for women volunteers to deal with sexual advances. Some women simply accepted and there was sometimes joy and freedom in interracial sex, an exhilaration born of breaking the last major social barrier between the races. Interracial sex for some women took on a kind of totality of integration in their lives which represented a unity of belief, work and life. For others, sleeping with black men was a way to "prove" their "commitment" to black and white equality; some women tried to demonstrate their liberalism in that way. It has also been suggested that white women expiated their "guilt" about racism by sleeping with black men. Indeed, Poussaint found this a component in what he ironically (and cruelly) called the "White African Queen Complex."[26]

Whether women volunteers accepted or rejected the advances of black men, sex became the metaphor for racial tension, hostility, and aggression. Nearly every project had real problems over interracial sex, and many white women volunteers were in a painful double bind from the moment they arrived. One FDP woman advised:

I think that the white female should be very well prepared before she comes down here to be bombarded. And she also has to be well prepared to tell . . .

[black men] to got to hell, and prepared to have them not give up.... I don't know from an intellectual point of view what the role of sex is.... I mean if you go into a community, they're going to be talking how you're going to bed with a Negro fellow ... and the Negro fellows are going to be hitting on you too.... I think it's because, just because, you're white....[27]

Another FDP woman, who was very bitter, described her situation, "I've seen the Negro fellows run after white women. It's quite obvious that they're after a white woman, not this particular woman. And I'm quite disillusioned about that...."[28] But it was not only a problem of the more radical projects, for a black staff member at the SCOPE orientation warned:

The only way or place a Negro man has been able to express his manhood is sexually and so you find a tremendous sexual aggressiveness. And I say, quite frankly, don't get carried away by it and don't get afraid of it either. I mean don't think it's because you're so beautiful and so ravishing that this man is enamored of you. It's not that at all. He's just trying to find his manhood.... So, in a sense, what passes itself off as desire quite often ... is probably a combination of hostility and resentment, because he resents what the society has done to him, and he wants to take it out on somebody who symbolizes the establishment of that society. And at the same time it's a search for his own personhood, for his own freedom.[29]

It was this scarcely veiled hostility that troubled most of the women.

The woman who simply accepted the advances and "slept around" faced grave consequences, for ultimately she failed the "sexual test." In most cases she was written off as an ineffective worker, and she often became the focal point for a great deal of bitterness for the black women on the project. Additionally, her behavior was seen as scandalous by many within the black community and this profoundly inhibited community organizing, one of the main goals of the projects. Finally, in some instances such open flouting of the prevailing mores physically endangered the project.[30] When that happened, the woman was usually chastised and in some cases sent home, while the man was rarely reprimanded. In one incident in 1964, a black man and a white woman had sexual relations in the man's car under a street light in a white section of Jackson, obviously jeopardizing themselves, the project, and the black community. The woman was sent home and the man remained on the staff. When a woman volunteer professor complained, she was told by Staughton Lynd, the director of Freedom Schools, "We just couldn't get along without Flukey, could we?"[31]

Although many women volunteers had sexual relationships with black men, there were obvious pressures against such affairs. They were seen as disruptive to the projects and the community. Reflecting the consensus of civil rights workers, one white FDP woman earthily explained: "I think that people like that, if they come down just to screw around, they ought to stay up North. They can screw around in their own communities. It's going to hurt the Movement. I don't care if they screw around themselves, but it's going to hurt the Movement, and that's what I care about."[32]

It was not easy, however, to escape problems. Women who did not wish to become sexually involved—at least not with several men—faced a classic dilemma. Black men "in search of their manhood" were persistent and aggressive. If a woman refused them, they called her a racist, and she generally became a focus for the hostility of the black men on the project. Furthermore, "racist" was an exceedingly effective epithet: it was, quite simply, the worst thing a volunteer could be.

Accusations and verbal abuse were not the only pressure women volunteers faced. Some white women were raped by black men in the movement.[33] In 1965, before the Jackson demonstrations, one black man, whose father had been shot by a white man and who was a long-time SNCC worker, violently attacked at least three women in one evening, though he was not successful in his attempt to rape them. As one of his victims explained, "he had a real deep-seated emotional hatred ... and bitterness against white people. So that he hated most of the girls who were white, and most of the guys who were white, but he took out his hatred on the girls. ...."[34]

Women who did not wish to have casual sexual encounters evolved tactics of their own to deal with their situations. Married women, whether or not their spouses were present, had the least trouble avoiding casual encounters, if that was their choice. Nearly everyone seemed to see extramarital sex negatively (although it certainly went on), and married women could refuse sexual encounters without fear of being branded racist. ...

Obviously unmarried summer volunteers did not get married to avoid problems, but many found that attaching themselves "steadily" to one man served nearly the same function. One woman, who found, "it took a little while ... sort of building a reputation," said,

> I find it's almost a necessity to associate yourself with one person, so the other people will not bother you as much if you have a boyfriend. ... In a sense, you're in a better position.[35]

Sometimes, women simply put up with their situations and wrote out all their problems to special confidants in the North. This was not a viable alternative for most, however, because they needed immediate help and also, paradoxically, because their problems were too painful emotionally to verbalize. ... Rather than writing to outsiders, a more typical response was to find one other woman on the project in whom to confide. The two would help each other and talk over their mutual problems. Very rarely, a group of women would join together, but this seemed only to happen in extreme cases, when there was a real possibility of physical violence toward one of the women.[36] And the reasons for this were obvious: attaining civil rights for brutally oppressed southern blacks was the goal of the summer projects and was held firmly by most volunteers. Even when women believed they were not being treated fairly, in their view, their personal situations were never as bad in any dimension as the local blacks' and thus clearly had to be a secondary concern. . . .

By far the most common response was to limit severely all social contact and to practice a form of self-imposed celibacy. Rather like the Victorian women who asserted themselves by denying their sexuality, women who wanted to assert some control over their sex lives and also to obey the project rules often found themselves living completely (if temporarily) celibate lives. Only by sleeping with no one could women avoid, or lessen the impact of, the charge "racist." . . .

Once they passed the sexual test, women volunteers performed their movement tasks well. The very competence of the volunteers, as well-educated northerners, often in fact stood in the way of effectively developing indigenous leadership, which was one of the main goals of the Freedom Summers. In the specific case of women volunteers, however, their competence was often doubly resented because of their sex. . . . Although most women volunteers tried to ignore the sex discrimination, a few strong women dealt with it directly. Generally, however, they saw the problem in individual terms and tried only to change their position, not the position of women volunteers as a whole. . . .

Black women, staff and volunteers, obviously did not have to deal with racial resentment from black men, and they were perhaps in a better position to examine sex discrimination than white women volunteers. Additionally, those long-term white women staff members, who had years before passed the sexual test, and were seen as powerful insiders, were also able to begin to question women's position within the movement, especially since the influx of white women volunteers made the disparities between women's and men's experiences clearer than ever.

Within this context, the first analysis of sex discrimination in SNCC came at the November 1964 staff retreat held to reevaluate the organization. The major topics of discussion were the future of SNCC and the role of whites in southern civil rights work. But in addition, an anonymous staff woman, widely assumed at the time to be Ruby Doris Smith Robinson, who was black, wrote a "SNCC Position Paper: Women in the Movement," for the group's consideration in a workshop. The memo began with a list of eleven transgressions by men in SNCC, including several instances of women being excluded from decision-making bodies within the organization and COFO, women being held responsible for office work and minutes-taking, experienced women being underutilized in field work, and women being primarily identified as "girls" rather than individuals.

Acknowledging that the "list will seem strange to some, petty to others, laughable to most," the author went on to analyze the problem of women's position and held that it was analogous to the position of black people in white society.

> The average white person doesn't realize that *he assumes he is superior* . . . doesn't understand the problem of paternalism. So too the average SNCC worker finds it difficult to discuss the woman problem because of the assumption of male superiority. Assumptions of male superiority are as widespread and deep rooted and every much as crippling to the woman as the assumptions of white supremacy are to the Negro.

She explained that the paper was anonymous, because of the "insinuations, ridicule, and over-exaggerated compensations" which would ensue if her identity were known: "Nothing so final as being fired or outright exclusion but the kinds of things which are killing to the insides. . . ." After more scrutiny of the problems, the author concluded:

> Maybe the only thing that can come out of this paper is discussion—amidst the laughter—but still discussion. (Those who laugh the hardest are often those who need the crutch of male supremacy the most.) And maybe some women will begin to recognize day to day discrimination and start the slow process of changing values and ideas so that all of us gradually come to understand that this is no more a man's world than it is a white world.[37]

Her paper did cause a great deal of laughter and some discussion. At the formal meeting to consider it, Stokely Carmichael is supposed to have said, "The position of women in SNCC should be prone," which cut off more debate, although the minutes of the staff retreat reported the workshop seriously.[38] While the movement was not a uniformly hospitable and supportive environment for assessing sex discrimination, black women in SNCC and long-term white staff women were pushed to analyze their position in the civil rights movement precisely because the large numbers of white female volunteers and the increased racial tensions made sex-roles, racism, and sexuality stand out in unavoidable stark relief. . . .

This beginning analysis of institutional sexism came from black women who did not have to wade through charges of racism, and it came from long-term white staff women, who had years before dealt with sexual advances and who saw their hard-fought place in the movement slipping away as a result of the Freedom Summers. For a brief time, they tried to deal with the issue head-on and together, as a group, unlike the few volunteers who tried to find individual solutions. The sexism that permeated the southern movement was seen and felt clearly by all female staff, black and white. . . .

While a few black and white women staff members identified themselves as a group with interests occasionally in conflict with black men, young black women in the movement did not generally join with northern white women in any effort to overcome sexist practices. When there were sexual problems on a project, for the most part young black women remained bitterly divided from white women, whom they saw as stealing their men.[39] As a black SNCC staff woman recounted in 1965:

> Sex in one thing; The Movement is another. And the two shouldn't mix. There's an unhealthy attitude in The Movement toward sex. The Negro girls feel neglected because the white girls get the attention. The white girls are misused. There are some hot discussions at staff meetings.[40] ...

The divisions that sexuality created ultimately meant that all women, black and white, staff and volunteer, could not unite in the civil rights movement to work on problems that were common to them as women. It also meant that the hurt some black women felt as a result of their experiences with white women volunteers would remain long after the Freedom Summers had passed. . . .

The concept of institutional sexism aids in understanding women's daily life in the movement. Job assignments and responsibilities were clearly sex-role stereotyped. Women volunteers were under double jeopardy for competent performance of their jobs and often caught full-force hostility generated against all whites—but vented only on them. In terms of interpersonal dynamics, black and white women alike were dehumanized and objectified by black and white men unable to escape their sexism in just the same way that white volunteers unconsciously carried their racism with them to the South. The tensions between black men and women and white women were impossible to overcome without an analysis of the sexism of society and the projects in particular. Indeed, at the time, it was impossible for most of the people who worked in the South to realize what was happening. While both black and white together, in their finer moments, tried to show the nation what true racial equality could be, it did not occur to those involved to strive for sexual equality as well. The Freedom Summers tried to bring black Americans into the mainstream of American society, but they never questioned the unequal status of women and men in that society.

## NOTES

1. My interpretation is based mainly on the analysis and compilation of four groups of sources: Stanford University's KZSU Interviews, Commitment Sheets, and Pre-South Interview Forms; Delta Ministry's COFO Files for 1964 and FDP Files for 1965; CORE's application files from the State Historical Society of Wisconsin; a study of the SCOPE project; and my own interviews.

See also Michael Aiken, N. G. Demareth III, and Gerald Marwell "Conscience and Confrontation," *New South* 21 (Spring 1966): 19–28. Their final study was published as *Dynamics of Idealism, White Activists in a Black Movement* (San Francisco: Jossey Bass, Inc., 1971). Also see Sara

Evans, *Personal Politics: The Roots of Women's Liberation in the Civil Rights Movement and the New Left* (New York: Knopf, 1979).

2. For a larger examination of this brief summary, see Mary Aickin Rothschild, "Northern Volunteers and the Southern 'Freedom Summers,' 1964–1965: A Social History" (Ph.D. dissertation, University of Washington, 1974).

3. COFO File Compilation; FDP File Compilation; State Historical Society of Wisconsin, National CORE Papers, 1963 Louisiana Summer Task Force Applications; Miriam Feingold Papers, Summer Field Report (1963); Aiken, Demareth, and Marwell, *Dynamics of Idealism,* pp. 25–26. Also Interviews with Otis Pease, Seattle, Washington, 13 February 1967 and 23 March 1967; and Miriam Feingold Stein, San Francisco, California, 6 April 1975.

4. COFO File Compilation; FDP File Compilation.

5. This is corroborated by the KZSU Commitment Sheet sample.

6. Aiken, Demareth, and Marwell, "Conscience and Confrontation," p. 22.

7. Ibid., pp. 22–23. In this respect, however, there is some evidence to indicate that volunteers were simply following family patterns as the volunteers' parents "over represented such occupations as teacher, clergyman, social worker, and at the doctoral level, those occupations requiring the Ph.D. rather than a professional degree (M.D., D.D.S.)." John L. Horn and Paul D. Knott, "Activist Youth of the 1960's: Summary and Prognosis," *Science* 171, no. 3975 (12 March 1971): 979.

8. These data are from compilation of various address lists: COFO Address List; FDP File Compilation; KZSU Commitment Sheets; SCOPE Address List.

9. KZSU Interview, no. 0258.

10. Aiken, Demareth, and Marwell, "Conscience and Confrontation," p. 26; KZSU Commitment Sheets; KZSU Interviews; FDP File Compilation.

11. Aiken, Demareth, and Marwell, "Conscience and Confrontation," p. 26; KZSU Commitment Sheets; KZSU Interviews; FDP File Compilation.

12. Aiken, Demareth, and Marwell, *Dynamics of Idealism,* p. 34; KZSU Pre-South Interview Forms.

13. Aiken, Demareth, and Marwell, *Dynamics of Idealism,* p. 34–36; KZSU Interviews; Rothschild Interviews, Seattle, Washington: Carol Koppel, 30 January 1967; Gary Good, 26 January 1967; Sally Shideler, 15 February 1967; Michael Rosen, 7 February 1967; Barbara Rosen, 26 January 1967; John Darrah, 21 February 1967; Timothy Lynch, November 1966; Billy Jackson, 14 February 1967; Mary Gibson, 9 February 1967; John and Ellen Fawcett, 25 January 1967; David Hood, 24 January 1967; Palo Alto, California: Richard Gillam, January 1967; Roger Dankert, January 1967; Mt. Beulah, Mississippi: Rev. Roger Smith, November 1969; Charles Horwitz, November 1969; Ruleville, Mississippi: Fannie Lou Hamer, November 1969; Tougaloo, Mississippi: Jan Hillegas, November 1969.

14. COFO File Compilation; FDP File Compilation; Aiken, Demareth, and Marwell, *Dynamics of Idealism,* p. 50.

15. FDP File Compilation; COFO File Compilation; KZSU Commitment Sheets; Aiken, Demareth, and Marwell, *Dynamics of Idealism,* pp. 34–36.

16. FDP File Compilation.

17. KZSU Interview, no. 0442, p. 6; CORE. In general, citations for this section refer to specific illustrative quotations only.

18. Minutes of SNCC Executive Committee Meeting, 10 April 1964, 5, Jan Hillegas Papers, Tougaloo, Mississippi.

19. FDP Compilation; COFO Files; *Delta Ministry Collection.* See also KZSU Interviews; COFO Staff mimeographs, Spring 1964 (series).

20. For an example of a black woman's autonomy and power as project director in Bolivar County, Mississippi, see Cynthia Washington, "We Started at Different Ends of the Spectrum," *Southern Exposure* 4, no. 4: 14–15.

21. Interview with Sally Shideler, Seattle, Washington, 17 February 1967; Otis Pease, Seattle, Washington, 13 February 1967 and 23 March 1967; Melish, "Memoirs"; Hodding Carter, *So the Heffners Left McComb* (New York: Doubleday and Co., Inc., 1965), passim.

22. SNCC Position Paper, Women in the Movement, undated [November 1964], Clay Carson Papers, Stanford, California. I am indebted to Clay Carson for sharing this memo with me.

23. KZSU Interviews, no. 0275, p. 13, SCOPE.

24. Interview with Florence Howe and Paul Lauter, Seattle, Washington, 28 June 1972. I

am indebted to Howe and Lauter for their frank discussion of sexual tensions on the projects and for their encouragement of this undertaking.

25. Robert C. Sorensen, "Adolescent Sexuality in Contemporary America," *Woman's Day* (March 1973): 73–74, 196–97; Nathaniel Wagner, Department of Obstetrics and Gynecology, University of Washington, unpublished studies; Lise Vogel, "Notes at 1964 Orientation for MSP," Lise Vogel Papers, State Historical Society of Wisconsin, KZSU Interviews, no. 0132, SCOPE Orientation, no. 0099, SCOPE, Sally Belfrage, *Freedom Summer* (New York: Viking Press, Inc., 1965), p. 19.

26. Alvin Poussaint, "The Stresses of the White Female Workers in the Civil Rights Movement in the South," *American Journal of Psychiatry* 123, no. 4 (October 1966): 401–407. In this article, Poussaint accurately describes the hostility between black women and men and white women. I think he deals unfairly with white women, however. While black men are excused from aggressive and hostile acts because of their historical experience, white women are not extended the same understanding and compassion. Instead, he sees all of the tensions as the result of white women working in the South. They are the instigators by their very presence, and, in his final analysis, Poussaint identified "many" as having what he called the "White African Queen Complex," which is meant to be as derogatory as it sounds. Although I found some women who perhaps fit that "complex," I found none who exhibited those traits in a vacuum. Just as black men had their historical reasons for their hostility—which I think, if anything, Poussaint downplays—those white women could not escape their historical experience either. More importantly, however, I found most of the white women I studied caught in a horrendous double bind: they could be sex objects or they could be labeled racists. Poussaint seems to have little understanding of the viciousness of that bind.

27. KZSU Interview, no. 0365, p. 36, FDP.

28. KZSU Interview, no. 9006, p. 20, FDP.

29. KZSU Interview, no. 0099, pp. 2–3, SCOPE.

30. KZSU Interview, no. 0099, p. 3., SCOPE; Interviews with Florence Howe, Donna Goodman, Miriam Feingold Stein, Jody Aliesan, Seattle, Washington.

31. Interview with Florence Howe.

32. KZSU Interview, no. 0360, p.19, FDP.

33. KZSU Interviews, nos. 9009, pp. 9–12; FDP; 9006, pp. 19–20, FDP, Alice Walker, "Advancing Luna—and Ida B. Wells," *Ms.*, July 1977, pp. 75–79, 93–97; Confidential Interviews, 1972–78.

34. KZSU Interview, no. 9009, p. 1–15. The attack by this black male volunteer on the three women volunteers had a sequel a few weeks later when the three women warned a young white female volunteer not to go out with him because he was dangerous. For their pains, one of the three was later attacked by the man with a hatchet; her hand was cut open. She said: "And at that point, I was really angry, 'cause my hand was bleeding, and 'cause I was badly frightened. He is a lot bigger than I am, and I do feel that he is mentally imbalanced.... He's been so frustrated, that he can't take any kind of action in a constructive way any longer. He's just got to hit. And, as I say, this is not a general case. I really think he is emotionally disturbed, but his emotional disturbance is a result of what the white people have done to him. And you know ... so what can I do?" The terrible irony of this case is that this woman volunteer was a fair-haired, fair-skinned woman whose father is black and whose mother is white. Because her parents did not want her and her sister, who looks black, to grow up with racism, they had lived in Europe until she was through high school. (It is not known whether the man was ever disciplined or how long he stayed with the project after these incidents).

35. KZSU Interview, no. 0365, p. 37, FDP.

36. See, for example, the case described in n. 34 above.

37. "SNCC Position Paper (Women in the Movement)." Underlining in original memo.

38. For a description of the meeting and Carmichael, see Julius Lester, *Revolutionary Notes* (New York: Grove Press, Inc., 1969), pp. 132–35. See also UCLA, "Special Collection on the Civil Rights Struggle and Black Movement in the United States, 1950 to 1970," 11: Mississippi, folder B: Item 51; "Summary of Staff Retreat Minutes," p. 1. I do not know if the secretary who wrote the minutes was a woman, but I would not be surprised if it were the case.

39. Poussaint, "Stresses," p. 403; KZSU Interview, no. 0099, p. 3., SCOPE.

40. Paul Jacobs and Saul Landau, *The New Radicals: A Report with Documents* (New York: Random House, 1966), p. 145.

# 17
## The Rebirth of the Women's Movement in the 1960s

### Sara Evans

*The contemporary women's movement, like its nineteenth-century predecessor, arose from diverse sources and attracted diverse supporters. Three points of origin seem especially important. First, growing labor force participation rates among married women of Betty Friedan's generation in the 1950s and 1960s generated among them an impatience with social attitudes that belittled women's contributions to their families and communities. Second, the Civil Rights Movement provided many younger women with a vision of social change that could easily be extended to embrace gender-specific as well as race-specific issues. Third, the antiwar and New Left movements of the 1960s and 1970s had the same effect on women in their ranks, creating ferment on campuses to match that among women in the workforce. By the mid-1970s, these three streams of women's activism combined to form a flood of social criticism that significantly altered the position of women in the paid labor force, in universities, and in American society as a whole. Sara Evans describes the empowerment women discovered through collective action in these decades.*

The election of John Fitzgerald Kennedy in 1960 marked a shift in the public mood. Change became a positive rather than a negative value. Together with the southern civil rights movement, programs like the Peace Corps and VISTA sparked a resurgence of idealism and active involvement in social change. The child-mother no longer fit the times. She was too static, too passive, maybe even too safe. A rising number of voices in the late 1950s urged the abandonment of outmoded myths, though usually with a qualifying clause about the importance of mothers to very young children and the primacy of the family. Many social scientists moved from using "role conflict" as an argument for women to refuse outside work, to a more realistic appraisal of the problems of the "working wife," who could not and would not evade such conflicts by returning to the home. Thus such observers had finally achieved the level of adjustment to changing reality accomplished already by millions of American families. Jobs for women were becoming legitimate as extensions of the housewife role.[1]

With the growing public acceptance of women's work outside the home, the mass media suddenly discovered the "trapped housewife." Betty Friedan pointed out that in 1960 the housewife's predicament was examined in *The New York Times, Newsweek, Good Housekeeping, Redbook, Time, Har-*

Excerpted from Chapters 1 and 9 of *Personal Politics: The Roots of Women's Liberation in the Civil Rights Movement and the New Left,* by Sara Evans (New York: Knopf, 1979). Reprinted by permission of the author.

*First Abortion Rights March, New York City, May 1972. Bettye Lane.*

*per's Bazaar,* and on CBS Television. *Newsweek* entitled a Special Science Report and cover story: "Young Wives with Brains: Babies, Yes—But What Else?" The editors reported that the American middle-class woman "is dissatisfied with a lot that women of other lands can only dream of. Her discontent is deep, pervasive, and impervious to the superficial remedies which are offered at every hand."[2] Both seriously and superficially, most articles in the issue treated women's problems of boredom, restlessness, isolation, over-education, and low esteem.

Educators also responded to the changing mood. Beginning in about 1960, a series of educational experiments and innovations appeared to meet the newly recognized malaise of the middle-class housewife. The "continuing education movement" focused on shaping the educational system to meet the demands of women's "dual role." Educational and career interruptions due to marriage and children were presumed inevitable. The problem, therefore, was to allow middle-class educated women to reenter the work force either full or part time without being forced into low-skilled, low-paid work.[3]

Even the federal government began to treat women's roles as a public issue and to explore public policy alternatives to meet changing conditions. On December 14, 1961, President Kennedy established the President's Commission on the Status of Women, chaired by Eleanor Roosevelt. The purpose, in fact, may have been to quell a growing pressure for an Equal Rights Amendment, but unwittingly the government organized its own opposition. The existence of the commission and in subsequent years of state commissions on the status of women provided a rallying point for professional women. Such commissions constituted a tacit admission that there was indeed a "problem" regarding women's position in American society, that the democratic vision of equal opportunity had somehow left them out. Furthermore, they furnished a platform from which inequities could be publicized and the need for women's rights put forth. The President's Commission's report, entitled *American Women* and published in 1963, was moderate in tone. Yet despite obeisance to the primacy of women's roles within the family, it catalogued in great detail the inequities in the lives of women, the discrimination women faced in employment, and the need for proper child-care centers.[4]

The importance of the report and the commission itself lay less in the specific changes they generated directly than in the renewed interest in "women's place in society" which they reflected. The following year women's rights advocates gained a crucial legal victory in the passage of Title VII of the Civil Rights Act, which prohibited discrimination by private employers, employment agencies, and unions on the basis of sex as well as race, color, religion, and national origin. Though introduced by a southern senator in a facetious gesture of hostility to the entire act, Title VII provided women with a legal tool with which to combat pervasive discrimination in hiring and promotion in all aspects of the economy.

The renewed discussion and activism took place primarily among professional women, who did not see themselves as housewives. Precisely because these professional women thought their work important and because they resented being patronized as if they had fled housework to get a little excitement, they felt even more acutely the discrimination leveled against them. Having openly admitted a certain level of drive and ambition, they were far more likely to experience discriminatory hiring, training, promotion, and pay rates as unfair. Other women could justify their unwillingness to fight against such barriers by saying, "I wouldn't be here if I didn't have to be," or "I'm only doing this for my family, not for myself." But for professional women, long-term careers were involved. Discrimination could close off opportunities they had invested years of training and hard work to attain. And it could deny them the positive reinforcement of respect from their colleagues. Since they took their work seriously, they were more vulnerable to the contempt that underlies patronage.

In general such women embraced the American ideology of equal opportunity, believing in advancement according to individual merit and achievement. Between 1940 and 1960, while the numbers of professional women declined relative to men, they also grew in absolute numbers by 41 percent. With more and more women in professional jobs, there were more examples to prove that women could excel at any occupation they chose. The individual professional woman was not a fluke or a freak of nature. On the other hand, there were also multiplying examples of blatant discrimination as their salaries and promotions increasingly lagged behind those of men with the same training and experience.[5]

The new public attention to women's roles finally generated an overtly feminist position in 1963 in Betty Friedan's book, *The Feminine Mystique*. In a brilliant polemic she declared that housework was intrinsically boring, that the home had become a "comfortable concentration camp" which infantilized women. She took dead aim at the educational establishment, Freudians, women's magazines, and mass advertising, which she believed had combined to limit women's horizons and to force them back into the home. More academic but equally critical reassessments of women's traditional roles soon followed.[6]

By the mid-sixties these angry professional women were developing an oppositional ideology and a strong network within governmental commission on the status of women. As participants and consultants, they articulated the discrepancy between the ideals of equal opportunity and the actual treatment of women by employers. They mobilized to press for the passage of Title VII and then for its enforcement. A growing circle of women, including Friedan, Rep. Martha Griffiths, and the lawyers Mary Eastwood and Pauli Murray, urged the creation of an action group to pressure a government that continued to issue provocative reports but showed little sign of taking effective action. When, at a national conference of state commissions on the status of women in 1965, activists were informed that they could pass no resolutions and take no action in their capacity as state commissioners, a group broke away to resolve to found the National Organization for Women (NOW). These women had become convinced that, for real change to occur, a new civil rights group must be formed that could pressure the government to enact and enforce laws against sexual discrimination. Thus NOW became the "women's rights" branch of a renewed feminism.[7]

In general, the professional women who created NOW accepted the division between the public and private spheres and chose to seek equality primarily in the public realm. Betty Friedan's devastating critique of housewifery ended up with a prescription that women, like men, should be allowed to participate in both realms. In effect she urged women to do it all—to be superwomen—by assuming the dual roles of housewife and professional. She made no serious assault on the division of labor within the home. For Friedan it was easier to imagine a professional woman hiring a "professional housewife" to take her place in the home than to challenge the whole range of sex roles or the division of social life into home and work, private and public, female and male domains.

In contrast, however, the oppression of most American women centered on their primary definition of themselves as "housewife," whether they worked solely inside the home or also outside it. Although they could vote, go to college, run for office, and enter most professions, women's primary role identification created serious obstacles both internally and in the outside world. Within themselves, women were never sure that they could be womanly when not serving and nurturing. And such doubts were reinforced by a long series of experiences: the advice and urging of high school and college counselors; discrimination on the job; pressure from family and friends; a lack of social services such as child care; and social expectations on the job that continually forced women back into traditional roles. Somehow women in every position from secretary to executive all too often ended up making the coffee.

At the same time that women acknowledged the social judgment that their work counted for very little—by accepting lower pay and poor jobs outside the home, or describing themselves as "just a housewife"—they also felt uncomfortable in any role other than that of the housewife. To admit discontent was to face a psychic void. The choices were there in a formal sense, but the price they exacted was a doubled workload and loss of both self-approval and public approval. Thus, though the *Newsweek* article on "Young Women with Brains" generated a storm of response from women, many who responded in writing denied the existence of a problem altogether. Others advised volunteer work and hobbies to fill the time, or else criticized women for their unhappiness. Only a few women echoed the article and discussed their distress.[8]

If women found housewifery unfulfilling, they also on some level believed it was their own fault, thus turning their guilt and anger back in upon themselves. In a culture that offered no support for serious alternatives, women clung to the older definitions. If such roles did not reflect changing options or their real desires, at least they were familiar.

The tenacity of traditional roles and their internalization by most women meant that any successful revolt that drew on women's discontent would finally neither accept a traditional view of "female nature" as particularly suited to home and motherhood nor restrict itself simply to a critique of inequities in the public realm. For this reason, the emergence of the National Organization for Women did not provoke a massive grass-roots feminist movement. As a civil rights lobbying group, it could and did raise the public policy issues of discrimination in education, employment, and media in accordance with its stated purpose:

> ... to take action to bring women into full participation in the mainstream of American society *now*, exercising all the privileges and responsibilities thereof in truly equal partnership with men.

But while the professional women in NOW's constituency militantly demanded equality in the public realm, they were not prepared to question the mainstream itself, nor to carry their critique into the operation of sex roles in every aspect of life.

Yet the initiation of a mass movement required that the problem be addressed at its core. The pressures on most women were building up not on the level of public discrimination but at the juncture of public and private, of job and home, where older structures and identities no longer sufficed but could not simply be discarded either. The growing emotional strains of providing nurture for others with nowhere to escape to oneself, of rising expectations and low self-esteem, of public activity and an increasingly private, even submerged, identity required a radical—in the literal sense—response. A new movement would have to transform the privacy and subjectivity of personal life itself into a political issue.

Women from the new left explained the sources of their new awareness by pointing to the discrepancy between the movement's egalitarian ideology and the oppression they continued to experience within it. What they failed to perceive, however, was the fact that the new left did more than simply perpetuate the oppression of women. Even more importantly, it created new arenas—social space—within which women could develop a new sense of self-worth and independence; it provided new role models in the courage and capability of southern black women and female community leaders; and having heightened women's self-respect, it also allowed them to claim the movement's ideology for themselves. The point at which they did so came when the movement that had opened for them a new sense of their own potential simultaneously thrust them into menial domestic roles. Feminism was born in that contradiction—the threatened loss of new possibility.

Moreover, as conditions within the new left permitted young women to reexamine and reinterpret their own experiences, their situation also proved parallel to that of millions of American women far beyond the enclaves of the left. Indeed, it represented in microcosm the dilemma of most American women, trapped in an obsolete domestic role while new realities generated an unarticulated sense of greater potential. Although women's liberation was shocking and alienating to many, especially as seen through the magnifying lens of a hostile media, the reactions to the outcry on behalf of women's equality indicated that feminism had tapped a vein of enormous frustration and anger. The Harris Survey found in 1971 that 62 percent of American women believed that women had to "speak up" in order to accomplish anything, although most of them disapproved the tactics of picketing and protest and did not support "efforts to strengthen and change women's status in society." Nearly five years later, after the intervening upsurge of activism, 65 percent endorsed such efforts. Previously, ambivalence and fear of change had made women even less likely than men to advocate greater sexual equality. But by 1975 a new sense of rights and possibilities had led women to assert their belief in equal rights and opportunities for females in greater numbers and with greater intensity than men. Similarly, on specific issues such as abortion, child care, and the Equal Rights Amendment, opinion polls recorded a steady shift in public opinion toward the endorsement of feminist programs. By the bicentennial year, 1976, the *Reader's Digest* conceded: "Women's Liberation has changed the lives of many Americans and the way they look at family, job, and sexual equality." Nearly a decade after the women's movement began, the confused response of most American women would be: "I'm not a women's libber, but . . . I believe women ought to be equal."[9]

Within the context of such massive shifts of opinion, as millions of women readjusted their view of themselves and of the world, many thousands also moved to activism and into the burgeoning women's liberation movement. But success was not without its problems: neither the leaders nor the organizational structures could maintain a unified movement. And at the same time that the issue of sexual equality had become a subject of dinner conversation in households across the nation, the new revolt suffered from internal weaknesses inherited from the new left.

The lack of structure and of responsible leadership led, inevitably, to a loss of internal coherence as the women's liberation movement expanded. This fragmentation was intensified by the obstacles and defeats that the women's movement encountered, analogous to those of the civil rights movement and the anti-war protest. New Left women, emerging from a movement high on visions of immediate revolution, failed to perceive initially that the profound changes they desired would arouse intense opposition and that the process of change itself would of necessity be long and laborious. As a result, they often deprecated their achievements and failed to claim the concrete victories that were won.

In the beginning, radical women believed that if they pointed out the inequities in women's position, at the very least their comrades on the left would understand. And with a united, egalitarian movement, they would quickly be able to revolutionize society. They rapidly met the full force of social tradition on the one hand, however, and the realities of the left culture on the other. After a child-care bill had sailed through Congress, Richard Nixon explained his ringing veto by saying that the family must be protected and women should stay at home with their children. And on the left, while a few men responded openly and honestly, others paid guilty lip service and many were obscenely hostile. "Take her off the stage and fuck her," shouted members of the audience as Marilyn Salzman Webb spoke to an anti-war rally in January 1969. Thus, young women in their small groups found themselves floundering in a morass of left-wing hostility and establishment derision. As both left and right labeled them "man-haters" when they demanded equality, they became acutely sensitized to the way in which it seemed that the whole culture was biased against women. One new recruit described her change in consciousness: "I couldn't walk down the street, read advertisements, watch TV, without being incensed ... at the way women are treated." Robin Morgan's anger grew in the year that she edited *Sisterhood Is Powerful,* an anger that came "from deep down and way back, something like a five-thousand-year buried anger." She continued, "It makes you very sensitive—raw, even, this consciousness."[10]

The rage, the sensitivity, and the overwhelming, omnipresent nature of "the enemy" drove parts of the women's movement into ideological rigidities, and the movement splintered as it grew.[11] Who could say what was *the* central issue: equal pay? abortion? the nuclear family? lesbianism? welfare policies? capitalism? Groups formed around particular issues, constituencies, and political styles, many sure that they had found the key to women's liberation. After 1970, women's liberation groups in all parts of the country suffered painful splits variously defined as politico/feminist, gay/straight, anti-imperialist/radical feminist.

Yet while some became disillusioned at the fragmentation, the movement continued to spread. Certain more radical branches mellowed and grew critical of their own purism. They recognized that consciousness-raising, as an essentially intellectual mode of radicalization, could not address the daily needs for health care, child care, equal pay, and decent housing of minority and working-class women. At the same time former conservatives were radicalized. The National Organization for Women gradually assumed primary responsibility for creating new consciousness-raising groups and absorbed much of the new left heritage with its slogan: "Out of the mainstream—and into the revolution." But no single organization was able to capture the energy and enthusiasm aroused by the women's revolt and convert it into a sustained power base from which women could demand political and social change.

The difficulties of achieving change grew further as the spread of feminist ideas provoked opposition. Predictably, the traditionalists organized a reaction to turn back the Equal Rights Amendment, proscribe abortion, punish homosexuality, and in general return women to a subservient domesticity.[12] But for all their vehemence and occasional victories, their arguments drew on visions of a mythic past in which women and men knew their places and the patriarchal family served as the stable foundation of a static social order. Although there was reaction, there could be no return.

## NOTES

    1. Alva Myrdal and Viola Klein, *Women's Two Roles: Home and Work* (London: Routledge & Kegan Paul, 1968), 2nd ed.; Robert B. Smuts, *Women and Work in America* (New York: Columbia University Press, 1954); National Manpower Council Reports, *Womanpower, A Statement with Chapters by the Council Staff; Work in the Lives of Married Women; Proceedings of a Conference on Womanpower Held October 20–25, 1957* (New York: Columbia University Press, 1957–8); Janet Zollinger Giele, "Introduction to Viola Klein, *The Feminine Character* (Urbana: University of Illinois Press, 1971), pp. xx–ix; Ravenna Helson, "The Changing Image of the Career Women," Journal of Social Issues 28 (1972) 34–26.

2. "Young Wives with Brains: Babies, Yes—But What Else?" *Newsweek* (March 7, 1960), pp. 57–60.

3. Jean W. Campbell, "Women Drop Back In: Educational Innovation in the Sixties," and Joan Huber, "From Sugar and Spice to Professor," in *Academic Women on the Move,* ed. by Alice S. Rossi and Ann Calderwood (New York: Russell Sage Foundation, 1973), pp. 93–104, 125–35.

4. Judith Hole and Ellen Levine, *Rebirth of Feminism* (New York: Quadrangle, 1971), pp. 16–81. Lois W. Banner, *Women in Modern America: A Brief History* (New York: Harcourt Brace Jovanovich, 1974), pp. 231–35.

5. Jo Freeman, *The Politics of Women's Liberation: A Case Study of an Emerging Social Movement and Its Relation to the Policy Process* (New York: McKay, 1975), pp. 44–71.

6. Ellen Keniston and Kenneth Keniston, "An American Anachronism: The Image of Women and Work," *American Scholar* 33 (1964), 355–75; and Alice Rossi, "Equality Between the Sexes: An Immodest Proposal," in *The Woman in American,* ed. by Robert J. Lifton (Boston: Houghton Mifflin, 1965), pp. 98–143.

7. NOW's formation and its early activities are described in great detail in Hole and Levine, *Rebirth,* pp. 81–95; Banner, *Women in America,* pp. 233–5; Freeman, *Politics of Women's Liberation,* pp. 71–102.

8. "Wives with Brains," reader response, *Newsweek* (March 21, 1960), pp. 2, 8; see also Peter G. Filene, *Him/Her/self: Sex Roles in Modern America* (New York: Harcourt Brace Jovanovich, 1975), pp. 192–3.

9. "The Harris Survey," May 20, 1971; December 11, 1975; December 8, 1975; "The Gallup Opinion Index," Report no. 92, February 1973; Report no. 113, November 1974; see also Cynthia Fuchs Epstein, "Ten Years Later: Perspectives on the Women's Movement," *Dissent* 22 (Spring 1975), 170; "The American Woman on the Move," *Reader's Digest,* 108 (March 1976), 54. The Harris Poll records the continued ambivalence of women who support efforts to improve their lot but are not attracted by most women's rights organizations (December 11, 1975).

10. Hole and Levine, *Rebirth,* pp. 133–4; quotes from Robin Morgan, ed., *Sisterhood is Powerful: An Anthology of Writings from the Women's Liberation Movement* (New York: Random House, 1970), p. xv., and Maren Lockwood Carden, *The New Feminist Movement* (New York: Russell Sage Foundation, 1974), p. 36.

11. See, for example, the discussion of Redstockings and the Feminists in Hole and Levine, *Rebirth,* pp. 136–47.

12. See Marabel Morgan, *The Total Woman* (Old Tappan, N.J.: Revell, 1975).

# 18

## Women at Farah:
## An Unfinished Story*

### Laurie Coyle, Gail Hershatter, and Emily Honig

*In "Women at Farah," Laurie Coyle, Gail Hershatter, and Emily Honig explore the empowerment and mobilization of a largely female, largely Chicana workforce in a major garment firm in Texas along the Mexican border. Utilizing intensive oral interviews with striking women workers, the authors trace the emergence of exploitative working conditions in the borderland garment factories, the place of factory work in the broader life cycles of recent immigrants, and the slow and steady growth of organization among them. They delineate the sources of internal and external support for the strike and show how the women were changed by the event. The narrative offers a view of the changing balance of power among employer, workers, and union, providing a framework for understanding future developments for women workers in similar, precariously situated, competitive industries.*

When four thousand garment workers at Farah Manufacturing Company in El Paso, Texas, went out on strike for the right to be represented by a union, many observers characterized the conflict as "a classic organizing battle."[1] The two-year strike, which began in May 1972 and was settled in March 1974, was similar in many ways to earlier, bloodier labor wars.

There was a virulently antiunion employer, Willie Farah, who swore in the time-honored manner that he would rather be dead than union. There was a company that paid low wages, pressured its employees to work faster and faster, consistently ignored health and safety conditions, and swiftly fired all those who complained. There was a local power structure that harassed the strikers with police dogs and antipicket ordinances, denied them public aid whenever possible, and smothered their strike and boycott activities with press silence for as long as it could. There were strikebreakers, and sporadic violence was directed at the striking workers. On the side of the strikers there was a union, the Amalgamated Clothing Workers of America, which mustered national support for the strikers and organized a boycott of Farah pants. There was support from organized workers and sympathizers throughout the United States. Finally, there was a victory—an end to the strike and a union contract.

*The authors wish to thank the real authors of this oral history—the women workers at Farah who generously shared their lives and opinions with three outsiders. Many of them asked to remain anonymous because they still live and work in El Paso, Texas.

Excerpted from "Women at Farah: An Unfinished Story," in *Mexican Women in the United States: Struggles Past and Present* (Los Angeles: University of California, Chicano Studies Research Center, 1980). Copyright by the authors. Reprinted by permission of the authors.

*Farah Strike Meeting, San Antonio. ACTWU/Labor Unity.*

However, any account of the Farah strike that focuses exclusively on its "classic" characteristics misses most of the issues that make it an important and unfinished story. The Farah strikers were virtually all Chicanas. They were on strike in a town whose economy is profoundly affected by proximity to the Mexican border, in a period when border tensions were on the rise. They were workers in an industry plagued by instability and runaway shops. They were represented by a national union committed to "organizing the unorganized," but which often resorted to tactics that undermined efforts to build a strong, democratic local union at Farah.

Perhaps most important, 85 percent of the strikers were women. Their experiences during and since the strike changed the way they looked at themselves—as Chicanas, as wives, and as workers—and the way they looked at their fellow workers, their supervisors, their families, and their community.

The following account . . . attempts to explore the effect of the strike on the women who initiated and sustained it. In extensive interviews (approximately seventy hours) conducted during the summer of 1977, the women described their working conditions, events leading to the strike, the strike itself, the development of the union, and their lives as Mexican American women in the Southwest. . . . The account appears here primarily as it was told by the Farah strikers themselves—eloquently, sometimes angrily, and always with humor.

The history of the Farah Manufacturing Company exemplifies the myth and reality of the American success story. Unlike many other southwest garment plants that ran away from the unionized Northeast, Farah got its start in El Paso. During the Depression, Mansour Farah, a Lebanese immigrant, arrived in El Paso and set up a tiny shop on the South Side. Farah, together with his wife and two sons, James and Willie, and a half-dozen Mexican seamstresses, began to turn out the chambray shirts and denim pants that were the uniform of the working West.

When Mansour died in 1937, James was twenty-one and Willie only eighteen, but they were well on the way to becoming kingpins of the needle trade. Winning government contracts for military pants during the war mobilization effort enabled the company to expand, and it emerged from World War II in the top ranks of the garment industry. In the postwar period, the rapid expansion of the garment industry transformed the South into the largest apparel-producing region of the United States. The Farah brothers shifted production to meet the growing demands of the consumer trade, and sold their product to the major chain stores, J. C. Penney, Sears, and Montgomery Ward, for retail under the store names. In 1950 the Farah brothers began marketing pants under their own name, and built a loyal and growing clientele in men's casual and dress slacks. The company expanded until it employed 9,500 workers in Texas and New Mexico.[2] Before the strike, it was the second largest employer in El Paso.

Many workers felt that the expansion ruined what had been warm relations between management and employees. One woman remarked on the changes: "In 1960, there were only two plants. They had time for you. But it started growing and they didn't give a damn about you, your health, or anything. They just kept pushing."

While some workers saw these changes as significant departures from happier days, many felt that the public image of Farah as one big happy family had never accorded with the reality on the shop floor. Willie ran his business like a classic *patron,* conducting unannounced plant inspections and instructing women in how best to do their jobs.

In fact, he would shower the workers with promises of liberal pay raises which never materialized. . . . For many, wages were never raised above the legal minimum, and workers were often misled to believe that legislated increases in the minimum wage were raises granted by management. Wages remained low under the quota system; since pay increases were based upon higher and higher production rates, workers' wages continually lagged behind spiraling quotas. Women were pitted against one another in the scramble to meet management demands and protect their jobs. . . . In the garment industry, where labor comprises a major portion of a firm's expenditures, southwestern companies like Farah keep their competitive edge over unionized plants in the Northeast by these cutthroat pay practices.

Many women who were pretty and willing to date their supervisors received preferential treatment. One seamstress, who had worked on a particular job operation for twenty years, received less than the attractive young woman who had begun the operation only a year before. The less favored women were subjected to constant harassment.

Rather than hire Chicanos who had worked on the shop floor, it was standard practice for the company to hire Anglo males as supervisors. Their treatment of Chicana workers was frequently hostile and racist. Women were humiliated for speaking Spanish. When they could not understand a supervisor's orders, he would snap his fingers, hurl insults, bang the machines and push them. . . .

Workers who challenged arbitrary decisions were dismissed on the spot. "When I was just learning to sew," a striker remembers, "I made a mistake on three pieces and the supervisor threw them in my face."

> I couldn't say anything, being new there. But an old man who worked with the seamstresses defended me, saying that I wasn't trained yet and there was no reason to throw them at me because everyone made mistakes at the start. They fired him for that, because he wasn't supposed to meddle in those things. He'd been there for fifteen years.

All of these racist and abusive practices played a role in helping to control the work force.

Health problems in the plant were numerous. Some workers contracted bronchitis from working directly under huge air conditioners, while others suffered from a lack of ventilation. The pressure to produce was so great that women were reluctant to take time to go to the bathroom or get drinks of water. As a result, many workers developed serious kidney and bladder infections after several years of work. Equipment was faulty and safety devices were inadequate. Needles often snapped off machines and pierced the fingers and eyes of the seamstresses. . . .

Several workers were fired after having been injured on the job. Others had their injuries and illnesses misdiagnosed and were sent back to work without proper treatment, sometimes with serious consequences:

> I saw several times people fainting. There was this time the doctor told this guy there was nothing wrong with him and kept giving him pain killers. In the afternoon, he was the guy who did cleanup and sweeping, he just bent over—he couldn't stand the pain anymore. They took him to the hospital and at the hospital he went into a coma. He was in a coma and they couldn't operate on him. I think it was his gall bladder.

Few Farah workers ever retired from the company. Usually workers were shoved out just before retirement age, so that Farah was not obliged to pay their pensions. Older workers were frequently the lowest paid and the least likely to be promoted despite their extensive work experience. Instead, they were expected to work long hours at the most demanding operations. Their health ruined by this ordeal, many workers quit prematurely. Farah absorbed new employees continually, and had little consideration for the needs of aging workers. Many women were bitter about the treatment of the older workers, and realized that their "benefits" were only guaranteed by their own wits, resilience, and ability to make the grade. . . . The factory conditions described by the women workers were by no means unique to Farah. Exploitation, low wages, no security, and minimal employer liability were the lot of working people whether they grew up in El Paso's *barrios* or across the Rio Grande in El Paso's sister-city Juarez.

The border economy affected the lives of women at Farah even before they entered the work force, shaping their family backgrounds and presenting them with enormous obstacles when they tried to act on their own behalf.

The boundaries policed by the border patrol scarcely disguise the historic integration and interdependency of the Mexico-Texas region. The border itself is marked by the Rio Grande River, which is a mere thirty feet wide and four feet deep on the outskirts of El Paso and Juarez. Today, more than ever, the United States economy depends on cheap labor from the Mexican side of the river to harvest its seasonal crops, replenish its industrial workforce, and maintain profits in its labor-intensive industries.

The close cooperation of authorities on both sides of the border, as well as the special privileges granted to twin plants, allows for the optimum flow of labor and goods between El Paso and Juarez. The state of Texas has protected these privileges by establishing the right-to-work law. This law stipulates that no worker in a plant be required to join a union, and furthermore that *all* workers, whether they are union members or not, are entitled to the benefits provided by a union contract. Collective bargaining efforts have frequently been undermined by this law, and El Paso remains a largely nonunion town.

The availability of unorganized workers on the El Paso side, many of whom are Mexican nationals without rights of permanent residence, and many others who are unskilled Chicanos, has created an ideal situation for companies investing in labor-intensive operations such as electronics and garments. El Paso has become the last frontier of United States industry on the move south and out of the United States. "Runaways?" asked one Farah worker incredulously. "Industries in El Paso don't need to move. They have the advantage that they can get people from Juarez to work for less."

Many Farah strikers maintained close ties with friends and family in Juarez. Women who had extensive personal contact with life in Mexico, either because their parents had crossed the Rio Grande or because they themselves had grown up there and come to the United States as adults, tended to see the Mexicans and Chicanos as one people. . . .

Many workers at Farah, as children, took part in the pilgrimage north to find work. . . . Other women at Farah came north as adults to seek work. Even when they succeeded in finding a stable job, the relocation entailed severe hardship and demanded major readjustments. Most of the women had grown up in the poverty-stricken rural areas of northern Mexico. They had almost no formal education, and many married very early in life. While the daily struggle to survive prepared them for the grinding labor of the factory, nothing in their backgrounds had prepared them to assume roles traditionally restricted to male heads-of-household: to leave the home, enter the industrial workforce, and, for some, become the major breadwinner of the family.

A major change for those who came from Mexico involved no longer being a "native" but being stigmatized as an "alien." This identification was applied to all Mexican people regardless of citizenship, and included a population indigenous to the region and more "native" than the later white settlement.

The pride of many Farah workers in their Mexican heritage—a pride often fostered by their parents—protected them somewhat from this hostility and enabled them to stand up to it. . . . Like their sisters in Mexico, Chicanas growing up in El Paso were expected to share responsibility for *la familia* at an early age. They were raised in poverty, received little formal education, began working when they were still children, married young, and spent their working lives in low status, low paying jobs.

Most of the Chicana workers at Farah had grown up in the *barrio* in south El Paso's Second Ward. Squeezed between the downtown area and the border, residents of "El Segundo" faced street violence, police indifference, or brutality, rip-offs from slumlords, and racism from uptown whites. . . .

Whether they were raised in the United States or Mexico, these women by no means suffered passively. To survive they had to struggle. They responded with anger to the racism, deprivation, and systematic oppression which they experienced as Raza women. While this anger was seldom expressed openly, it was always present and potentially explosive. The advent of a unionization campaign helped to give organized expression to this anger.

Despite most workers in the El Paso region not being organized into unions, some women had been exposed to labor-organizing drives. Women from Mexico had parents who had fled to the United States after their attempts to organize workers in Mexico had failed. They had lost everything in the process. Some women, as children, had witnessed bloody strikes in the textile mills and mines of northern Mexico. Among those women, some had even worked as children in these industries. Others had undergone the dislocation and hardship of migrant life in the United States.

Among Chicanas at Farah, some had fathers, mothers, brothers, and husbands who belonged to unions in El Paso's smelting and packing plants. There was the example of the prolonged and successful strike of garment workers for union recognition at the Top Notch clothing plant in the 1960s. But experience with organized labor was by no means widespread among workers at Farah. . . .

The earliest attempt by workers at Farah to present an organized response to management attacks was a brief petition campaign among markers at the Gateway plant in 1968. A more systematic effort to address workers' grievances began in 1969 when male workers from the cutting and shipping departments contacted organizers from the Amalgamated Clothing Workers of America (ACWA).[3] They acted in spite of Farah's repeated violent tirades against unions. Farah presented films about union corruption on company time and pronounced to his workers, "See what a union does? You don't want anything to do with that!" But Farah overestimated the impact of his blitz on organizing. He was sufficiently confident of union defeat in an upcoming election that he urged cutters to vote, insisting that not to vote was to vote for the union. The cutters turned out in force for the election, and on October 14, 1970, they voted overwhelmingly to affiliate themselves with the union. Not about to accept the unexpected turn of events, Farah immediately appealed the election result with the National Labor Relations Board (NLRB). The cutting-room election was tied up in court until 1972, when the election victory was set aside on grounds that the cutting room was not an appropriate bargaining unit. But by that time, organizing had long since spread to the rest of the plant.

The campaign to unionize the Farah plants intensified in the spring of 1972. In March, twenty-six workers were fired when they attempted a walkout at the Northwest plant in El Paso. But it was a series of events in San Antonio that triggered the large-scale strike in El Paso.

One weekend, members of the union organizing committee in El Paso sponsored a march. Farah workers from San Antonio made the twelve-hour drive between the two cities to join the demonstration. Some of them did not return to San Antonio in time for work on Monday morning. On Tuesday, a supervisor confronted a worker with pictures of him marching under union banners in El Paso and then promptly fired him. Workers who objected to his dismissal were also fired. More than 500 San Antonio Farah workers walked out in protest.

Six days later, when El Paso Farah workers learned of the San Antonio strike, their frustration with working conditions and with Farah's continued suppression of union activity exploded into a spontaneous strike. On May 9, the machinists, shippers, cutters, and some of the seamstresses walked out. The walkout, which continued for almost a month, initially took the company by surprise. Women who had worked docilely at their machines for years, women who had been reduced to tears by a supervisor's reprimand, women who had never openly spoken a word in favor of the union, suddenly began to speak up.

The Amalgamated Clothing Workers of America quickly moved to support the Farah workers; the strike was declared an unfair labor practice strike. One month later a national boycott of Farah products was begun, endorsed by the AFL-CIO. In El Paso the strikers began to picket the Farah plants and local stores that carried Farah products. But in a town where many regarded Willie Farah as a folk hero, the strikers found that public reaction to the walkout was often hostile. One woman remembers:

> People were just very cruel. Everybody thought that Farah was a god or something. I swear, they'd even turn around and spit on you if they could. There was one lady, I was handing out some papers downtown and she got her purse and started striking me. When she started hitting me, she said, "Ah, you people, a bunch of dumb this and that! Farah's a great man!"

Passers-by told the picketers that they were lazy bums who just wanted welfare and food stamps. The strikers were repeatedly reminded that Farah was a major employer in the area where unemployment was high, and that they should be grateful to him for giving them jobs.

... The strike split the Chicano community. Many workers at Farah crossed picket lines and continued to keep the plant operating. They were known as the "happies" because they wore buttons which featured a smiling face and the slogan, "I'm happy at Farah." Especially at Farah's Third Street plant, where many of the people had worked for Farah since World War II, vehement opposition to the strike was expressed....

The strike divided families. Several women told of walking out while their sisters remained inside the plant. There was even one family where the husband was on strike and his wife was continuing to work at Farah. "He'd drive his wife up to the door," one striker recalled, "and get out of there as fast as he could. Now this was ridiculous!"

Striking workers were quickly replaced by strikebreakers from El Paso and ... Juarez. There was no lack of applicants for the jobs: El Paso unemployment figures have soared as high as 14 percent in recent years, while Juarez, like much of Mexico, has a current unemployment rate of 40 percent.

Until shortly before the strike, Willie Farah, who liked to style himself as a superpatriot, had refused to hire Mexicans to work in his plant even if they had green cards. But when the strike began and he needed workers, he abruptly changed his policy, and willingly hired Mexican nationals....

People on the picket lines faced continuing harassment from company personnel. Farah hired guards to patrol the picket line with unmuzzled police dogs. Several strikers were hit by Farah trucks, and one woman was struck by a car driven by Willie Farah's mother. Farah obtained an injunction limiting pickets to one every fifty feet; 1,008 workers were cited for violations, and many were ordered to report to the police station in the middle of the night and require to post four-hundred-dollar bonds. One woman was jailed six times. (The Texas law which permitted such injunctions was later declared unconstitutional, and all charges were dropped.)

Although the strikers suffered physical and psychological harassment from opponents of the strike, they also discovered new sources of support. The ACWA sent organizers to El Paso, gave weekly payments of thirty dollars to each striker, administered a Farah Relief Fund, and sponsored classes for the strikers on labor history and union procedures....

Immediately after the strike began, the union organized a national boycott of Farah pants which became a crucial factor in the success of the strike. By January 1974, forty union representatives were working on boycott campaigns in more than sixty cities.[4] ...

The Catholic Church was another source of help for the strikers. Father Jesse Muñoz, a priest at Our Lady of the Light Church, made church facilities available for union meetings and participated in several national speaking tours to promote the boycott of Farah products. He also came to the picket line at the Gateway plant to bless the strikers on Ash Wednesday. Bishop Sidney Metzger of El Paso publicly endorsed the boycott in a letter to his fellow bishops....

The strikers were also encouraged by messages of solidarity and financial support from other unions around the country. Particularly important to them was the visit to El Paso of Cesar Chavez. In addition, a variety of Chicano, student, and leftist organizations in El Paso and around the country supported the strike by publicizing the boycott and the conditions at Farah.

But the most profound changes among the Farah strikers began when they took on new responsibilities for organizing strike activities. Some women went to work for the union on a volunteer basis, writing strike relief checks, keeping records, and distributing the goods that arrived from outside El Paso. Almost immediately they began to realize that their capabilities were not as limited as they had been taught to believe. One striker asserted, "If I had not walked out, I would not have been able to realize all those things about myself." ...

Other strikers went on speaking tours organized by the union or by strike support groups to publicize the boycott and raise funds....

One woman observed that antiunion harassment took similar forms all over the country; when she stopped to talk to workers at a nonunion plant, a supervisor appeared and shooed the workers back inside. When she spoke on the East Coast she noticed that racial and ethnic differences often kept workers isolated from one another. She returned to El Paso with a heightened perception of the difficulties involved in building a strong union. . . .

As women became more and more involved in running strike support activities, and as they developed new friendships among the strikers, they began to spend more time outside the home. This was a source of tension in many households. . . . In some cases, differences of opinion about the merits of the walkout were fueled by financial insecurity. In other homes the husbands did not think that attending public meetings was an appropriate way for their wives to spend their time.

> Well, at the beginning they didn't like it. They thought [the women] should be at home, because here they were kind of old-fashioned, the women were always supposed to be home. The only time she'd be working was if she had to work to keep up with the bills, and both wife and husband had to work. Otherwise there was no way that the man himself could support the house. But that's about all they thought about, just for them to work—they didn't think they could go to meetings.

But the women felt strongly enough about their involvement in the strike to put up a spirited defense of their activities.

> My ex-husband told me, "You're not gonna make it, and I'm not gonna help you!" And I said, "If God made it, and his followers made it, like Peter, he left his boat behind, all his belongings to follow God, yet he didn't die! Right now he's in better shape than we are. He's in heaven, holding that door—isn't that true!"

. . . Most marriages survived the ordeals of the strike, and many women feel that their growth as individuals has strengthened their relationships with their husbands. But it was also not uncommon for husbands threatened by the new eloquence, assertiveness, and political awareness of their wives simply to walk out.

The strike also transformed the relationship of women workers to their children. Many brought their children to meetings and to the picket line. "My little boy was only three months, and you should have seen me, I had him always in my arms, going everywhere," remembers one striker. Children who were slightly older took an active part in strike support work, and formed their own opinions about unionization. . . .

One teenager commented, "Mom used to be a slave. But since the strike she thinks for herself. It's a lot better." . . .

Women strikers turner a critical eye on their personal lives and their home; as they became more experienced they developed criticisms of the union campaign as well. Some women felt that the ACWA was not promoting the strike and boycott actively enough, particularly in El Paso. . . .

Some strikers began to meet independently of the union, in a group which was known simply as the rank-and-file committee. (This group took the name Unidad Para Siempre—Unity Forever—when it was reactivated after the strike.) The members of the group—about forty—shared a strong sense of themselves as workers and a desire to build a strong and democratic union. They put out their own leaflets, participated in marches and rallies, helped to found the Farah Distress Fund, and talked to other strikers about the need for a strong union. "We wanted a union with action, not just words. That's why we were having meetings and going out, really doing more, making our own papers." . . .

The strike made women more conscious of political and social movements that they had regarded as "outside" and irrelevant to their own lives. These ranged from the support of local union struggles to the struggles of the United Farm Workers (UFW) and Texas Farmworkers to the women's movement. . . .

For all of the women, the strike made them more conscious of themselves as working people with interests distinct from other classes. One woman began to argue with her dentist, who complained to her that her strike was causing him to lose money he had invested in Farah Manufacturing Company. She commented that he could afford to lose money, and added,

> It's like I tell him, "Just because you happen to be one Mexican out of many that made it to the top—and I bet you worked your butt off to get up there. I'll respect you for your ideas as long as you respect me for mine. I happen to be of the working class, and I happen to be one of the minority (i.e. Chicana), that I feel work at the lowest type of job there is, and I feel that we have a right to fight.

. . . By the beginning of 1974, the nationwide boycott organized by the ACWA was having a noticeable effect on Farah's business. Sales which were $156 million in 1972, dropped to $126 million in 1974.[5] By the end of 1973 four Farah plants outside of El Paso had been closed, and the El Paso plants had been put on a four-day week. . . .

The final blow came at the end of January 1974, when an administrative judge of the National Labor Relations Board issued a decision which accused Farah of "flouting the (National Labor Relations) Act and trampling on the rights of its employees as if there were no Act, no Board, and no Ten Commandments." Farah was ordered to offer reinstatement to the strikers (whom the company asserted had voluntarily quit), to reinstate with back pay several workers who had been fired for union activity, and to allow the union access to company bulletin boards and employee lists.

Farah initially indicated that he would appeal the decision, but several weeks later he abruptly changed course. On February 23, apparently after preliminary discussion with union officials, he recognized the ACWA as the bargaining agent for Farah employees. The union simultaneously announced that it would terminate the boycott.

The strikers, exultant and relieved, celebrated the fact that they had outlasted El Paso's major business figure. . . .

When the negotiating committee for the first contract was elected, strikers discovered to their dismay that happies were to be represented on the committee. In the few weeks before Farah recognized the union, his supervisors had been ordering people to sign union cards, telling them that if they didn't comply the factory would close. As nominal union members, these people had the right to participate in contract negotiations. The committee was thus badly split. . . .

The final contract included pay increases of fifty-five cents an hour over three years, a medical insurance plan financed by the company, job security and seniority rights, and a grievance procedure. It also gave union representatives the right to challenge production quotas for individual operations. It was ratified at a meeting of employees on March 7.

Many workers were angry that there was little time taken to explain the contract or hear people's questions and objections. . . . Strikers felt that two years of suffering entitled them to a stronger contract. But Farah was in financial trouble as a result of the boycott and a series of management mistakes, and his threat to close the factory was a real one. The strikers, inexperienced at contract negotiations, felt outmaneuvered by a process in which the company set the terms and the union lawyers made most of the decisions.

In spite of their misgivings about the contract, and a pervasive feeling that the situation was no longer under their control, most strikers concluded that the contract was "all right for a first try," and that it was "a beginning." They realized that their fight for better working conditions was by no means over, but at least they now had the protection of a union and a grievance procedure. . . .

When the strikers returned to the factory, they found that the organization of production had changed dramatically during the two years of the strike. In an attempt to keep up with the changing men's clothing market, Farah was diversifying production to include men's leisure suits and jackets. Workers were placed in new production lines without adequate retraining. Women who had been sewing straight seams for ten years were suddenly expected to set sleeves. One woman said, "They just sat me on the machine and said, 'Try to do this.' That was my training.". . .

These changes in materials, patterns, and techniques were not taken into account when new production quotas were established. Women whose wages had been based on their ability to produce a certain number of pieces at one operation were expected to produce just as many at a new operation. As a result, quotas were often impossibly high. . . .

At the same time that Farah was changing production, the company plunged into a serious financial disaster. The recession of 1974–1975 hurt the company, and in addition, Willie Farah made major miscalculations in production and marketing.[6] . . .

Farah's financial predicament was exacerbated by marketing problems. In the past, Farah had been known for the high quality of its merchandise. But under severe pressure to meet quotas on new operations, workers were simply unable to concern themselves with perfection. "When you're pushing people they can't get their work out right," one ex-striker commented. . . .

All of these management problems resulted in a 40 percent decline in sales and a $3.5 million loss in the last quarter of 1976. Five thousand of the original nine thousand employees were laid off. Several Farah plants were closed, including plants in San Antonio, Victoria, and Las Cruces, New Mexico.

These financial setbacks hindered the efforts of union activists to continue organizing. First, there was a visible cutback in services provided for the workers by the company. Bus service to and from the plant was curtailed, coffee and donuts no longer were served during breaks, the already inadequate medical care available to workers was cut back, and Thanksgiving turkeys and Christmas parties were no longer provided. . . .

A more serious consequence of Farah's financial setback was that it required a drastic reduction in the size of the work force. This need to lay off workers provided Farah with an opportunity to harass and eliminate his most vocal opponents among the union activists. Some were given extremely erratic work schedules. Some days they would be required to work until noon, other days until three o'clock, and frequently they were called to work on Saturdays. They were rarely given much advance notice of their hours. Some ex-strikers were switched to production lines that were scheduled to be phased out. Others were placed on extended layoff and after one year were let go by the company. . . .

Militant union members were left in a particularly vulnerable position. The rank-and-file group, Unidad Para Siempre, pushed for reforms that had not been included in the contract. These reforms included elimination of the quota system, compensation and training for shop stewards, and greater rank-and-file participation in settling grievances between workers and the company. In this way, they hoped to build a stronger and more responsive union. The continued growth of Unidad was hampered by the fact that a large number of its members—the most vocal and militant union activists—were among the first to be laid off by Farah during his cutbacks in production. Unidad members feel that the union did not actively prosecute their cases because, like the company, it felt threatened by their presence. By 1977, few members of Unidad still worked in Farah plants. . . .

The continuing layoffs, loss of rank-and-file activists, tensions among workers in the plant, and inadequate support from the international union all combined to weaken the position of the workers during contract negotiations in early 1977.

Negotiations took place with both sides assuming that Farah was in serious financial difficulties. Workers on the negotiating committee spent several days listening to detailed descriptions of Farah's woes, and finally were told, "You can ask for the moon, but we give it to you we'll fold tomorrow and you'll all be out on the street. . . ." The 1977 contract granted the workers a scanty thirty-cent pay raise over a three-year period. It eliminated dental benefits and retained the hated quota system. Most damaging of all, it permitted Farah to lay off experienced workers and call them back to work on a different production line—at the minimum wage. . . .

Since March 1977, Farah has closed another of its El Paso plants. The number of workers at Farah, particularly union members, continues to decline.

Events at Farah since the strike show the continuing difficulty of union organizing in the Southwest. The right-to-work law, the consolidated opposition of powerful employers, the timidity of union officials, and the many incipient tensions in the border area which employers can use to divide the work force—all of these are formidable obstacles in the way of a strong workers' organization.

The story of the ACWA at Farah also illustrates some of the problems specific to organizing workers in the garment industry. In contrast to relatively monopolized, capital-intensive industries such as auto and steel, the garment industry is highly competitive, volatile, and labor intensive. In this context of constant business fluctuations, it is possible for a large and established company like Farah to suffer a dramatic decline within a period of several years. . . .

While the Farah strike did not produce a strong, mature rank-and-file movement, it did help to create the conditions under which one can develop. The workers who made the strike were irreversibly changed by it. All of them say that they would organize and strike again; most of them recognize the need for strong support from an international union like the ACWA, as long as it does not undermine the independent organization of rank-and-file workers. "We're sticking in there and we're not going to get out and we're not giving up!" one ex-striker insisted.

> I believe in fighting for our rights, and for women's rights. When I walked out of that company way back then, it was like I had taken a weight off my back. And I began to realize, "Why did I put up with it all these years? Why didn't I try for something else?" Now I want to stay here and help people to help themselves.

The Chicanas who comprise the majority of strikers learned that they could speak and act on their own behalf as women and workers, lessons they will not forget.

## NOTES

1. El Paso, Texas, is located on the western tip of Texas, near the point where the boundaries of Texas, New Mexico, and Mexico intersect. In July 1975, the population was estimated by the U.S. Bureau of Census at 414,700 people, of whom 57 percent were "Spanish American." El Paso is directly across the U.S.-Mexico border from Ciudad Juarez, which has an estimated population of 600,000.

2. General Executive Board Report, "Farah Boycott: Union Label," Amalgamated Clothing Workers of America, 1974 Convention, 1.

3. In June 1976, ACWA merged with the Textile Workers Union of American, and became the Amalgamated Clothing and Textile Workers Union. Since the events in this article occurred before the merger, the union will be referred to as ACWA.

4. "Farah Boycott," ACWA Report.

5. *Moody's Industrial Manual* (New York: Moody's Investors Service, Inc., 1975), 1099.

6. Critics of the union have blamed the strike and boycott for the company's business troubles. The boycott never actually destroyed Farah's profit margin, however, In fact, some analysts argue that the short-term effect of the strike was beneficial because it forced the company to stop overproduction. They note that "during the only full year of the boycott (1973), the company jumped from $8 million in losses to a modest $42,000 profit." (Allen Pusey, "Clothes Made the Man," *Texas Monthly* (June 1977), 135.) The losses predate the union and can be traced to management errors on Farah's part.

# 19

## *Women in the Labor Force, 1950–1980*

### Suzanne M. Bianchi and Daphne Spain

*In the post-World War II years, the single most important source of women's power in their personal and public lives has derived from their increasing participation in the paid labor force. Bianchi and Spain show the components of this change. In the 1950s substantial increases occurred among women 35 to 55 years of age. Then in the 1960s this trend was augmented by an increase in women's labor force participation at all ages. Finally, and most impressively, the 1970s saw dramatic increases in the proportion of working women aged 20 to 35 who chose to remain in the paid labor force during years when childrearing demands were most intensive. These changes mean that in the 1990s a woman's presence in the paid labor force can no longer be predicted on the basis of the age of her children. Two out of every three women will remain employed throughout their life cycle.*

Women have entered the labor force in dramatic numbers since World War II and the very fabric of American society has been revolutionized. . . .

The new story of the past two decades has been the rise in participation by younger women and the increased continuity of participation over their life course. Many women now postpone family formation to complete education and establish themselves in the labor force. Despite family obligations, a majority of women work outside the home during their childrearing years. Women's labor market involvement is still dissimilar to men's involvement, but the convergence in many of the indicators is truly the remarkable story of the 1960s, and even more so of the 1970s. . . .

TRENDS IN LABOR FORCE PARTICIPATION

During this century, the number of women in the labor force has increased dramatically—from about 5 million women in 1900 to 48.5 million in 1983. (See Table 1.) At the turn of the century, about one worker in five was a woman. By the mid-1970s, two workers in five were female, and the representation of women in the work force has continued to increase since that time. The proportion of women in the labor force, which was about 20 percent in the early part of the century, increased only slightly until the 1940s. Since World War II, participation of women in the paid work force has accelerated greatly.

Taken from *American Women in Transition*, by Suzanne M. Bianchi and Daphne Spain (The Russell Sage Foundation, 1986). Used with permission of the Russell Sage Foundation.

TABLE 1  Women in the Labor Force, Selected Years Since 1900

| YEAR | NUMBER (IN THOUSANDS) | PERCENTAGE OF TOTAL LABOR FORCE | PERCENTAGE OF ALL WOMEN |
|------|----------------------|----------------------------------|--------------------------|
| 1900 | 4,999 | 18.1% | 20.0% |
| 1910 | 8,076 | 21.2 | 23.4 |
| 1920 | 8,229 | 20.4 | 22.7 |
| 1930 | 10,396 | 21.9 | 23.6 |
| 1940 | 13,007 | 24.6 | 25.8 |
| 1950 | 18,389 | 29.6 | 33.9 |
| 1955 | 20,548 | 31.6 | 35.7 |
| 1960 | 23,240 | 33.4 | 37.7 |
| 1965 | 26,200 | 35.2 | 39.3 |
| 1970 | 31,543 | 38.1 | 43.3 |
| 1975 | 37,475 | 40.0 | 46.3 |
| 1980 | 45,487 | 42.5 | 51.5 |
| 1983 | 48,503 | 43.5 | 52.9 |

*Note:* Labor force data for 1900–30 refer to gainfully employed workers aged 10 and over; data for 1940 include the labor force aged 14 and over; data for 1950–83 refer to the civilian labor force aged 16 and over and are based on annual averages derived from the Current Population Survey; data for 1900–40 are based on the decennial census.

*Source:* U.S. Department of Labor, Bureau of Labor Statistics, "Women in the Labor Force: Some New Data Series," report 575 (October 1979), table 1; *Handbook of Labor Statistics* (Washington, DC: U.S. Government Printing Office, 1983), tables 1 and 2; *Employment and Earnings* vol. 31 (January 1984), table 1; U.S. Bureau of the Census, *Historical Statistics of the United States* (Washington, DC: U.S. Government Printing Office, 1976), series D11-25 and D29-41.

Women are less likely to be in the labor force than men, but as women's rates have increased, men's participation rates have decreased. In 1948, 87 percent of men were in the labor force compared with 33 percent of women—a difference of over 50 percentage points. By 1983, 76 percent of men and 53 percent of women were in the labor force—a difference of a little over 20 percentage points.

The decline in men's participation rates is accounted for almost entirely by rates of older men. Rates for men aged 25 to 54 remained about 95 percent, but rates have declined from 71 to 43 percent for those 55 and over. This reflects, among other things, the increased number of workers covered by Social Security, private pension plans, and disability benefits, allowing for earlier withdrawal from the labor force than was possible in the past.

Women's labor force participation has increased at all ages under 65, but there have been significant changes in the age groups accounting for the increase. Figure 1 shows 1950–80 changes in the age pattern of labor force participation of women and men. Typically, men's patterns look like an arch or an inverted U. That is, rates increase as men finish school and enter the labor force. By their late 20s most men are in the labor force and

*FIGURE 1.* Trend in Labor Force Participation Rates by Age and Sex

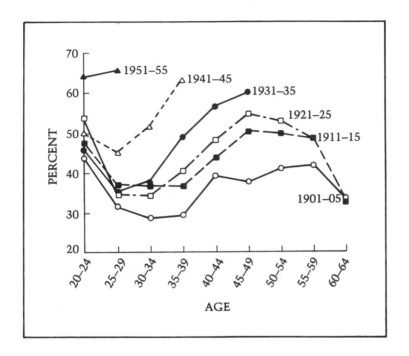

*Source:* Gertrude Bancroft, *The American Labor Force: Its Growth and Changing Composition* (New York: Wiley, 1958), tables A-1, D-1, and D-1A; U.S. Department of Labor, Bureau of Labor Statistics, "Labor Force and Employment in 1960," *Special Labor Force Report,* no. 14 (Washington, DC: U.S. Government Printing Office, 1961), table A-2; "Employment and Unemployment in 1970," *Special Labor Force Report,* no. 129 (Washington, DC: U.S. Government Printing Office, 1971), table A-2; and *Employment and Earnings,* vol. 28 (January 1981), table 3.

most will remain there more or less continuously until they retire in their late 50s and 60s. Women's patterns, on the other hand, have often been described as U-shaped, at least up to age 50. That is, they are highest in the early 20s before women start having children. They drop off as women leave the labor force to have children, but begin to increase again as some of these women return to work after their children have entered school. . . .

Women's labor force participation increased in each decade shown in Figure 1, and this U pattern is apparent in 1950, 1960, and 1970. During the 1950s and early 1960s the increase in women's labor force participation was largely the result of the increase in the rates of older women—women over age 45, beyond the years of most intensive childrearing responsibilities. But in the mid-1960s this pattern began to change. Since then the largest increase has been among women in their 20s and 30s—women most likely to be raising small children. The increase in the 1970s was particularly dramatic—so much so that the age pattern of labor force rates has lost the U-shaped pattern and is beginning to resemble men's pattern, albeit at a much lower level.

The disappearance of the drop in women's participation during the childbearing years is significant in relation to women's earnings. One reason given for women's lower wages is that women leave the labor force to have children and lose seniority and valuable experience in the labor market. A generation of young women is currently emerging for which this explanation will be less adequate because they will have worked continuously over their lifetime in contrast to previous cohorts of women. If continuity of work experience serves to explain wage differentials by sex, women's wages vis-à-vis those of men would be expected to rise.

### Black-White Differences in Participation

Figure 2 depicts the trends in labor force participation of Black and White men and women. Historically, Black women have been more likely than White women to participate in the labor force, but the difference has narrowed. In recent decades participation has risen faster for White women than for Black women. Hence, rates have converged over time.

The age profile of labor force participation for Black women has not exhibited the U-shaped pattern that has characterized White women's participation. There is no trough in the childbearing years for Black women as evidenced in both period and cohort data.[1] Studies of women's labor force participation rates, such as Sweet's, have noted that children do not seem to be the deterrent to Black women's participation that they have been to White women's participation.[2] The 1970–80 change in the age profile of participation of White women, with the loss of the trough in the childbearing years, is another way in which White women's participation has become more similar to that of Black women.

### Cohort Patterns

Thus far we have focused on measures of the increase in female labor force participation over time, but the data can be rearranged to show how birth cohorts compare in terms of their labor force participation at each age. This is done in Figure 3, which shows the age profiles of participation of five-year birth cohorts of women born between 1901 and 1960. Age profiles for later cohorts are incomplete since these women have not yet reached older ages.

*FIGURE 2. Trend in Labor Force Participation Rates by Race and Sex*

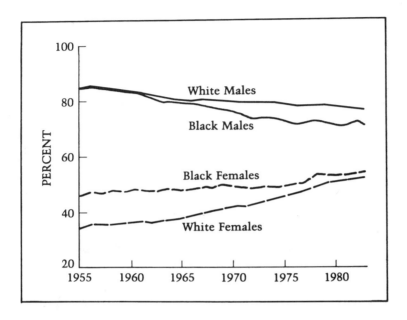

*Note:* Black and other races; persons aged 16 and over.

*Source:* U.S. Department of Labor, Bureau of Labor Statistics, *Employment and Training Report of the President* (Washington, DC: U.S. Government Printing Office, 1982), table A-5; *Employment and Earnings*, vol. 29 (January 1982), table 3.

The cohort patterns suggest that the upturn in female labor force participation has resulted in large part from the fact that, at least for cohorts born since 1930, each succeeding group of women started out with higher rates of participation and maintained higher rates at older ages than their predecessors. Analyses of cohort patterns for women born since 1870 show that even the gradual increase in labor force participation prior to World War II occurred because each cohort was a little more likely to participate at young ages than the previous one. Age patterns were quite similar for these cohorts but were shifting slowly upward.[3]

Smith and Ward show that for cohorts born in 1870 and 1880, women's participation rates peaked about age 20 and then declined and remained relatively flat throughout the rest of their lives.[4] But for cohorts born in 1890 and 1900, there was a surge in participation which coincided with World War II (that is, a surge just after age 50 for women born in 1890 and just after age 40 for women born in 1900). These cohorts of women

*FIGURE 3.  Labor Force Participation Rates of Birth Cohorts*

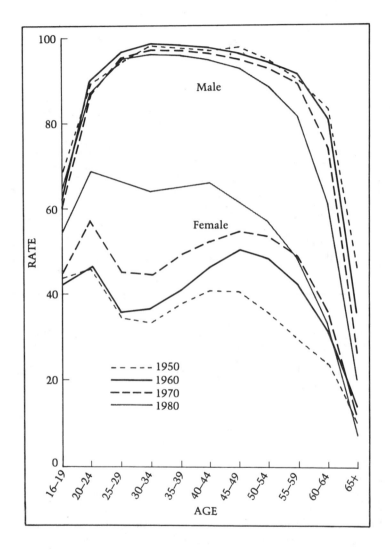

*Source:* U.S. Department of Labor, Bureau of Labor Statistics, *Perspectives on Working Women: A Databook,* bulletin 2080 (Washington, DC: U.S. Government Printing Office, 1980), table 5; *Employment and Earnings,* vol. 27 (January 1980), table 1; J. Gregory Robinson, "Labor Force Participation Rates of Cohorts of Women in the United States: 1890 to 1979," paper presented at the annual meeting of the Population Association of America, Denver, April 1980, table 2.

remained in the labor force as they aged, and hence their age profiles of labor force participation exhibit a double peak or U-shape. Thus, the first appearance of the U-shaped pattern actually came with the war and continued to characterize women's employment until only recently.

There is disagreement as to how much World War II per se affected the work patterns of women. Bancroft argued that the experience women gained in the labor market during World War II changed both individual workers' and employers' attitudes about women's place in the labor force.[5] Hence, World War II was crucial in creating a more hospitable environment for women workers and thus contributed to the higher labor force participation rates of cohorts reaching labor force age after the war. But others point to factors operating throughout the twentieth century, such as the increasing educational attainment of women and the increase in wages, as the more important inducements to women to work outside the home.[6]

... The increase in women's labor force participation has resulted from the replacement of successive cohorts of women, each with higher rates of participation and average work experience than preceding generations. At least since the late 1960s, the period for which we have actual measures of labor force experience, ... the increase in female labor force participation has coincided with an increased likelihood that once women enter the labor force, they remain there. Recent cohorts of women workers are exhibiting more continuous attachment to the work force than did women of earlier generations.

## SEX DIFFERENCES IN LABOR FORCE PARTICIPATION

Women's participation in the labor force over the life course still remains more discontinuous than men's, as women continue to exit and reenter the labor force more times than men. Estimates from 1980 suggest that the average man will enter the labor force 3.9 times and exit voluntarily 3.6 times. The average woman will enter 5.5 times and exit voluntarily 5.4 times. In the teenage years, women's and men's entry and exit rates are similar with the pace of entries slowing by age 20 for both sexes. However, female exit rates start to rise so that by age 25 the share of men in the labor force substantially exceeds that of women.[7]

Women's higher quit rates are often regarded as one reason why women earn less than men. Employers pay women less because women are less experienced, less stable workers, and employers believe they will lose investments that they make in the skills of these workers. But the causality is probably not unidirectional: Women earn less than men because they have less experience, but their lower wages also increase their probability of quitting a job. Recent studies of voluntary exit rates of men and women show that women with job characteristics equivalent to those of men are no more likely to quit their jobs than are men.[8] Osterman finds that women's voluntary exit rates are greatly reduced in industries in which there is greater pressure from the federal government for affirmative action programs. This suggests that if women perceive opportunities for advancement, they are less likely to change jobs or exit the labor force altogether.[9]

The average number of years that women work over their lifetime is lower than the number for men. Recent estimates . . . suggest that a female born in 1980 is likely to spend 29.4 years in the labor force compared with 39.8 years for a male—a difference of almost 10 years. However, as with labor force participation rates, there has been convergence in the work-life expectancies of women and men. Women's work-life expectancy increased from only 32 percent of men's in 1940 to 59 percent in 1970. Trends accelerated during the 1970s, primarily because of the strengthening of female labor force attachment, so that by 1980 women's work-life expectancy was up to 76 percent of that of men's.[10] . . .

A crucial component of experience levels is the extent of learning or on-the-job training that takes place during those years in the labor force. That is, it is not just the differential quantity of time men and women spend in the labor force but also the differential quality of that time which may be a key to wage differentials between the sexes. Although imperfect, a measure of on-the-job training was ascertained in the 1976 Panel Study of Income Dynamics. Respondents were asked to indicate how long it would take the average new employee to learn the respondent's job. Duncan and Hoffman analyze this indicator and find that White males are in jobs which are reported to require an average of two and one-quarter years of training; all other race-sex groups are in jobs requiring less than one year of training. When years of training are subtracted from tenure on the job to arrive at a measure of who is receiving training, Duncan and Hoffman find that 25 percent of White men are receiving on-the-job training compared with 14 percent of White women and 9 percent of Black men and women. Their multivariate results suggest that all race-sex groups receive similar payoffs for on-the-job training. However, commitment to the labor force, as measured by past years of work experience, does not increase the probability that a worker will receive on-the-job training for minorities and women as much as it does for White males. Women (and Black men) receive less on-the-job training than White men and part of the reason is that their work experience is treated differently.[11]

## OCCUPATIONS

What has happened to the occupational distribution of women since 1970? Have women moved into male-dominated occupations in greater numbers than they had in previous decades? . . .

During the 1970s women increased their representation among most major occupational groups. A very significant increase occurred in the proportion of managers who were women—an increase from 19 to 31 percent. Another large increase took place among technicians: In 1970, 34 percent of technicians were women; by 1980 this was up to 44 percent.

Relative to the overall increase in the female proportion in the labor force, there was very little change in the percentage female within two of the major occupational groups with very high proportions of male workers— handlers (laborers) and precision production (craft) workers. Likewise, among major groups that are largely composed of women—administrative support (clerical) and private household workers—there was little change in the female proportion during the decade.

Overall, as shown in the third column of Table 2, women accounted for more than half of the growth in professional specialties, technical and related support, sales, administrative support, and other service occupations. Among protective service and transportation major groups, the percentage of women among workers added during the decade was low, but much higher than the overall percentage of women in these groups in 1970. The percentage female was lowest among net additions to the precision production (craft) major group. In 1970 only 7 percent of precision produc-

*TABLE 2 Growth in the Percentage of Women in Major Occupational Groups, 1970–1980*

| MAJOR OCCUPATIONAL GROUP | 1970 | 1980 | 1970–80 NET GROWTH |
|---|---|---|---|
| Executives, Managers | 18.5% | 30.5% | 46.9% |
| Professional Specialty | 44.3 | 49.1 | 61.2 |
| Technicians | 34.4 | 43.8 | 57.5 |
| Sales | 41.3 | 48.7 | 75.4 |
| Administrative Support, Including Clerical | 73.2 | 77.1 | 89.2 |
| Private Household | 96.3 | 95.3 | |
| Protective Service | 6.6 | 11.8 | 23.2 |
| Other Service | 61.2 | 63.3 | 67.5 |
| Farming, Forestry, Fishing | 9.1 | 14.9 | |
| Precision Production, Including Craft | 7.3 | 7.8 | 10.2 |
| Machine Operators | 39.7 | 40.7 | 48.5 |
| Transportation Workers | 4.1 | 7.8 | 23.9 |
| Handlers, Laborers | 17.4 | 19.8 | 38.8 |
| Total | 38.0 | 42.5 | 57.5 |

*Note:* Percentage shown in column 3 is calculated in the following way: the number of women in the occupational group in 1970 is subtracted from the number in 1980 to form the numerator of the fraction; the denominator is the total civilian labor force in the occuaptional group in 1980 minus the total in 1970; this fraction is multiplied by 100; percentage female is not calculated for occupational groups which declined in size between 1970 and 1980.

*Source:* U.S. Bureau of the Census, "Detailed Occupation of the Experienced Civilian Labor Force by Sex for the United States and Regions: 1980 and 1970," *Census of Population: 1980,* Supplementary Report, PC80-S1-15 (Washington, DC, U.S. Government Printing Office, 1984).

tion workers were women, and of the workers added to this group during the decade 10 percent were women. . . .

. . . The change that occurred in the sex composition of detailed occupations . . . arose from the fact that some women moved into male-dominated occupational spheres. The reverse did not occur: Men did not rush into jobs typically filled by women. Indeed, some occupations, such as office clerks, that had a higher than average proportion female in 1970 became even more female by 1980.[12]

In 1980, 46 percent of the female experienced civilian labor force was still concentrated in occupations which were 80 to 100 percent female. Nearly 50 percent of male workers in 1980 remained in occupations which had been 0 to 10 percent female in 1970. But these male-dominated occupations did become more female by 1980, so that only 37 percent of male workers were in occupations which remained 0 to 10 percent female in 1980.

### SUMMARY

Women's labor force participation has increased dramatically over the century and, in recent years, the continuity of attachment over the life course also appears to be increasing. What has brought about these changes?

Perhaps the most important factor explaining the increase in labor force participation throughout this century has been the increase in the wages paid to women working outside the home.[13] Smith and Ward argue that few married women were in the labor force at the turn of the century because wages of married women were so much lower than those of single women. As this differential narrowed, married women increased their participation dramatically.[14] Rising educational attainment of women has also increased women's "tastes" for market work and increased the costs to them of not working outside the home, since better educated persons tend to command higher salaries in the workplace. The development and lowered cost of labor and time-saving devices in the home may also be related to the increase in women's market work. However, it is difficult to determine whether new technology was a cause or response to women's increased work outside the home.[15]

The importance of World War II—and the greater need for women workers during that time—has been noted as a catalyst for participation at older ages in the 1950s. Economic growth during the 1950s also created many jobs. Oppenheimer has argued that the 1940–60 period was one of immense growth in clerical and service sector jobs, jobs typically filled by women.[16] This increased demand for female workers coincided with a period of relative shortage of the type of female worker preferred in the past—young single women or married women without children. That is, just as the demand for female labor was growing to new heights, young women of the 1950s were marrying and starting families earlier. Hence, older women, who had their appetites for paid work awakened during the war and whose families were already grown, filled the gap.

How does one explain the large influx of young women workers during the past two decades and the more continuous labor force participation of these women? Some of the suggested explanations . . . include the rising educational attainment of women, the increasing divorce rate and women's ensuing realization that they must be able to support themselves financially, the women's movement and changing attitudes about the desirability of working outside the home, the slow wage growth of males during the past decade, rising consumption aspirations requiring both husbands and wives to be in the labor force, lower fertility, and later marriage.

. . . In recent years young women have been waiting longer to marry and start families than did women of their mother's generation. However, these would seem reasonable responses to, as much as causes of, an increased desire to participate in the labor force. Demographers, who point to the importance of the marriage squeeze or to the postponement of marriage because of the poor labor force prospects facing young men of the baby boom generation as they entered the job market, contend that young women funneled the time they would have otherwise spent in marrying and rearing children into getting a college education and starting a job. However, such an explanation paints a very passive picture of women, suggesting that they spend their lives waiting to marry and have children and everything else is secondary. More reasonable, in our estimation, is that as more women became aware of alternatives to marriage and early childbearing, and as they were increasingly able to exert effective control over the timing of these events, particularly childbearing, more women invested in education and acted on desires to enter the world of paid work. Indeed, as we have shown, delayed marriage and childbearing are not the real key to labor force increases among women, for the sharpest growth in rates has been among married women with children. Michael has shown that standardizing for changing marital and parity statuses of women does not diminish the increase in women's labor force participation rates.[17] Increased educational attainment of women does, however, contribute to the explanation of labor force increases and accounts for about one-quarter of the growth.

Changing attitudes about women's place and about equality between the sexes have no doubt influenced women's propensity to earn higher degrees and subsequently embark on a career track. Additionally, legislative initiatives may have opened doors previously closed to women.

Women may also be assessing the possible costs attached to discontinuous labor force participation and making a realistic appraisal of their need to be able to support themselves. Divorce rates remain high by historical standards. Behavior of women, such as staying in school longer, working for pay, and working more continuously throughout life, certainly seems economically rational in a world in which half of women who marry eventually divorce and the other half tend to outlive their husbands. Greater attachment to work provides women more independence and marital choice—they can delay marriage or leave an unhappy marriage more easily. Working also provides women with more financial security in those situations in which they are propelled by circumstances beyond their control into providing for a family on their own.

Finally, some would point to the slow or nonexistent growth in wage rates for men during the past decade as an additional impetus for wives to enter the labor force. Also, rising standards of living and desires for consumer goods have contributed to the perceived need among married couples for two wage earners rather than one. In general, women's labor force participation is more responsive to their own wage opportunities than to those of their spouse—and this has become more the case over time.[18] Still, families do save and spend as a unit and labor supply decisions are influenced by such things as mortgage payments and college tuition. More women are working today because they want to, but also because they feel they have to. The perceived pressure to work outside the home is another way in which women's work motivations have become similar to those of men.

## NOTES

1. U.S. Department of Labor, Bureau of Labor Statistics, *Handbook of Labor Statistics* (Washington, DC: U.S. Government Printing Office, 1983), table 4; and J. Gregory Robinson, "Labor Force Participation Rates of Cohorts of Women in the United States: 1880 to 1979," paper presented at the annual meeting of the Population Association of America, Denver, 1980.

2. James A. Sweet, *Women in the Labor Force* (New York: Seminar Press, 1973).

3. James P. Smith and Michael P. Ward, "Women's Wages and Work in the Twentieth Century," report prepared for the National Institute of Child Health and Human Development, R-3119–NICHD (Santa Monica, CA: Rand Corporation, 1984); and Robinson, "Labor Force Participation Rates."

4. Smith and Ward, "Women's Wages."

5. Gertrude Bancroft, *The American Labor Force: Its Growth and Changing Composition* (New York: Wiley, 1958).

6. Smith and Ward, "Women's Wages"; and Claudia Goldin, "The Changing Economic Role of Women: A Quantitative Approach," *Journal of Interdisciplinary History* 13 (Spring 1983):707–33.

7. Shirley J. Smith, "New Worklife Estimates Reflect Changing Profile of Labor Force," *Monthly Labor Review* 105 (March 1982): 15–20; and Shirley J. Smith, "Revised Worklife Tables Reflect 1979–80 Experience," *Monthly Labor Review* 108 (August 1985): 23–30.

8. Francine D. Blau and Larry Kahn, "Race and Sex Differences in Quits by Young Workers," *Industrial and Labor Relations Review* 34 ( July 1981):563–77; and W. Kip Viscusi, "Sex Differences in Worker Quitting," *Review of Economics and Statistics* 62 (August 1980):388–98.

Also, Haber, Lamas, and Green look at overall separation rates (quits + layoffs) using CPS data and find only small sex differences. Women are more likely to leave the labor force entirely, however, whereas men are more likely to leave one job to take another. Sheldon E. Haber, Enrique J. Lamas, and Gordon Green, "A New Method for Estimating Job Separation by Sex and Race," *Monthly Labor Review* 106 (June 1983):20–27.

9. Paul Osterman, "Affirmative Action and Opportunity: A Study of Female Quit Rates," *Review of Economics and Statistics* 64 (November 1982):604–12.

10. Smith "Revised Worklife Tables."

11. Greg J. Duncan and Saul D. Hoffman, "On-the-Job Training and Earnings Differences by Race and Sex," *Review of Economics and Statistics* 61 (November 1979): 594–603.

12. U.S. Bureau of the Census, "Detailed Occupation of the Experienced Civilian Labor Force by Sex for the United States and Regions: 1980 and 1970," *1980 Census of Population Supplementary Report,* PC80–S1–15 (Washington, DC: U.S. Government Printing Office, 1984).

13, Victor Fuchs, *How We Live* (Cambridge, MA: Harvard University Press, 1983), pp. 127–40.

14. Smith and Ward, "Women's Wages."

15. Fuchs, *How We Live,* pp. 130–31; and Glen G. Cain, "Women and Work: Trends in Time Spent in Housework," Discussion Paper no. 747–84 (Madison: Institute for Research on Poverty, University of Wisconsin, 1984).

16. Valerie K. Oppenheimer, *The Female Labor Force in the United States* (Westport, CT: Greenwood Press, 1970).

17. Robert T. Michael, "Consequences of the Rise in Female Labor Force Participation Rates: Questions and Probes," *Journal of Labor Economics* 3 (January 1985 supplement):S117–46.

18. June O'Neill and Rachel Braun, "Women and the Labor Market: A Survey of Issues and Policies in the United States," United States Country Report to the Conference on "Regulation of the Labor Market: International Comparison of Labor Market Policy Related to Women," IIMV/LMP, Berlin, 1983.

# 20
## *Equality and Feminist Legal Theory*
### Christine A. Littleton

*Feminist legal theory is one of the most vital areas of feminist activity today because the rights of women are now, more than ever before, being advanced and contested in the legal domain. Like feminists everywhere, feminist legal scholars do not always agree on how best to advance women's interests. In this article Christine Littleton offers an important new concept, "equality as acceptance," to bridge the gap between legal strategies that emphasize sexual equality based on the similarities between men and women and legal strategies that seek to advance women's interests by recognizing differences between the sexes.*

## I. INTRODUCTION

The inequality of women in this society wears many faces: the seemingly intractable wage gap between employed women and men;[1] the "feminization of poverty" (which might more accurately be termed "the impoverishment of women"); the double burden of workplace and family responsibilities that women who work outside the home shoulder, usually alone;[2] the scarcity of women in decision-making positions in law schools, law firms and on the bench;[3] the daily undermining of women's employment status and intellectual self-confidence through sexual harassment in the workplace and in academia;[4] widespread physical abuse by husbands[5] and rape by friends as well as strangers,[6] and the pervasive fear that results. The forms are many, varied and, unfortunately, ubiquitous.

In responding to these myriad and interlocking forms of inequality, feminists have developed a correspondingly rich and interwoven repertoire of theories, strategies and practices designed to expose and ultimately eliminate the methods of social control whereby half the human race has been sacrificed to the interests of the other half.

The law has been slow to respond to women's claims, and even slower to acknowledge the depth and diversity of feminist critique. In 1873, the United States Supreme Court upheld the barring of women from the practice of law.[7] Myra Bradwell was the editor-in-chief of the influential *Chicago Legal News*[8] and sought admission to the Illinois bar, but Justice Bradley's concurring opinion quickly put her in her "proper place"—"[t]he natural and proper timidity and delicacy which belongs to the female sex evidently unfits it for many of the occupations of civil life."[9] Not until 1971 did the Court strike down a law on the basis of discrimination against women.[10]

Excerpted from "Equality and Feminist Legal Theory," by Christine A. Littleton, *University of Pittsburg Law Review* 48 (1987): 1043–1059.

The need for women to call the social and legal system to account has not disappeared over the last hundred years. Our culture claims to embrace the notion of equality as a social ideal, and our legal system expressly holds out the promise of "equal protection of the laws." Yet, the hypocrisy of these proclamations is evident. Even when widespread inequality is recognized, legal redress is available only in limited situations. In 1979, the Supreme Court upheld a state veteran's preference system that effectively locked women out of all upper-level civil service positions, on the ground that the legislature had not "intended" to discriminate against women.[11] The task of feminist legal theory and practice is to develop the critiques that will lead to making the promise of equality a reality.

## II. FEMINIST LEGAL THEORY

The richness and diversity of feminist legal theory that has developed over the last two decades is hard to reduce to a simple schema. The sorting and classifying of intricate analysis inevitably leads to distortion. Nevertheless, it may be useful to view the body of feminist legal theory as developing three interrelated theories to explain and resist women's inequality.

First, theories of *sex discrimination* address those forms of inequality that arise from irrational prejudices against women in public arenas,[12] as well as the unjustified stereotypes used to exclude women from employment and other areas of social life.[13] For example, in the 1971 case of *Reed v. Reed*,[14] the United States Supreme Court recognized sex discrimination in a state provision that automatically preferred men over women as estate administrators, all other things being equal. The irrationality of the decision to prefer men over women without justification[15] allowed the Court to strike down the decision in its first use of the Equal Protection Clause on behalf of women.

Second, theories of *gender oppression* address those forms of inequality that arise from the restriction of women to particular social roles defined somehow as "ours."[16] For instance, the legal system responded to gender oppression in *Hopkins v. Price Waterhouse*.[17] A female accountant had been denied partnership in an accounting firm, in part because she was described by the male partners as acting to "too much" like a man.[18] The court found such attitudes to be discriminatory toward women, and the denial of partnership on that basis to violate equal employment opportunity law. Unfortunately, courts may be more sympathetic to employers who engage in another form of gender oppression by discriminating against someone who acts "too much" like a *woman*. In *De Santis v. Pacific Telephone & Telegraph Co.*,[19] for example, the court refused to find discrimination in the firing of a male nursery school teacher considered "effeminate."[20]

Finally, theories of *sexual subordination* address those forms of inequality that arise from the devaluation and disaffirming of anything associated with women (the classic case being the care and raising of children), or from the identification of women with anything that is devalued, disaffirmed or disempowering.[21] For example, Catherine MacKinnon's work on reconceptualizing pornography as a violation of women's civil rights[22] partakes of a theory of sexual subordination. She views pornography's harm as lying more in its devaluation of women, its targeting us for abuse, than in its restriction on women's social role choice or its irrational preference for one sex over the other in situations where they are functionally interchangeable.

These three strands of feminist legal theory, while they may clash in particular circumstances, are at least potentially complementary, because they address different aspects of the complex social phenomenon that constitutes inequality. All three can be brought to bear on a particular issue. Consider the example of comparable worth, or pay equity. In *County of Washington v. Gunther*,[23] the Supreme Court held that a potential cause of action existed under Title VII (the federal equal employment opportunity law)[24] in a case in which female prison guards alleged that their pay had been decreased compared to the pay of male guards on the basis of sex. The County had undertaken a job evaluation survey, and claimed to rely on it in setting wage scales for various occupations. The survey itself set a lower wage scale for the all-female job than for the all-male job based on differences in the jobs themselves.[25] *But* the County added insult to injury by paying the male guards 100% of the survey recommendation, while paying the female guards only 90% of the lower survey scale for their job.

Under a sex discrimination theory, the County's action can easily be seen as differential treatment of very similar situations. The survey set scales for each job in the same manner, yet the County did not apply that evaluation in the same way to male and female occupations. The Court thus held that if the plaintiffs could establish that *sex* was the reason for this differential treatment, the County would be in violation of Title VII. By restricting its inquiry to sex discrimination, the Court avoided any ruling on "the controversial concept of 'comparable worth.'"[26] It also avoided dealing with the concepts of gender oppression or sexual subordination.

Looking at a similar situation, but using a theory of gender oppression, an additional problem comes to light—that of channeling women into jobs that tend to be lower-paid. In *Sears Roebuck & Co. v. EEOC*,[27] for example, one of the allegations made by the EEOC was that Sears, in effect, handed female applicants application forms for only "female" jobs and handed male applicants forms for the "male" jobs. Of course, it "just so happened" that the male jobs were much higher-paying. These jobs tended to be big-ticket commission positions, selling refrigerators, washing machines, and tires. The female jobs tended to be either non-commission, or selling low-commission items, such as cosmetics. As a result, men's and women's pay scales turned out to be substantially different. Theories of gender oppression focus on the restriction of women into particular roles. Here, both sexes experience the restriction, that is, neither males nor females were encouraged to cross into the sphere of the other, although (as usual) the restriction on women had a greater adverse effect.

Finally, looking at pay equity issues using a theory of sexual subordination, an even deeper problem appears—the process by which pay scales themselves are set. If the evaluation that the County of Washington undertook in *Gunther* and the wage scales Sears used established different and lower pay scales for predominately or all-female job categories, the question becomes whether the skills or skill combinations are ranked as they are *because* of their perceived status as "male" or "female."[28] There is strong evidence that skills associated with women, or that come in combinations that appear to be associated with women, are systematically devalued on that basis.[29] As a blatant example, an informal study done some years ago from the Dictionary of Occupational Titles found that the job of marine mammal handler was ranked as more complex and calling for a higher skill level than the job of kindergarten school teacher.[30] The results can only be explained as a result of sexual subordination—unless, of course, dolphins require greater interaction of a more complex nature than children do.

## III. "EQUALITY" AND "DIFFERENCE"

Implicated in all three strands of feminist legal theory—sex discrimination, gender oppression and sexual subordination—is the question of difference, and the relationship of difference to inequality. This question is important to feminist legal theory because women's inequality has been traditionally both explained and justified by our supposed "difference" from men.[31]

One might ask how it was decided that *we* were the ones who were different, since it appears that if there is a difference, men are just as different from women as women are from men, but that way of posing the issue is itself a part of the story of how sexual inequality works. *Assuming* men are the norm, women appear different, and indeed appear abnormal and inferior.

This is not just a reference to the "bad old days" of Justice Bradley's insistence on the "natural and proper timidity of women" rendering us unfit for the practice of law. In the 1970s, the notion of difference as justifying inequality was used by the Supreme Court yet again in *Dothard v. Rawlinson*.[32] In that case, a prison[33] excluded women from particular "contact" guard positions, and had minimum height and weight requirements for all prison guards. The Court easily struck down the minimum height and weight requirements, reasoning that they were unrelated to the job, because what the prison really wanted was strength, not size. Because many short people could be just as strong as tall ones, and some heavy people are weaker than thin ones, the Court ruled that the employer should test applicants for strength, rather than relying on height and weight.[34] But when it came to the total exclusion of women from positions that required contact with prisoners, the Court saw things differently.

Title VII has a very narrow exception that allows an employer to exclude employees of one sex if sex is a *bona fide occupational qualification* (BFOQ) for the job.[35] Although the legislative record is sketchy, it appears that what Congress had in mind was that ethnicity or sex might be relevant in certain limited situations for "authenticity" purposes.[36] This exception appears most applicable in entertainment and the arts where, for example, the role of "husband" might be limited to male actors. But the Court somehow found this exception applicable to a job as a prison guard, in this respect: the Court said that because it was presented with a prison in which violent sex offenders were intermingled with the rest of the prison population, a female's "very womanhood" would make her less effective on the job.[37] Reading between the lines, what Justice (now Chief Justice) Rehnquist seemed to be saying is that women are rapable, and that "fact" justifies their exclusion.

On a sex discrimination analysis, this finding of difference can be seen as irrational, because anyone who thinks seriously about the issue would not be likely to think of rape *in prisons* as something that only happens to women.[38] From this perspective, Justice Rehnquist's implied assertion is simply untrue, and therefore not a proper justification for the exclusion of women from this job.

A gender oppression perspective adds that even if it *were* true that women are more at risk in this setting, that may be a function of women's social conditioning away from meeting force with force and toward accommodation or submission in the face of violent behavior.[39] Therefore, a valid response to supposed concern for and about women as guards might be to require the employer to hire women into these positions *and* to give them karate or self-defense training, to make up for prior social disadvantaging.[40]

Finally, if looked at from the perspective of sexual subordination, one might ask, "If women in this context are vulnerable to rape, what is it that creates that vulnerability?" It cannot be something inherent in women; women are not the ones who rape. Therefore, one should look at the structure of the workplace itself. In this case, it is particularly easy to do that because the very conditions that the Court assumed were inherent, unchangeable, and justifying the exclusion of women, had been declared in previous litigation a violation of the *prisoners'* rights, under the Eighth Amendment.[41] These conditions were too cruel and unusual for prisoners, but were taken as given when it came to women's economic opportunities. So long as the Court can see women as *different* from men, then it can somehow (the logic escapes me) use conditions that it has been unable to justify in any other context to exclude women.

This analysis leads me to make a very simple statement about difference: there is no logical, inherent link between *difference* and *inequality*. Jefferson wrote, "We hold these truths to be self evident, that all men are created equal." (Well, he got it *half* right.) In any event, he did not say that we are all created the *same*. It is true that the *ir*rationality of inequality is easy to comprehend when similar things are being compared. If I had two pens, both of which were blue, fine-point and felt-tipped, and I expressed a preference for one, you might question the basis for that preference. But it is the next step in the chain of reasoning which does not hold. Simply because it is silly to create inequality between two groups that are the *same* does not mean that it is wise to create inequality between two groups that are different.

This is not to say that the inequality that is explained and justified by pointing to difference is simply silly. On the contrary, it has very real consequences and serves a very real function. If you belong to the group that is seen as the norm from which difference is measured, that is, if you are male, it makes a great deal of sense to adopt an approach to equality that requires *sameness* in order to apply. A society constructed from the male point of view is acting quite *rationally* when it first constructs the social categories of "male" and "female" and then says to those it has defined as female, "All you have to do to be included is to prove that you 'really' are the same as we are." In other words, "prove that you really belong in the category that we have constructed in order to exclude you." This is a neat trick. In effect, it guarantees that equality will continue to be the preserve of "men," however the male-defined culture chooses to define "male."[42]

I am not suggesting that male is always a biological category. In talking about a male perspective, and a male-defined point of view, I do not mean biologically male, but rather that view constructed from the standpoint of those who historically occupied space in the public discourse, who were, of course, men. The category is social, not biological.[43]

A notion of "equality" limited and bounded in this way can scarcely be dignified with that label. It should come as no surprise that legal application of this truncated and skewed version of equality has operated to keep *most* women "out and down,"[44] even as it allows some women a few steps beyond the gate.

This notion of equality has provided access for *some* women into formerly male bastions, like the practice of law, but has not permitted challenges to the structure of law firm practice—a structure that moves you *off* the partnership track if you call any attention to the fact that you are, either biologically or socially, female. You could call attention to the fact that you are biologically female by doing something as radical as having a baby. You could call attention to the fact that you are acting in a socially female way by asking for parental leave, whether you are a mother or a father. Despite significant progress in combatting overt sex discrimination at the hiring stage, it seems clear that young attorneys are moved off the "fast track" to partnership if they behave in such a socially female manner.[45]

## IV. EQUALITY AS ACCEPTANCE

If this concept of equality as assimilation to male norms is not the *only* possible one (i.e., it is a social construction), then the *de*construction of that concept by feminist critique can provide a path to *re*construction. The proposal I have been developing seeks to replace the current judicial model of equality as assimilation (of women to male structures) with a model of "equality as acceptance."[46] This model can be briefly described as requiring that social institutions react to gender differences, whether arising from biological or cultural sources, in such a way as to create equality between complementary male and female persons, skills, attributes and life patterns. Inequality is created; it is not natural. Consequently, equality can be created (and its legal meaning re-created). Thus in employment, for example, employers could be required to restructure workplaces so that they fit female persons and life patterns to the same extent they now fit male ones, rather than simply being required to allow women to compete with men on male terms.

The need for redefinition of equality guarantees is readily apparent from even the most cursory examination of existing case law. Under current interpretations of Title VII, an employer may not refuse to hire women with young children, at least so long as the employer hires men with young children.[47] It is, however, not at all clear that an employer could not refuse to hire any person, male or female, who was a primary parent, that is, a person with primary responsibility for the care of an infant or very young child. While it is, of course, very unlikely that an employer would even question male applicants for employment about their parental responsibilities, there is something deeply disturbing about the possibility that an employer could cure the discrimination of a rule barring women with small children by simply adding into the disfavored category those rare fathers who are primary parents and subtracting out those rare mothers who are not.[48]

What is disturbing about this possibility is that the method of analysis in *Phillips v. Martin Marietta Corporation*[49] (the case referred to above) presupposes the legitimacy of the employment structure itself. That structure is seen as inherently legitimate, and the only question is, "Can women fit into it?"[50] But the employment structure is built on the assumption that people who take care of children need not be considered at all. While employers as a class have not been known for their willingness to consider any worker's "private" nonemployment situation, it still seems clear that the fact that people who take care of children usually are women contributes significantly to the ease with which employers now ignore the entire issue. The *per curiam* opinion in *Phillips* states in part:

> Section 703(a) of the Civil Rights Act of 1964 requires that persons of like qualifications be given employment opportunities irrespective of their sex. The Court of Appeals therefore erred in reading this section as permitting one hiring policy for women and another for men—each having pre-school age children. *The existence of such conflicting family obligations, if demonstrably more relevant to job performance for a woman than for a man, could arguably be a basis for distinction. . . .*[51]

Practically speaking, courts might be quite suspicious of evidence presented to demonstrate that "conflicting family obligations" were "more relevant to job performance" for women. Be that as it may, what are the implicit statements made to women in this supposed victory? First, that family obligations are inherently conflicting with employment obligations. And second, that if employment obligations and family obligations do in fact place women in a double bind, it is women who must go, not the structure that placed them in that untenable position.

Thus, women are told that all we can hope for from guarantees of "equal employment opportunity" is the right to be considered for employment on the same basis as men *if* we will emulate their forced non-involvement in child care—the very forced non-involvement that has made child care "women's work." This may be the Supreme Court's definition of equal employment opportunity, but it is hardly a feminist one.

If social institutions, such as employment, are more compatible with culturally male life patterns than with culturally female ones, that is discrimination against women.[52] This conclusion is not affected by the fact that men may not have freely chosen "male" lives or that women may not have freely chosen "female" ones.[53] Nor is it affected by the fact that some men, at great cost to their economic and social status, choose to be primary parents, or that women can choose not to be.[54] The fact remains that a great number of women (and a small number of men) who are identified as "female" in social terms must pay a significant price for that identification. Their selves, however those selves are skewed by the current sex-gender system, are simply not accepted in public arenas to the extent that similarly skewed, but culturally male, selves are.

The Supreme Court's recent decision in *California Federal Savings & Loan Association v. Guerra (Cal Fed)*[55] indicates that the Court may be more open to claims of equal acceptance when limited to biological difference *and* presented in the context of affirmative state equalizing action rather than federal mandate.[56] *Cal Fed* involved an employer's challenge to a California state law requiring employers to provide a reasonable period of unpaid leave with guaranteed reinstatement to any employee temporarily dis-

abled by "pregnancy, childbirth or related medical conditions."[57] The
employer alleged that this law forced any employer who did not guarantee
reinstatement for disability arising from illness and injury to discriminate
in favor of pregnant women, in conflict with federal equal opportunity
law.[58]

The case uncovered a divergence in the feminist legal community, between those who urged "equal treatment" of disabilities regardless of their
cause,[59] and those who urged accommodation of women's unique childbearing role.[60] Using a model of equal acceptance, however, it is possible to
make a third argument, which includes both the first group's concern about
stressing women's differences and the second group's concern about ignoring women's concrete conditions. Any employer whose leave policy is inadequate to the temporary disability of pregnancy has created a situation in
which the procreative rights of female employees are burdened, while the
*same* rights of male employees are not affected. Such an inadequate leave
policy affects not only women who *are* pregnant, but also those who are
deciding whether or not to become pregnant. Knowledge of impending job
loss may impact on the decision whether to attempt or forgo pregnancy, as
well as whether to terminate the pregnancy or carry to term.

> A female employee subject to an inadequate leave policy must choose be-
> tween exercising a fundamental right and keeping her job. This is a choice
> that no male employee is forced to make. For this reason, when a state acts
> to reduce or eliminate such a differential impact, it acts to *increase* equality
> between female and male employees.[61]

In a 6-3 decision, the Court upheld California's pregnancy disability
leave statute. The majority opinion, authored by Justice Marshall, provided
two grounds for the decision. First, Title VII did not prohibit equalizing
actions. Indeed, "[b]y 'taking pregnancy into account,' California's pregnancy disability leave statute allows women, as well as men, to have families
without losing their jobs."[62] Second, even if Title VII were read to require
the *same* treatment for pregnancy and non-pregnancy related disabilities,
an employer could comply with both the California statute and Title VII by
providing adequate leave for all temporary disabilities.[63]

Read in combination with the Court's decision in *Wimberly v. Labor &
Industrial Relations Commission*[64] (decided the following week), *Cal Fed* seems
limited to approving, but not requiring, a state's recognition of and attempts to remedy asymmetry between women and men, at least where procreation is concerned.

However, it is not only with respect to pregnancy that women and men
stand in asymmetric relations to social institutions such as employment. To
the extent that asymmetry is ignored, therefore, some group must be subjected to a Procrustean bed in order to "fit" the institution. Given the cur-

rent power imbalance between the sexes, that group is almost always women.

The theory of equality as acceptance requires social institutions to ad-just themselves to the fact that people come in two sexes, not one, or one and a half. Even if—perhaps especially if—male and female are wholly so-cial constructions, a society embracing equality as an ideal cannot fulfill that ideal by elevating one social category (male) to the level of public norm, and subordinating the other (female) to it. . . .

The model of equality as acceptance incorporates and transcends sex discrimination theory by insisting that equality need not be limited to same-ness, but can in fact be applied across difference. Equality analysis can *start* at the finding of difference; it certainly should not stop there. Equal accept-ance also incorporates and broadens theories of gender oppression, by in-sisting on "open borders" between male and female workers. Both the fe-male accountant considered "too male" and the male teacher considered "too effeminate" are victims of gender oppression. Thus gender oppression cannot be combatted in one direction alone. In order to address fully the implications of this broadened notion of gender oppression, equality analy-sis must finally include a perspective of sexual subordination. Until both biological and social manifestations of the "female" are treated as equally worthy, both women and men who choose to pursue traditionally female occupations will be punished economically as well as socially. . . .

Under the model of equality as acceptance, equality analysis does not end with the discovery of a "real" difference, but rather begins to assess the "cultural meaning"[65] of such difference and how to achieve equality despite it. This formulation locates difference in the *relationship* between women and men, not in women themselves. Women do not carry difference as part of some genetic code; difference is created only in relationship. We only know what is different in relationship to something else. Thus, equality as acceptance in the athletic sphere could not only support arguments for equal resources to two programs (women and men), but to three (male sports, female sports, and genuinely co-ed sports).[66] Wherever a "different game"[67] develops—in male, female or co-ed programs—equal acceptance would recognize a claim to full participation.

Finally, equality as acceptance recognizes that women and men fre-quently stand in asymmetrical positions to a particular social institution, and insists that such asymmetries justify equalizing efforts, rather than justi-fying the perpetuation of inequality. To carry the athletics example forward, equality as acceptance would tend to support equal division of resources among male, female and co-ed programs, rather than dividing up the avail-able sports budget per capita. Since women and men do not stand in sym-metry to the social institution of athletics, per capita distribution would simply perpetuate the asymmetry, diverting more resources to male pro-grams, where the participation rate is already high, and away from female programs, where the participation rate has been depressed by both the exclusion of women from certain forms of athletic activity and the subordination or devaluation of those forms women have developed for themselves.

## V.    CONCLUSION

The model of equality as acceptance provides for arguments that include the entire range of theories that feminists have developed to respond to different forms of social inequality, but it does not yield a particular right answer. There may be, depending on the situation, many ways of achieving equality. Equal acceptance does, however, provide a way for advocates on behalf of women to challenge the structures that create inequality, rather than being limited to arguments that in this particular case, women and men are in fact the same, or that women have simply been denied the opportunity to become more like men.

In making claims on behalf of women, we need to use the full arsenal of feminist legal theory—not *just* theories of sex discrimination, not *just* theories of gender oppression, not even *just* theories of sexual subordination. To be able to strike at the entire spectrum of the myriad faces of sexual inequality, we need to be able to use all three. We need to ask, in each situation, whether what is going on is simply an irrational refusal to acknowledge the similarity of the skills being offered by women and men, or a restriction of women to particular roles that have been identified as female (along with the corresponding restriction of men to roles that have been identified as male), or (and?), a devaluation of what has been identified as female and an overvaluation of what has been identified as male. If we use these tools of analysis in combination, we might achieve a reconstructive form of equality that *starts* at the point at which we find ourselves and does not end there.

### NOTES

1. *See* Note, *Toward a Redefinition of Sexual Equality,* 95 Harv. L. Rev. 487, 489 n.15, 490 no.20 (1981) (authored by Christine A. Littleton).
2. *See* P. Roos, Gender & Work 16–19 (1985).
3. In 1985, only 1% of the partners in New York law firms and only 4% of the partners in Los Angeles firms were women. *See* Littleton, *Reconstructing Sexual Equality,* 75 Calif. L. Rev. (forthcoming 1987).
4. On sexual harassment in the workplace, see generally C. MacKinnon, Sexual Harassment of Working Women (1979); on sexual harassment in academia, see generally B. Dziech & L. Weiner, The Lecherous Professor (1984).
5. *See* DuBois, Dunlap, Gilligan, MacKinnon, Menkel-Meadow, *Feminist Discourse, Moral Values, and the Law—A Conversation,* 34 Buffalo L. Rev. 11, 26 (1985) [hereinafter *Feminist Discourse*].
6. *See generally* Estrich, *Rape,* 95 Yale L.J. 1087 (1986).
7. Bradwell v. Illinois, 83 U.S. 130 (1873).
8. *See* K. Morello, The Invisible Bar 14–21 (1986).
9. 83 U.S. at 141 (Bradley, J., concurring).

10. Reed v. Reed, 404 U.S. 71 (1971).

11. Personnel Adm'r v. Feeney, 442 U.S. 256 (1979).

12. *See* Note, *supra* note 1, at 500–01.

13. Sometimes the courts recognize this process, *see, e.g.,* Frontiero v. Richardson, 411 U.S. 677, 685–86 (1972) (rejecting "gross, stereotyped distinctions between the sexes"); sometimes they do not. *See, eg.,* Bucha v. Illinois High School Ass'n, 351 F. Supp. 69, 75 (N.D. Ill. 1972) (relying on isolated physiological differences to justify sex separation in *all* sports).

14. 404 U.S. 71 (1971).

15. The Court did consider, and reject as insufficient, a proffered justification of administrative convenience, *Id.* at 76.

16. *See* Dem & Dem, *Homogenizing the American Women,* in Feminist Framework 10 (A. Jaggar & P. Rothenberg 2d ed. 1984).

17. 618 F. Supp. 1109 (D.D.C. 1985).

18. *Id.* at 1117.

19. 608 F.2d 327 (9th Cir. 1979).

20. *Id.* at 331 (employee wore an earring to work).

21. *See Feminist Discourse, supra* note 5, at 25.

22. *See generally* MacKinnon, *Not a Moral Issue,* 2 Yale L. & Pol'y Rev. 321 (1984).

23. 452 U.S. 161 (1981).

24. Title VII of the Civil Rights Act of 1964, 42 U.S.C. §§ 2000e to 2000e-17(1982), makes it an unfair labor practice for an employer with more than 15 employees to discriminate against any individual applicant or employee with respect to "terms and conditions of employment" on the basis of race, color, sex, religion or national origin.

25. 452 U.S. at 180–81.

26. *Id.* at 166.

27. 581 F.2d 941 (D.C. Cir. 1978). *See* Littleton, *Equality Across Difference: Is There Room for Rights Discourse?,* 2 Wisc. Women's L. J. 28–30 (1987).

28. Of course, this perceived status is socially determined and may have little or nothing to do with the biological gender of the individual employees or applicants. For further explication of the concept of "socially male" and "socially female" categories, see Littleton, *supra* note 3.

29. *See* Note, *supra* note 1, at 490.

30. *See* Briggs, *Guess Who Has the Most Complex Job,* unpublished manuscript (1971), *reprinted in* B. Babcock, A. Freedman, E. Norton & S. Ross, Sex Discrimination and the Law 203, 204 (1973).

31. *See* Littleton, *supra* note 3, at Part II.

32. 433 U.S. 321 (1977).

33. Prisons and airlines seem to generate a significant number of sex discrimination cases. *See, e.g.,* Dothard v. Rawlinson, 433 U.S. 321 (1977) (prison); County of Washington v. Gunther, 452 U.S. 161 (1981) (prison); Gerdom v. Continental Airlines, Inc., 692 F.2d 602 (9th Cir. 1982), *cert. dismissed per stipulation,* 460 U.S. 1074 (1983); Harriss v. Pan Am World Airways, Inc., 649 F.2d 670 (9th Cir. 1980); Wilson v. Southwest Airlines Co., 517 F. Supp. 292 (N.D. Tex. 1981).

34. *Dothard,* 433 U.S. at 331–32.

35. *See generally* Case Summaries, *Bona Fide Occupational Qualification (BFOQ),* 1 Women's Rights L. Rep. (Rutgers University) 36–40 (1972–73).

36. *See* Wilson v. Southwest Airlines Co., 517 F. Supp. 292, 297–98 (N.D. Tex. 1981) (discussion of legislative history of BFOQ defense).

37. *Dothard,* 433 U.S. at 336.

38. "The apparent invisibility of the problem of male rape, *at least outside the prison context,* may well reflect the intensity of the stigma attached to the crime and the homophobic reactions against its gay victims." Estrich, *supra* note 6, at 1089 n.1 (emphasis added). Two qualifications on Estrich's observations are in order: first, it is apparent that, at least for the Supreme Court, male rape *in* the prison context also is invisible; second, just as not all women who are raped are heterosexual, so not all men who are raped are gay.

39. *See* Estrich, *supra* note 6, at 1091–94. *Cf.* Lemaire, *Women and Athletics: Toward a Physicality Perspective,* 5 Harv. Women's L.J., 120, 138 (1982) ("The fact is that women are not socialized to overpower anyone.")

40. *See* Note, *supra* note 1, at 494–95.

41. *See* Pugh v. Locke, 406 F. Supp. 318 (M.D. Ala. 1976), *off 'd,* 559 F.2d 283 (5th Cir. 1977), *modified per curium,* 438 U.S. 781, *cert. denied,* 438 U.S. 915 (1978).

42. *See* Littleton, *supra* note 3.

43. *See supra* note 28. *See also* Estrich, *supra* note 6, at 1091 n.9: In referring to "male" standards . . . I do not mean to suggest that every man adheres to them. A "male view" is nonetheless distinct from a "female view" not only by the gender of most of those who adhere to it, but also by the character of the life experiences and socialization which tend to produce it.

44. I heard Catherine MacKinnon once use this incredibly succinct description of women's situation.

45. *See* Project, *Law Firms and Lawyers with Children: An Empirical Analysis of Family Work Conflict,* 34 Stan. L. Rev. 1263, 1273–74 (1982).

46. For a more fully developed explanation of this model of equality, see Littleton, *supra* note 3.

47. Phillips v. Martin Marietta Corp., 400 U.S. 542 (1971).

48. Ann Scales has used the *Phillips* case in a similar way, arguing eloquently for a standard that "reaches the worse injustice: The fact that women who fit the stereotype [of conflicting family responsibilities] are precluded from advancement in our economic system." Scales, *The Emergence of Feminist Jurisprudence: An Essay,* 95 Yale L.J. 1373, 1395 (1986).

49. 400 U.S. 542 (1971).

50. Similarly, the Court in Dothard v. Rawlinson, 453 U.S. 321 (1977) (discussed *supra* at text accompanying notes 32–37), presupposed the legitimacy of the structure itself, and *then* asked whether women fit into that structure.

51. 400 U.S. at 544 (emphasis added).

52. *Cf.* Lynn v. Regents of the Univ. of Cal., 656 F.2d 1337 (9th Cir. 1981), in which the University of California denied tenure to a female scholar in women's studies, based in part on disdain for the field itself. While the district court found no discrimination "because the University would have had the same objection if a man concentrated his studies on women's issues," the Ninth Circuit disagreed: "A disdain for women's issues, and a diminished opinion of those who concentrate on those issues, is evidence of a discriminatory attitude towards women." *Id.* at 1343.

53. These two aspects of lack of choice are not as parallel as the sentence structure might indicate. As a result of male power, *both* "male" and "female" life patterns may be constructed from the male point of view.

54. For some women that choice is also costly, but in emotional rather than economic terms. For others the same choice is not. I do not think that all women have a deep psychic need or desire to care for children, but to the extent that those who do must abandon it in the name of equal employment opportunity, equality begins to look like a bad joke.

55. 107 S. Ct. 683 (1987).

56. About a week after the *Cal Fed* decision, the Court decided, in Wimberly v. Labor & Indus. Relations Comm'n, 107 S. Ct. 821 (1987), that states were not *required* to take equalizing action. The plaintiff was terminated while on pregnancy leave, and Missouri law treated that termination as a voluntary resignation, thereby making her ineligible for unemployment compensation. She claimed that denial of benefits was precluded by the Federal Unemployment Tax Act, which prohibits states from denying unemployment benefits "solely on the basis of pregnancy." In a unanimous opinion authorized by Justice O'Connor, the Court concluded that Missouri was not required to grant unemployment benefits when the termination was a result of absence from work, even if the reason for the absence was pregnancy. *Id.* at 825.

57. Cal. Gov't Code § 12945(b)(2) (West 1980).

58. The Pregnancy Discrimination Act, Pub. L. No. 95–555, 92 Stat. 2076 (1978) (codified at 42 U.S.C § 2000e(k) (1982)) (amending Title VII of the Civil Rights Act of 1964), prohibits discrimination on the basis of pregnancy.

59. *See, e.g.,* Williams, *Equality's Riddle: Pregnancy and the Equal Treatment/Special Treatment Debate,* 13 N.Y.U. Rev. of Law & Soc. Change 325 (1985).

60. *See, e.g.,* Krieger & Cooney, *The Miller-Wohl Controversy: Equal Treatment, Positive Action and the Meaning of Women's Equality,* 13 Golden Gate U. L. Rev. 513 (1983).

61. Brief Amicus Curiae of Coalition for Reproductive Equality in the Workplace (CREW) at 14, California Fed. Sav. & Loan Ass'n v. Guerra, 107 S. Ct. 683 (1987). I was the attorney of record for CREW, and principal author of the brief.

62. *California Federal Savings*, 107 S. Ct. at 694.

63. *Id.* at 694–95.

64. 107 S. Ct. 821 (1987). *See supra* note 56.

65. Cf. Lawrence, *The Id, the Ego and Equal Protection: Reckoning with Unconscious Racism*, 39 Stan. L. Rev. 317 (1987).

66. Interestingly, equality as acceptance would provide little support for the argument that traditionally male sports (such as football) should be modified so as to accommodate women (or vice versa). Equality as acceptance is not a model of the superiority of socially female categories, nor even of the superiority of androgynous categories, but rather a model of the equal validity of men's and women's lives.

67. *See* Littleton, *supra* note 27.

# Suggestions for Further Reading

ANDERSON, KAREN. *Wartime Women: Sex Roles, Family Relations, and the Status of Women During World War II* (Westport: Greenwood Press, 1982).

BENSON, SUSAN PORTER. *Counter Cultures: Saleswomen, Managers, and Customers in American Department Stores, 1890–1940* (Urbana: University of Illinois Press, 1986).

BERGMANN, BARBARA R. *The Economic Emergence of Women* (New York: Basic, 1986).

BLAIR, KAREN. *The Clubwoman as Feminist: True Womanhood Redefined, 1868–1914* (New York: Holmes and Meier, 1979).

BORDIN, RUTH. *Frances Willard: A Biography* (Chapel Hill: University of North Carolina Press, 1986).

———. *Woman and Temperance: The Quest for Power and Liberty, 1873–1900* (Philadelphia: Temple University Press, 1981).

BUECHLER, STEVEN. *The Transformation of the Woman's Suffrage Movement: The Case of Illinois, 1850–1920* (New Brunswick: Rutgers University Press, 1986).

BUHLE, MARI JO. *Women and American Socialism, 1870–1920* (Urbana: University of Illinois Press, 1983).

BUTLER, ANNE M. *Daughters of Joy, Sisters of Mercy: Prostitution in the American West, 1865–1890* (Urbana: University of Illinois Press, 1985).

COTT, NANCY F. *The Grounding of Modern Feminism* (New Haven: Yale University Press, 1987).

COWAN, RUTH SCHWARTZ. *More Work for Mother: The Ironies of Household Technology from the Open Hearth to the Microwave* (New York: Basic, 1983).

D'EMILIO, JOHN, and ESTELLE FREEDMAN. *Intimate Matters: A History of Sexuality in America* (New York: Harper and Row, 1988).

DANIEL, ROBERT. *American Women in the Twentieth Century* (New York: Harcourt, Brace, and Jovanovitch, 1987).

DAVIES, MARGERY W. *Woman's Place is at the Typewriter: Office Work and Office Workers, 1870–1930* (Philadelphia: Temple University Press, 1982).

DAVIS, ALLEN F. *American Heroine: The Life and Legend of Jane Addams* (New York: Oxford University Press, 1973).

———. *Spearheads of Reform: The Social Settlements and the Progressive Movement, 1890–1914* (New York: Oxford University Press, 1967).

DEGLER, CARL. *At Odds: Women and the Family in America from the Revolution to the Present* (New York: Oxford University Press, 1980).

DINER, HASIA. *Erin's Daughters in America: Irish Immigrant Women in the Late Nineteenth Century* (Baltimore: Johns Hopkins University Press, 1983).

DYE, NANCY SCHROM. *As Equals and As Sisters: Feminism, the Labor Movement, and the Women's Trade Union League of New York* (Columbia: University of Missouri Press, 1980).

EISENSTEIN, SARAH. *Give Us Bread, But Give Us Roses: Working Women's Consciousness in the United States, 1890 to the First World War* (Boston: Routledge and Kegan Paul, 1983).

EVANS, SARA. *Personal Politics: The Roots of Women's Liberation in the Civil Rights Movement and the New Left* (New York: Vintage, 1979).

EWEN, ELIZABETH. *Immigrant Women in the Land of Dollars: Life and Culture on the Lower East Side* (New York: Monthly Review Press, 1985).

FLEXNER, ELEANOR. *Century of Struggle: The Woman's Rights Movement in the United States* (Cambridge: Harvard University Press, 1959).

FRANKFORT, ROBERTA. *Collegiate Women: Domesticity and Career in Turn-of-the-Century America* (New York: New York University Press, 1977).

FREEDMAN, ESTELLE. *Their Sisters' Keepers: Women's Prison Reform in America, 1830–1930* (Ann Arbor: University of Michigan Press, 1981).

GLAZER, PENINA, and MIRIAM SLATER. *Unequal Colleagues: The Entrance of Women into the Professions, 1890–1940* (New Brunswick: Rutgers University Press, 1987).

GLENN, EVELYN NAKANO. *Issei, Nisei, War Bride* (Philadelphia: Temple University Press, 1986).

GORDON, FELICE. *After Winning: The Legacy of New Jersey Suffrage, 1920–1947* (New Brunswick: Rutgers University Press, 1987).

GORDON, LINDA. *Heroes of Their Own Lives: The Politics and History of Family Violence, 1880–1980* (New York: Viking, 1988).

———. *Woman's Body, Woman's Right: Birth Control in America* (New York: Viking, 1976).

HAGOOD, MARGARET. *Mothers of the South: Portraiture of the White Tenant Farm Woman* (Chapel Hill: University of North Carolina Press, 1939).

HALL, JACQUELYN DOWD. *The Revolt Against Chivalry: Jessie Daniel Ames and the Women's Campaign Against Lynching* (New York: Columbia University Press, 1979).

HALL, JACQUELYN DOWD et al. *Like a Family: The Making of a Southern Cotton Mill World* (Chapel Hill: University of North Carolina Press, 1987).

HARTMAN, SUSAN. *The Homefront and Beyond: American Women in the 1940s* (Boston: G. K. Hall, 1982).

HAYDEN, DOLORES. *The Grand Domestic Revolution: A History of Feminist Designs for American Homes, Neighborhoods, and Cities* (Cambridge, MA: M.I.T. Press, 1981).

HILL, MARY A. *Charlotte Perkins Gilman: The Making of a Radical Feminist, 1860–1896* (Philadelphia: Temple University Press, 1979).

HOBSON, BARBARA MEIL. *Uneasy Virtue: The Politics of Prostitution and the American Reform Tradition* (New York: Basic, 1987).

HUNTER, JANE. *The Gospel of Gentility: American Women Missionaries in Turn-of-the-Century China* (New Haven: Yale University Press, 1984).

JANIEWSKI, DOLORES. *Sisterhood Denied: Race, Gender, and Class in a New South Community* (Philadelphia: Temple University Press, 1985).

JENSEN, JOAN, ed. *A Needle, a Bobbin, a Strike: Women Needle Workers in America* (Philadelphia: Temple University Press, 1984).

———. *With These Hands: Women Working on the Land* (New York: Feminist Press, 1981).

JENSEN, JOAN, and LOIS SCHARF, eds. *Decades of Discontent* (Westport: Greenwood Press, 1983).

JONES, JACQUELYN. *Labor of Love, Labor of Sorrow: Black Women, Work and the Family, from Slavery to the Present* (New York: Vintage, 1985).

KATZMAN, DAVID. *Seven Days a Week: Women and Domestic Service in Industrial America* (Urbana: University of Illinois Press, 1978).

KESSLER-HARRIS, ALICE. *Out to Work: A History of Wage-Earning Women in the United States* (New York: Oxford University Press, 1982).

KRADITOR, AILEEN. *The Ideas of the Woman's Suffrage Movement, 1890–1920* (New York: Columbia University Press, 1965).

LEACH, WILLIAM. *True Love and Perfect Union: The Feminist Reform of Sex and Society* (New York: Basic, 1980).

LEMONS, J. STANLEY. *The Woman Citizen: Social Feminism in the 1920s* (Urbana: University of Illinois Press, 1975).

LEVINE, SUSAN. *Labor's True Woman: Carpet Weavers, Industry and Labor Reform in the Gilded Age* (Philadelphia: Temple University Press, 1984).

MAY, ELAINE TYLER. *Great Expectations: Marriage and Divorce in Post-Victorian America* (Chicago: University of Chicago Press, 1980).

MELOSH, BARBARA. *The Physician's Hand: Work Culture and Conflict in American Nursing* (Philadelphia: Temple University Press, 1982).

MEYEROWITZ, JOANNE. *Women Adrift: Industrial Wage Earners in Chicago, 1880–1930* (Chicago: University of Chicago Press, 1988).

MILKMAN, RUTH, ed. *Women, Work and Protest: A Century of United States Women's Labor Activism* (Boston: Routledge and Kegan Paul, 1985).

———. *Gender at Work: The Dynamics of Job Segregation by Sex During World War II* (Urbana: University of Illinois Press, 1987).

MORANTZ-SANCHEZ, REGINA. *Sympathy and Science: Women Physicians in American Medicine* (New York: Oxford University Press, 1985).

PEISS, KATHY. *Cheap Amusements: Working Women and Leisure in Turn-of-the-Century New York* (Philadelphia: Temple University Press, 1986).

PIVAR, DAVID. *Purity Crusade: Sexual Morality and Social Control, 1868–1900* (Westport: Greenwood Press, 1973).

REED, JAMES. *The Birth Control Movement and American Society* (Princeton: Princeton University Press, 1978).

ROSEN, RUTH. *The Lost Sisterhood: Prostitution in America, 1900–1918* (Baltimore: Johns Hopkins University Press, 1982).

ROSENBERG, ROSALYN. *Beyond Separate Spheres: The Intellectual Roots of Modern Feminism* (New Haven: Yale University Press, 1982).

SCHARF, LOIS, *To Work and to Wed: Female Employment, Feminism, and the Great Depression* (Westport: Greenwood Press, 1980).

SCOTT, ANNE FIROR, and ANDREW MACKAY SCOTT. *One Half of the People: The Fight for Woman Suffrage* (Urbana: University of Illinois Press, 1982).

SELLER, MAXINE SCHWARTZ. *Immigrant Women* (Philadelphia: Temple University Press, 1981).

SOLOMON, BARBARA MILLER. *In the Company of Educated Women: A History of Women and Higher Education in America* (New Haven: Yale University Press, 1985).

STRASSER, SUSAN. *Never Done: A History of American Housework* (New York: Pantheon Books, 1982).

TENTLER, LESLIE WOODCOCK. *Wage Earning Women: Industrial Work and Family Life in the United States, 1900–1930* (New York: Oxford University Press, 1979).

WANDERSEE, WINIFRED. *Women's Work and Family Values, 1920–1940* (Cambridge: Harvard University Press, 1981).

WARE, SUSAN. *Beyond Suffrage: Women in the New Deal* (Cambridge: Harvard University Press, 1981).

————. *Partner and I: Molly Dewson, Feminism, and New Deal Politics* (New Haven: Yale University Press, 1987).

WEINER, LYNN. *From Working Girl to Working Mother: The Female Labor Force in the United States, 1820–1980* (Chapel Hill: University of North Carolina Press, 1985).

# Index

Readers of this book may be interested in its companion volume, Kathryn Kish Sklar and Thomas Dublin, eds., *Women and Power in American History*, volume 1, which includes an introduction, suggestions for further reading and the following articles:

1. "Native American Women and Agriculture," Joan M. Jensen.
2. "The Weaker Sex as Religious Rebel," Lyle Koehler.
3. "'A Friendly Neighbor': Social Dimensions of Daily Work in Northern Colonial New England," Laurel Thatcher Ulrich.
4. "The Planter's Wife: The Experience of White Women in Seventeenth-Century Maryland," Lois Green Carr and Lorena S. Walsh.
5. "The Beginnings of the Afro-American Family in Maryland," Allan Kulikoff.
6. "Divorce and the Changing Status of Women in Eighteenth-Century Massasschusetts," Nancy F. Cott.
7. "Butter Making and Economic Development in Mid-Atlantic America from 1750 to 1850," Joan M. Jensen.
8. "The Sexual Division of Labor and the Artisan Tradition in Early Industrial Capitalism: The Case of New England Shoemaking, 1780–1860," Mary H. Blewett.
9. "The Domestic Balance of Power: Relations between Mistress and Maid in Nineteenth-Century New England," Carol Lasser.
10. "Women, Work, and Protest in the Early Lowell Mills," Thomas Dublin.
11. "Female Slaves: Sex Roles and Status in the Antebellum Plantation South," Deborah G. White.
12. "The Political Activities of Anti-Slavery Women," Gerda Lerner.
13. "Beauty, the Beast, and the Militant Woman: A Case Study of Sex Roles and Social Stress in Jacksonian America," Carroll Smith-Rosenberg.
14. "The Founding of Mt. Holyoke College," Kathryn Kish Sklar.
15. "Women and Indians on the Frontier," Glenda Riley.
16. "Victorian Women and Domestic Life: Mary Todd Lincoln, Elizabeth Cady Stanton, and Harriet Beecher Stowe," Kathryn Kish Sklar.
17. "Chinese Immigrant Women in Nineteenth-Century California," Lucie Cheng.
18. "The Social Character of Abortion in America, 1840–1880," James C. Mohr.